On the Alternative Punishment to the Death Penalty in China

Gui Huang

On the Alternative Punishment to the Death Penalty in China

Springer

Gui Huang
Law School
Yunnan University
Kunming, Yunnan, China

ISBN 978-981-97-1626-5 ISBN 978-981-97-1627-2 (eBook)
https://doi.org/10.1007/978-981-97-1627-2

This work is supported by China Scholarship Council (CSC No. 202107035010; No. 201500500019) and the Stipendium Hungaricum Scholarship (Reference number: 2015-SH-14036).

This Springer imprint is published by the registered company Springer Nature Singapore Pte Ltd.
The registered company address is: 152 Beach Road, #21-01/04 Gateway East, Singapore 189721, Singapore

To my parents,
for giving me life, raising and supporting me;
To Prof. Zhongqi Xu,
who led me to academia, enlightening and inspiring me;
To my wife Dr. Sini Song,
the great person behind me.

Life is given by parents, education is given by teachers.

Foreword

You are now reading a unique book. No book on the sanctions indicated in the title being so comprehensive was published which would have intended to analyze the legal environment of such sanctions in a complex manner, present the peculiarities of those sanctions, and, thereby facilitate the establishment of adequate regulation of the same.

The analyzed sanctions go way back in time both domestically and internationally. The author is correct when delineating that the social, political, and legal contexts have a greater significance in case of the most severe criminal penalties than in case of other sanctions. The related complex review in the first part of the book helps us to be able to understand the background of such issue.

The determination of death penalty as the point of reference is both reasonable and necessary. In this respect, the author first presents the changes that occurred following WWII focusing on China and, later the reader is granted the chance to have an insight into the legal environments of various countries. Thereafter, the chapters qualifying as the foundations of the book—relating to life imprisonment—are to follow. The author is correct when leaving the most space for this topic in line with the title of the book. The reader gets closer to the peculiarities of life imprisonment as the internationally acknowledged alternative of death penalty by the author's detailed delineation of the same. The analytic presentation of the regulations of various countries—partly European, partly non-European—is also included. However, in parallel with the application of historic and comparative methods, the author strives to conduct theoretic and pragmatic analysis as well.

The book is characterized by a critical tone, the presentation of the author's individual opinion, and a series of suggestions by the author which primarily appear during the analytical and evaluating presentation of the currently effective regulations.

While analyzing the topic indicated in the title of the book, the review of the regulations of various countries may not be eliminated which is realized by way of presenting the legal environment of certain countries; in case of each and every country analyzed there is a rational explanation why the same has been included in the necessarily arbitrary selection. At the same time, however, this "round trip" does not qualify as a static snapshot but gives excellent basis for the composition of de lege feranda recommendations.

The conclusions of the detailed research may be read at the end of the book which does not come down exclusively to the complex statements—which otherwise could have rarely been found in domestic legal literature to date—but also contains a multi-level system or recommendations which covers all segments of criminal law in the broader sense; at the same time, however, it also delineates practical solutions aiming at the improvement of the efficiency of execution.

February 2024

Prof. Dr. Madai Sándor
Head of Department of Criminal
Law and Criminology
University of Debrecen
Debrecen, Hungary

Preface

Background and Hypotheses

Since 2011, China has adopted two important amendments to the criminal law, i.e., the Eighth Amendment and the Ninth Amendment, and gradually repealed the death penalty for 22 crimes; however, the abolition carried out by these two amendments has had a limited influence on the control of death penalty and has not substantially reformed the death penalty as used frequently by the judicial authorities. On the one hand, there are still 46 crimes punishable by the death penalty according to the Chinese Criminal Law. On the other hand, this is especially true given that, in judicial practice the death penalty is used most widely for crimes of intentional homicide, intentional injury, drug-related offenses, robbery, and rape, for which the number of death sentences accounted for 90% of all 152 death cases in sampling research; so, in practice, the abolition of the death penalty has not yet gone to the core of the issue. Undeniably, this is in accordance with the gradualist approach to abolition, which was declared in the relevant political documents. Consequently, the legislators and judicial authorities do not have to face an urgent question of how to control serious and lethal crimes immediately after completely abolishing the death penalty; this problem, however, cannot be neglected. Because the issue of completely repealing the death penalty de jure and de facto can hardly be avoided, the issue of how to control crime without the death penalty in China's complicated society, and its alternative punishment, have to be considered during the process of removing the death penalty.

The initial hypotheses are that the death penalty will be gradually removed from the penalty system, and life imprisonment with the possibility of release will be the alternative punishment to the death penalty. However, all the hypotheses have to be placed in the context of China's reality, including theories influenced by the special ideology and the judicial practice. Actually, to a certain extent, the common Western theories and standards cannot be used to explain and understand Chinese issues, including the reform of the penalty system and human rights, so the hypotheses and their related issues need to be placed in the reality of contemporary China. And the most important reality is China's special political system. In other words, the Communist Party of China's (CPC) viewpoint has a great influence on legislation, because China's political and legal regimes are completely different from the West's. In China, the CPC's policies play a guiding role in the process of the enactment and implementation of the law through the main methods used to codify the Party's policies into law, and the ways in which the laws are implemented. Conversely, the process of the rule of law also restricts the Party's policies; however, where there is a conflict between the rule of law and policies, the influence of the former on the latter will always show that the former effectively promotes and ensures the implementation of the latter.

The Aims and Subject

Given the above background and hypotheses, the ultimate aim of the book is to solve the question of how to deal with the most heinous crimes without the death penalty in China, and thus, the book is centered around the issues of what the alternative punishment to the death penalty is, and how to replace the death penalty with another punishment in China's penalty system, which is also the subject that the book develops.

Actually, in a super-country such as China, with a complex social structure, a weakened social regulating mechanism and a huge population, any in-depth reform of the death penalty will be accompanied by the question of how to control crime without the use of the death penalty, and this question will become an important and difficult challenge for legislators and the rulers of the state. Looking outside China, we can see that an alternative punishment to the death penalty has always been the option in order to control crime without the use of the death penalty. Considering the coming problems in China and international legislative experience, in recent years some Chinese scholars have already started to research the issue and attempted to find an appropriate alternative punishment to the death penalty, but they have not yet reached a consensus on this question. Some scholars have argued that if the term "death penalty" merely refers to immediate execution without including the death penalty with reprieve, the alternative punishment, in practice, already exists. In this sense, an alternative sanction is not a punishment replacing the death penalty in a situation in which it is repealed completely, but one that can restrict the application of the death penalty from the judicial and legislative perspective of retaining it as a punishment. They have argued that the death sentence with reprieve and strict life imprisonment would be the appropriate alternative punishment to immediate execution. Other critics have pointed out that when considering an alternative measure to the death penalty, measures should not be taken that restrict the application of the death penalty or ensure that it is never used in judicial practice. The alternative sanction to the death penalty should be a punishment that legislatively replaced the death penalty as stipulated for a certain and concerete crime in the Chinese Criminal Law. This is the debate regarding the legal concept of an alternative punishment to the death penalty in which Chinese criminal law scholars are currently involved. Another debate concerns what kind of punishment measure could be adopted as the alternative to the death penalty, and here different scholars have different opinions.

Based on these academic debates and legislative facts, in order to approach the research aims and develop the subject, this book starts by investigating the general theory on criminal punishment in China, which serves as the basic theoretical grounding and thinking for further considering the potential punishment to replace the death penalty. It then looks to the possibility of the abolition of the death penalty and develops a potential map for abolishing it. Based on the main background of the abolition of the death penalty and its theoretical foundation, this book comes to its core, i.e., what the alternative punishment to the death penalty is and how to replace it. For the former question, this book starts with a discussion of the definition of an alternative punishment to the death penalty and its relevant issues and then turns to the punishment option, life imprisonment. Finally, the study explores the approach of replacing the death penalty with life imprisonment with the possibility of release (LWPR).

The Methodologies Adopted in the Book

The book focuses on the reforms of specific legal issues, which thus may be carried out from three perspectives, i.e., the theoretical level, which should be a discussion among scholars; the institutional level, which is related to the relevant laws and regulations; and judicial practice, which deals with the problems of the issues discussed as they occur in judicial practice. Therefore, this book mainly adopts historical studies, comparative studies, a literature review, case analysis as well as a data statistical analysis to approach its aims.

Historical studies is a type of research method that, based on the historical materials at hand, researches or studies the same issue as it occurs in different historical periods, with the aim of explaining the current situation of the legal system and anticipating its future potential trends. To research the legal issues through a historical studies approach, it is necessary to find the causal relationships among the relevant factors or elements regarding the same issues, then analyze the causes which make the current situation happen, and finally, anticipate the future potential trends of the issues. In this book, the historical studies approach is a very useful and important way for me to explain the issues of the nature of criminal punishment as I explore them from the Mao Zedong era to the present day and show the changes which have occurred in the death penalty policies and related legislation in different periods of China's history, which I analyze from 1949 to now, and anticipate that the death penalty will be completely repealed. I also deal with the development of human rights in China, which I outline from a historical perspective, as well as the ideas behind the penalty which I mainly explain by reference to the traditional and foundation culture and the theoretical thinking in relation to the penalty.

To a certain extent, historical studies seem also to be a type of comparative study, but in fact it is a kind of longitudinal perspective to investigate the same issues taking place in different times; by contrast, comparative studies have a much stronger tendency toward a horizontal perspective to investigate the same issues existing or occurring in different places at the same time. In the field of legal research, comparative studies are a very common and frequently used research methodology. In this book, comparative studies is an important approach taken to realize the aim of the book, and it is mainly used to compare the death penalty and its reform in China, Japan, Indonesia, and the USA as retentionist states and also study the same issues in Europe and Central Asia; meanwhile, this book also uses it to compare life imprisonment in China, Japan, Singapore, and some member states of Europe, as well as long-term imprisonment in Norway and Portugal. In addition, it is also used to compare theoretical debates, such as those comparing the theoretical arguments on the alternative punishment from a judicial perspective and a legislative perspective.

Focusing on the issue of the alternative punishment to the death penalty and its relevant issues, this book systematically reviews the relevant scholarly papers and research reports, in order to clearly outline the state of the art regarding the issues relevant to the book, in particular reviewing the scholarly papers on the issues of the nature and purpose of criminal punishment, penalty discretionary, the definition of the alternative punishment and the factors influencing the punishment option to replace the death penalty, as well as the theoretical arguments on the issue of how to replace the death penalty with other punishments. So, literature review is a very significant methodology to approach the research aims of this book and present its subject.

Case analysis is another important research methodology in legal research, and it is an important way of uncovering problems in law and in practice and explaining legislative intentions by analyzing specific cases. This book also adopts the method of case analysis to support or explain the author's arguments, but there is a certain limitation; i.e., it is not possible to analyze every case, and so it mainly focuses on the relevant main points and just refers to the cases rather than analyzing them deeply. This book uses 25 cases to support or explain its arguments.

Finally, in order to support the author's arguments, the author adopts data statistical analysis, in particular for arguments on the number of executions in China and around the world, changes in crime rates in China in a certain period, changes in the number of criminal cases in the last several decades, the distribution of crimes punishable by life imprisonment, and so on.

The Main Structure and Conclusions of the Book

Apart from the Introduction, the book contains other five chapters. Chapter 2 is a general theoretical discussion of criminal punishment in China; Chap. 3 focuses on the death penalty and its reform in China and other countries; Chap. 4 focuses on the issues of an alternative punishment to the death penalty; Chap. 5 explores issues surrounding life imprisonment; Chap. 6 explores the approach to life imprisonment as an alternative to the death penalty.

The main conclusions of the book are the following:

Chapter 2: General Views on Criminal Punishment in China

Since the founding of New China in 1949, in a one-party system state, almost every area has been greatly influenced by socialist ideology, which takes Marxism–Leninism as its guiding thought. In the first thirty years, from 1949 to 1979, the whole society of China was in a stage in which there was a key link with the class struggle and revolutionary thought played a leading and predominant role. In this context, China adopted only a few special criminal laws to deal with the terrible situation in the first decade of the founding of New China, and in this situation of a lack of law, certain words used by the national and political leaders were always considered as the highest order and their legal effect was unofficially higher than that of the law, and they were even written into judgment. Criminal punishment at this time functioned as a rule instrument for the ruling class to run the country and society. In the 1960s and 1970s, a sociopolitical movement, *the Great Proletarian Cultural Revolution*, took place in China. In this political meltdown, the Constitution and other laws, as well as regulations were laid aside and neglected, and the whole country and society was in a lawless state. After this period had passed, China passed its first Criminal Law in 1979 and then adopted 25 specific criminal laws and other subsidiary criminal provisions, which are provided in 107 non-criminal laws. Even though the "class struggle" and "revolutionary thought" were not the dominant theme in the political area, and economic construction and reform were considered the main task for the government and even the whole of society, to a large extent the instrumental rule character of law in these two decades was greatly emphasized by the 1979 Criminal Law and a series of special criminal laws and other subsidiary criminal provisions. An obvious example is that heavy punishments, including the death penalty and life imprisonment, were widely stipulated for crimes, especially economic crimes and other nonviolent crimes. In 1997, China amended the 1979 criminal law and specific criminal laws and some subsidiary criminal provisions and it became the present Criminal Law. Its character as a rule instrument seems to have been weakened to a certain extent; an example of this is that this character was no longer emphasized in political documents and the legislative practice no longer emphasized the death penalty as the heavy punishment for crimes, including for new crimes. However, we can still find some "trace" of the rule instrument since the 1997 Criminal Law still had many crimes (68 crimes, accounting for 16.46% of a total of 413 crimes); on the other hand, in judicial practice, the government and the judicial authorities always adopted "strike-hard" as the policy to control crime, which implies that the heavy punishment is the only useful way to control crime and protect the social and ruling order. It also seems that the character of the rule instrument of the penalty is further weakened in the Eighth and Ninth Amendments because they removed the death penalty from the 22 crimes for the first time. However, it still appears in other aspects, for instance, in the heavy punishments stipulated for offenses against food safety and corruption crimes in recent years; and in some special political contexts, the character of the rule instrument appears in another way, referred to as the "new instrument" by some scholars. Meanwhile, its penal nature and use as a rule instrument determine the purpose of the punishment, which, in fact, always takes retributivism as its main penal purpose. On one hand, its "rule instrument" nature requires that the penalty should be a measure that can crack down on and even eradicate crimes, and asks that the crime should be given a corresponding punishment; on the other hand, the current structure of the penalty system is a kind of retributive one, given that the application of the death penalty, the combined punishment of fines and other principal punishments, life imprisonment without release for corruption crimes and a heavier penalty for recidivists do not only make the penalty system heavy, but also retributive. Since the Mao era, a basic line of the Party, i.e., the "Mass Line," has always been emphasized in different areas and at different times. Under this requirement, a political requirement for penalty discretion, i.e., "unifying the legal effect and the social effect," becomes an important factor reflecting the implementation of the "Mass Line" in judicial practice and is also an important element in evaluating the justice of sentencing from a political perspective, especially for cases causing great concern among the public. However, some risks caused by "unifying the legal effect and the social effect" should be considered. How to balance the legal effect and the social effect is an important problem; and sometimes, under some political circumstances, the judgment is inclined to emphasize the social effect and neglect the legal requirement, so this dilutes public sentiment; sometimes, the judgment strictly applies the law and focuses on the legal effect, but the result of the sentencing causes the victim's family members to complain about the injustice of the sentencing and then complain to different governments and judicial authorities. At the same time, in examining the justice problem of sentencing in judicial practice, we can see that Chinese criminal procedure faces some serious problems concerning the sentencing system. Judges often fail to provide acceptable reasons and arguments to support their decisions on punishments. Judicial decisions are influenced by many internal and external factors and judges do not pay attention to making their decisions regarding sentences according to a coherent and consistent system of values. Their sentencing practice leads to an unpredictable, disproportional, and unjust punishing system. The failure to provide rational reasons for particular sentences in judicial decisions can undermine the justice of the decisions and provide the opportunity for the public and the legal community to call the rightfulness of the decision into question. To avoid this kind of unjust sentencing system judicial practice needs to be reformed in some ways. Improving the quality of judicial reasoning on sentencing includes the need to reform the appointment system of judges, construct an effective communication channel between the judges and society, and develop judicial skills by setting up an effective training system. These reforms in the judicial system would contribute to creating a more just and predictable sentencing practice in China.

Chapter 3: The Death Penalty and Its Reforms in China and Other Countries

Historically, China is a capital punishment country, which has never removed the death penalty from its legal system. China will not completely abolish the death penalty de facto and de jure in the near future (some scholars say that it will take at least 30 years). This is the background to death penalty reform in China. In the Mao Zedong era, China was in a lawless period (even though there were some laws and regulations, they were barely used) and thus countless people were executed without any legal procedure and legal judgment; however, we cannot ignore the fact that the country implemented a policy of cautious and strict execution. Post Mao, the death penalty policy of cautious and strict execution was still taken as the effective policy. This changed a little in the Deng Xiaoping era, in which the execution legislation was expanded and the death penalty was used more frequently in judicial practice. Since the Deng era, the "strike-hard" movement—which is in fact a kind of revolution in the approach to crime—was introduced and implemented, and the death penalty in this period was deemed to be the best deterrent to curb crime. After Deng, in the Jiang Zemin era, a death penalty policy of cautious and strict execution was implemented again, but was expressed in another form, i.e., "killing cautiously and killing less." In the Jiang era, the number of crimes punishable by death was kept at a same level and this situation continued to the early period of Hu Jintao's premiership.

In the middle of the Hu era, in 2007, China took the first step to effectively control the use of the death penalty, namely the power to review for all death sentences was restored to the SPC from the local High People's Courts and the Military Courts, such that the Supreme People's Court can now uniformly exercise the power to review and further improve the standards and conditions of evidence and the procedure involved in sentencing someone to death. Actually, this was a reform conducted from the perspective of judicial practice. At the end of the Hu era, China took the second step to reduce the possibility of the use of the death penalty, namely repealing the death penalty for 13 crimes. Then, in 2015, the Ninth Amendment removed the death penalty from a further nine crimes. In fact, these were two great steps for the reform of China's punishment system. However, we cannot ignore the fact that the abolition of the death penalty for these 22 crimes is almost useless in reducing the possibility of the use of the death penalty, because the death penalty for these crimes was almost never used in judicial practice. At present, there are 46 crimes punishable by death, but we do not know how many people are sentenced to death and executed every year because this information is treated as a secret in China. According to the Amnesty International Report, around 1500 offenders are sentenced to the death penalty and executed annually. Even though China will not completely abolish the death penalty in the near future, the Party's political document promises that China will gradually reduce the number of charges that could lead to the death penalty. Some scholars have pointed out that China will strategically remove the death penalty from the penalty system; namely, firstly repealing the death penalty for nonviolent crimes, then abolishing the death penalty for violent but non-lethal crimes, and finally removing the death penalty for lethal crimes. Consequently, China will be able to completely abolish the death penalty de facto and de jure.

Outside of China, at the international level, as an obviously inhuman punishment, the death penalty is gradually being abolished de jure and de facto by more and more states. Even though it is still provided for in the Criminal Law, the judicial authorities have already taken many steps to limit and control its use. In the future, we can say that the death penalty will be completely removed from the penalty system around the world under the influence of the concept of human rights. Obviously, however, the moment at which a state abolishes the death penalty does not have any connection with its economic and social development, or even with its democratic development. For instance, the USA and Japan are two important and democratic developed countries, but the death penalty is still provided in their criminal laws and used frequently, and many citizens in these countries are in favor of the death penalty. Therefore, to a great extent, the abolition of the death penalty is still in process and steps to abolish it are also being taken slowly. However, we can also see that the reform of the death penalty has already been launched in these states.

Chapter 4: The Alternative Punishment to the Death Penalty

The issue of the alternative punishment to the death penalty is the core and also the main topic of this book. Due to the differences of the research approaches and habits of thought, Chinese scholars would normally prefer to start their research with a discussion of the notion of the alternative to the death penalty, which Western scholars seldom do. In the notion of the alternative punishment to the death penalty, there are two main arguments, i.e., a judicial alternative punishment to the death penalty and a legislative alternative. As to the former, some scholars argue that the alternative punishment to the death penalty should refer to the kind of punishment which could be used to replace the death penalty with immediate execution; but for the latter, scholars believe that the alternative punishment to the death penalty refers to a punishment replacing the death penalty for a crime that has already been removed from the list of the most heinous crimes punishable by death under the law. Both two arguments are based on the aim of reducing the use of the death penalty. However, the judicial argument is based on the fact that the death penalty is still stipulated in the criminal law and applicable in the judicial practice; in this case, the argument is about controlling or reducing the use of the death penalty rather than abolishing it; therefore, this book disagrees with this argument, but tends to agree with the argument of a legislative alternative punishment. The alternative punishment to the death penalty should be the punishment that replaces the death penalty for the most heinous crimes, which should be the most serious violent and lethal crimes. After clarifying the notion of the alternative punishment to the death penalty, we need to explore the potential factors that influence the punishment options to replace the death penalty. Actually, in China, the factors influencing punishment options to replace the death penalty are varied. However, all of these factors should be understood on the basis of Chinese realities, in particular the special political regime, culture, and social development. The book focuses on four factors, i.e., human rights, the ideas behind the penalty, criminal policy, public opinion, and political concerns in terms of the anti-corruption campaign. Human rights is the most important factor influencing punishment options to replace the death penalty, and it can be said that human rights has pushed the abolition of the death penalty forward in the world and now it also influences the punishment options to replace the death penalty in the retentionist states and influences the imprisonment penalty reform in the abolitionist states. As for China, because of its special political regime, the CPC's views on human rights play a dominant role throughout the country and have a great influence on all aspects of life. The development of human rights has a very short history in China; the CPC admits and accepts human rights, although focus is given to different aspects of these rights. The CPC always emphasizes that national development and stability are guarantees of all citizens' human rights, and consequently, protecting the majority of citizens' human rights and the people's right to subsistence and development are always the CPC's priority. However, the development and changes in the CPC's views on human rights will give correct guidance to China's legislation to choose the right punishment to replace the death penalty. The second important factor is the ideas behind the penalty, which are analyzed from the perspective of historical culture and society, as well as the political factors. The ideas behind the penalty mainly include the traditional concept of the penalty system, i.e., the foundation culture and philosophical thinking on the penalty, and the position of the nation-state regarding the penalty; i.e., China's penal system has always had a very strong tendency toward, and obvious characteristics of, the representation of state interests and regime supremacy. The third important influencing factor is the criminal policy, which plays a crucial role in criminal legislation and judicial practice. "Combining leniency and severity" is the current policy and will greatly influence the potential punishment option to replace the death penalty for the most heinous crimes, so that it can keep the severe punishment for serious crimes. Public opinion is the fourth most important factor influencing the potential punishment option to replace the death penalty. However, so far there has been no exact social survey on the alternative punishment to the death penalty, only a few surveys on death penalty reform. In these surveys, most respondents support the death penalty. In this case, public opinion seems to present a great challenge to abolition and to the punishment option to replace the death penalty. Finally, a new factor which is found in the Ninth Amendment is the particular political concern related to corruption crimes. The fact that life imprisonment without release (LWOR) is stipulated for corruption crimes is mainly caused by political concerns in the context of anti-corruption campaigns.

After exploring the issues of the alternative punishment to the death penalty in China, this book looks to other states for guidance by analyzing the same issues in the abolitionist states and retentionist states. Most abolitionist states have adopted LWPR as the punishment option to replace the death penalty, and some of these states have already abolished life imprisonment, leaving only long-term imprisonment as the maximum punishment in their penalty system. In some retentionist states, there is a debate about the abolition of the death penalty, and some propose to adopt LWPR as the punishment to replace the death penalty, although some of them support LWOR as the punishment to replace the death penalty.

Chapter 5: General Issues Concerning Life Imprisonment

The book believes that life imprisonment will be the most appropriate punishment option to replace the death penalty. Except for a few states which have abolished life imprisonment, most states provide life imprisonment in their criminal laws for serious crimes. Compared with other punishment measures, life imprisonment, generally, is a punishment which incarcerates the inmate in prison for the rest of his or her natural life, which thus removes the inmate's right to hope, and so it is almost the severest punishment. In light of this, we also can observe that the fact that it involves lengthy incarceration, that it is almost the severest penalty, and that it is only used for the most serious crimes represent three obvious and important characteristics of life imprisonment. Based on different criteria, life imprisonment includes three main types, LWOR and LWPR, (relating to the terminating mechanism of life imprisonment), life imprisonment with work and without work, as well as mandatory life imprisonment and discretionary life imprisonment, (relating to whether life imprisonment is the only or an alternative punishment for the crimes). Even though there are different types of life imprisonment, its effects are almost the same, and it normally and mainly impacts on three kinds of people, i.e., directly impacting on the inmate and his or her family, indirectly impacting on the victims and their family, and indirectly impacting on the public. All of these are the basic and brief theories about life imprisonment. In practice, most states stipulate life imprisonment in their Criminal Laws for serious crimes. In fact, three important factors need to be examined when we examine life imprisonment in the penalty system, i.e., the prevalence of life imprisonment in the criminal law, the conditions for passing a sentence of life imprisonment, as well as the terminating mechanism. This book does not only examine life imprisonment in China, but also analyzes life imprisonment in other states, including retentionist states such as Japan and Singapore and in some abolitionist states such as various members of the EU; in addition, this book also examines long-term imprisonment in some states. After analyzing life imprisonment in the law, this book also looks to the facts of its application in judicial practice. In addition, it also discusses various international conventions or treaties and other documents concerning life imprisonment, which mainly include the ECHR, the ICCPR, and the Rome Statute of the International Criminal Court.

Chapter 6: The Approaches of Life Imprisonment as an Alternative to the Death Penalty in China

What kind of potential punishment could be chosen to replace the death penalty, and how to replace are the questions that the book has to answer. In the limited theoretical debates, except for the suggestion from the judicial perspective which proposes the death penalty with reprieve as the multiple alternative punishment, most scholars have favored and proposed life imprisonment as an alternative punishment to the death penalty; however, as regards its terminating mechanism, different scholars have different opinions. Some scholars propose LWOR, but some propose LWPR. As regards LWPR, different scholars have different arguments in terms of the length of incarceration before release. Some scholars argue for 15 years, some argue for 25, some for 30 years, and so on. However, in legislative practice, the legislator, on one hand, extends the punishment term for an inmate who is sentenced to a fixed term imprisonment and so serves life imprisonment in prison; on the other hand, the legislator stipulates LWOR for corruption crimes. From my perspective, I propose that an aggravated life imprisonment which puts many more restrictions on commutation, could be chosen to replace immediate execution, with no parole granted; i.e., if the nature of the crime involves serious violence and is lethal, the death penalty for it should be replaced by aggravated life imprisonment, i.e., a convict who is sentenced to this sentence can be released after serving in prison for not less than 30 years on commutation. And no parole would be granted. Meanwhile, the penalty system, in particular the imprisonment system needs to be reformed; on the one hand, it is necessary to reduce the number of crimes punishable by life imprisonment; on the other hand, it is necessary to clearly demarcate the circumstances and degrees of crimes punishable by life imprisonment and their corresponding punishments. From the procedural perspective, the jurisdiction of the courts of the first instance over crimes punishable by life imprisonment and the review courts should be changed to a certain extent.

Fribourg, Switzerland Dr. Gui Huang
January 2024

Acknowledgments

Time goes pretty fast, and it seems nothing has been changed.

Wherever I will be in the future, the experience of studying at the Faculty of Law, University of Debrecen, Hungary, and doing research at the Faculty of Law, University of Fribourg, Switzerland, will be my most wonderful memories.

However, at this moment, first and foremost I want to immensely thank my supervisor, Prof. Dr. Madai Sándor, who is not merely a good supervisor but also a pretty good brother. It has been an honor to be his first Ph.D. student from Asia, specifically from China. He has taught me, both consciously and unconsciously, how good academic research is done. I appreciate all his contributions of time, ideas, and his mother's delicious food and support to make my Ph.D. experience productive and stimulating. I am also thankful for the excellent example he has provided as a great brother and successful supervisor.

I would also like to thank the committee members of my doctoral dissertation defense, in particular I immensely thank Prof. Dr. Horváth M. Tamás (Chairman), Prof. Dr. Gál István László and Prof. Dr. Nagy Anita, Prof. Dr. Görgényi Illona as well as Prof. Dr. Blaskó Béla and other opponents for their great comments and suggestions. I would also extend my gratitude to Prof. Dr. Zhou Zhenjie (Beijing Normal University, China) and Prof. Dr. Li Rong (Minzu University of China).

The members of the Faculty of Law have contributed immensely to my personal and professional time in Debrecen. The faculty family, especially my department members, Dr. Sipos Ferenc and Dr. Pápai-Tarr Ágnes, have been a source of friendship as well as good advice and collaboration. I would like to thank all faculty members, and I am especially grateful to our Dean, Dr. Szikora Veronika, the Secretary of our Doctoral School, Dr. Zaccaria Márton Leó, and the Head of the Géza Marton Doctoral School Of Legal Studies, Prof. Dr. József Szabadfalvi D.Sc., and the administration office, Dr. Kissné dr. Tóth Tímea, Csonka Brigitta Katalin, Szabad-Andrási Tünde, and our professors, Prof. Dr. Várnay Ernő, Prof. Dr. Bencze Mátyás, Prof. Dr. Fézer Tamás, and I would also like to acknowledge my best friends and colleagues: Dr. Ficsor Krisztina and Dr. Gócza Ágnes.

I gratefully acknowledge Prof. Dr. Marcel Alexander Niggli, who support me to do research at the Faculty of Fribourg, Switzerland, and Prof. Dr. iur. Hubert Stöckli,

Prof. Dr. Gerhard Fiolka, Prof. Dr. Bettina Hürlimann-Kaup, Prof. Dr. Joëlle Vuille, and Dr. Patricia Meylan, as well as my colleagues Larissa Fricke, Paul Stübi, Emile Moorhouse, Jérôme Léger, Stefanie Bernet.

I would like to thank Misi Bácsi and his wife, who were like my grandparents in Debrecen.

My sincerest thanks to my brothers' and sisters' love and encouragement, in particular I appreciate my uncle, Wang Yi, just like my father, who has always been sponsoring me to study, so that I can have the opportunity to change my destiny through knowledge from a poor family's child.

Lastly, I do sincerely appreciate the following journals for kindly allowing materials, previously published in them, to be reprinted in this book in a substantially modified version: *Acta Juridica Hungarica* (Gui Huang: On the Problem of Just Sentencing in China, Acta Juridica Hungarica, Vol.56, Issue 2–3, 2015, pp.177–190), *University of Bologna Law Review* (Gui Huang: On Recent Changes to Life Imprisonment in the Context of the Gradual Reduction in the Use of the Death Penalty in China, Vol.3, Issue 1, 2018, pp.24–63), *Lawasia Journal* (Gui Huang: On the Alternative Punishment to the Death Penalty in China, Lawasia Journal, Vol.2017, pp.19–48), *Asia-Pacific Journal on Human Rights and the Law* (Gui Huang: The Communist Party of China's Approach to Human Rights and the Death Penalty, Asia-Pacific Journal on Human Rights and the Law, Vol.18, Issue 2, 2017, pp.117–154), *Jura* (Gui Huang: Life Imprisonment System in Continental Europe and Asia: Examples from Various States, Jura: A Pecsi Tudomanyegyetem Allam-es Jogtudomanyi Karanak Tudomanyos Lapja, Vol.2018, Issue 1, 2018, pp.269–279).

Fribourg, Switzerland Dr. Gui Huang
January 2024

Contents

1 Introduction 1
1.1 Background and Hypotheses 1
1.2 A Reality Should not Be Ignored: The Relationship Between the CPC's Viewpoint and Legislation 5

2 General Views on Criminal Punishment in China 11
2.1 The Nature of Criminal Punishment 12
2.2 The Purpose of Criminal Punishment 24
2.2.1 The Retention of the Death Penalty 24
2.2.2 Combined Punishments Involving a Fine and Other Principal Punishments 26
2.2.3 LWOR for the Crime of Embezzlement and Bribery 28
2.2.4 A Heavier Penalty for a Recidivist 29
2.3 A Political Requirement of Penalty Discretion: Unifying the Legal Effect and the Social Effect 30
2.3.1 The Rise and Causes of "Unifying the Social Effect and the Legal Effect" 31
2.3.2 The Risks and Correction of the Unity of the Legal Effect and the Social Effect in Punishment Decisions 34
2.4 De Facto: The Problems of the Justice of Penalty Discretion and Its Solutions 36
2.4.1 The Limitations of Deductive Reasoning in the Sentencing 38
2.4.2 The External and Internal Factors Influencing the Judicial Reasoning of Punishment Decisions 42
2.4.3 Values Fostered by Judges 47
2.4.4 The Solutions for the Dilemma of Sentencing Justice in China 48
2.5 Conclusion 51

3 The Death Penalty and Its Reforms in China and Other Countries 55
3.1 The Death Penalty System and Its Reforms in China 56
3.1.1 The Death Penalty Policies and Legislation: From 1949 to 2011 56
3.1.2 The Death Penalty Legislation and Reform After 2015 70
3.1.3 The Death Penalty and Its Reforms in Other Countries 74
3.1.4 The Death Penalty and Its Reforms in Europe and Central Asia 80
3.1.5 The Death Penalty and Its Reform in the USA 87
3.2 Conclusion 91

4 The Alternative Punishment to the Death Penalty 93
4.1 Controversy over the Notion of an Alternative Punishment to the Death Penalty 93
4.2 The Influencing Factors on the Punishment Options to Replace the Death Penalty 96
4.2.1 Human Rights 97
4.2.2 The Ideas Behind the Penalty 108
4.2.3 Criminal Policy 115
4.2.4 Public Opinion 118
4.2.5 Political Concerns 121
4.3 The Issues of Alternative to the Death Penalty in Other States 123
4.3.1 The Alternative Punishment to the Death Penalty in Abolitionist States: The European Perspective 124
4.3.2 The Potential Alternative Punishment to the Death Penalty in Retentionist States: Taking India, Japan and the United States as Examples 126
4.4 Conclusion 128

5 General Issues Concerning Life Imprisonment 131
5.1 The Notion of Life Imprisonment 132
5.2 The Characteristics of Life Imprisonment 135
5.2.1 Lengthy Incarceration 135
5.2.2 In Its Severity Life Imprisonment Ranks Only Second to the Death Penalty 137
5.2.3 Only for the Most Serious Crimes 138
5.3 The Forms of Life Imprisonment 139
5.3.1 LWPR and LWOR 139
5.3.2 Life Imprisonment with Work and Without Work 140
5.3.3 Mandatory Life Imprisonment and Discretionary Life Imprisonment 141
5.4 The Effects of Life Imprisonment 141
5.4.1 The Effects of Life Imprisonment on the Convict 142
5.4.2 The Effects of Life Imprisonment on the Victims 144
5.4.3 The Effects of Life Imprisonment on the Public 145

5.5 Life Imprisonment in China and Other Countries 146
5.5.1 Life Imprisonment in China 146
5.5.2 Life Imprisonment in Other States 159
5.5.3 International Documents Relating to Life Imprisonment 179
5.6 Conclusion 180

6 The Approaches of Life Imprisonment as an Alternative to the Death Penalty in China 183
6.1 In theory 183
6.2 In Practice 186
6.3 My Proposals 190
6.4 The Potential Changes Caused by the Alternative Punishment to the Death Penalty 192
6.4.1 Substantive Perspective 192
6.4.2 Procedural Perspective 195
6.5 Conclusion 196

7 Conclusion 197

References 199

control of death penalty, and has not substantially reformed the death penalty as used frequently by the judicial authorities. This is especially true given that, in judicial practice the death penalty is used most widely for crimes of intentional homicide, intentional injury, drug-related offenses, robbery and rape, for which the number of death sentences accounted for 90% of all 152 death cases in sampling research,[9] so the abolition of the death penalty has not yet gone to the core of the issue. Undeniably, this is in accordance with the gradualist approach to abolition, which was declared by the political document. Consequently, the legislator and judicial authorities do not have to face an urgent question of how to control serious and lethal crimes after completely abolishing the death penalty; this problem, however, cannot be neglected.

It is particularly worth mentioning that, except for reforming the death penalty system, the two amendments also amend the relevant systems of life imprisonment and fixed-term imprisonment with the aim of "making up the deficiencies of the custodial sentences".[10] To a certain extent, it cannot be denied that the country has already confronted the potential problems of the penalty structure as a whole which are caused by the abolition of the death penalty, and become aware of the importance and urgency of the coming issue of the alternative punishment to the death penalty.

In a super-country with a complex social structure, a weakened social regulating mechanism[11] and a huge population, such as China, with an in-depth reform of the death penalty, the issue discussed above, i.e. how to control crime without the use of the death penalty, will become an important and difficult challenge for legislators and the rulers of the state. Looking outside China, we can see that an alternative punishment to the death penalty has always been the option in order to control crime

说明》*[The Explanations for the Draft of the Ninth Amendment to Criminal Law of the People's Republic of China]*, available at: 中国人大网 [The National People's Congress of the People's Republic of China]. http://www.npc.gov.cn/npc/lfzt/rlys/2014-11/03/content_1885123.htm (Last visited: November 10th, 2023).

[9] See 苏永通, 任重远 [SU Yongtong and REN Zhongyuan], *《152份死刑复核裁定书分析报告公开的死刑密码》[Death Sentence Code Disclosed by the Analysis Report on 152 Judgments of Death Case Review]*, available at: 凤凰网 [ifeng Net]. http://ent.ifeng.com/a/20141016/40331612_0.shtml (Last visited: Novermber 15th, 2023) This report notes that the sampling research was carried out on the 152 judgments of death case review conducted by the Supreme People's Court published in China Judgements Online (中国裁判文书网) in the period from 2 July 2013 to 30 September 2014. These judgments include 45 judgments made in 2014, 101 judgments in 2013, 4 judgments in 2012 and 2 judgements in 2011. There are 12 capital crimes in these 152 death cases, and 5 of them are the crimes of intentional homicide, intentional injury, drug-related offenses, robbery and rape.

[10] 赵秉志[ZHAO Bingzhi], *《中国刑法改革新思考——以 < 刑法修正案(八)(草案) > 为主要视角》[New Thinking on the Reform of Criminal Law of China: With the Perspective of the Eighth Amendment (Draft) to the Criminal Law]*, 北京师范大学学报(社会科学版) [Journal of Beijing Normal University(Social Sciences)] 2011, No.1, 96.

[11] See 田中重好, 朱安新 [TIANZHONG Chonghao and ZHU Anxin], *《中国社会结构变动和社会性调节机制的弱化》[The Changes of the Social Structure in China and the Weakening of the Social Regulating Mechanism]*, 学习与探索 [Study & Exploration] 2010, No. 4, 35.

without the use of the death penalty.[12] Considering the coming problems in China and international legislative experience, in recent years some Chinese scholars have already started to research the issue and attempted to find an appropriate alternative punishment to the death penalty, but they have not yet reached a consensus on this question. Some scholars have argued that, if the term "death penalty" merely refers to immediate execution without including the death penalty with reprieve, the alternative punishment, in practice, already exists. In this sense, an alternative sanction is not a punishment replacing the death penalty in a situation in which it is repealed completely, but one that can restrict the application of the death penalty from the judicial and legislative perspective of retaining it as a punishment. They have argued that the death sentence with reprieve and strict life imprisonment would be the appropriate alternative punishment to immediate execution.[13] Other critics have pointed out that when considering an alternative measure to the death penalty, measures should not be taken that restrict the application of the death penalty or ensure that it is never used in judicial practice. The alternative sanction to the death penalty should be a punishment that legislatively replaces the death penalty as stipulated by the Criminal Law for a certain and concrete crime.[14] This is the debate regarding the legal concept of an alternative punishment to the death penalty in which Chinese criminal law scholars are currently involved. Another debate concerns what kind of punishment measure could be adopted as the alternative to the death penalty, and here different scholars have different opinions.

Based on these academic debates and legislative facts, we can see that even though some literature has already done some researches on the issue of the alternative punishments to the death penalty, it is still not the hottest topical one like the issues on the reform of the death penalty in China, but it could not be ignored and need to be focused in the near future with the further steps of the death penalty abolition. Because the issue of completely repealing the death penalty *de jure and* de facto can hardly be avoided, the issue on how to control the crime without the death penalty in China's complicated society and its alternative punishment have to be considered during the process of removing the death penalty. The main question of this present book is what the alternative punishment is and how to replace the death penalty with

[12] See, generally, *Alternatives to the Death Penalty Information Pack (Second edition 2015)*, available at: https://cdn.penalreform.org/wp-content/uploads/2015/03/PRI_Alternatives_to_death_penalty_info_pack_WEB.pdf (Last visited: November 17th, 2023).

[13] See, especially, 高铭暄 [GAO Mingxuan], *《略论中国刑法中的死刑替代措施》[Brief Discussion on the Alternative Measures to the Death Penalty in Chinese Criminal Law]*, 河北法学 [Law Science] 2008, Vol. 26, No. 2, 18; See also 高铭暄, 王秀梅 [GAO Mingxuan and WANG Xiumei], *《死刑替代利弊分析》[Advantages and Disadvantages of Replacing the Death Penalty*], 江苏行政学院学报 [Journal of the Jiangsu Administration Institute] 2008, No.1, 98. In this paper, the scholars argue that only the mandatory imposition of the death penalty and no other punishment should be available for certain crimes (the crime of aircraft skyjacking and kidnapping); and that it should be replaced legislatively by other alternative measures. For the other capital crimes, there are other punishments stipulated by law as an alternative to the death penalty.

[14] See especially 李希惠 [LI Xihui], *《论死刑的替代措施:以我国刑法立法为基点》[Study on the Alternative Measures to the Death Penalty: Standpoint on the Ground of Criminal Law Legislation in Our Country]*, 河北法学 [Hebei Law Science] 2008, Vol. 26, No. 2, 27.

other punishment in China's penalty system. The initial hypotheses are that the death penalty will be gradually removed from the penalty system and life imprisonment with possibility of release will be the alternative punishment to the death penalty. However, all the hypotheses have to be placed on China's reality, including the theories influenced by the special ideology and the judicial practice.

1.2 A Reality Should not Be Ignored: The Relationship Between the CPC's Viewpoint and Legislation

Actually, China's reality cannot be ignored if you want to research the issues on China. In other words, it, to a certain extent, cannot use the Western common theories and standards to explain and understand the China's issues, including the reform of penalty system and human rights, but it needs to place the hypotheses and their related issues on the China's realities. And the most important reality is China's special political system. In other words, the CPC's viewpoint has a great influence on the legislation. Therefore, here would like to explain the relationship between the CPC's viewpoint and the legislation. In order to better to explain this relationship, this section would like to take the relationship between the CPC's view on human rights and the death penalty as the analysis example.

Given the existence of two factors discussed below, it seems a false dichotomy that there are certain relationships between the CPC's view on human rights and the death penalty. Firstly, the concept and standards of human rights should be the same throughout the word, and so the CPC should not have its own view on the subject; secondly, if the former principle is valid, the relationships between the view taken on human rights and the death penalty will be met with much skepticism because of the existence of judicial independence; in other words, it seems impossible to explain the relationship between the Party's view and the specific system, particularly the specific punishments adopted. In considering these two potential problems, we need a full understanding of human rights development in China, and the country's political regime.

As regards the first question, human rights should have no frontiers, although this principle seems to change when it comes to China. This can be explained by China's history and the CPC's attitudes to human rights and their practical application. In China, with its long history of feudal dictatorship, a feudal culture developed to an extreme degree, and there has been neither the opportunity nor the appropriate conditions for democratic forces to develop, nor even for the concept of democracy itself to breed and develop, due to its suppression and destruction by feudal influences and despotism. In modern times, along with foreign intervention, Western civilization was introduced into China, including its political thought and the concept of human rights. Guo Songtao, the first Chinese diplomat and statesman during the

Qing dynasty, introduced Jean-Jacques Rousseau into China[15] and was the first to propose the concept of "civil rights (民权)".[16] Following this, such Chinese scholars and revolutionaries as Kang Youwei and Liang Qichao continued research on this subject. Sun Yat-sen, first president and founding father of the Republic of China, tried to establish a rich and powerful state incorporating the Western approach to Liberty, Equality and Fraternity. From 1908 to 1946, there were dozens of publications dealing with human rights and civil rights protection.[17] The concept of human rights, however, could not take hold among the Chinese people. One of the chief reasons for this is that the concept of human rights, just like that of the constitution, was shaped and developed in Western cultural soil and is exotic; this led to it being challenged and excluded by the feudalistic culture in China. So, it is clear that there were no conditions for the development of human rights in modern China, let alone constitutionally protected human rights, and the theory of human rights has not taken hold in China due to the lack of an appropriate cultural environment for these rights and their practical application.

The development of human rights in China enjoys only a relatively short history, stretching back no more than three decades. Compared with the West, where "human rights as values are rooted in the historical development of human society, being theorized by both natural law doctrine and the doctrine of positivism",[18] in China the issue of human rights has been considered a bourgeois slogan and was excluded from the field of jurisprudence studies after the founding of the New China; this situation changed somewhat on 10 November 1989, when the Propaganda Department of the CPC Central Committee organized a small expert panel to discuss human rights issues.[19] Subsequently, due to the lack of an indigenous concept of human rights from China's own cultural resources, Chinese scholars once again began to pay attention to the West, the theoretical source of human rights. Western human rights theory became a significant and key resource in Chinese academic circles; for example, the majority of Western works on human rights have been translated into Chinese and

[15] 吴雅凌 [WU Yaling], *《卢梭 <社会契约论 > 的汉译及其影响》 [Chinese Translation of the Social Contract by Jean-Jacques Rousseau and its influences]*, 现代哲学 [Modern Philosophy] 2009, Vol. 104, No. 3, 86.

[16] 赵小波[ZHAO Xiaobo], *《近代中国 "民权"内涵演变考论:从维新到革命的话语转换》 [On the Evolution of the Concept of Civil Rights in Modern China: The Discussion on Conversion from Restoration to Revolution]*, 法学家 [The Juris] 2015, No. 2, 140–141.

[17] These documents chiefly include the Outline of the *Constitution by Imperial Order [钦定宪法大纲]* adopted on August 27, 1908; The *Provisional Constitution of the Republic of China [中华民国临时约法]* adopted on March 11, 1912; The *'Temple of Heaven' Draft Constitution [天坛宪法草案]* adopted on October 31, 1913; *The Constitution of Republic of China [中华民国宪法]* adopted on October 10, 1923; The *Constitution of Republic of China [中华民国宪法]* adopted on December 25, 1946, and so on.

[18] PAVEL Nicolae, *Defining the Concept of Human Rights in the Light of Juridical Values Theory*, Contemporary Readings in Law and Social Justice, 2012, Vol. 4, No. 1, 508.

[19] 郭道晖, 陶威 [GUO Daohui and TAO Wei], *《人权禁区是怎样突破的——建国以来法学界重大事件研究》 [How Could the Exclusion Zone for Human Rights be Broken? On Significant Cases Occurring in the Field of Jurisprudence after the Foundation of the PRC]*, 法学 [Law Science] 1999, No. 5, 2.

introduced into China. Furthermore, Chinese scholars have long been researching Western human rights theory from all kinds of perspectives, and exploring the causes of the development of human rights and the conditions for their implementation and for the creation of a system to safeguard them. This research has also investigated the considerable experience and practice of human rights in the West. In addition, various Chinese scholars have conducted research on human rights issues from the perspective of the West, or in terms of the international standards set by various international treaties or conventions. All of these approaches promote the development of human rights in China. However, the influence exerted by this activity is, in fact, only limited, and mostly confined to academic research.[20] Consequently, it is easy to create a false impression that human rights issues in China can be completely and definitively answered and solved simply by learning from, and copying or following, Western or international standards.

On the other hand, international critics, observers, activists and relevant organizations always focus on human rights issues in China from their own perspectives, and criticize China according to the standards set by Western or relevant international treaties or conventions, or according to the so-called "double standard".[21] This approach puts a great deal of international pressure on China and drives human rights in China forward. However, it also seems to have already created an erroneous impression that the human rights process in China can be quickly advanced by international criticism and pressure.

China does indeed have to draw lessons from the successful Western experience of human rights protection and needs to fulfill its obligations and commitments under relevant international treaties. We really cannot deny that the development of human rights in China would benefit from academic research and international criticism; however, to research the issue of human rights in China and to identify the essential facts and their causes and to offer a perspective which is academically appropriate, one has to understand the brief developmental history of human rights in China, and the country's present condition.

As regards China's present condition, a significant point is the country's special political regime. According to *the Preamble of the Constitution of China*, the country is a one-party state, and the system is one of multiparty cooperation and political consultation led by CPC.[22] As far as human rights is concerned, therefore, based on this theoretical guidance, the CPC has its own outlook. The Party not only plays

[20] In this sense, the CPC's political documents have already stated that, 'we should draw from the quintessence of Chinese legal culture, learn from beneficial experiences in the rule of law abroad, but we can absolutely not indiscriminately copy foreign rule of law concepts and models. See *《中共中央关于全面推进依法治国若干重大问题的决定》[The CCP Central Committee Decision Concerning Some Major Questions in Comprehensively Moving Government of the Country According to the Law Forward (hereinafter abbreviated to CCP-CDC)]*, available at: 中国社会科学网 (China Social Science Net) http://www.cssn.cn/fx/fx_ttxw/201410/t20141030_1381703.shtml. (Last visited: November 25th, 2023).

[21] PEERENHOOM Randall, *Assessing Human Rights in China: Why the Double Standard?* Cornell International Law Journal, 2005, No. 38, 71.

[22] *《中华人民共和国宪法》[Constitution of the People's Republic of China]*, 2004.

a political leadership role, but also directs legislation and law enforcement, and its view or standpoint is considered the national will and so becomes law.[23] Party-led legislation is a system with Chinese characteristics. In accordance with the *Constitution of the CPC*, "leadership by the Party means mainly political, ideological and organizational leadership".[24] Political leadership by the Party refers to leadership over political principles, political orientation and major policy decisions. Political leadership can normally be carried out by legalizing the implementation of policies. Organizational leadership refers to formulating and implementing the correct line, principles and policies, i.e. carrying out organizational, publicity and educational work effectively. Ideological leadership means that the Party guides thinking. "The CPC takes *Marxism-Leninism, Mao Zedong's Thought, Deng Xiaoping's Theory, the Important Thought of the Three Representatives ((三个代表重要思想; hereinafter: Three Representatives)* and *the Scientific Outlook on Development (科学发展观, hereinafter: SOD)* as its guide to action."[25] The CPC has its own position on human rights, based on the Party's theoretical guidance and China's reality and history. It is clear that the CPC's outlook on human rights must be incorporated into the relevant human rights legislation and judicial practice. However, one point must be made clear in this book, and that is that the difference between the CPC's perspective on human rights and the West's is not based on a different literal definition of the notion and terminology of human rights; in other words, in examining the CPC's outlook on human rights, this book does not focus on a didactic conceptual explanation of human rights, but rather concentrates on the CPC's understanding and attitude towards the practice of human rights at different times.

In the light of this analysis, it has already been demonstrated that the first question is valid, i.e. the CPC's perspective on human rights deeply influences and even leads the legislation concerning guarantees of human rights; the second question is hence very easily answered and demonstrated. On the one hand, in international terms, i.e. in terms of basic standards and safeguards, the concept of international human rights

[23] The CCP-CDC demonstrates that letting the Party leadership penetrate the entire process and all aspects of ruling the country according to the law is a basic experience of the construction of our country's Socialist rule of law. Persisting with the Party leadership is a basic need for the Socialist rule of law; it is where the foundations and the life-line of the Party and the State lie...... Party leadership and the Socialist rule of law are identical, the Socialist rule of law must persist in Party leadership; Party leadership must rely on the Socialist rule of law...... We must persist with the idea of the Party leading legislation, guaranteeing law enforcement, supporting the judiciary...... being good at making the Party's standpoints become the national will through statutory procedures. See *《中共中央关于全面推进依法治国若干重大问题的决定》[The CCP Central Committee Decision Concerning Some Major Questions in Comprehensively Moving Government of the Country According to the Law Forward]*, above no.20. In relation to this, one Chinese scholar has said that the role of political guarantees for the Party leadership lies in the fact that the Party's guiding thought should also be the guide for the rule of law. See刘家征 [LIU Jiazheng], *《党的领导和依法治国高度统一》[On the High Unity of the Party's Leadership and Rule by Law]*, available at: 求是网 (Qiu Shi Net). http://www.qstheory.cn/laigao/2015-02/10/c_1114315500.htm (Last visited: November 29th, 2023).

[24] *《中国共产党党章》[Constitution of the Communist Party of China]*.

[25] Ibid.

is an essential element in the strategy to abolish the death penalty, and has enabled abolition and saved lives.[26] In other words, protecting human rights by abolishing capital punishment or limiting its use, which has already been prescribed by some international treaties or conventions, has already, and for a long time, been recognized and accepted by the international community. On the other hand, China itself is still ruled by an authoritarian regime.[27] Under this regime, two important elements decide whether a policy will be implemented or not, namely, the determination made by the highest level of government, and time demands.[28] This is also the case with the reform of the death penalty. When exploring China's death penalty reform from the perspective of human rights, the CPC's human rights perspectives and relevant policies should be focused on, rather than Western standards of human rights, because China's political and legal regimes are completely different from the West's. In China, the CPC's policies play a guiding role in the process of the enactment and implementation of the law through the main methods used to codify the Party's policies into law, and the ways in which the laws are implemented. Conversely, the process of the rule of law also restricts the Party's policies; however, where there is a conflict between the rule of law and policies, the influence of the former on the latter will always show that the former effectively promotes and ensures the implementation of the latter.[29]

---

[26] SHETTY Salil, *The Value of International Standards in the Campaign for Abolition of the Death Penalty,* The Brown Journal of World Affairs, 2014, Vol. XXI, No. 1, 42.

[27] 于建嵘 [YU Jianrong], *《共治威权与法治威权——中国政治发展的问题与出路》[Condominium Authoritarian Regime and the Authoritarian Regime of the Rule of Law: the Problems and Outlooks of Political Development in China],* 当代世界社会主义问题 [Issues of Contemporary World Socialism] 2008, Vol. 98, No. 4, 17. The author pointes out in this paper that China had already changed from a "*paternalistic authoritarian regime (家长式的威权体制)*" in the Mao Zedong and Deng Xiaoping era to the "*condominium authoritarian regime (共治式的威权体制)*" in the of post-Deng period, and now is trying to drive forward the "*authoritarian regime of rule of law (法治式的威权体制).*".

[28] 聂辉华 [NIE Huihua], *《郑永年先生站着说话不腰疼》[Mr. Zheng Yongnian Spoke Irresponsibly and Sarcastically]*, available at: 新浪博客 (Sina blog). http://www.21ccom.net/html/2016/gqmq_0129/1317.html (Last visited: Devember 1st, 2023).

[29] 沈宗灵 [SHEN Zongling], *《法理学》[Jurisprudence],* 北京大学出版社[Beijing University Press], Beijing, 2000, 272–273.

Chapter 2
General Views on Criminal Punishment in China

Abstract This chapter is a general theoretical discussion of criminal punishment in China. Based on China's realities, this chapter intends to analyse the nature of criminal punishment in China, which is considered "a dictatorship punishment instrument" and the purpose of criminal punishment, which always has a retributive goal, and punishment decisions, which focus on the political requirements of discretionary punishment and practical problems in judicial practice, i.e., problems related to the justice of punishment decisions.

In a Party-state[1] like China, the leadership of the CPC is considered the strongest foundation and the most fundamental guarantee of the construction of the rule of law with its special Chinese characteristics,[2] and its decision and policies should be implemented and embodied in all areas of legislation and judicial practice. After President Xi Jinping came to power in late 2012, the CPC officially launched the Party's important political document in 2013 and declared its intention "to build a China under the rule of law…and safeguard the people's rights and interests, and ensure that the people are satisfied with equality and justice in every court verdict"[3]; in 2014, the CPC released another important political document and set a new blueprint for the socialist rule of law. This political document emphasizes that rule of law "insists on the dominant position of the people…makes guaranteeing the people's basic rights and interests into a starting point and stopover point … [and] insists on

---

[1] TREVASKES Susan, *Lenient Death Sentencing and the "Cash for Clemency" Debate*, The China Journal, 2015, Vol. 73, 39.

[2] See 陈翼平 [Chen Yiping],《坚持党的领导》*[Upholding the Leadership of the Party]*, available at: 求是网 (Qstheory.cn). http://www.qstheory.cn/dukan/qs/2014-11/16/c_1113228486.htm (Last visited: December 3rd, 2023).

[3] *Decision of the Central Committee of the Communist Party of China on Some Major Issues Concerning Comprehensively Deepening the Reform*, above no. 5.

G. Huang, *On the Alternative Punishment to the Death Penalty in China*,
https://doi.org/10.1007/978-981-97-1627-2_2

starting from China's reality."[4] According to these two political documents, China has been building a state under "the socialist rule of law" since 2013. In addition, these two political documents also emphasize that the socialist rule of law theory provides the theoretical guidance and academic support for ruling the country according to the law; it can absolutely not indiscriminately copy foreign rule of law concepts and models but draws from the quintessence of Chinese legal culture.[5] In this context, in order to correctly review and analyze criminal punishment in China, one needs to adapt to the Chinese "language system" and its reality. The "language system" here is, in fact, a kind of ideological one, which "plays a leading role in building the socialist rule of law in China",[6] and "puts the development of the rule of law" on "the path designed by the ideology and following the CPC's pursuit of values."[7]

Even though the so-called "class struggle" aspects have already been withdrawn from the language system in present-day China, "the Maoist ideology has helped to package criminal justice language and practice across disparate agendas, across the different political priorities of Party leaders from Deng Xiaoping, Hu Jintao and Xi Jinping, and so across … time."[8] In fact, however, Maoist ideology is only one important part of China's socialist ideology, which includes *Marxism-Leninism, Mao Zedong's Thought, Deng Xiaoping's Theory, the Three Representatives, the SOD* and the *spirit of the series of important speeches by Xi Jinping*, all of which have "helped to frame and justify the way the party-state punishes those it has identified as offenders in order to preserve political and social stability."[9] On this basis, this part will examine the criminal punishment system in China in the context of building a state under the rule of law from the perspectives of the nature, aim and function of criminal punishment, and examine the problems of the justice of the penalty discretion in judicial practice.

2.1 The Nature of Criminal Punishment

Regarding the Chinese socialist rule of law, a Chinese scholar has explained and clearly pointed out that in the context of contemporary society, social complexity and other important special facts mean that China must take and expand the positions and

[4] *The CCP Central Committee Decision concerning Some Major Questions in Comprehensively Moving Governing the Country According to the Law Forward*, available at: https://chinacopyrightandmedia.wordpress.com/2014/10/28/ccp-central-committee-decision-concerning-some-major-questions-in-comprehensively-moving-governing-the-country-according-to-the-law-forward/ (Last visited: December 10th, 2023).

[5] See ibid.

[6] 蒋传光, 王逸飞 [JIANG Chuangang and WANG Yifei], *《论社会主义意识形态对当代法治发展的主导作用》[On the Leading Role of Socialist Ideology in the Development of Rule of Law in the Contemporary of China]*, 学习与探索 [Study & Exploration] 2011, No. 5, 97.

[7] Ibid, 99.

[8] TREVASKES Susan, *Using Mao to Package Criminal Justice Discourse in 21st Century China*, China Quarterly, 2016, Vol. 226, 299.

[9] Ibid.

orientation of the pragmatic application of the rule of law against the background of the conception and practice of the socialist rule of law.[10] These special facts include: 1) that the reality of the operation of the law is conducted under the guidance of the Party's policies[11]; 2) that the law advocated or approved by the mainstream ideology is still considered as expressing the opinions of the "will" and "instrument" initiated by Marxism-Leninism, i.e., the law is the will of the ruling class and it is an instrument for them to rule the country.[12] In addition, China is a traditional society with a history of being ruled by man.[13] In this light, criminal law has more obvious pragmatic characteristics in the context of the socialist rule of law. Even though the class features of criminal law have faded and been replaced by other new Marxist theories for the development of society, they still show through in unexpected forms and places, "like wolves in sheep's clothing".[14]

The nature of criminal punishment refers to an inherent and internal feature of criminal punishment and this can distinguish it from other punishments. In the era of "class struggle", the concept of the offense is bound together with class and the "class struggle",[15] and the offense refers to "a struggle done by an isolative individual against the rule relationship."[16] The "rule relationship" is considered a class oppression relationship, i.e., the ruling class which grasps state power sets up or approves of a social relationship reflected by the law for the sake of protecting the ruling class's interest; it is a kind of relationship of rights and obligations, which are stipulated by the ruling class in accordance with their will and interests, in a society that protects the political and economic interests of the ruling class.[17] These relationships of rights and obligations constitute a social relationship and social order which benefit the ruling class; therefore, an offense is a kind of behavior that harms this social relationship and defies the social order.[18] As a legal result of the

[10] 顾培东[GU Peidong], *《当代中国法治共识的形成及法治再启蒙》[On the Formation of the Consensus of Rule of Law and its Re-enlightenment in Contemporary China]*, available at: 中国社会科学网(Chinese Social Sciences Net) http://ex.cssn.cn/fx/201708/t20170830_3624561.shtml (Last visited: December 12th, 2023).

[11] Ibid.

[12] Ibid.

[13] Ibid.

[14] GARDINER Gerald, *The Purposes of Criminal Punishment*, The Modern Law Review, 1958, Vol. 21, No. 2, 8.

[15] 刘耀彬 [LIU Yaobin], *《马克思主义犯罪学思想研究》[On Marxist Thought on Criminology]*, 南京航空航天大学博士论文 [Ph.D. Dissertation, Nanjing University of Aeronautics and Astronautics] 2010, 46.

[16] *《马克思恩格斯全集》[The Collected Works of Marx And Engels]*, Vol. 3 (391), available at: http://cpc.people.com.cn/GB/64184/180145/180168/10864948.html (Last visited: December 13th, 2023).

[17] 邓定一, 康松林 [DENG Dingyi and KANG Songlin], *《马克思的犯罪概念是刑法理论的根本变革》[The Marxist Notion of the offense is a Fundamental Change of the Criminal Theory]*, 现代法学 [Modern Law Science] 1983, No. 2, 21–22.

[18] See 赵延光 [ZHAO Yanguang], *《论"犯罪是孤立的个人反对统治关系的斗争"》[On the Argument that "crime is a struggle done by an isolative individual against the 'rule relationship']*, 贵州大学学报: 社会科学版 [Journal of Guizhou University (Social Sciences)] 1984, No. 1, 69.

offense, criminal punishment is always considered by Karl Marx as "the law or state's self-defence means and an important means which is used by the state against the blasphemer."[19] In this sense, Vladimir Lenin said that "criminal punishment is used by all the oppressive class to protect its rule."[20] These opinions are cited by most Chinese scholars as the representative views of orthodox Marxism on criminal punishment, which is a necessary measure for social self-defence.[21]

Mao Zedong's thought on criminal punishment is considered the first expression of Marxist thought on criminal punishment with Chinese characteristics, which refers to the fact that Marxism is integrated with China's reality and the characteristics of the time.[22] In the paternalistic authoritarian regime of the Mao period, Mao's thought on punishment, which is based on his dialectical materialist ideology, is considered the Chinese government's outlook on punishment, and he extended and developed Marxist thinking on the subject. Mao identified a social contradiction among people (good people and bad people) and between us and the enemy, both of which were completely different in nature.[23] Mao had different attitudes to, and adopted different punishments for, these two contradictions. For counter-revolutionaries and reactionaries, such as class enemies, he always emphasized punishment as a dictatorial instrument; for example, on July 23, 1950, the document entitled "Instructions on Suppressing the Counter-Revolutionary" stipulated that "we must suppress the counter-revolutionary who is the tough criminal and remains impenitent; we must kill the reactionaries who should be sentenced to death."[24] In the movement of struggle against the "three evils" and the "five evils", he emphasized that "the struggle against corruption, waste, and bureaucracy should be stressed as much as the struggle to suppress counter-revolutionaries…the worst among them should be shot. These problems can only be solved in this way."[25] Mao pointed out that "we must suppress the reactionaries and their accomplices, who are called the enemy,

---

19 *《马克思恩格斯全集》[The Collected Works of Marx And Engels]*, Vol. 3 (391), above no. 45.

20 *《列宁全集》[The collected Works of Vladimir Lenin],* Vol. 18 (259)", available at: http://cpc.people.com.cn/GB/64184/180146/180248/10899743.html (Last visited: December 17th, 2023).

21 袁江华 [YUAN Jianghua], *《马克思主义刑罚思想中国化研究综述》[Literature Review on Marxist Thought on Criminal Punishment with Chinese Characteristics],* 毛泽东邓小平理论研究 [Studies on Mao Zedong's and Deng Xiaoping's Theories] 2010, No. 5, 49; and see also 江礼华[JIANG Lihua],《毛泽东的刑罚思想》[On Mao Zedong's Thought on Criminal Punishment], 中央检察官管理学院学报 [Journal of the Central College of the Procurator] 1993, No. Z1, 7.

22 See 袁江华 [YUAN Jianghua], *《马克思主义刑罚思想中国化论纲》[On the Sinicization of Marxist Thought on Punishment],* 扬州大学博士论文 [Ph.D. Dissertation, Yang Zhou University] 2011, 77.

23 MAO Zedong (MAO Tse-tung), *Contradictions under Socialism, in "Selected Works of Mao Tse-tung: Vol. 7*, available at: https://www.marxists.org/reference/archive/mao/selected-works/volume-7/mswv7_466.htm (Last visited: December 19th, 2017).

24 毛泽东[MAO Zedong], *《关于镇压反革命》[Comment on Suppressing and Liquidating Counterrevolutionaries],* 毛泽东选集 [Selected Works of Mao Tse-tung: Vol. 6], available at: http://cpc.people.com.cn/GB/64184/64185/189966/11568071.html (Last visited: December 20th, 2023).

25 Mao Zedong (Mao Tse-tung), *On the Struggle against the 'Three Evils' and the 'Five Evils'*, "Selected Works of Mao Tse-tung: Vol. 5", available at: https://www.marxists.org/reference/archive/mao/selected-works/volume-5/mswv5_17.htm (Last visited: December 29th, 2023).

allowing them only to behave themselves and not to be too unruly in word or deed. If they speak or act in an unruly way, they will be promptly stopped and punished. We [will adopt an attitude of] dictatorship over the reactionaries".[26] He also emphasized that "counter-revolutionaries must be eliminated wherever found. Kill few, but on no account repeal the death penalty or grant any general pardon."[27] However, for normal offenses committed by bad people, Mao said that "it is necessary to exercise dictatorship as well over thieves, swindlers, murderers, arsonists, criminal gangs and other scoundrels who seriously disrupt public order,"[28] because "the function of this dictatorship is to protect our country from subversion and possible aggression by external enemies."[29] As for the other law-breakers among the people, they "will also be punished according to law, but this is different in principle from the exercise of dictatorship to suppress enemies of the people."[30] Mao's policies on punishment for these two contradictory cases had an obviously utilitarian character, and Professor Susan Trevaskes refers to this as "utilitarian dialectics".[31] Based on Mao's dialectical view on punishments for these contradictions, we can say that the views of Mao on the nature of criminal punishment are not confined to Marx's view of "a necessary measure of social self-defence", but take it further, i.e., "criminal punishment is not only the dictator's instrument for class enemies, but also the measure of social self-defence for the offender who is the member of the ruling class."[32] Mao's views on punishment not only emphasized the effectiveness of the ruling class's self-defence by punishing the enemy and reactionaries but paid attention to the function of social self-defence for normal crimes.[33] However, an undeniable fact that must be pointed out is that the dictatorial nature of the punishment was over-emphasized and its use was devoid of any legal basis, let alone "any concept of proportionality or procedural safeguards for criminal defendants",[34] i.e., thousands of people were executed on various unwarranted grounds and even without any trial in a society which was almost a "legal vacuum". Almost a legal vacuum, because

---

[26] See MAO Zedong, *On the People's Democratic Dictatorship*, Selected Works of Mao Tse-tung: Vol. 7, available at: https://www.marxists.org/reference/archive/mao/selected-works/volume-4/mswv4_65.htm (Last visited: December 30th, 2023).

[27] MAO Zedong, *The Situation in the Summer of 1957,* Selected Works of Mao Tse-tung: Vol. 5, available at: https://www.marxists.org/reference/archive/mao/selected-works/volume-5/mswv5_66.htm (Last visited: December 30th, 2023).

[28] MAO Zedong, *On the Correct Handling of Contradictions among the People*, Selected Works of Mao Tse-tung: Vol. 5", available at: https://www.marxists.org/reference/archive/mao/selected-works/volume-5/mswv5_58.htm#v5_89 (Last visited: January 1st, 2024).

[29] Ibid.

[30] Ibid.

[31] TREVASKES Susan, *Using Mao to Package Criminal Justice Discourse in 21st-century China,* above no. 37, 300.

[32] 江礼华 [JIANG Lihua], above no. 50, 8.

[33] See ibid.

[34] FLORIA Ryan, *The Capital Punishment Fits the Crime: A Comparative Analysis of the Death Penalty and Proportionality in the United States of America and the People's Republic of China,* University of Miami International and Comparative Law Review, 2008, Vol. 16, No. 1, 68.

there were some special criminal laws, such as the Instruction on Suppression of Counter-revolutionary Activities of July 23rd, 1950, *the Regulations for Suppression of Counterrevolution of the PRC,* of February 20th, 1951, *the Interim Regulations on Punishment for the Impairment of the State Currency of the PRC of April 19th, 1951,* and *the Regulations for Suppression of Corruption of the PRC of April 21st, 1952.* In the Maoist era, the ideology of "continuing the revolution under the proletarian dictatorship" was dominant, and it was generalized into all spheres of society at that time,[35] and "made the legal construction of China nearly suffer from extinction."[36] However, as the founding father of China, Mao's thoughts on punishment have had a great influence on the subsequent and even current legislation and judicial practice. For example, Mao said that "kill few, but on no account repeal the death penalty",[37] which is still the current death penalty policy. Furthermore, following his dialectical approach, Mao proposed "a policy of combining suppression with leniency",[38] i.e. "a policy of certain punishment for the main culprits, no punishment for those accomplices who act under duress and rewards for those who render positive services".[39] This policy was written into the first Criminal Law in China which was passed in 1979, of which Article 1 stipulated that "it takes Marxism-Leninism-Mao Zedong Thought as its guide and the Constitution as its basis, and is formulated in accordance with the policy of combining punishment with leniency",[40] while Article 2 provided that it "uses criminal punishments to fight against all counterrevolutionary and other criminal acts in order to defend the system of the dictatorship of the proletariat…"[41] In fact, Mao's criminal policy is the original of the present policy of "balancing leniency and severity".[42]

"After Mao's death, Deng Xiaoping emerged as the country's paramount leader, initiating a gradual repudiation of orthodox Marxism"[43] and of Mao's theory of the class struggle, and China entered into an era of more pragmatic policies under Deng's

---

35 See 徐增文, 房博 [XU Zengwen and FANG Bo], *《社会主导意识形态变迁与中国经济发展::1978–2008》 [The Changes of the Socially Dominant Ideology and the Development of the Economy in China: From 1978 to 2008],* 南京政治学院学报 [Journal of PLA Nanjing Institute of Politics] 2008, No. 6, 5.

36 GAO Mingxuan and ZHAO Bingzhi, *The Evolution of Chinese Criminal Legislation,* Law Press. China, Beijing, 2007, 69.

37 MAO Zedong, *The Situation in the Summer of 1957,* Selected Works of Mao Tse-tung: Vol. 5, above no. 56.

38 MAO Zedong, *Fight for A Fundamental Turn for the Better in the Nation's Financial and Economic Situation,* Selected Works of Mao Tse-tung: Vol. 5", available at: https://www.marxists.org/reference/archive/mao/selected-works/volume-5/mswv5_06.htm (Last visited: January 2nd, 2024).

39 Ibid.

40 *《中华人民共和国刑法》 [The Criminal Law of the People's Republic of China], Order No. 5, 1979,* Article 1.

41 Ibid, Article 2.

42 See generally TREVASKES Susan, *The Shifting Sands of Punishment in China in the Era of 'Harmonious Society,* Law & Policy, 2010, Vol. 32, No. 3, 332–361.

43 *After Mao: The Rise of Deng Xiaoping,* available at: Facts and Details http://factsanddetails.com/china/cat2/sub7/entry-5537.html (Last visited: January 2nd, 2024).

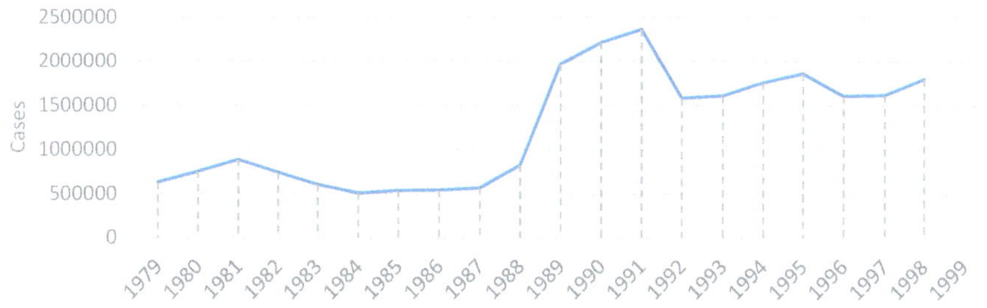

Graph 2.1 The changes in crimes rates from 1979 to 1999 (From the above graph, we can see that crime rates showed a rapid increase from 500,000 cases in 1987 to 2,400,000 cases in 1991. Before that, there was a small increase from 550,000 cases in 1979 to 900,000 cases in 1981, but after 1981 the crime rate decreased to its lowest point of 500 000 in 1984. After 1991, the crime rate also showed a marked decrease and then entered a period of fluctuating change.)

leadership.[44] Deng changed the socialist dominated ideology from the orthodox ideology, which unilaterally emphasized the revolution towards an emphasis on building the economy,[45] and launched a policy of reform and opening-up in 1979. Following this, all kinds of social contradictions arising from the consciousness of freedom, rights, and profit-seeking, which had been oppressed and held down for a long time, were gradually awakened and released, and the people's thoughts were released from the confines of the theory of the class struggle. Furthermore, people seized and competed for limited social resources. These also resulted in crimes occurring frequently and rampantly, as can be seen in the following graph.

Criminal cases reported to and filed by the public security authorities between 1979 and 1998 in China (Graph 2.1).[46]

As for the extreme changes in the social situation at that time, Deng had to face two important and urgent problems, i.e., he had to maintain a stable political environment and to develop the economy for the whole country. In order to solve these two problems, he inherited and carried forward Marx's view on criminal law, i.e. that criminal law is the ruling instrument for the ruler to protect the ruling order. At the beginning of the policy of reform and opening up, Deng still emphasized the class struggle but had already weakened it, saying, for example that,

> We must recognize that in our socialist society there are still counter-revolutionaries, enemy agents, criminals and other bad elements of all kinds who undermine socialist public order, as well as new exploiters who engage in corruption, embezzlement, speculation and profiteering... The struggle against these individuals is different from the struggle of one class

---

[44] Ibid.

[45] See 徐增文, 房博 [XU Zengwen and FANG Bo], above no. 64, 5.

[46] These data are from 董方, 徐建 [DONG Fang and XU Jian], *《对改革开放以来我国刑事犯罪增减变化的评析》[Analyzing the Changes of the Criminal Cases since the Reform and Opening-up in China]*, 青少年犯罪问题 [Issues on Juvenile Crimes and Delinquency] 1995, No. 2, 1; 夏菲 [XIA Fei], *《观念误区与犯罪现象关联的分析: 我国改革开放进程中犯罪问题的回顾与反思》[Analyzing the Relationship between Wrong Concepts and Crime Phenomena: Reviewing and Rethinking the Crime Issues in the Process of the Reform and Opening up in China]*, 犯罪研究 [Criminal Research] 2001, No. 2, 21.

> against another, which occurred in the past (these individuals cannot form a cohesive and overt class). However, it is still a special form of class struggle or a special form of the leftover, under socialist conditions, of the class struggles of past history. It is still necessary to exercise dictatorship over all these anti-socialist elements, and socialist democracy is impossible without it.[47]

And in the following year, 1980, he pointed out that,

> Our present struggles against the various kinds of counter-revolutionaries and saboteurs, criminals and criminal gangs guilty of serious offenses do not all constitute class struggle, but they contain elements of class struggle.[48]

In 1986, Deng continued to emphasize that "if we practice democracy within the ranks of the people without exercising dictatorship over the saboteurs, we cannot maintain political stability and unity or succeed in the modernization drive."[49] Ten years after launching the policy, the domestic conflicts and contradictions showed a rapid increase after 1988, and a typical example of this was the Tian Anmen Case in 1989. This case made Deng clearly understand China's situation and he pointed out that "in China, the overriding need is for stability. Without a stable environment, we can accomplish nothing and may even lose what have gained".[50] This approach has had a great influenced on China to date, and Deng's successors have also frequently emphasized this policy. For all the social changes under Deng's pragmatic policies, and although he weakened and even denied the existence of the orthodox class struggle, he could not deny and, in fact, even emphasized the dictatorial nature of punishment, and even more so than Mao, because of China's political regime and social structure as well as its network of interests. China is a "one-party state", which allows allied parties to exist as part of a permanent "popular front" coalition, but they are completely subservient to the ruling party, the Communist Party, and must accept its monopoly of power. Consequently, China's political regime is an exclusive and closed one, which takes the monopoly of political power as its ultimate aim and does not allow anyone to challenge it. Therefore, "maintaining political stability", as Deng pointed out, is the most important political task for China, and is also the core element of "the overriding need … for stability" which is referred to by some Chinese scholars as "stiff stability".[51] A famous Chinese sociologist and political

[47] DENG Xiaoping, *Uphold the Four Cardinal Principles", Selected Works of Deng Xiaoping: Volume II*, available at: https://dengxiaopingworks.wordpress.com/2013/02/25/uphold-the-four-cardinal-principles/ (Last visited: January 2nd, 2024).

[48] DENG Xiaoping, *The Present Situation and the Tasks before Us*, Selected Works of Deng Xiaoping: Volume II, available at: https://dengxiaopingworks.wordpress.com/2013/02/25/the-present-situation-and-the-tasks-before-us/ (Last visited: January 3rd, 2024).

[49] DENG Xiaoping, *Talk at a Meeting of the Standing Committee of the Political Bureau of the Central Committee*, Selected Works of Deng Xiaoping, available at: https://dengxiaopingworks.wordpress.com/2013/03/18/talk-at-a-meeting-of-the-standing-committee-of-the-political-bureau-of-the-central-committee/ (Last visited: January 4th, 2024).

[50] DENG Xiaoping, *The Overriding Need is for Stability*, Selected Works of Deng Xiaoping: Volume III, available at: https://dengxiaopingworks.wordpress.com/2013/03/18/the-overriding-need-is-for-stability/ (Last visited: January 4th, 2024).

[51] 于建嵘 [YU Jianrong], *《当前压力维稳的困境与出路——再论中国社会的刚性稳定》[The Problems and the Solution of the Present Pressure on Stability: Reviewing again the Stiff Stability in*

sciencitist, Professor Yu Jianrong, pointed out that there have been some serious cases of "mass disturbance" in China, but they are only isolated cases which cannot easily become social movements on a nationwide scale. They protest at negative and/or random acts of the government, and they do so in order to deal with the problems of pragmatic interests, rather than to make political claims or topple the government.[52] However, under the requirements of the "stiff stability" which takes absolute social stability as its governmental aim, and based on the concept of state violence, all protest activities, such as demonstrations, strikes, shopkeeper's strikes and so on, are considered contrary to good order and essentially chaotic, and the government must adopt all kinds of measures to suppress and crack down on them,[53] and maintain its dictatorship position.[54] Following this political logic, Deng argued that "we cannot do without dictatorship; we must not only reaffirm the need for it but exercise it when necessary."[55] These arguments on the dictatorship nature of punishment were fully implemented into contemporary legislation and judicial practice. From 1981 onwards, the SCNPC successively adopted 25 Special Criminal Laws up to the time the present Criminal Law was passed in 1997; other subsidiary criminal provisions are provided in 107 non-criminal laws.[56] All these Special Criminal Laws brought a great change to the 1979 Criminal Law; for example, 163 new crimes were added to it. As regards legally prescribed punishments for crimes, the maximum penalty for some crimes has been increased, and for several crimes even to the death penalty.[57] Since 1983, China has launched two nationwide "strike hard" campaigns, in 1983 and 1996. When launching these campaigns in 1983, Deng pointed out that "combating crime will be a long-term struggle and require the efforts of people in all fields. Since the current situation is unusual, we have to strike hard, fast and according to law. The only way to stop crime is to be tough about it. If we go easy, we'll lose the support of the people. This is what we mean by strengthening the people's democratic dictatorship."[58] With the gradual repudiation of the orthodox theory of the class struggle, the maintenance of stability and economic development became

---

China's Society], available at: 爱思想 [Aisixing.com] http://www.aisixiang.com/data/58296.html (Last visited: January 4th, 2024).

52 于建嵘 [YU Jianrong], *《从刚性稳定到韧性稳定——关于中国社会秩序的一个分析框架》[From Stiff Stability to Flexible Stability: An Analyzing Framework on the Social Order in China],* 学习与探索 [Study & Exploration] 2009, No. 5, 113–115.

53 Ibid.

54 于建嵘 [YU Jianrong], *《当前压力维稳的困境与出路——再论中国社会的刚性稳定》[The Problems and the Solution of the Present Pressure on Stability: Reviewing again the Stiff Stability in China's Society],* above no. 80.

55 DENG Xiaoping, *Take A Clear-Cut Stand against Bourgeois Liberalization,* Selected Works of Deng Xiaoping, available at: https://dengxiaopingworks.wordpress.com/2013/03/18/take-a-clear-cut-stand-against-bourgeois-liberalization/ (Last visited: January 5th, 2024).

56 GAO Mingxuan and ZHAO Bingzhi, above no. 65, 79–80.

57 See ibid, 92–93.

58 DENG Xiaoping, *Crack down on Crime,* Selected Works of Deng Xiaoping, available at: https://dengxiaopingworks.wordpress.com/2013/03/08/crack-down-on-crime/ (Last visited: January 5th, 2024).

the most important political issues for Deng and even for his successors. The nature of punishment was also gradually released from the confines of the class dictatorship theory, but its dictatorial nature has not, in fact, been changed because its theoretical basis, the political regime which it serves and the social and interest structures which it responds to have not been substantially changed, and this essential nature still shows through in unexpected ways and places.

With the death of Deng Xiaoping in 1997, China arrived at "a collective leadership model with Chinese characteristics",[59] in which the leaders are expected to "maintain a balanced and cooperative leadership style, but play decisive leadership roles within their own portfolios."[60] In this leadership structure, although there are no authoritative political leaders, like Mao Zedong and Deng Xiaoping in the paternalistic authoritarian regime,[61] we still can understand their views on criminal punishment from their speeches and political documents. In the post-Deng era, China's leadership is still facing two important problems, which are same as in the Deng era, i.e., maintaining stability and developing the economy. Consequently, Deng's successors adhere to a policy in which "the overriding need is for stability" and use the criminal law to protect the development of the economy.

Since Jiang Zemin, the theory of class struggle has been completely absent from the political language system, but Jiang—Deng's successor—still emphasized the dictatorial nature of punishment, just as Deng Xiaoping did. In 1998, for serious smuggling and related criminal activities, Jiang stated that,

> The smuggling crimes and corruption crimes have already eroded into the organs of the people's democratic dictatorship... The people's democratic dictatorship must be managed well; if there are some problems with it, the Party and the country will be destroyed. The political-legal organs are the competent bodies of the people's democratic dictatorship, and they are the barrel of a gun and knife handle which is held by the Party and the people. ... What does the people's democratic dictatorship do? Its chief task is to punish all kinds of criminals and punish all the hostile force and saboteurs who commit behaviors which damage the state, society and the people's interests.[62]

When the public security situation became worse and worse in 2001,[63] Jiang stated that the issue of public security is not only an important social problem, but also a

---

[59] CHAI Winberg, *China after Deng Xiaoping: Some Encouraging-and Not-So-Encouraging-Signs*, Asian Affairs: An American Review, 1997, Vol. 24, Issue 2, 90.

[60] Ibid.

[61] 于建嵘 [YU Jianrong], *《共治威权与法治威权——中国政治发展的问题与出路》[Condominium Authoritarian Regime and the Authoritarian Regime of the Rule of Law: the Problems and Outlooks of Political Development in China]*, above no. 27, 22.

[62] 江泽民 [Jiang Zemin], *《坚决打击走私犯罪活动》[Resolutely Crack down on Smuggling Crime Activities]*, 江泽民选集 [Selected Works of Jiang Zemin], available at: http://cpc.people.com.cn/GB/64184/64185/180138/10818637.html (Last visited: January 6th, 2024).

[63] See 史丹顿 [SHI Dandun], *《2001年第三次 '严打': '打黑除恶' 再掀高潮》[The Third "Strike Hard" Campaign in 2001: The Campaign of Cracking down on Criminal Syndicates Had Another Major Shift]*, 国家.

人文历史 [National Humanity History] 2013, No. 16, 31. In this paper, the author states that, "in 2000, there were in all 3.63 million criminal cases which were reported to and filed by the police security organs.

critical political problem, claiming that the people's democratic dictatorship would not work if political and judicial staff have relationships with criminals, and that as a consequence the socialist state power would be changed.[64] Subsequently, the whole country launched the third round of the "Strike Hard" campaign in 2001. To a great extent, Jiang Zemin inherited and extended Mao's and Deng's views on punishment as an instrument of dictatorship, under which, "the offense is not the behavior that damages the victim's rights and interest at all, but rather the individual is against the ruling class."[65] In this case, the dictatorship instrument of punishment is frequently emphasized, and it becomes further embedded in judicial practice when the social and ruling order deviates from the expectations of the ruling class.

Post-Jiang, China entered the Hu Jintao era (from 2002 to 2012) and the Xi Jinping era (from 2012 to date). In the Hu and Xi eras, with the development of the economy, China's political formation has become a responsive one. The most important feature is that the economy drives policy, and policy frequently responds to the ever-growing requirements of society, and consequently, society and the body politic, power and rights, are balanced.[66] This is caused by the fact that political authority, which was created by paternalistic authoritarianism, has sharply decreased, while populism has risen dramatically.[67] Meanwhile, an empirical study shows that the number and the intensity of cases involving social conflicts has dramatically increased since 1990, from 14.15 million cases in 1990 to 34.02 million in 2010, a 4.5% average annual growth; despite this, "the number of the 'contradictions between ourselves and the enemy' is very few."[68] In accordance with these social changes, the CPC has changed its ideological language from "the state ruling (国家统治)" to "political governance(政治治理)".[69] The former expression emphasizes that power runs in one direction, i.e., from above to below; however, the latter requires that power should

---

[64] 江泽民 [JIANG Zemin], *《切实加强社会治安工作》[Practically Improving the Works of Public Security],* 江泽民选集 [Selected Works of Jiang Zemin], available at: http://cpc.people.com.cn/GB/64184/64185/180139/10818572.html (Last visited: January 7th, 2024).

[65] 黎宏 [LI Hong], *《刑事和解:一种新的刑罚改革理念》[Criminal Reconciliation: A New Penalty Reform Notion],* 法学论坛 [Legal Forum] 2006, Vol. 21, No. 4, 13.

[66] See 许晓龙 [XU Xiaolong], *《从"统治"到"治理":中国行政思维的历史嬗变》[From 'Ruling' to 'Governance': The Historical Evolution of the Administration Logic of China],* 观察与思考 [Observation and Ponderation] 2014, No. 6, 60.

[67] See ibid.

[68] See 胡联合, 胡鞍钢, 魏星 [HU Lianhe, HU Angang and WEI Xing], *《国家治理::社会矛盾的实证研究》[National Governance: Empirical Study of National Social Contradiction],* 新疆师范大学学报 (哲学社会科学版) [Journal of Xinjiang Normal University (Philosophy and Social Sciences)] 2014, Vol. 35, No. 3, 12.

[69] See 许晓龙 [XU Xiaolong], above no. 95, 56; see also 王学荣 [WANG Xuerong, *《从统治到治理: 国家政治理念的上升——以十八届三中全会的相关论述为起点》[From Ruling to Governance: The Increase of the Political Idea of the State—Starting with the Relevant Point of the Third Plenary Session of 18th CPC],* 机构与行政[Organizations and Administration] 2015, No. 4, 18–22; 孔繁斌 [KONG Fanbin], *《 治理对话统治:一个政治发展范式的阐释》[Conversation between Governance and Ruling: An Exploration of the Approach to Political Development],* 南京社会科学[Social Sciences in Nanjing] 2006, No. 11, 62–67.

operate interactively between the government and the citizens.[70] As regards criminal legislation, the former concept encourages the rule of the state as its legislative standard, and so punishment is always considered an instrument of dictatorship; in contrast, the latter encourages political governance as its standard and is based on the principle of legality. As a result, it has to consider the social and legal effects of punishment. For example, *the Decision concerning Some Major Questions in Comprehensively Moving Governing the Country According to the Law Forward* requires that the authorities "strive to make the people feel fairness and justice in every judicial case."[71] "In a society of benefit priority,"[72] the dictatorship instrument of punishment has been gradually weakened under the influence of the ideology of political governance, but its conciliatory political aim has acquired value, as can be seen, for example, in the criminal reconciliation system established in China in recent years, which is known as the new punishment reform.[73] With the development of the internet and the "we media", public opinion has a great impact on the use of punishments,[74] and thus the authorities have to balance the legal effect and public opinion when using punishment, because "the public pay attention to social problems which lie behind the individual case, and which are beyond the issues of the facts and the application of the law in that case; and they hope the current social problems, such as the social structure, can, to a great extent, be solved by the judiciary in individual cases."[75] Therefore, the dictatorship instrument of punishment is greatly weakened. Consequently, Hu and Xi have not directly stated the nature of criminal punishment or directly emphasized the instrument of the democratic dictatorships as Deng and Jiang did, and they have actually weakened the official expression of the dictatorship nature of punishment by formulating *the SOD* launched by Hu, and *the Decision on Comprehensively Moving Governing the Country According to the Law Forward (DCM-ALF),* launched by Xi. According to *the SOD*, Hu attempted to create a "harmonious society". "Both of them take 'the people-first and fairness and justice' as their value aims."[76] In accordance with these aims, punishment is required to protect human rights, which is also a constitutional obligation since

---

[70] Ibid.

[71] *The CCP Central Committee Decision concerning Some Major Questions in Comprehensively Moving Governing the Country According to the Law Forward,* above no. 33.

[72] 王庆德 [WANG Qingde], *《人民内部矛盾并非仅是利益问题》[The Internal Contradictions among the People are not only Interest Problems],* available at: http://theory.people.com.cn/GB/49154/49156/13467113.html (Last visited: January 8th, 2024).

[73] 黎宏 [LI Hong], above no. 94, 13–18.

[74] 徐光华 [XU Ganghua], *《个案类型特征视阈下的刑事司法与民意——以2005至2014年130个影响性刑事案件为研究范本》[Criminal Justice and Public Opinion from the Perspective of the Type-features of Individual Cases: Taking 130 Criminal Cases Having Great Impact from 2005 to 2014 As the Study Example],* 法律科学 (西北政法大学学报) [Science of Law (Journal of Northwest University of Political Science and Law)] 2015, No. 5, 30.

[75] Ibid.

[76] 黄凯峰 [HUANG Kaifeng], *《关于改革开放以来意识形态建设的几点认识》[Some Understandings of the Developments of Ideology since the Reform and Opening-up],* available at: 中国社会科学网[Chinese Social Science Net] http://www.cssn.cn/ddzg/ddzg_ldjs/ddzg_wh/201105/t20110514_812709.shtml (Last visited: January 8th, 2024).

respecting and protecting human rights was included in the Constitution in 2004, and is fairly and justly applied. As a result, the criminal policy of "balancing leniency and severity" was launched in 2006. According to *DCM-ALF*, Xi is attempting to build a socialist country under the rule of law, under which punishment is required to be fairer and more just, so that "the people feel fairness and justice in every judicial case." However, we have to point out that the dictatorship nature of punishment will not be repudiated and, in fact, has taken a new course, because the political regime and the ideology have not changed in the one-party state. In addition, "when facing the challenges caused by the social transformation, China has to ease the internal social pressures through political governance, and ease the various risks of social transformation; consequently, the criminal legislation will be gradually shifted to policy aims and its policy effect will be legislatively emphasized."[77] For example, drunk driving and refusing to pay labor remuneration were newly criminalized by the Eighth Amendment.[78] The criminalization of these two behaviors does, to a great extent, respond to public requirements and policy demands.[79] In judicial practice, Hu "inherited and extended Deng Xiaoping's and Jiang Zemin's thoughts on "cracking seriously down on crimes".[80] For example, China launched the fourth and fifth rounds of the "strike hard" campaign in 2004 and 2010, respectively. Because of the serious terrorism crimes which took place in 2014, China officially launched the "people's war on terror" in May 2014, after Xi visited Xinjiang Province in China.[81] All in all, even though the dictatorship nature of punishment has gradually weakened since Hu, it has not disappeared and it will emerge in a new form in the context of building a state under the socialist rule of law.

---

[77] 魏昌东[WEI Changdong],《新刑法工具主义批判与矫正》*[Criticizing and Correcting the New Criminal Instrumentalism]*, 法学 [Law Science] 2016, No. 2, 87.

[78]《中华人民共和国刑法修正案(八)》*[The Eighth Amendment to the Criminal Law of the People's Republic of China]*, above no. 1, Articles. 8 and 22. For the criminalization of refusing to pay labor remuneration, many Chinese sholars raised their objection, they argued that refusing to pay labor remuneration is a kind of the private legal behavior and can be dealed with by the Civil Law and relevant Administration Law. See 王海军[WANG Haijun],《拒不支付劳动报酬罪的规范性解读—基于"双重法益"的新立场》*[Normatively Analyzing the Crime of Refusing to Pay Labor Remuneration: On the New Basis of the Dual Legal Interests]*, 法学评论[Law Review] 2013, No. 5, 122.

[79] See 魏昌东 [WEI Changdong], above no. 106, 87.

[80] 王超强, 周宏, 倪晓一 [WANG Chaoqiang, ZHOU Hong and NI Xiaoyi],《胡锦涛刑法思想探析》*[Examining the Criminal Thought of Hu Jintao]*, 学理论 [Theory Research] 2012, No. 16, 131.

[81]《习近平: 打好反恐人民战争》*[XIN Jinping: Making a Good People War on Terror]*, available at: http://money.163.com/14/0504/08/9RD094QG00253B0H.html (Last visited: January 9th, 2024).

2.2 The Purpose of Criminal Punishment

"Regarding what the penal purposes should be for China, those scholars studying criminal law have already debated for a long time and formed more than 10 opinions, but they have not reached a consensus to date."[82] Among these debates, however, most scholars' arguments are trapped within three main perspectives, i.e., retributivism, prevention, and eclecticism.[83] However, these arguments are mainly on the level of "subjective requirements"—i.e. what the purpose of the criminal punishment "should be", which is a kind of ideal value pursuit—, rather than the "objective facts"—what the purpose is "in fact". Therefore, this book will analyse and explore the actual purpose of punishment by analyzing the punishment structure stipulated in the present criminal law. In fact, criminal punishment in China always takes retributivism as its purpose, which will be explored by analyzing the present punishment structure in the following sections.

2.2.1 The Retention of the Death Penalty

The existence of the death penalty, which includes immediate execution and the death penalty with a reprieve, is a significant factor which reflects a retributivist approach, because this approach "has traditionally furnished arguments in favor of the death penalty."[84] At present, there are 46 crimes punishable by death under the present Criminal Law of China, mainly involving crimes of endangering national security (7 crimes punishable by death), crimes of endangering public security (14 crimes), crimes of infringing upon citizens' personal and democratic rights (5 crimes), and crimes involving breaches of duty among service personnel (10 crimes).[85] Regarding retention of the death penalty, one of the vice presidents of the Supreme People's Court (hereinafter: SPC) has pointed out that the degree of the public's ideological

---

82 周少华 [ZHOU Shaohua], *《刑罚目的观之理论清理》[Theoretically Reviewing the Opinions on the Penalty Aims]*, 东方法学 [Oriental Law] 2012, No. 1, 13.

83 李永升, 冯文杰 [LI Rongsheng and FENG Wenjie], *《刑罚目的新界说》[New Definitions of the Purposes of the Criminal Punishment]*, 湖南警察学院学报[Journal of Hunan Police Academy] 2016, Vol. 28, No. 2, 23. Although there are also other arguments, such as the reinstatement of social justice, implementation of justice, correction (rehabilitation) of the convict, resocialization, punishing, and expressing public condemnation, etc., this paper only focuses on the retributivism, prevention, and eclecticism. See 周少华 [ZHOU Shaohua], above no. 111, 15–18.

84 BRUDNER Alan, *Retributivism and the Death Penalty*, The University of Toronto Law Journal, 1980, Vol. 30, No. 4, 339.

85 See HUANG Gui, *The Death Penalty in China after the Ninth Amendment: Legislative Abolishing and Judicially Limiting,* Journal of Forensic Science & Criminology, 2016, Vol. 4, Issue. 3, 3.

understanding is one important reason for retention.[86] In fact, the distribution of the death penalty confirms her statement, since 11 crimes—accounting for 23.9% of a total of 46 crimes punishable by death—take the lethal consequence, i.e., causing the victim or another person to die, as a circumstance for applying the death penalty. This, to a great extent, reveals the deep influence of the traditional culture and the lex talionis—"an eye for an eye, a life for a life"—approach, which has a long-established tradition among Chinese people,[87] especially among the deceased's family members. For example, the father of Xu Yuyu—who died of cardiogenic shock because she was distraught at being the victim of phone fraud—said he did not want the compensation money if the perpetrators were sentenced to death[88]; in the case of Lin Senhao, who poisoned his roommate, the victim's father, Huang Guoqiang, said that he would launch a counter-appeal if the perpetrator was not sentenced to death.[89] To a great extent, the traditional ethical conception of the equivalent value of separate lives and the concept of "atoning for the offender's sin with life" are considered by many Chinese people as a justifiable basis for favoring the death penalty. However, the death penalty for the crimes of endangering national security has an obvious retaliatory and punishment nature, and strongly reflects the dictatorship nature of the punishment. This is because crimes of endangering national security—which aims to "protect state sovereignty, territorial integrity, and consolidate state power",[90] are, to a great extent, illegal on the basis of political concerns, and because acting against these crimes "is a significant measure to suppress the political opponents who are involved in political and factional struggle, particularly to suppress people who criticize the government."[91] In addition, another significant element which shows that China's death penalty has an obviously retributory character is that the death penalty is an absolutely determined statutory punishment, i.e. there is only one punishment measure without any other alternative punishment for the judge to consider under certain

86 *《最高人民法院:中国相当时期内不具备废除死刑条件》 [Supreme People's Court: China Does Not Have Any Conditions to Abolish the Death Penalty in A Considerably Long Time]*, available at: 人民网 [People Net] http://society.people.com.cn/GB/42735/6979231.html (Last visited: January 9th, 2024).

87 王文华 [WANG Wenhua], *《"法外复仇"传统与 "仇恨犯罪"的抗制——以中国传统复仇文化为视角》 ['Extrajudicial Revenge' and the Prevention of Hate Crime: From the Perspective of the Culture of Revenge in Chinese Tradition]*, 法学论坛 [Legal Forum] 2011, Vol. 26, No. 6, 54.

88 See 沈寅飞 [SHEN Yinfei, *《徐玉玉案9900元追回 徐父::如骗子判死刑 我不要钱》[9900 Yuan was Returned in the Case of Xu Yuyu, the Father of Xu said I Do not Want Money if the Perpetrator is Sentenced to Death]*, available at: 南方网[South Net] http://news.southcn.com/china/content/2016-10/12/content_157394962.htm (Last visited: January 11th, 2024).

89 See *《复旦投毒案今日宣判受害人家属称不判死刑就抗诉》[Judgement in the Poisoning Case in Fudan was Pronounced Today; the Victim's Family Said That They Will Make a Counter-appeal if the Death Penalty Is Not Imposed]*, available at: SOHU Net http://news.sohu.com/20140218/n395162155.shtml (Last visited: January 11th, 2024).

90 王世洲 [WANG Shizhou], *《危害国家安全罪的信条学考察》[Dogmatically Review the Crimes of Endangering National Security]*, 中国刑事法杂志 [Criminal Science] 2012, No. 8, 13.

91 Ibid, 9.

circumstances,[92] and for 4 crimes under special circumstances.[93] Under the special circumstances provided by the criminal law, the judge does not have any choice but to apply the death penalty when passing sentence, this is "typically retributive legislation."[94]

2.2.2 Combined Punishments Involving a Fine and Other Principal Punishments

As one of the supplementary punishments, a fine can be imposed independently, but also as a supplement to the other principal punishments, such as the death penalty, life imprisonment, fixed-term imprisonment and so on. In the present Criminal Law, there are 214 crimes,[95] accounting for 45.7% of a total of 468 crimes,[96] for which a fine shall be supplementarily imposed with other principal punishments, and 7 crimes,[97] accounting for 1.5%, for which a fine may be supplementarily imposed with other principal punishments, and 170 crimes,[98] accounting for 36.3%, for which a fine can be independently imposed, mostly on an entity (legal person), which amounts to around 159 crimes, accounting for 93.5% of a total of 170 crimes. Consequently, the fine is mostly used supplementarily with other principal punishments and can be independently imposed on a natural person for only a few crimes, (around 11 in total). In this case, adding a fine increases the severity of the principal punishment and constitutes a double punishment. Considering the crime of counterfeiting or duplicating tickets as an example, this is a crime committed for profit, and the perpetrator shall generally be sentenced to fixed-term imprisonment of not more than two years, criminal detention or public surveillance, and shall also, or shall only, be required to pay a fine equal to not less than the value of the tickets, but not more than five

---

[92] See 李华 [LI Hua], *《论我国刑法中的绝对确定法定刑》[On the Absolutely Determined Statutory Punishment Provided in China's Criminal Law],* 法律适用 [Law Application] 1995, No. 9, 17.

[93] These crimes include the crime of hijacking aircraft (Article 121 provides that any hijacker who causes serious injury to, or the death of, any other person or serious damage to the aircraft shall be sentenced to death), the crime of abducting and trafficking in woman and children (Article 240 provides that if the circumstance is especially serious, the culprit shall be sentenced to death), the crime of instigating a riot to escape from prison and the crime of gathering people to raid a prison with weapons (for these two crimes, Article 317 provides that the ringleaders shall be sentenced to death if the circumstances are especially serious). See *《中国人民共和国刑法》[Criminal Law of the People's Republic of China]*, Oder No. 30, 2015.

[94] 樊文 [FAN Wen], *《犯罪控制的惩罚主义及其效果》[The Punitive Nature of Crime Control and its Effectiveness],* 法学研究 [Chinese Journal of Law] 2011, No. 3, 122.

[95] *《中国人民共和国刑法》[Criminal Law of the People's Republic of China],* Oder No. 30, 2015.

[96] *《 刑法最新罪名一览表》[Chart Showing the New Crimes in the Criminal Law],* available at: http://www.zuiming.net/51.html (Last visited: January 12th, 2024).

[97] *《中国人民共和国刑法》[Criminal Law of the People's Republic of China],* Oder No. 30, 2015.

[98] Ibid.

times their value.[99] However, in practice, counterfeiting tickets is an illegal activity which is normally resolved by confiscation, and any illegal benefits from these tickets are recovered; in this case, if the offender is given a fixed-term imprisonment and a fine, this will increase the severity of the principal punishment and constitute a double punishment, i.e. by depriving him or her of property rights and the right to freedom. For example, in the case of Huang Guangyu, the culprit was convicted of committing an illegal act in a business operation, the crime of insider trading and crime of offering bribes to an organization and sentenced to 14 years imprisonment and fined 600 million CNY (Chinese Yuan); he also had personal property of 200 million CNY confiscated.[100] Obviously, this double punishment is not conducive to the offender's rehabilitation. In addition, for many crimes, the Criminal Law does not provide any limit to the fine but provides that the amount of the fine shall depend on the circumstances of the offense,[101] and, obviously, this has tended to increase the degree of severity of the punishment and violates the principle of legality, and it is also simply the result of the legislator's idea of severe punishment.[102] In this case, an unlimited fine will result in different punishments being given to different offenders according to different circumstances and different economic situations. This "will easily result in unjust sentencing, and it also reveals the systemic character of pure retribution without any idea of prevention". Furthermore, according to Article 53, there is no deadline for the payment of the fine if a person is not able to pay it in full.[103] In fact, it is "contrary to the contemporary criminal concept of 'rejecting indeterminate sentence'",[104] and it has an obvious character of retribution.

[99] Ibid, Article 227.

[100] See 《北京市第二中级人民法院刑事裁定书》 *[Criminal Ruling of Beijing Second Intermediate People's Court]*, (2015) 二中刑减字第1634号 [*The Second Intermediate Criminal Commutation*, No. 1634, 2015].

[101] See 高永明 [GAO Yongming], *《罚金刑的基底性批判——罚金刑执行难的另一种解读》 [Thorough Animadversion to the Penal Fine: Another Understanding of the Difficulties in the Execution of the Penal Fine]*, 河北法学 [Hebei Law Science] 2014, Vol. 32, No. 10, 74. In this paper, the author reports that there are 277 provisions (including the paragraphs) in the Code providing unlimited penal fines, 42 provisions (including the paragraphs) providing proportion penal fines, and 46 provisions (including the paragraphs) providing specific amounts.

[102] Ibid, 75.

[103] *《中国人民共和国刑法》 [Criminal Law of the People's Republic of China]*, Oder No. 30, 2015, Article 53. This provides that, "if a person is not able to pay the fine in full, the People's Court shall demand the payment whenever it finds the person has property for execution of the fine.".

[104] 王衍松, 吴优 [WANG Yansong and WU You], *《罚金刑适用研究——高适用率与低实执率之二律背反》 [On Application of the Penal Fine: The Antinomy of the High Rate of the Application and the Low Rate of Implementation]*, 中国刑事法杂志 [Criminal Science] 2013, No. 6, 13.

2.2.3 LWOR for the Crime of Embezzlement and Bribery

Life imprisonment without possibility of release (LWOR) is a new method of punishment[105] provided by the Ninth Amendment in 2015, in which Article 44 provides that, "when imposing the death penalty with reprieve on a convict, the people's court may simultaneously decide to impose life imprisonment without parole or commutation on the convict after the death penalty commuted to the life imprisonment."[106] LWOR is only for the serious crime of embezzlement and bribery, when the cumulative amount involved is especially large, and causes especially heavy losses to the interests of the state and the people.[107] In fact, LWOR was provided following the request to "aggravate the criminal punishment for corruption crime" made during the Third Plenary Session of the 18th National Congress of the Communist Party of China,[108] and it takes the death penalty with reprieve as the applicable condition, and thus cannot be independently used, like the death penalty, fixed-term imprisonment, criminal detention and public surveillance. So far, three offenders have been sentenced to LWOR after their death penalty sentences were commuted with reprieve to life imprisonment, in three different cases. In such a political context, with its obviously punitive character, LWOR carries high expectations as regards punishing corruption crimes. However, if the death penalty is still retained, establishing LWOR as a punishment only increases the tendency towards retributivism. LWOR, as Professor Jason Iuliano pointed out after analyzing lifers' comments on their experiences in prison, "is viewed as a slow, torturous death sentence that is far worse than the traditional death penalty".[109] As for China's LWOR, on the basis of its applicable preconditions, one Chinese scholar has pointed out that "LWOR seems by its nature like the death penalty, and is a method of the death penalty with reprieve."[110] Stipulating LWOR for corruption crimes makes no sense in preventing corruption crimes, but is, in fact, simply the result of retributivism and also violates human rights.

---

[105] Chinese scholars and the officials deny LWOR is a new punishment measure but say that LWOR is a new method of carrying out the punishment. See 余文唐 [YU Wentang], *《终身监禁逆用之法理辨思》[Juridically Reviewing the Reversal Use of Life Imprisonment without Release]*, available at: http://ywt0207.fyfz.cn/b/876139 (Last visited: January 15th, 2024).

[106] *《中华人民共和国刑法修正案(九)》[The Ninth Amendment to Criminal Law of the People's Republic of China]*, above no. 6, Article 44.

[107] *《中国人民共和国刑法》[Criminal Law of the People's Republic of China]*, Order No. 30, 2015, Article 383.

[108] See *《关于 中华人民共和国刑法修正案(九) 草案 > 的说明》[The Explanations for the Draft of the Ninth Amendment to the Criminal Law of the People's Republic of China]*, above no. 8.

[109] IULIANO Jason, *Why Capital Punishment is no Punishment at All*, American University Law Review, 2015, Vol. 64, Issue.6, 1438.

[110] 黎宏[LI Hong], *《终身监禁的法律性质及适用》[On the Legal Nature of Life Imprisonment without Release and its Application]*, 中国检察官 [The Chinese Procurators] 2016, No. 17, 23. The applicable precondition for LWOR is that the convict should be sentenced to the death penalty with reprieve.

2.2.4 A Heavier Penalty for a Recidivist

According to Article 65 of the current Criminal Law, a recidivist is a convict who was sentenced to fixed-term imprisonment or a heavier penalty, and who, within five years of finishing serving his or her sentence or being pardoned,commits a crime again, for which a fixed-term imprisonment or a heavier penalty shall be given,[111] or a convict, who has committed a crime involving the endangering of national security, terrorist activities or organized crime of a gangland nature, and then committed any these crimes again at any time after he or she has finished serving his or her sentence or has been pardoned.[112] The former case is known as general recidivism; the latter special recidivism. Recidivists shall not be granted probation[113] and shall be given a heavier penalty unless it is a negligible crime, or if he or she commits the crime under the age of 18.[114] For the justifiable basis for "a heavier penalty for a recidivist", some Chinese scholars "are inclined to take utilitarianism as its legitimate ground",[115] and argue that a recidivist should receive a heavier punishment because of the threat he or she represents, which is reflected in the criminal circumstances[116]; however, some scholars criticize this, arguing that if we take utilitarianism as a legitimate ground, this will lead to the possibility of destroying social justice and violating human rights because the punishment for the recidivist will be discretionary and heavier punishments will be imposed without limits.[117] Therefore, they argue that "the recidivism system should preferentially take retributivism as its theoretical basis,"[118] and point out that the heavier punishment given to a recidivist shall be on the basis of the harmful consequences caused by the criminal behavior rather than the offender's personal dangerousness,[119] and they also argue that utilitarianism could be taken as the basis of the punishment purpose of the recidivist system.[120]

However, no matter what the basis for "a heavier punishment for a recidivist" should be, "a heavier punishment for a recidivist" system is, undeniably, based on the fact that the previous criminal behavior and its punishment are taken as important grounds for aggravating the punishment for the subsequent crime, and thus the same

---

[111] 《中国人民共和国刑法》*[Criminal Law of the People's Republic of China]*, Order No. 30, 2015, Article 65.

[112] Ibid, Article 66.

[113] Ibid, Article 74.

[114] Ibid, Article 65.

[115] 劳佳琦 [LAO Jiaqi], 《累犯从严量刑适用实证研究》*[Empirical Study on the Sentencing Application of A Heavier Punishment for A Recidivist]*, 中国法学 [Chinese Legal Science] 2016, No. 1, 274.

[116] Ibid; see also, 贾宇, 舒洪水 [JIA Yu and SHU Hongshui], 《累犯制度研究》*[On the Recidivist System]*, 山东警察学院学报 [Journal of Shandong Public Security College] 2005, No. 5, 28.

[117] 苏彩霞 [SU Caixia], 《累犯制度设立根据之探究》*[Exploring the Basis for the Establishment of the Recidivist System]*, 中国法学 [Chinese Legal Science] 2002, No. 5, 175.

[118] Ibid, 174.

[119] Ibid.

[120] Ibid.

crime and behavior are reassessed repeatedly. This "obviously violates the principle of prohibiting repetitive assessment."[121] Consequently, the legitimacy of "a heavier punishment for a recidivist" is seriously challenged. This is especially so for special recidivism, because there is no time limitation on establishing what constitutes a recidivist, and he or she shall be punished as a recidivist at any time for the special crimes provided by Article 66.[122] On this ground, the punitive function of "a heavier punishment for a recidivist" has far more emphasis than that of prevention.

2.3 A Political Requirement of Penalty Discretion: Unifying the Legal Effect and the Social Effect

The establishment and legislation of criminal punishment, have, to a great extent, already been brought together with the value propositions of punishment by the state ruler, legislator, and the public. As an important method for transferring these value propositions into individual cases, punishment decisions should be reached by strictly applying the rules and principles provided in the Criminal Law and its relevant judicial interpretations so as to realize them and their penal purposes within legal bounds, so that the legal effects of the punishment decision are realised, i.e. decisions "refer [back] to the results which are generated by the judge sentencing the convict and which are in line with the penal purpose, and which chiefly includes the punishment's special protection, general protection and the effect of realizing fairness."[123] However, in the content of China's judicial practice, punishment decisions must carry a political responsibility, unifying the legal effect and the social effect, "which is considered an important judicial policy."[124] The social effect of punishment decisions refers to the results achieved beyond the legal effect, and it chiefly includes whether the sentence is accepted by the public or not, whether the stability of the social order is maintained, or not, whether or not the sentence satisfies both parties concerned, whether or not the sentence is in harmony with the current political and economic situation, etc..[125] Considering China's reality, which is that politics leads the rule of law rather than being limited by the latter, most judicial personnel and some scholars favor this judicial policy, unifying the legal effect and the social effect;

---

[121] 樊文[FAN Wen], above no. 123, 124.

[122] *《中国人民共和国刑法》[Criminal Law of the People's Republic of China]*, Oder No. 30, 2015, Article 66.

[123] 尤金亮 [YOU Jinliang], *《刑罚裁量中法律效果与社会效果的比较与选择》[On the Comparison and the Choice between the Legal Effect and the Social Effect during Sentencing]*, 学术界 [Academics] 2013, No. 3, 181.

[124] 吕方 [LV Fang], *《穿行于理想和现实之间的平衡——从法律文化的视角解读"法律效果和社会效果的统一"》[The Balance Between the Ideal and the Reality: Reviewing the Unity of the Effect and the Social Effect from the Perspective of Legal Culture]*, 法学论坛 [Legal Forum] 2005, Vol. 20, No. 3, 128.

[125] Ibid.

however, some scholars criticize it as "being a kind of expediently practical instrument rather than a self-consciously, autonomously judicial choice"[126]; some scholars even criticize that "it leads the judge into a dilemma when he or she sentences, and it may also violate the spirit of the rule of law and the judging principle."[127] This book agrees with the critics' arguments and intends to analyze the causes and the risks of this judicial policy of unifying the social effect and legal effect.

2.3.1 The Rise and Causes of "Unifying the Social Effect and the Legal Effect"

The principle of "unifying the social and legal effect" was firstly put forward by the SPC's meeting to discuss civil trials in 1999. In this meeting, the SPC required that all the civil trials should pay attention to the social effect.[128] Following this, the then Vice-president of the SPC, Li Guoguang, published a paper and pointed out that "upholding 'unifying the legal effect and social effect' is an elementary trial requirement with Chinese characteristics, and it is also a concentrated reflection of emphasizing political awareness, and an important standard of the quality of [the] handling [of] the case."[129] Since then, it has become an important guiding ideology and a judicial policy for all trials, including criminal trials.[130] A famous case can be taken as an example to demonstrate the results of this policy—the Liu Yong Case, which occurred in Shen Yang City in 2002 and 2003. On April 17, 2002, the convict, Liu, was sentenced by the Immediate People's Court of Tie Ling City to immediate execution for murder and other crimes.[131] On August 15, 2002, the Higher People's Court of Liu Ning Province, which was the location of the second and the final trial, changed the first sentence to the death penalty with a reprieve because there were circumstances involving confession by torture. Many famous Chinese criminal law

---

[126] Ibid.

[127] 尤金亮 [YOU Jinliang], above no. 152, 185.

[128] See, *《全国民事案件审判质量工作座谈会纪要》[The Work Symposium Summary of the National Trial Quality of Civil Cases]*, 1999 (法 [1999]231号) [Legal No. 231], available at: http://www.law-lib.com/law/law_view.asp?id=17091 (Last visited: January 15th, 2024).

[129] 李国光 [LI Guoguang], *《办案的重要标准:法律效果与社会效果的统一》[An Important Standard of Handling the Case: the Unity of the Legal Effect and Social Effect]*, available at: 光明新闻 [News.gmw.cn] http://www.gmw.cn/01gmrb/2000-01/25/GB/01%5E18312%5E0%5EGMB1-210.htm (Last visited: January 15th, 2024).

[130] 黄晓亮, 王霖 [HUANG Xiaoliang and WANG Lin], *《死刑适用法律效果与社会效果问题研究》[On the Problems of the Legal Effect and the Social Effect of the Use of the Death Penalty]*, 法治研究 [Research on Rule of Law] 2013, No. 1, 62.

[131] See *《最高人民法院再审刘涌案刑事判决书》[The SPC's Criminal-retrial Judgement in the Case of liu Yong]*, (2003) 刑提字第5号 [Criminal Interrogation No. 5, 2003], available at: 中国法院网 (China Court) http://old.chinacourt.org/public/detail.php?id=96393 (Last visited: January 15th, 2024).

professors agreed with and supported this second sentence.[132] However, the public was not satisfied by the second judgment and deemed it unjust, and they expressed their dissatisfaction and anger on the internet, in newspapers, and in other public media. Finally, the SPC arraigned the case and sentenced the convict to immediate execution.[133] The public was satisfied with the SPC's final judgment, but most rational jurists were very disappointed and concerned about the rule of law in China; for example, some scholars pointed out that everything that "happened with the case of Liu Yong [is] the chaotic phenomena of the rule of law"[134]; some scholars criticized the SPC's final judgment, saying that, "it will make the people who have infinite faith in criminal clauses and rules feel shocked and angry."[135] However, the policy of unifying the legal effect and social effect was not challenged but continued to be emphasized. In 2006, in the political context of "constructing a harmonious society", the then CPC's Secretary of the Central Political and Legal Affairs Commission (中共中央政法委, hereinafter: CPLAC), Luo Gan, clearly pointed out the need to, "firmly establish a consciousness that political and legal work serves the Party and the nation, and to always adhere to the unity of the legal effect and the social effect, and resolutely overcome and effectively prevent a tendency to a simple professional view."[136] Based on this requirement, this kind of judicial activism with Chinese characteristics, which "is mainly aimed to adapt to the Chinese reality, to respond to the changes of the age, to meet the requirements of society, and to answer the political call of the Party",[137] is advocated as the judicial philosophy. It also creates

---

[132] See 汪明亮 [WANG Mingliang], *《论死刑量刑社会学模式——以"刘涌案"为分析视角》[On the Sociological Model of the Death Sentence: From the Perspective of the Case of Liu Yong]*, 中国刑法学年会文集 (第1卷: 死刑问题研究) [Collected Works of the 2004 Annual Conference on China's Criminal Law: On the Death Penalty (Volume 1)], 中国人民公安大学出版社 [China's People's Public Security University Press], Beijing, 2004, 692.

[133] *《最高人民法院再审刘涌案刑事判决书》[The SPC's Criminal-retrial Judgement in the Case of Liu Yong]*, (2003)刑提字第5号 [Criminal Interrogation, No. 5, 2003], available at: 中国法院网 (China Court) http://old.chinacourt.org/public/detail.php?id=96393 (Last visited: January 16th, 2024).

[134] 冯军 [FENG Jun], *《评最高人民法院再审刘涌案刑事判决书》[Review on the Supreme People's Court's Judgement on the Case of Liu Yong]*, 刑事法评论 [Criminal Law Review], edited by 陈兴良 [CHEN Xingliang], 中国政法大学出版社 [China University of Political Science and Law Press], Beijing, 2004, Vol. 14, 130.

[135] 汪明亮 [WANG Mingliang], *《论死刑量刑社会学模式——以"刘涌案"为分析视角》[On the Sociological Model of the Death Sentence: From the Perspective of the Case of Liu Yong]*, 中国刑法学年会文集(第1卷: 死刑问题研究) [Collected Works of the 2004 Annual Conference on China's Criminal Law: On the Death Penalty (Volume 1)], 中国人民公安大学出版社 [China's People's Public Security University Press], Beijing, 2004, 696.

[136] See 冒丽 [MAO Li], *《从许霆案透视法律效果与社会效果的统一> [Reviewing the Unity of the Legal Effect and the Social Effect from the Case of Xu Ting]*, 天水行政学院学报 [Journal of Tianshui College of Administration] 2009, No. 5, 96.

[137] 顾培东 [GU Peidong], *《能动司法若干问题研究》[On the Problems of the Active Judiciary]*, 中国法学 [China Legal Science] 2010, No. 4, 5. In China's context and reality, the active judiciary is very different from the Western concept of judicial activism because Chinese judges do not have power to conduct a judicial review of the constitution, and establish the legal rules in individual cases. See 姚莉 [YAO Li], *《当代中国语境下的"能动司法"界说》[On the Definition of the Active*

a phenomenon in which "the understanding of the law and its application conducted by the judge is beyond the law's actual words rather than [being based on] the laws' 'linguistic meaning', and it seems that the law has come back to the situation that it is only a reference for handling affairs"[138]; This also has a very negative impact on the authority of the legal text,[139] and thus judicial authority is widely queried and diminished. This is especially so, given the political requirement to "ensure that the people are satisfied with equality and justice in every court verdict".[140] In the political context of "the Party's Mass Line",[141] the social effect tends to be incorrectly considered to be equivalent to social equality and justice, and assumes that the people are satisfied with these standards. Consequently, the social effect is widely given the first priority and is even excessively emphasized and misused. As a result, some judges argue that "strictly applying the law in accordance with the legal rules is nor certain to reflect equality and justice because the law itself has certain defects, but the purpose of the law is difficult to realize if the social effect is not given any attention."[142] Meanwhile, public concerns and debate regarding the case is always deemed by the judge to be an important factor when considering the social harm caused by the crime, which is a significant element of the sentence. Consequently, sentences for the same crime in the same case vary widely before and after the case has been reported by the media, as occurred, for example, with the case of Xu Ting. Xu was sentenced to life imprisonment for the crime of larceny in the first trial, but in the second trial, after the case was reported in the media, he was sentenced to a fixed-term imprisonment of 5 years for the same crimes.[143] The unity of the legal effect and the social effect is especially emphasized by the SPC for murder,

---

Judiciary in the Content of Contemporary China], 法商研究 [Studies in Law and Business] 2011, No. 1, 130.

[138] 陈金钊 [CHEN Jinzhao], *《被社会效果所异化的法律效果及其克服——对两个效果统一论的反思》[On the Alienation of the Legal Effect Conducted by the Social Effect and Overriding it: Rethinking the Unity of the Two Effects]*, 东方法学 [Oriental Law] 2012, No. 6, 45.

[139] Ibid, 46.

[140] *Decision of the Central Committee of the Communist Party of China on Some Major Issues Concerning Comprehensively Deepening the Reform*, above no. 5.

[141] *《沈德咏与人大代表、政协委员座谈强调司法审判工作必须坚持群众路线》[Shen Deyong Emphasizes "Judicial Works Must Uphold the Mass Line" When He Holds a Symposium with Members of the National People's Committee]*, available at: 中华人民共和国最高人民法院 [The Supreme People's Court of the People's Republic of China] http://www.court.gov.cn/zixun-xiangqing-1755.html > ; see also, *《全面贯彻党的群众路线 让人民群众在每一个司法案件中都感受到公平正义》[Completely Implement the Party's Mass Line, Ensure that the People are Satisfied with Equality and Justice in Every Court Verdict]*, available at: 中华人民共和国最高人民法院 [The Supreme People's Court of the People's Republic of China] http://www.court.gov.cn/zixun-xiangqing-6149.html (Last visited: January 16th, 2024).

[142] 马艾地 [MA Aidi and WU Cunzai], *《从法律规则的局限性谈法律效果与社会效果》[On the Legal Effect and Social Effect from the Perspective of the Limitation of the Legal Rules]*, 人民法院报 [People's Court Daily], February 21st, 2004.

[143] See *许霆案 [The Case of XU Ting], (2008) 穗中法刑二重字第00002号 [Hui Intermediate Court—The Second Criminal Court Second Trial No. 2 2008]*, available at: 广州审判网 [Guangzhou Judgement Net] http://www.gzcourt.gov.cn/cpws/wsjs/ (Last visited: January 16th, 2024). The reasons for the changes are not explained in the judgment, but it did say that, "according to the

intentional injury and crimes of a gangland nature. The SPC provides that for these kinds of crimes, when the judge deals with them strictly according to the law, they shall fully consider whether or not the end result of the process is supported by the public and maintains stability … and whether or not it is beneficial in reducing social confrontation, promoting social harmony and achieving a better social effect.[144] Even though the priority of the social effect is not obviously stated, it has always been considered more important than the legal effect when the case concerns the public, until the recent case of Yu Huan, who was sentenced to life imprisonment for murder and intentional injury at the first trial.[145] Since it was reported by the media, the Supreme People's Procuratorate (hereinafter: SPP) and Shan Dong local judicial authorities attached great significance to this case, and now the relevant authorities are reviewing it. On April 5, 2017 the then Vice-president of SPC, Shen Deyong, delivered a speech on the case and emphasized that, "when trying to achieve the unity of "the two effects", we have to uphold the priority of the legal effect, and must not unilaterally pursue the social effect at all costs to the detriment of the legal effect."[146] This speech, to a great extent, rectifies the previous view on the unity of the two effects and restores the legal effect to the place it deserves.

2.3.2 The Risks and Correction of the Unity of the Legal Effect and the Social Effect in Punishment Decisions

For a long time, the policy of unifying the legal effect and the social effect has placed judges in an embarrassing dilemma. That is to say, if the judge strictly complies with the letter of the law to make a decision on punishment, this will not be accepted by the public and the judge will be deemed a mechanical device or a "slot machine of the law"; if, however, the judge pays more attention to the aims of the law, to common social values, and to public expectations and claims and to other considerations beyond the limits of the law, the judge will be criticized and deemed to

special situation in this case, approved by the Supreme People's Court, the convict is sentenced to fixed-term imprisonment of 5 years".

144 See *《最高法: 审判故意杀人等案件要注重法与社会效果的统一》 [Supreme People's Court: It Should Pay Attention to the Unity of the Legal Effect and the Social Effect when Handling Murder and other Crimes]*, available at: 中华人民共和国最高人民法院 [The Supreme People's Court of the People's Republic of China] http://www.court.gov.cn/zixun-xiangqing-728.html (Last visited: January 16th, 2024).

145 See *山东省聊城中级人民法院刑事附带民事判决书 [The Criminal Incidental Civil Judgment of Liao Cheng Intermediate People's Court, Shandong Province], (2016) 鲁15刑初33号 [Lu No. 5 Criminal First Trial, No. 33, 2016].*

146 *《沈德咏: 让热点案件成为全民共享法治公开课》 [Shen Deyong: To Make a Hot Case become an Open Course for the Public to Share in the Rule of Law]*, available at: 中华人民共和国最高人民法院 [The Supreme People's Court of the People's Republic of China] http://www.court.gov.cn/zixun-xiangqing-39292.html (Last visited: January 16th, 2024).

have perverted the law.[147] Faced with this dilemma, most judges tend to take the social effect as the priority, because they are expected to have political consciousness, overall awareness, and responsibility,[148] and they have to take political responsibility for the maintenance of stability. This is also due to the long-term instrumental effects of the punishment, which have been explained in the second section. Regarding this, some scholars have pointed out that "the substance of thinking about the unity of these two effects [concerns the questions of] 'being in power for whom; and implementing the law for whom'"[149] Under political pressure to maintain stability and reduce the number of complaints and requests (上访、信访),[150] the judge may make a decision on punishment beyond the sentencing rules in order to forestall any potential trouble, and to cater to political requirements.[151] This is especially true with the policy of "strike hard", where judges may also impose heavier punishments on the convict than in normal circumstances.[152] The legal effect yields to the social effect which results in an inappropriate balance in the sentences, and thus the authority of the law is damaged and challenged.

A speech delivered by the then Vice-president of the SPC, Shen Deyong, attempts to change previous practice, i.e. to make the legal effect the priority, which is a kind of judicial process respecting the authority of the law and "reflects that judicial practice is limited by legislation and the principle of independent adjudication."[153] To make the legal effect the priority is, to a great extent, a kind of correction of punishment instrumentalism, and also an important measure in policy to prevent extreme sentence deviation, as well as making judges understand and evaluate sentencing by referring

---

[147] See 杜月秋 [DU Yueqiu], *《论裁判的正当性基础: 以法律效果和社会效果的相互关系为视角》[On the Legitimate Base of the Judgment: From the Perspective of the Interrelationship of the Legal Effect and the Social Effect],* 法律适用 [National Judges College Law Journal (Journal of Law Application)] 2007, No. 3, 38.

[148] 李国光 [LI Guoguang], above no. 158.

[149] 吕忠梅 [LV Zhongmei], *《论实现法律效果和社会效果的有机统一》 [Reanalyzing the Organic Unity of the Legal Effect and the Social Effect],* 人民法院报 [People's Court Daily], Version 5, November 4th, 2008.

[150] See generally 刘正强 [LIU Zhengqiang], *《信访的"容量"分析——理解中国信访治理及其限度的一种思路》[Analyzing the 'Capacity' of People's Complaints Vis Letters or Visits: Towards Understanding the Handling of People's Complaints and its Limits],* 开放时代 [Open Times] 2014, No. 1, 130–144.

[151] Even though we do not the exact number of these kind of cases to prove this statement, some individual cases have already shown this tendentiousness, such as the case of Xu Ting, and the case of Li Changkui. In the latter case, the criminal, Li Changkui, intentionally killed two people. The behavior of the criminal caused great public outrage, and he was sentenced to immediate execution in the first trial but in the second trial, the sentence was commuted to the death penalty with a reprieve; however, the local Higher People's Court was asked by the SPC to review the sentence, and he was finally sentenced to immediate execution in the third judgment. See 李昌奎案 [LI Changkui An] [The Case of Li Changkui], available at: http://baike.so.com/doc/5430314-5668573.html (Last visited: January 16th, 2024); *李昌奎 [LI Changkui] (2010) 昭中刑一初字第52号 [(2010) Zhao intermediate Criminal Court First Trial. No. 52; (2010) 云高法终字第1314号 [(2010 Yun High Court Second Trial No. 1314).*

[152] 尤金亮 [YOU Jinliang], above no. 152, 186.

[153] Ibid.

back to the legal framework. It also means sentencing can be foreseeable and certain, as well as preventing the tyranny of conviction and sentencing carried out in the name of the social effect, because "the social effect ... is based on imaginary conjecture, and lacks empirical facts, [which means] we cannot exactly know the social effects."[154] Therefore, China needs to clarify the rules regarding punishment decisions, such as implementing the standardization of sentences, i.e. creating sentencing guidelines.[155] Furthermore, the legislature and the judicial authorities should refine the provisions of the Criminal Law regarding legislative or judicial interpretations; and judges should clearly state the reasons for the sentence in their judgment. This is because in China, in most criminal judgments, the reasons for the sentencing and the reasoning procedures themselves are very simple, and some even lack any kind of explanation of social harm and the responsibility attached to the crime.[156] In this way the judge can be prevented from emphasizing the social effect in the name of social harm.

2.4 De Facto: The Problems of the Justice of Penalty Discretion and Its Solutions

The criminal law and criminal norms affect citizens' life and freedom in the most forceful way. By creating criminal norms, the state imposes the most severe and rigorous sanctions on citizens. Imposing criminal sanctions (imprisonment, forfeiture, etc.) by which the state constrains its citizens' freedom or takes their property always has to be justified. In modern constitutional democracies criminal procedure and criminal legislation are required to be subject to constitutional principles and they only can function within the framework of human rights. In the European legal culture, the European Convention on Human Rights (hereinafter: ECHR) declares: "No one shall be subjected to torture or to inhuman or degrading treatment or punishment"[157] and "No one shall be held guilty of any criminal offense on account of any act or omission which did not constitute a criminal offense under national or international law at the time when it was committed. Nor shall a heavier penalty be imposed than the one that was applicable at the time the criminal offense was committed."[1582] The fundamental principles of criminal justice—e.g. legality, *nullum crimen* and

[154] 陈金钊[CHEN Jinzhao], above no. 167, 46.

[155] See *《最高法通知要求进一步扩大量刑规范化范围》 [The Supreme Court Requires the Further Extension of the Scope of the Standardization of Sentencing],* available at: 中华人民共和国最高人民法院 [The Supreme People's Court of the People's Republic of China] http://www.court.gov.cn/zixun-xiangqing-39112.html (Last visited: January 16th, 2024).

[156] HUANG Gui, *On the Problems of Just Sentencing in China*, Acta Juridica Hungarica [Hungarian Journal of Legal Studies], 2015, Vol. 56, Issue 2–3, 181. "Social harmfulness" is an important circumstance of the penalty discretion provided in China's Criminal law.

[157] *The European Convention on Human Rights*, Article 3.

[158] Ibid, Article 7.

nulla poena sine lege, proportionality of punishments, etc.—are the most important legal guarantees against arbitrary power of the state. These principles demand accessibility, predictability and legal certainty in criminal legal practice.

The fundamental principles of criminal law do not apply only to the legislator enacting criminal statutes but also to judges when they decide criminal cases. Judges are required to justify their decisions in every case. This requirement includes highlighting the relevant legal and factual basis of the decisions and throwing light on the arguments that led the judge to inflict a particular punishment on an offender. Although judges—when interpreting criminal statutes—are required to adhere to the text of criminal norms[159] and they are bound by the law, they have a relatively broad discretionary power when deciding the proper amount of punishment. This does not entail the possibility that judges have the power to determine any type and amount of punishment in a particular case. Punishments should be proportional to the harm caused by the criminal conduct and to the level of culpability that characterized the offender's mind when s/he committed the crime. Judges have to be able to justify their decisions regarding the sentences they determine as the right legal answer to criminal conduct.[160] In this book I will concentrate on the problem of justifying judicial decisions concerning the infliction of penalties on offenders. My analysis will focus on the problems of justifying sentences imposed by criminal judges in Chinese judicial practice. I contend that these problems relating to justification undermine the rightfulness of the decisions.

In China, the justice of sentencing decisions has always been questioned by the whole of society in recent years. One notable feature of unjust sentencing in judicial practice is the inconsistency in the results of sentences, namely, different judges determine different penalties for crimes that have been committed under similar circumstances.[161] Because of this very serious problem of injustice, the judicial authorities in China, for the sake of ensuring impartial sentencing, have embarked upon a bottom-up judicial reform of the practice of sentencing. However, the problems of how to promote the judicial reform of sentencing in China, and which conception of justice—the formal or the substantial conception of justice or both of them—the judicial reform wishes to pursue have always been debated by theorists and practitioners.

---

[159] For instance, it is not allowed in criminal law to apply analogies or to convict and punish a person for a conduct which cannot be qualified as a crime according to the text of the criminal rules.

[160] In 1992 the Council of Europe drafted a recommendation on the consistency of sentencing with the aim of achieving a greater consistency between the sentencing practice of courts in Europe. It contains suggestions concerning the rationales of sentencing, the structure of penalties, aggravating and mitigating factors and so on. This recommendation expects European judges to determine particular punishments according to common European principles which can lead to a coherent and justified sentencing system in the EU. [Council of Europe Committee of Ministers, Recommendation Nr. R (92) 17].

[161] As Jerome Frank demonstrated, this kind of inconsistency can arise even within the sentencing practice of judges who work in the same court. See FRANK Jerome, Law & the Modern Mind, Transaction Publishers, St. Louis, 1963, 120.

Based on the above-mentioned problems and in order to analyze the problems of sentencing justly in China, this book plans to explore the limitations of reasoning behind particular sentences and to study the external and internal factors which affect the justification of sentences determined by judges. After that, this book will take the conceptions of justice into consideration. Finally, this book will attempt to find the solutions that are able to guarantee that judges will sentence justly under the guidance of the conception of justice, which should be pursued by the judicial reform in China.

2.4.1 The Limitations of Deductive Reasoning in the Sentencing

Although a lot of guiding cases have been issued recently by the SPC, they do not serve as the legal basis of sentencing, but only as a reference guide for the judges. The Criminal Law and its judicial interpretations in China, actually, are the primary legal grounds for the judges to justify particular sentences. So, the basic model of reasoning behind the infliction of sentences in China is determined by the legal system. This is, and can only be deductive reasoning. In other words, the basic paradigm of the reasoning style in China can be described as the following. Firstly, judges have to find the sentencing rules which can be applied to the individual case from the relevant sentencing laws and regulations, and then they have to interpret them. This will serve as the major premise of reasoning. After this, the judges have to establish the facts of the case, which will serve as the minor premise of reasoning. Finally, they have to deduct the results according to the process of deductive reasoning.

According to the legal culture, China's judges cannot deviate from the model of reasoning used in the determination of sentences. This is the so-called deductive legal reasoning. However, it is inevitable that this model of reasoning has its own inherent limitations in judicial applications of law, and these limitations figure in the reasoning process.

2.4.1.1 Problems of Interpreting the Abstract Terms of Sentencing Laws and Regulations

The sentencing laws and regulations are the major premise and the vital basis of the reasoning which underlies sentencing decisions in judicial practice. If they are inappropriately interpreted the justice of sentencing results would be significantly violated. The sentencing laws and regulations, which are all formed in a very abstract way, are totally determined by a series of legal concepts and other legal elements. That is why it is a relatively complicated process to interpret legal concepts and apply them to facts. These interpretations depend mostly on the judges' knowledge, experience and their intuition. As Jaques Ghestin and Gilles Goubeaux state "the choice of premises, to a great extent, depends on the judges' intuitions, and it would make the reasoning result become uncertain".[162]

During the sentencing process, different interpretations of sentencing laws and regulations differently influence the judges to choose the basic line and level of severity of the penalty. For example, if judges make different interpretations of the concept and extension of "banking institution" in the provision of "robbing a bank or any other banking institution", they will have different choices between the sentencing margin of the fixed-term imprisonment of not less than three years but no more than five years and of the fixed-term imprisonment of not less than ten years but not more than twelve years.

In judicial practice, although there are many judicial interpretations and *the Guiding Opinions of the People's Court for Sentencing on Trial [hereinafter: the Sentencing Guide (on trial)]*[163] made by the SPC and regional high courts, they cannot make an exhaustive list of the legal concepts and legal elements, and they even have to use more obscure concepts to make clear the original concepts.[164] For instance, the term "general" in the sentence "circumstances of crime and its results are general" makes difficult for a judge to give it a clear meaning. So, it is becoming increasingly important whether or not the connotation and denotation of the concept are able to contain the legally relevant facts of sentencing in an individual case.

Even if these legal concepts and elements, as well as the useless, obscure and abstruse components were excluded judges still have to use a set of special professional vocabularies to interpret the laws and regulations. If they use everyday expressions, these expressions have to be given a correct meaning. However, this may not always be possible. So, in interpreting statutes, the supplementary and benefit equilibrium of the legal provisions and extra judicial factors are very important impact factors and grounds which influence the judge to interpret the sentencing provisions which serve as the major premise.

These factors and grounds usually also lead different judges to give different interpretations. The consequence of this is that the sentencing results will be different as well. Sometimes judges inflict an abnormally lenient or abnormally severe punishment on the offenders. According to the analysis of some complex cases, there are still relatively many cases in which sentencing results differ from each other due to the different interpretation of sentencing laws and regulations. This is the main reason for the public to question the justice of the sentencing result.

---

[162] STITH Kate and CABRANES Jose A., *Fear of Judging. Sentencing Guidelines in Federal Courts*, University of Chicago Press, Chicago, 1998, 38.

[163] 最高人民法院司法改革办公室 [The Office of Judicial Reform of the Supreme People's Court of P.R.C.], 《人民法院量刑指导意见(试行)》 [The Guiding Opinions of the People's Court for Sentencing on Trial], available at: 中国法院网 [China Court Net] http://www.chinacourt.org/article/detail/2013/04/id/948052.shtml (Last visited: January 17th, 2024).

[164] About the relevancy and efficiency of a sentencing guideline in judicial sentencing practice see STITH Kate and CABRANES Jose A., *Fear of Judging. Sentencing Guidelines in Federal Courts*, University of Chicago Press, Chicago, 1998, 104–142.

2.4.1.2 Difficulties in Identifying the Legally Relevant Facts

The facts related to the sentencing in an individual case, which serve as the minor premise of reasoning, cannot be solely described by using ordinary vocabulary. When ordinary terms are used to describe the facts of the case they have to get special legal characteristics. It, thus, is far more important to identify the legally relevant facts which are related to the sentencing decision. The concepts and elements of the sentencing laws and regulations are specified and listed exhaustively by judicial practice and the sentencing guidance. But, the actual facts, which are related to the case, are not always consistent with legal concepts and provisions, so there have been always discussions about whether or not to apply the legal concepts to the facts of the case.

For example, in a robbery case, the fact that an offender broke into a property which served both as a place of residence and the site of a business operation can cause difficulties in interpretation. The question is whether the offender could be convicted according to the provision "intruding into another person's residence to rob" provided by the Article 263 of the *Criminal Law*.[165]

Concerning this, some people believe that the fact that the offender broke into a house at "business time" could be covered by the meaning of the concept of "house-breaking", namely the offender having intruded into another person's residence to rob. But some people think that the right interpretation could depend on the time: when the offender stepped into the property during the period of business, this should have been qualified as a public place, and thus it could not be interpreted as "house-breaking." However, they say, if the offender entered the place and robbed outside of business hours, he or she could be convicted as a person who "has intruded into another person's residence to rob". Thus, due to the legal terminology and its expression, it is extremely difficult to identify the legal facts in judicial practice. This leads to a very incoherent sentencing system in judicial practice.

2.4.1.3 Problems of Deductive Reasoning

Deductive reasoning is a process by which the judge deduces a conclusion from a certain major premise and a minor premise. In a legal system which is based mostly on the legislated law legal decisions are inferred from the laws and regulations which serve as the major premise, and the legally relevant facts which serve as the minor premise. So, in the process of deductive reasoning the judges have to interpret the abstract legal concepts, meanwhile summarizing and extracting the specific facts related to sentencing, and then deciding whether or not these facts can be contained by the sentencing provisions. If the sentencing provision can be applied the judge can make further deductions. Subjected to the inherent constraints of the positive

[165] 《中华人民共和国刑法》 *[Criminal Law of the People's Republic of China]*, Order No. 83, 14 March 1997, Article 263.

law judges cannot make law when they apply the laws and regulations of sentencing, however, it is possible for them to cite the corresponding judicial interpretations.

The judges evaluate the effects of the crime on society according to their personal intuition and then make a sentencing decision. Meanwhile, due to the highly recapitulated nature of the legal language, the procedures of summarizing and extracting legally relevant facts become simple, lacking legal reasoning and rigorous logical procedure. For these defects, according to the conclusion of my analysis of cases published by the SPC and regional high courts, in most of the criminal judgments the reasons for the sentencing results and the reasoning procedures are very simple, some of the decisions contain simply a short sentence without any reasoning, and even if judges cite the relevant provision, they particularly declare whether "the social harmfulness is great or not." This serves as the justification of sentencing decisions, without any explanation of the meaning of social harmfulness and without exploring the responsibility aspects of the crime.

2.4.1.4 Deficiencies of the Legal Background of Sentencing

As I stated above, the sentencing legal norms serve as the major premise of deductive reasoning and should be interpreted by the judges when they are sentencing. If the sentencing regulations are extremely abstract and they lack any corresponding interpretation or instruction, it would prevent judges from understanding the sentencing regulations. This makes the application of laws and regulations controversial, and finally it would lead to huge differences between the results of sentencing decisions.

In China the reform of sentencing has been brought into effect since 2009 and the *Sentencing Guide (on trial)* has been issued by the SPC, which provides the concrete sentencing steps and the applicable standards of penalty for common crimes. However, it failed to put this reform into practice around the whole country and it has not included all crimes. Furthermore, there are many abstract concepts which contain value judgments, such as "the circumstances of crimes in general" and "the social harmfulness is not so serious".

To some extent, this gives much more space for the judges to make decisions, but, to a great extent, it also easily leads to the result that judges understand the sentencing laws and regulations in a different way. The result of this practice is that the legal system cannot fulfill its function.

2.4.2 *The External and Internal Factors Influencing the Judicial Reasoning of Punishment Decisions*

2.4.2.1 The Internal Factors

The internal factors influencing the reasoning behind the determination of sentences refer to the factors that affect how the judge is interpreting abstract provisions, summarizing and extracting legally relevant facts, and deducing the results of sentencing.

(1) Personal knowledge as the background of judicial decisions. The background knowledge of the judge refers to educational attainment, range of knowledge and so on. The background of the judges' knowledge affects the judicial decision by influencing the judges' ability to perceive sentencing provisions, to identify the legally relevant facts in an individual case, and to deduce the sentencing result from the abstract provision, which serve as the major premise, and specific facts, which serve as minor premise.

Beside the legal knowledge, which is the basis of understanding, other kinds of knowledge, such as basic medical knowledge, financial knowledge and so on, could be helpful for judges to understand the laws and regulations and to summarize sentencing facts in an individual case. Generally speaking, the judges who graduate from law school and become highly educated, as they have a scientific training in law and even did some special legal research, can understand the legislative intent and spirit in a more sophisticated way. Such training helps to guarantee that judges will choose and apply abstract laws and regulations correctly.

(2) The judge's personal experience. The judicial experience of judges makes it possible for a judge to grasp and understand the legal provisions through the concrete judicial operation, and it is also an important way for the judges to know that the same hypothesis of the sentencing provision has different results in different cases. So, it can enable the judges to understand the abstract provisions and to understand that the same crime can be committed in various ways. So, it can improve the judges' ability to summarize legally relevant facts in an individual case, so that they can correctly apply the laws and identify the legal facts and then deduce a just sentence.

However, extensive judicial experience does not necessarily enable the judges to infer just sentences from the statutes. One important reason for this is that having a serious attitude towards one's work plays a vital role in adjudication. It is inevitable that the rich judicial experience is in proportion to years of work experience, which means that the longer the working years are, the richer the experience becomes. But it is also able to make judges develop a monotonic attitude towards their work, and thus, drive judges to adopt an indifferent, passive or perfunctory attitude. For instance, when the judge believes him- or herself to have rich judicial experience due to which he or she is able to grasp and understand the laws and regulations and the specific facts in a single case, she or he may be led to think that judicial decision making is simple or that arriving to a particular decision does not require an in-depth analysis. This attitude would easily result in unjust sentencing.

In comparison, the judge who has less experience in judicial practice and believes that she or he lacks the ability to identify the laws and regulations and specific facts in an individual case, tends to possess a cautious and serious attitude, and deals with the case in a most careful manner. Thus, to a great extent, this kind of cautious judicial attitude can lead to sentencing decisions strictly in accordance with the law. Some researchers have explored this issue, and the result of the survey is that.

> Most of the judges said that the working life had a significant influence on judicial decisions. If the years of judicial work experience are only few, judges are likely to deal with the case mechanically, they decide according to the laws and regulations when they are sentencing; but the judges who have a long time of work, they would give much more consideration to the extra judicial factors, and they do not sentence only according to the laws and regulations, but have to pay close attention to the attitude of the leaders and the public.[166]

(3) The judge's special personal experiences. What do we mean by "special experiences"? For instance, if a judge or his or her family was ever violated by a criminal, or the judge personally saw somebody being violated by a crime, then this could have an impact on judicial decision making. These special experiences, to a great extent, make the judges personally feel some pain because of the crimes and then create resentment against the offender. This attitude provokes the sense of justice of the judges.

Thus, judges are likely to resonate with the pain suffered by the victims. Because of this, their sense of disgust towards the crime and the offender is stimulated, which would make the judges understand and apply the laws and regulations with much more emotion rather than rationality.

Considering the term "social harmfulness", judges who were victims of certain crimes would tend to interpret this concept according to their own experience. However, judges who did not suffer from violation are usually confined to the legal language and decide according to the text of the law. In addition, regarding the summarizing and extracting facts in a single case, judges who have special experiences are more or less influenced by some emotions and thus it leads them to make inappropriate judgments. Due to these attitudes of judges the justice of the result can be violated.

(4) The attitude of judges to the crime itself. The attitude of judges can be influenced by not only the whole crime situation, but also by understanding the cause of the crime, the personality of the criminal and the victim of the specific crime. Generally speaking, when judges believe that the level of crime in their society is exceptionally high and thus needs to be controlled by strict punishment, they are likely to exaggerate the interpretation of social harmfulness of criminal behavior when they ascertain the legally relevant facts related to sentencing, and they are

---

166 李荣 [LI Rong],《公正量刑机制研究》[*Research on the Guaranteeing System of Sentencing Justly*], 中央民族大学出版社 [Minzu University of China Press], Beijing, 2013, 67.

likely to apply more severe punishment when they choose and apply sentencing laws and regulations.

2.4.2.2 The External Factors

The external factors affecting the reasoning of sentencing means the extra judicial factors which are not part of the judges' personality. They have an influence on judges when they apply the abstract sentence provision and identify the sentence factors, and deduce the result of sentencing.

(1) The attributes of the victim. The attributes of the victim, which have an influence on sentencing, include the background, social status, reasons for suffering a criminal offense and the victim's attitude towards the criminal.

Background and social status usually determines someone's material wealth, literacy and reputation, which to a great extent also determines someone's social attributes, namely, whether he or she is part of a vulnerable group. The members of a vulnerable group are inferior to other people in terms of economic and social status, literacy, etc. In China, most of the time, for this group of people it is difficult to settle the confronting social problems, and they suffer pressure from other groups. All of these would lead them to get into more trouble and worse circumstances.

In criminal cases, usually, victims have already been a member of a vulnerable group and when they are violated by crimes their family is usually involved as well. So, this often has an influence on judges when they interpret the social harmfulness of the crime and then it also has an influence on judges when they impose a criminal sanction. In addition, the victim of a vulnerable group could easily receive sympathy from judges, which also would have an influence on judges when they make decisions.

The reasons for suffering a violation do not only urge judges to determine the nature of behavior in a crime, but also influence judges when they identify the facts which are relevant in sentencing. These reasons could include legal factors and non-legal factors as well. For example, in the case of the crime of creating disturbances, if the judge finds out that the victim provoked the offender he will take this into consideration when convicting the defendant; or in the crime of causing traffic casualties the illegal behavior of the victim, which contributed to the traffic casualty, would also influence the judge when s/he engages in balancing the legal facts and makes a decision about the punishment.

However, the reasons for suffering from a crime have both legal factors and non-legal factors. The attitude of the victim to the criminal is also a significant factor that influences the judges when they make decisions about the right punishment. One such example is the case of criminal reconciliation. The *Sentencing Guide (on trial)* has clearly defined criminal reconciliation as a circumstance for lighter punishment. Furthermore, in judicial practice, criminal reconciliation cannot be taken as an agreement on criminal settlement, but when the crime took place between the relatives and neighbors, if the victim forgives the criminal it would also influence the judge when s/he makes a sentencing decision.

For instance, the case of *State v Hao Weidong,*[167] in which Hao Weidong stole his uncle's money, the SPC reviewed this case and stated that, "Hao Weidong stole a huge amount of money, but it took place in a close relationship which includes a common background and living circumstances, and the victim, Hao Xihou, intended to forgive his nephew and asked the court not to investigate the criminal responsibility". According to the special situation this case should be identified as "the circumstances of a person's crime are counted as mitigating factors and do not require criminal punishment", which is provided by Article 37. However, the punishment in the original judgment, which sentenced Hao Weidong to a punishment less than the prescribed punishment, is still a heavy punishment."[168]

(2) The attributes of the criminal's personality. One important factor affecting judicial decision making concerning sentences is the factor of the criminal's personality, which includes the criminal's background, social status, duties and habitual behavior. In judicial practice the cases in which the features of the criminal's personality influence judges in adjudication are very common. For example, the cases of Wu Ying[169] and Gao Xiaosong[170] were of great concern to the broader community because of their special status and identity, which also inevitably urged the judge to take their situation seriously and deal with these cases more carefully.

The main features of these factors are that they are able to induce public resentment against a particular group, for instance, bribery and corruption can generate public resentment against the corrupt officials; or they could raise public doubts about the judicial justice and bring about public condemnation against the public authorities, for example, in the case of Li Qiming,[171] who caused traffic casualties. Li caused the death of one person and one serious injury with his car when he drove to a campus. His reaction was the following: "my father's name is Li Gang, who is the head of the police." After that, the whole society condemned Li Qiming and his father, but most of the public condemned the public authorities and judicial corruption represented by the statement "My father's name is Li Gang."

Moreover, it can occur that celebrities commit crimes, such as in the case of Gao, who drove under the influence of alcohol, and in the case of Huang, who was one of China's richest persons. The habitual behavior of the defendants can have an influence on judicial decisions concerning sentences. Good habits in daily life, to a great extent, can easily explain the contingency of crime and the possibility of repentance, but the

---

167 《中华人民共和国最高人民法院公报》[*The Bulletins of the Supreme People's Court of the People's Republic of China*], 2013年卷[Vol. 2013], 人民法院出版社[People's Court Press], Beijing, 2014, 463.

168 Ibid.

169 *吴英 [WU ying], (2009) 浙金刑二初字第1号 [(2009) Zhejin the Second Criminal Court First Trial. No. 1]; (2010) 浙刑二终字第7号 [(2010) Zhe the Second Criminal Court Second Trial. No. 27].*

170 *高晓松 [Gao Xiaosong] (2011) 东刑初字第438号 [(2011) East Destrict the Second Criminal Court First Trial. No. 438].*

171 *李启铭 [LI Qiming] (2010) 河望刑初第10号 [Hewang Criminal Trial. No. 10, 2010].*

bad daily behavior, to a great extent, can make judges think that the defendant tends to commit crimes easily and is reluctant to show repentance. When judges make discretionary decisions on penalties, all of these behavioral attitudes will be taken into consideration by them and these factors will to a great extent have an influence on their decisions.

(3) The intervention of external power. The "intervention of external power" refers to other persons or organizations that intervene in adjudication and violate the right to fair trial and judicial independence. In China, these kinds of intervention come mostly from the superior departments of the internal system of the courts or the leaders of courts, or the leaders of organizations of state power or from the government.

The reasons behind interventions of superior departments or leaders are the following: there is a system of "asking instructions from the superior departments" in the internal system of the courts, or presiding judges ask instructions about the special case from the head of the department, or the leaders intervene or are involved in special cases in various forms with certain aims.

The organizations of state power or governments' intervention come mostly from the Political and Legal Committee or from the coordination meeting organized by the Political and Legal Committee. The results of these interventions usually make judges deal with the case in a manner that fits the decisions of the committee and the will of the leadership.

Thus, judges are influenced to estimate the social harmfulness of the crime and to ascertain the facts related to sentencing, meanwhile they also influence judges in adjudication of sentences. So, the existence of deviation between sentencing results will be inevitable.

(4) The opinion of the public. Recently it is a very common phenomenon that public opinion influences the judiciary, particularly in the criminal judicial field. Moreover, the impact of public opinion has grown with even more intensity nowadays, such as in the case of Xu Ting,[172] in the case of Yao Jiaxin,[173] and in the case of Li Changkui,[174] which reflect the influence of the public opinions on the criminal practice.

---

[172] *许霆案 [The Case of XU Ting], (2007) 穗中法刑二重字第196号 [Hui Intermediate Court The Second Criminal Court Second Trial No. 196, 2007; (2008) 穗中法刑二重字第2号 [Hui Intermediate Court The Second Criminal Court Second Trial No. 2 2008], (2008) 穗法高刑重审字第 197 号 [Hui Intermediate Court The Second Criminal Court Second Trial No. 2 2008]*, available at: 广州审判网 [Guangzhou Judgement Net]. http://www.gzcourt.gov.cn/cpws/wsjs/ (Last visited: January 17th, 2024).

[173] *药家鑫 [Yao Jiaxin An] [The Case of Yao Jiaxin], available at:* http://baike.so.com/doc/7016976-7239865.html; *药家鑫 [Yao Jiaxin], (2011) 西刑一初字第68号 [(2011 Xi the First Criminal Court First Trial. No. 68).*

[174] *李昌奎 [Li Changkui] (2010) 昭中刑一初字第52号 [(2010) Zhao intermediate Criminal Court First Trial. No. 52; (2010) 云高法终字第1314号 [(2010 Yun High Court Second Trial No. 1314).*

The most important signs of the impact of public opinion on judicial decision making are the case of Xu, in which the judge changed the punishment of life imprisonment to a fixed term of 5 years; the case of Yao, where the public was concerned about the death penalty in the two trials; the case of Li, where the sentencing result changed from death penalty with immediate execution to death penalty with suspension, and then at the retrial procedure the sentence was altered to death penalty with execution. These cases prove that public opinion has played an important role in changing sentencing results.

The fact that public opinion influences judges in adjudication to a great extent expresses the public's dissatisfaction with the criminal justice system, but actually, it shows that it is the laymen who deliver sentences to the criminals in an offensive manner.

There are two ways to form public opinions about criminal decisions: one is the traditional way, such as the television, broadcast and newspapers; another one is the community media, which is the most important channel to express public opinion and is also an important way to influence judicial practice.

Public opinion not only influences judges when they interpret and apply the sentencing laws and regulations, but also influences judges when they evaluate the concept of social harmfulness described by the criminal law, and also affect judges when they ascertain the legally relevant facts. The opinions expressed by the public on criminal judicial practice include both rationality and sensibility. The prime causes of both rational opinions and perceptual opinions are that the public worries and doubts the justice of current criminal judicial practice, and, to a great extent, reflects the gaps between the social justice which the public wants to achieve and the justice of current criminal judicial practice.

2.4.3 Values Fostered by Judges

2.4.3.1 The Value of Desert: Guaranteeing the Justice of the Results of Sentencing

The justice of the results of sentencing decisions can be divided into two levels, namely substantial justice and formal justice. Formal justice can be interpreted in terms of concrete cases. It means that the result of sentencing reflects that the punishment fits the nature of the particular crime and the dangerous character of the criminal's personality in anindividual case. The results also should meet the requirements of substantial rationality and the requirement of justice of the individual case.

The latter conception of justice figures in terms of similar individual cases. It means that a unified standard should be applied to situations and circumstances in similar cases. It also should realize the principle that "the same or similar crimes should be punished in the same or similar way". The two forms of justice, the formal and substantial conceptions, are complementary.

2.4.3.2 The Actual Value in an Individual Case: Guaranteeing the Proportionality of the Results of Sentencing

The uniformity between the results of sentencing means—according to some scholars—that concerning the same crimes and same cases judges should reach the same sentencing decision, and different crimes and different cases should be sentenced differently, moreover, the judicial decisions should be consistent and in continuity with space and time. The requirement that the results of sentencing should be established in a coherent and consistent manner can be inferred from the principle that punishments should be in proportion to particular crimes.

The Criminal Law declares that "the degree of punishment shall be commensurate with the crime committed and the criminal responsibility of the offender."[175] This article, to some extent, requires the punishment and crime to be commensurable in an individual case which should be realized as the basic requirement of justice in individual cases. And pursuing the relative uniformity between the individual cases, especially between the same or similar cases is now the core task of criminal judicial practice.

In judicial practice, the severity of punishments differs significantly in the same or similar cases. The problems of sentencing incoherently and the significant disparity in making decisions about punishments are the main causes of violating social justice. The aim of balancing the practice of sentencing is to deal with the problem of the severity of punishments differing significantly in the same or similar cases.

2.4.4 The Solutions for the Dilemma of Sentencing Justice in China

2.4.4.1 Improving the Legal Background of Sentencing

In China, the legal background of sentencing, now, is comprised by *Criminal Law* and its judicial interpretations. The SPC issued the *Sentencing Guide (on trial),* which declares the judicial procedures of sentencing, and offers judges referential data to improve the reasoning of sentencing decisions. It tightens the gaps of sentencing results between decisions, but it still needs further suggestions for real improvement.

Firstly, it should shorten the trial period of the reform of sentencing standardization and it should realize the reform in judicial practice. Secondly, it is important to promulgate a far more detailed *Sentencing Guideline* and allow the regional high courts to make a far more detailed implementation of rules within the scope of the *Sentencing Guide* according to the local economic, social and criminal situation, so that it is required to make *the Sentencing Guideline* fully operational.

---

175 《中华人民共和国刑法》 *[Criminal Law of the People's Republic of China],* Order No. 83, 14 March 1997, Article 5.

Furthermore, it needs to compile all the provisions of the *Sentencing Guideline* and its detailed implementation of rules made by regional high courts into a volume so that it can tighten the gaps between sentencing rules and decisions. By creating this compilation, it would be possible to decrease the rate of imbalanced sentencing results due to the defects of sentencing laws and regulations. Thirdly, it is necessary to establish a case-guiding system. It is necessary that judges be allowed to cite the cases that are involved in the case-guiding system, and rely on these cases as important reasons and grounds for determining punishments. This system would enable judges to interpret the disputed issues and legal concepts in a far more comprehensive and detailed way. Furthermore, it would foster deducing the results of sentencing in a more coherent manner.

Meanwhile, in order to eliminate the disadvantages of ambiguous terms, judges could be allowed to use the previous cases which can help them understand and interpret presumptions described by legal terms. So, the legal system needs to build a database with previous legal decisions, which could be searched on the internet.

In addition, the legal system also needs to establish an institution which would serve as an authority guiding judicial interpretations. This institution could be responsible for formulating, amending and interpreting the *Sentencing Guideline* and sentencing policies, and supervise the implementation of the *Detailed Implementation Rules of the Sentencing Guideline* formulated by the regional high courts. This authority would also have the right to make suggestions for correcting inappropriate sentencing cases.

2.4.4.2 Standardizing Judicial Skills of Establishing Sentences

According to the results of my research and the results of the analysis of the judgments published by regional courts, it has come to light that judicial decisions lack real reasoning when judges state the reasons for their decisions about punishments. It is clear that judicial decisions lack interpretation of sentencing laws and regulations, judges usually cite the sentencing provisions and seldom interpret the legislative intent.

To a great extent, my research proves that judges are not confident in their legal knowledge and the ability to interpret the sentencing laws and regulations, and it also shows that judges do not pay much attention to the reasoning procedure of sentencing.

So, the legal system needs to improve judges' ability to interpret sentencing laws and regulations. The interpretative ability can only be improved by teaching and training and by judges learning how to apply their legal knowledge to individual cases. By setting up a special training system judges will learn to avoid resorting only to the literal meaning of statutes and applying regulations in a doctrinaire manner. By interpreting and understanding deeply the legislative spirit and intent judges would be able to apply sentencing laws and regulations accurately.

2.4.4.3 Improving the Criteria of Judges' Appointment

In the process of justifying sentences judges play a decisive role. The rules and regulations of punishments and legally relevant facts as objective and external factors in the process can only have an effect on judicial reasoning if judges have a subjective consciousness in relation to the results of their decisions on sentences.

The character and justice of the results of sentencing usually depend on conscious activity. During the procedure of reasoning that justifies sentences, one of the most important embodiments of the judges' subjective initiative is their academic preparation, judicial experience, and personal judicial competence, the ability to settle disputes, social perception and so on. It requires a relatively long period of time to form and improve all these personal qualities, and they can be improved by rich judicial experience and legal academic preparation, so it is necessary to improve the criteria of the appointment of judges, and the overall quality of judicial skills. This will decrease the possibility of there being an imbalance and variation in sentencing.

2.4.4.4 Constructing an Effective Communication Channel Between Judges and Society

As was mentioned above, one of the most important external factors affecting judges in sentencing is public opinion. So, we have to coordinate the relationship between the courts, who exercise judicial power independently, and the public, who supervise judicial activities. In order to make the criminal judgment acceptable to society without causing extensive concern to public, it is necessary to construct and improve the ways and channels of communication, so that public opinions can be heard by judges.

However, this does not mean that judges have to completely accept public opinions, but only that these opinions can serve as a point of reference. In order to achieve this goal judges should communicate with and reply to the public. In this way the professional rationality of judges and the conceptions of the public could reach a consensus and agree mutually during these communications, and even bridge the gaps of the conceptions of values between judges and the public.

The methods for constructing effective communication channels could be the following: firstly, it is necessary to improve and reform the assessment system of the people. For instance, a dualistic assessment system should be implemented, namely, a simultaneously existing system of the people's assessors and the people's jury. This means that in some complex, important cases which attract the widespread attention of society, the people's jury should be applied.

Secondly, it is inevitable to construct so-called hearing procedures about sentences, namely, the courts should organize hearing procedures for the complex, important cases in which the result of the decision about the punishment is a bit more controversial. This hearing procedure would enable judges to collect the public opinions about the sentencing problems.

Overall, just sentencing is, in practice, always questioned, as sentencing practice leads to an unpredictable, disproportional and unjust punishing system. In order to avoid these situations, the proposal for judicial reform would greatly change the current situation, i.e. it will provide rational reasons for particular sentences in judicial decisions and provide the opportunity for the public and the legal community to call the rightfulness of the decision into question. These reforms in the judicial system would contribute to creating a more just and predictable sentencing practice in China.

2.5 Conclusion

Since the founding of New China in 1949, in a one-party system state, almost every area has been greatly influenced by socialist ideology, which takes Marxism-Leninism as its guiding thought. In the first thirty years, from 1949 to 1979, the whole society of China was in a stage in which there was a key link with the class struggle and revolutionary thought played a leading and predominant role. In this context, China adopted only a few special criminal laws to deal with the terrible situation in the first decade of the founding of New China, and in this situation of a lack of law, certain words used by the national and political leaders were always considered as the highest order and their legal effect was unofficially higher than that of the law, and they were even written into judgments. Criminal punishment at this time functioned as a rule instrument for the ruling class to run the country and society. In the 1960s and 1970s, a socio-political movement, *the Great Proletarian Cultural Revolution*, took place in China. In this political meltdown, the Constitution and other laws, as well as regulations were laid aside and neglected, and the whole country and society was in a lawless state. After this period had passed, China passed its first Criminal Law in 1979 and then adopted 25 specific criminal laws and other subsidiary criminal provisions, which are provided in 107 non-criminal laws. Even though the "class struggle" and "revolutionary thought" were not the dominant theme in the political area, and economic construction and reform were considered the main task for the government and even the whole of society, to a large extent the instrumental rule character of law in these two decades was greatly emphasized by the 1979 Criminal Law and a series of special criminal laws and other subsidiary criminal provisions. An obvious example is that heavy punishments, including the death penalty and life imprisonment, were widely stipulated for crimes, especially economic crimes and other nonviolent crimes. In 1997, China amended the 1979 criminal law and specific criminal laws and some subsidiary criminal provisions and it became the present Criminal Law. Its character as a rule instrument seems to have been weakened to a certain extent; an example of this is that this character was no longer emphasized in political documents and the legislative practice no longer emphasized the death penalty as the heavy punishment for crimes, including for new crimes. However, we can still find some "trace" of the rule instrument since the 1997 Criminal Law still had many crimes (68 crimes, accounting for 16.46% of a total of 413 crimes[176]); on the other hand, in judicial practice, the government and the judicial authorities always adopted "strike-hard" as the policy to control crime, which implies that the heavy punishment is the only useful way to control crime and protect the social and ruling order. It also seems that the character of the rule instrument of the penalty is further weakened in the Eighth and Ninth Amendments because they removed the death penalty from the 22 crimes for the first time. However, it still appears in other aspects, for instance, in the heavy punishments stipulated for offenses against food safety and corruption crimes in recent years; and in some special political contexts the character of the rule instrument appears in another way, referred to as the "new instrument" by some scholars. Meanwhile, its penal nature and use as a rule instrument determines the purpose of the punishment, which, in fact, always takes retributivism as its main penal purpose. On one hand, its "rule instrument" nature requires that the penalty should be a measure that can crack down on and even eradicate crimes, and asks that the crime should be given a corresponding punishment; on the other hand, the current structure of the penalty system is a kind of retributive one, given that the application of the death penalty, the combined punishment of fines and other principal punishments, life imprisonment without release for corruption crimes and a heavier penalty for recidivists do not only make the penalty system heavy, but also retributive. Since the Mao era, a basic line of the Party, i.e. the "Mass Line", has always been emphasized in different areas and at different times. Under this requirement, a political requirement for penalty discretion, i.e. "unifying the legal effect and the social effect" becomes a important factor reflecting the implementation of the "Mass Line" in judicial practice, and is also an important element in evaluating the justice of sentencing from a political perspective, especially for cases causing great concern among the public. However, some risks caused by "unifying the legal effect and the social effect" should be considered. How to balance the legal effect and the social effect is an important problem; and sometimes, under some political circumstances, the judgement is inclined to emphasize the social effect and neglect the legal requirement, so this dilutes public sentiment; sometimes, the judgement strictly applies the law and focuses on the legal effect, but the result of the sentencing causes the victim's family members to complain about the injustice of the sentencing and then complain to different governments and judicial authorities. At the same time, in examining the justice problem of sentencing in judicial practice, we can see that Chinese criminal procedure faces some serious problems concerning the sentencing system. Judges often fail to provide acceptable reasons and arguments to support their decisions on punishments. Judicial decisions are influenced by many internal and external factors and judges do not pay attention to making their decisions regarding sentences according to a coherent and consistent system of values. Their sentencing practice leads to an unpredictable, disproportional and unjust punishing system. The failure to provide rational reasons for particular sentences in judicial decisions can undermine the justice of the decisions and provides the opportunity

[176] This number includes the 1997 Criminal Law and the 7 Amendments to the Criminal Law, which adopted from 1999 to 2009.

for the public and the legal community to call the rightfulness of the decision into question. To avoid this kind of unjust sentencing system judicial practice needs to be reformed in some ways. Improving the quality of judicial reasoning on sentencing includes the need to reform the appointment system of judges, construct an effective communication channel between the judges and society and develop judicial skills by setting up an effective training system. These reforms in the judicial system would contribute to creating a more just and predictable sentencing practice in China.

Chapter 3
The Death Penalty and Its Reforms in China and Other Countries

Abstract This chapter focus on the death penalty and its reform in China and other countries. Since 1949, China has had different death penalty policies in different phrases of its history. In the first thirty years, from 1949 to 1979, China's implementation of its policy on carrying out the death penalty was cautious and strict. During these thirty years, there was no criminal code until 1979, and China was a "disorderly and lawless society", although we can at least see that the application of the death penalty was accompanied by the expression "cautious and strict" in political documents. Even the first Criminal Law, which was adopted in 1979, only stipulated only 28 crimes punishable by death. It was considered by far the best code to be adopted in the history of China. When, in 1979, China launched its policy of opening up and reform, the whole of society underwent great changes and the crime rate dramatically increased. In order to control crime, China frequently adopted specific Criminal Laws and provided the death penalty for many crimes, which was considered an expansion of the execution legislation. China's first step to reduce the use of the death penalty legislatively was in 2011, when the Eighth Amendment was adopted. This amendment removed the death penalty from 13 crimes. Then, in 2015, the Ninth Amendment was adopted and repealed the death penalty for 9 crimes. Currently, there are 46 crimes punishable by death. In the near future, China will gradually and strategically abolish the death penalty. This chapter also looks at death penalty reform in other states, considering, for instance, Japan and Indonesia as retentionist states, and death penalty reform in the abolitionist states in Europe, death penalty reform in Central Asia, and death penalty reform in the USA.

G. Huang, *On the Alternative Punishment to the Death Penalty in China*,
https://doi.org/10.1007/978-981-97-1627-2_3

3.1 The Death Penalty System and Its Reforms in China

3.1.1 The Death Penalty Policies and Legislation: From 1949 to 2011

3.1.1.1 The Death Penalty Policies and Legislation in the Period from 1949 to 1979: The Policy on Execution is Cautious and Strict

In the paternalistic authoritarian regime of the Mao period, Mao and even the CPC did not have any conception of human rights and the execution legislation was not influenced by the CPC's outlook on human rights at all. Meanwhile, there was no Criminal Code, except for some specific regulations; there thus was no systematic execution legislation; we can even argue that the death penalty was effectively a lawless punishment.

Human rights protection had in fact no any connection with legislation, and in particular, with execution legislation; however, we cannot ignore CPC attitudes towards, and policy regarding, the death penalty in the Maoist era; indeed, we can even claim that the attitude of both the CPC and Mao himself towards execution was more cautious and stricter than that of the post-Mao period. In Mao's paternalistic authoritarian regime, the CPC's most important policies, such as its death penalty policy, were normally promulgated through the Party's or the national leaders' speeches or reports, especially those of Mao himself. In what follows, therefore, we will trace the death penalty policy of that period, using some of Mao's speeches or documents relating to capital punishment.

In 1951, in his paper, *"the Party's Mass Line must be followed in Suppressing Counter-revolutionaries (镇压反革命必须试行党的群众路线)"*, Mao said that.

> The number of counter-revolutionaries to be killed must be kept within certain proportions. The principle to follow here is that those who owe blood debts or are guilty of other extremely serious crimes and have to be executed to assuage the people's anger and those who have caused extremely serious harm to the national interest must be unhesitatingly sentenced to death and executed without delay.[1]

This is considered the policy for the application of the death penalty for counter-revolutionaries. As for the anti-corruption movement, on 8 December 1951, Mao said that the struggle against corruption, waste and bureaucracy should be emphasized as much as the struggle to suppress counter-revolutionaries; in major cases the guilty should be dismissed from office, punished, or sentenced to prison terms (to be reformed through labor), and the worst among them should be shot. The problem

[1] MAO Zedong, *The Party's Mass line must be followed in Suppressing Counter-revolutionaries*, Selected Works of Mao Tse-tung: vol. 5, available at: https://www.marxists.org/reference/archive/mao/selected-works/index.htm (Last visited: January 17th, 2024).

could only be solved in these ways.[2] In 1956, in his paper, *On the Ten Major Relationships (论十大关系),* Mao argued that "from now on there should be fewer arrests and executions in the suppression of counter-revolutionaries in society at large … All the same, we cannot announce that there will be no more executions, and we must not abolish the death penalty."[3] Mao's statements about capital punishment are taken to constitute the death penalty policy at that time.[4]

As to the law on the death penalty, in the 30 year period from 1949 to 1979 there was no criminal code and there was also a lack of relevant regulation on capital punishment, although some death penalty provisions could be found in certain special criminal laws, including the Instruction on Suppression of Counter-revolution Activities, of July 23 1950, which was the legal basis for dealing with counter-revolutionary cases in the early days following the foundation of the PRC, *the Regulations for Suppression of Counterrevolution of the PRC, of February 20 1951, the Interim Regulations on Punishment for the Impairment of the State Currency of the PRC, of April 19 1951*, and *the Regulations for Suppression of Corruption of the PRC, of April 21, 1952.* In February, 1956, the SPC systematically summarized the crimes, penalties and the extent of the sentences which were to be applied in judicial practice, and then issued a summary report. In this report, those crimes punishable by death were not only the crimes which were stipulated in the above special criminal laws, but also included the offenses of intentional killing, of intentionally causing injury (which caused death), and so on.[5] "After 1958, the criminal legislative work was weakened; except for several amnesty decrees, no special criminal law had been issued, even non-criminal laws issued had seldom included criminal law norms, too."[6] All of these comprised the main criminal system at that time and, to great extent, they were beginning to establish the death penalty system. In practice, in this period, capital punishment was considered an important measure in fighting the enemy, and was widely applied. In this sense, "the death penalty was applied on a ground of political legitimacy and reasonableness, and this period is considered as the process of the politicization of capital punishment, but with a lack of attention to the legal character of execution."[7]

---

[2] Ibid.

[3] Ibid.

[4] 张守文, 米传勇[ZHANG Shouwen and MI Chuanyong],《中国死刑政策的过去、现在及未来》*[The Past, Present and Future of the Death Policy in China]*, 法学评论 [Law Review] 2006, No. 2, 40; See also 陈兴良 [CHEN Xingliang],《死刑政策之法理解读》[The Death Penalty Policies: A Jurisprudential Perception], 中国人民大学学报 [Journal of Renmin University of China] 2013, No. 6, 3.

[5] 高铭暄[GAO Mingxuan],《死刑60年:新中国死刑立法的变迁与展望》*[60 years of the Death Penalty: the Evolution of and Prospects for the Capital Legislation of New China*], available at: 人民网[People Net] http://history.people.com.cn/n/2014/1030/c372326-25936904.html (Last visited: January 17th, 2024).

[6] Gao Mingxuan and Zhao Bingzhi, above no. 65, 69.

[7] 陈兴良[CHEN Xingliang],《死刑政策之法理解读》[The Death Penalty Policies: A Jurisprudential Perception], above no. 209, 3.

Even though Mao Zedong died in 1976, his thought still had a deep influence on death penalty legislation in 1979, when the new China passed its first Criminal Law. However, the 1979 Criminal Law was actually made on the basis of "the 33rd draft and also considering the new conditions, new experiences and new problems".[8] The 33rd draft was drawn up on October 9, 1963; Mao Zedong noted that "not only Criminal Law but also Civil Law is needed. There is lawlessness nowadays and things are very difficult without laws. Criminal Law and Civil Law have got to be established. Law needs to be instituted, so do cases."[9] Here, we can see that the attitude of Mao towards the law differed from the speeches made in 1958, and had clearly changed. Hence, the 1979 Criminal Law, particularly the execution legislation, still retained some of the characteristics and traces of the Maoist era, as can be seen in the "explanatory note to the Seven Draft Laws" made by Peng Zhen, the former Vice-Chairman of the Fifth National People's Congress, in the Second Session of China's Fifth National People's Congress (hereinafter: NPC). In this explanatory note, he argued that,

> China can't and shouldn't abolish death penalty, and yet should try to reduce its use. In 1959, The Central Committee of CPC and Comrade Mao Zedong already and repeatedly made similar demands for a reduction in the use of the death penalty. Now, in the almost three decades since the foundation of New China, particularly after crushing the 'Gang of Four', the nationwide situation of public safety and public order has become increasingly stable and better day by day; the Criminal Law hence decreases the number of the crimes punishable by death….it also keeps the provisions of death with a suspension of execution.[10]

In addition, Article 1 of the 1979 Criminal Law provided an explicitly party-minded reference to "taking Marxism-Leninism-Mao Zedong Thought as its guide".[11] Obviously, even though the 1979 Criminal Law was issued in the post-Mao era, it still retained Maoist legislation, and consequently, based on the above analysis; the 1979 Criminal Law was influenced by Mao's thought at some level.

Without exception, the legislation regarding the death penalty in the 1979 Criminal Law also implemented the death penalty policy of Mao and of the so called Central Committee of the CPC. In accordance with the 1979 Criminal Law, the death penalty "shall only be applied to criminals who have committed the most heinous crimes (罪大恶极)",[12] and "not imposed on persons who had not reached the age of 18 at the time the crime was committed or on women who are pregnant at the time of trial."[13] The death sentence review system was first established explicitly by the 1979 Criminal Law, but this review system was adapted by the NPC Standing Committee

---

[8] GAO Mingxuan and ZHAO Bingzhi, above no. 65, 77.

[9] *《人民日报》[People's Daily],* Beijing, October 29th, 1978, Cited in GAO Mingxuan and ZHAO Bingzhi, above no. 65, 74.

[10] 彭真[PENG Zhen], *《关于七个法律草案的说明》[An Explanatory note to the Seven Draft Laws],* available at: 中国共产党新闻网 [News of Communist Party of China] http://cpc.people.com.cn/GB/69112/99985/100003/9739230.html (Last visited: January 17th, 2024).

[11] *《中华人民共和国刑法》[The Criminal Law of the People's Republic of China],* Order No. 5, 1979, Article 1.

[12] Ibid., Article 43.

[13] Ibid., Article 44.

and the SPC over the next few years.[14] There were only 28 crimes[15] punishable by death in the 1979 Criminal Law, which meant that the number of crimes punishable by death reached its lowest point. As for the circumstances relating to these crimes, they mainly concern 'causing particularly grave harm to the State and the people, or if the circumstances are especially serious', or "inflicting serious injury or death on people, or causing heavy losses of public or private property, etc.",[16] provisions which partly limited the use of the death penalty. Some scholars have noted that the provisions on crime and its corresponding punishment, in particular the provisions on the punishment for general crimes, are very close to the legislation level of developed states.[17]

Even though the 1979 Criminal Law provided for the lowest number of crimes punishable by death, it was still full of political utilitarianism and had a heavily political complexion. These features can be found in some Chinese criminal scholars' research papers. Some contemporary scholars maintained that 'retaining or abolishing the death penalty by a state, is decided by the state's specific situation in

[14] Article 44(2) of the Criminal Law 1979 provided that 'all death sentences, except for those that according to law should be decided by the Supreme People's Court, shall be submitted to the Supreme People's Court for approval'. However, on June 10th, 1981, the NPC Standing Committee formulated an adaptation on reviewing the death sentence by issuing a Decision, which provided that, within the period from 1981 to 1983, in any case where a person who commits the crimes of homicide, robbery, rape, arson, causing an explosion, poisoning, breaching a dike, or sabotaging any means of transport, any transportation facility or electric power facility, is sentenced to death by High People's Courts in the provinces, autonomous regions and special municipalities, or by the Intermediate People's Court in the first instance, and if the defendant does not appeal, and the sentence is verified and approved by the High People's Court, or the sentence is imposed by the High People's Court in the first instance, and the defendant does not appeal, all of these sentences do not have to be submitted to the Supreme People's Court for verification and approval. See *《全国人民代表大会常务委员会关于死刑案件核准问题的决定》[The Decisions of the NPC Standing Committee on the Issues of Verifying and Approving Death Sentences]*, adopted by the 19th Session of Standing Committee of China's National Fifth National People's Congress (NPC), on June 10th, 1981. In addition, on September 7 1983, the Supreme People's Court made a notification to authorize the High People's Courts in the provinces, autonomous regions and special municipalities, and the Military Court to verify and approve the death sentence in accordance with the laws imposed on criminals who commit homicide, robbery, rape, causing an explosion and other crimes which cause serious damage to public safety. See *《最高人民法院关于授权高级人民法院核准部分死刑案件的通知》[The Supreme People's Court's Notification on the Authorization the High People's Courts to Verify and Approve some Death Sentence Cases]*, on September 7th, 1983.

[15] In accordance with the Criminal Law of 1979, there were 10 articles, which were Articles 90, 91, 92, 93, 94, 95, 96, 97, 100 and 101, providing for 15 crimes punishable by death in Chap. 1 (crimes of counter-revolution), 2 articles (Article 106 and Article 110) providing 8 crimes punishable by death in Chap. 2 (crimes of endangering public security), 2 articles (Article 132 and Article 139) providing 3 crimes punishable by death in Chap. 4 (crimes of infringing upon citizens' personal and democratic rights), and 2 articles (Article 150 and Article 155) providing 2 crimes punishable by death in Chap. 5 (crimes of property violation). See *《中华人民共和国刑法》[The Criminal Law of the People's Republic of China]*, Order No. 5, 1979.

[16] See Articles 103, 106, 110, 132, and others of the 1979 Criminal Law.

[17] 李洁 [LI Jie], *《慎重修改刑法论》[On Modifying Cautiously the Criminal Law]*, 刑事法评论[Criminl Law Review], edited by 陈兴良[CHEN Xingliang], 中国政法大学出版社[China University of Political Science and Law Press], Beijing, 2002, Vol. 11, 314.

its political history, and exists to meet the objective requirements of combating crimes. As for the limited retention of the death penalty in the Criminal Law of China, it is a result of the situation of the class struggle now existing in China and the crime situation. Imposing the death sentence in accordance with the law on counter-revolutionaries and other criminals is a current demand of the state economic construction, and is necessary to consolidate the dictatorship of the proletariat, and also responds to the requirements of the Masses.[18]

3.1.1.2 The Death Penalty in the Deng Era: Expansion of Execution Legislation

Deng's thinking on human rights was also implemented through the CPC's death penalty policy. After the implementation of reforms and the opening-up of 1978, although all kinds political control imposed on the individual were relaxed and Chinese society also changed from a repressive to a more open attitude, the social system was brought into a state of anomie, and public security and criminality deteriorated. All these changes can be observed in the increasing number of criminal cases which were dealt with by the People's Courts in the period from 1979 to 1997, as the Graph 3.1 shows.[19]

In the deteriorating social environment, the Central Government of China had to apply the death penalty as the most severe punishment to control the increasing crime rate. At that time, "the view of Deng Xiaoping on the death penalty could in principle represent the attitude of central government."[20] As regards the social situation in 1983, Deng Xiaoping said:

> The number of crimes, including serious ones, has increased substantially, and the people are very disturbed about this. Over the past few years, far from being checked, the tendency has grown. Why is that? Chiefly because we have hesitated to take prompt and stern actions to combat criminals and have given them very light sentences. ..... Serious offenders...... should be severely punished according to law. A number of criminals should be executed according to law ...... The only way to stop crime is to be tough about it.[21]

---

[18] 葛平, 王洪谷[GE Ping and WANG Honggu], *《谈死刑》[On the Death Penalty]*, 法学研究[Chinese Journal of Law] 1980, No. 1, 29; See also 力康泰 [LI Kangtai], *《正确认识和适用死刑》[Understanding and Applying Correctly the Death Penalty]*, 北京政法学院学报[Tribune of Beijing Colleague on Political Science and Law] 1983, No. 2, 18. In this paper, the authors said that, in China, at the present stage, the death penalty still cannot and shall not be abolished due to the existence of the remnants of the exploiting class and the existence of internal class struggle and international reactionaries.

[19] 中华人民共和国最高人民法院[The Supreme People's Court of P.R.C], *《数说人民法院审批工作60年》[Showing the People's Courts' Trail Works by Statistics Over 60 Years]*, available at: 最高人民法院网[Supreme People's Court Net] http://www.court.gov.cn/fabu-xiangqing-119.html (Last visited: January 17th, 2024).

[20] 张守文, 米传勇[ZHANG Shouwen and MI Chuanyong], above no. 209, 40.

[21] DENG Xiaoping, *Bourgeois Liberalization Means Taking the Capitalist Road*, The Selected Works of Deng Xiaoping, available at: https://dengxiaopingworks.wordpress.com/2013/03/18/bourgeois-liberalization-means-taking-the-capitalist-road/ (Last visited: January 17th, 2024).

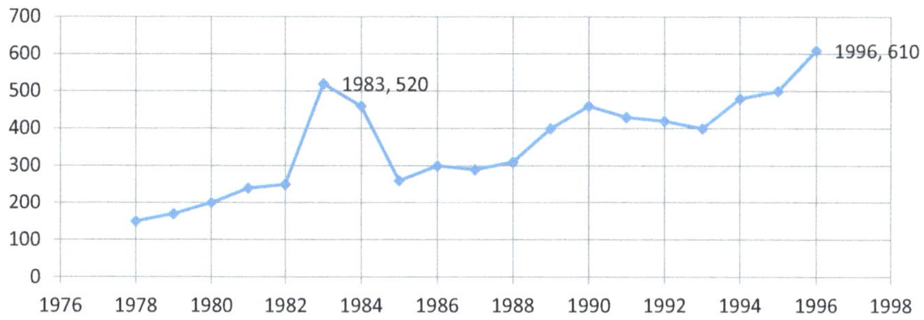

Graph 3.1 The number of first instance criminal cases in the whole country from 1978 to 1996 (in thousands). This graph shows the number of criminal cases before 1983, in which Chinese government implemented "strike-hard" anti-crime campaign, was dramatically increase to around 520,000 cases since 1978, especially in period from 1982 to 1983; but after the campaign in 1983, the number declined to approximately 260,000 cases in 1985, almost similar with the number of 1982. After 1985, the number of criminal cases showed a steadily increase to another highest in 1996, around 610,000 cases, even though it had a short term decrease during 1990 to 1993

Basic on the speech quoted from above, given by Deng on July 19, on August 25, 1983, the CPC launched *the Decision on Cracking Down Severely on Crimes*, which claimed that "cracking down severely on crimes is as serious a struggle of opposites as that between us and the enemy in the political area."[22] Hence, the criminal was deemed the enemy of the people.

As to the death penalty, in 1986 Deng pointed out that:

> The death penalty cannot be abolished, and some criminals must be sentenced to death…. Some criminals must be executed, but of course we have to be very careful in such matters. Some of the perpetrators of serious economic or other crimes must be executed as required by law. As a matter of fact, execution is one of the indispensable means of education…… Executing some of them can help save many cadres. As the saying goes, execute one as a warning to a hundred.[23]

From the speeches above, it is obvious that Deng tended to emphasize the death penalty as a severe punishment to control crime, an approach which differs totally from Mao's attitudes towards the death penalty. The execution policy was correspondingly changed from a restrictive one in the Maoist era to an extensive application in the Deng era. Regarding this change in the execution policy, one Chinese scholar criticized the fact that "the ruler expects to contain crimes and restore social order by the death penalty, and has come to somewhat depend on the death penalty during the process of social government."[24]

---

[22] *《中共中央发出 < 关于严厉打击刑事犯罪活动的决定 》[CPC's Decision on Cracking Down Severely On Crimes]*, available at: 中国共产党新闻网[News of the Communist Party of China] http://cpc.people.com.cn/GB/64162/64165/68640/68665/4739396.html (Last visited: January 18th, 2024).

[23] DENG Xiaoping, *Bourgeois Liberalization Means Taking the Capitalist Road*, above no. 226.

[24] See also 陈兴良 [CHEN Xingliang],《死刑政策之法理解读》[The Death Penalty Policies: A Jurisprudential Perception], above no. 209, 4.

Starting in 1981, the NPC Standing Committee had successively adopted 25 Specific Criminal Laws up to time the present Criminal Law was passed in 1997, 18 of which could be punishable by death. All of these Specific Criminal Laws brought significant changes in terms of the number of crimes punishable by death and the conditions in which the death penalty could be applied. There are three important points to note about this: (1) the number of crimes punishable by death increased dramatically. According to these Specific Criminal Laws, 33 crimes in total could be punishable by death,[25] and together with the 1979 Criminal Law, the total number of crimes punishable by death was raised to around 80 before the 1997 Criminal Law was passed with its dramatic rate of increase; (2) some Specific Criminal Laws stipulated the death penalty as an mandatory penalty. These laws included Article 2 of *the Decision Strictly Prohibiting Prostitution and Visiting Brothels ([1991] No. 51),* Article 1 of *the Decision on Punishing Criminal Elements Abducting and Selling or Kidnapping Women or Children ([1991] No. 52),* and *the Decision on Punishing Criminal Elements Hijacking Aviation Vehicles ([1992] No. 67).* The death penalty for these crimes was mostly a mandatory penalty; (3) another significant change was in the terms of judicial practice. In contemporary judicial practice, in order to crack down severely on ordinary crimes such as theft, the relevant judicial authorities applied the death penalty to these kinds of crimes through their interpretation of the law. For example, the death penalty could not be applied for theft in accordance with the 1979 Criminal Law, but could be applied in the light of *the Decision on Severely Punishing Criminals Who Seriously Undermine the Economy (1982).*

China adopted its second Criminal Law at the 2nd Session of the Fifth NPC on July 1 1997. Effectively, the 1997 Criminal Law was based upon the 1979 Criminal Law and a serious of Specific Criminal Laws passed successively from 1981 to 1996. Based on the 1979 Criminal Law, the execution legislation in the 1997 Criminal Law continued the death penalty policy contained in the Specific Criminal Laws, with some modifications and adjustments. In the 1997 Criminal Laws there were 68 crimes punishable by death, which were distributed across 9 different chapters—excluding Chapter IX *(Crimes of Dereliction of Duty)*—and the percentage of crimes punishable by death from the total number of crimes (414) was 16.4%.[26] It might appear that the number of crimes punishable by death is fewer than the total in the 1979 Criminal Law and the 25 Specific Criminal Laws (i.e. around 80 crimes), but actually, "it neither increased nor decreased in principle; the conditions were not right for us to decrease the number of crimes punishable by death due to the current severe situation regarding social order and economic crimes."[27] However, the applicable condition

---

25 高铭暄[GAO Mingxuan], *《死刑60年:新中国死刑立法的变迁与展望》[60 years of the Death Penalty: the Evolution of and Prospects for the Capital Legislation of New China*], above no. 210.

26 *《中华人民共和国刑法》[Criminal Law of the People's Republic of China],* Order No. 83, March 14th 1997.

27 王汉斌[WANG Hanbin], *《关于 < 中华人民共和国刑法(修订草案)的说明》[Introduction on the Draft to the Criminal Law of P.R.C],* available at: Law library http://www.law-lib.com/fzdt/newshtml/20/20050812041456.htm (Last visited: January 18th, 2024). However, apparently, the number of crimes punishable by death has become fewer than ever due to two important considerations; namely, some crimes punishable by death according to the Special Criminal Laws were abolished,

for imposing the death penalty was changed from "the most heinous crimes (罪大恶极)' in the 1979 Criminal Law to 'extremely serious crimes (罪行极其严重)",[28] which means that the conditions for execution were broadened and the number of possible executions increased.[29] Although the 1997 Criminal Law does not reduce the executions carried out, it limits to some extent the scope of applicable cases and reduces the conditions required for commuting the death penalty to life imprisonment or fixed-term imprisonment, i.e. (1) as regards limitations, it deleted the following provision: "Persons who have reached the age of 16 but not the age of 18 may be sentenced to death with a two-year suspension of execution if the crime committed was particularly serious,"[30] so a person who had not reached the age of 18 at the time the crime was committed would not be sentenced to death, including death penalty with a suspension of execution; (2) in terms of reducing the conditions, it changed the phrasing of the 1979 Criminal Law from "shows true repentance" or "shows true repentance and performs meritorious service",[31] to "does not intentionally commit a crime",[32] so commutation can occur if the person does not intentionally commit a crime, even if true repentance does not occur.

All things considered, the expansion of execution legislation in China was not changed legislatively by the 1997 Criminal Law, and we can even argue that the

---

or the death penalty itself was abolished for a few crimes; and some crimes punishable by death were merged or certain provisions or articles were merged by legislative technicality.

[28] Article 43 of Criminal Law 1979 provided that 'the death penalty shall only be applied to criminals who have committed the most heinous crimes', but Article 48 of Criminal Law 1997 provided that 'the death penalty shall only be applied to criminals who have committed extremely serious crimes'. See《中华人民共和国刑法》*[The Criminal Law of the People's Republic of China]*, Order No. 5, 1979 and《中华人民共和国刑法》*[Criminal Law of the People's Republic of China]*, Order No. 83, March 14th, 1997.

[29] Scholars have pointed out that the concept of "the most heinous crimes (罪大恶极)" emphasizes both of two facts: objectivity and subjectivity; specifically, that the objectively harmful consequence of the crime is extremely serious, and that the subjective culpability of the offender's mind is extremely serious, but the concept of 'extremely serious crimes (罪行极其严重)' only emphasizes the objective consequences of harm to society. So the change from 'the most heinous crimes' to 'extremely serious crimes' already lowers the applicable standards of death penalty. Moreover, some scholars noted that, compared with 'extremely serious crimes', 'the most heinous crimes' had stricter demands in terms of the number of crimes punishable by death and the concrete applicable conditions for the death penalty, and imposed more stringent restrictions on the stipulation of crimes punishable by death in the Specific Provisions of the Criminal Law and on the death sentence in judicial practice. See 张远煌[ZHANG Yuanhuang],《我国死刑适用标准的缺陷及其弥补方法》*[On* the Defects of Applicable Standards of the Death Penalty in China and their Solution], 法商研究[Studies in Law and Business] 2006, No. 6, 40; 储怀值[CHU Huaizhi],《死刑司法控制: 完整解读第四十八条》*[Judicial Control of Death Penalty: A Comprehensive Understand*ing of Article 48 of Penal Code], 中外法学[Bejing University Law Journal] 2012, No. 5, 1014; 赵秉志 [ZHAO Bingzhi],《刑罚总论问题探索》*[Exploring the Issues of Punishments in the General Provisions of Criminal Law]*, 法律出版社 [Law Press], Beijing, 2002.

[30]《中华人民共和国刑法》*[The Criminal Law of the People's Republic of China]*, Order No. 5, *1979*, Article 44.

[31] Ibid, Article 46.

[32] Ibid, Article 50.

execution was somewhat strengthened. However, we should note that the 1997 Criminal Law preserved, to a great extent, the scope of crimes punishable by death, but did not completely preserve the legislative pattern of the death penalty after 1979, due to the decrease in the number of crimes punishable by death. This change might appear insignificant, but it really does show that the death penalty needs to be limited and even abolished. The expansion of legislation was inevitable to give much more possibility of death sentence to the judges. Information about the number of executions is a state secret until now, but according the available reports estimated by Amnesty International, the execution numbers is 3500 in 1996,[33] but in 1997, it is 1644,[34] showing a dramatically decrease, and in 1998, it increased again to 1769.[35]

3.1.1.3 The Death Penalty Policies and Legislation in the Period from 1979 to 2011: From Expansion of Execution Legislation to Limiting Its Use.

In a state—in this case, China—which only emphasizes the national interest or the interests or human rights of the majority, the interests or human rights of the few, such as criminals, are seen as opposed to those of the majority, and are in most cases neglected or not taken seriously, and so "the criminals' human rights protection" is denied[36]; in a state which only focuses on economic and state development, or on the stability of the state, the instrumental efficacy of criminal law and its punishment will be highlighted and taken full advantage of. In terms of crime and public security, the state is expected to control crime and protect public security by launching a national anti-crime campaign[37]; on the other hand, the traditional concept of "governing the country with severe law during troubled times (治乱世用重典)" still plays an important role in contemporary China. "Culture is a rather vague concept, but certain legal and religious traditions can influence whether the death penalty is considered a culturally accepted part of the penal system."[38] The death penalty is always considered the main option in an anti-crime campaign, because it is the most effective and direct measure for controlling crime. It is true, to some extent, that the death penalty has always received the attention and has been a favored policy of national rulers and

---

[33] Amnesty International, *The Death Penalty Worldwide: Developments in 1996*, Al Index: ACT 50/05/97. We have to note that Chinese government launched "cracking down severely" policy on Crimes, so the execution number is higher than the following years.

[34] Amnesty International, *The Death Penalty Worldwide: Developments in 1997*, Al Index: ACT 50/04/98.

[35] Amnesty International, *Death Sentences and Executions in 1998*, Al Index: ACT 51/01/99.

[36] *《江泽民论人权》[On Human Rights by Jiang Zemin]*, available at: 人民网[People's Net] http://politics.people.com.cn/GB/8198/5139784.html (Last visited: January 18th, 2024).

[37] Since the first anti-crime campaign was launched in 1983, China has launched four similar campaigns; in 1983, 1996, 2004 and 2010. In addition, in 2014, the country launched an anti-terrorist campaign in Xin Jiang province.

[38] NEUMAYER Eric, *Death Penalty: The Political Foundations of the Global Trend towards Abolition*, Human Rights Review, 2008, Vol. 9, No. 2, 253.

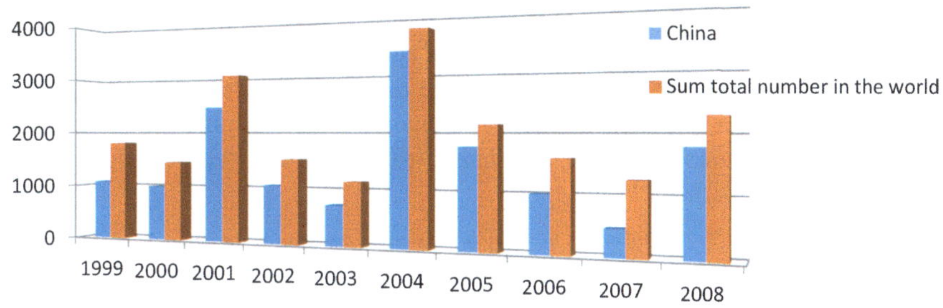

Graph 3.2 The execution numbers in China and the world (in execution) (all these dates are from *Amnesty International Death Sentences and Executions from 1999 to 2008*, AI Idex respectively: ACT 50/08/00, ACT 50/001/2001, ACT 50/001/2002, ACT 50/002/2003, ACT 50/007/2004, ACT 50/005/2005, ACT 50/002/2006, ACT 50/004/2007, ACT 50/001/2008, and ACT 50/003/2009). This graph shows the execution number of China in 2007 is the lowest, around 470 but in the world, it is in 2003, approximately 1146, at the same year, China's amount is around 726; the highest in China is in 2004 with 3400 due to it implemented "strike-hard" anti-crime campaign at that year, and in 2001, it also implemented this policy so is showed the second highest number, around 2468

the public. The public expect the authorities to be able to crack down on and control crimes by using the death penalty; and the rulers also want to govern and control crime by applying heavy punishments to protect the social order and public security. To a great extent, these expectations on the part of the public and the rulers formed the basic reasoning behind the death penalty and expanded the scope of its application. In the post-Deng era, the national leaders of China still face serious public security issues; however, they need to launch different policies. Jiang, in his time in office, still continued the policy of "stability overwhelming the wholeness", which was proposed by Deng Xiaoping; in the Hu era, the emphasis was on the strategic idea that "development is an absolute principle and stability is an absolute task."[39] Therefore, in these two eras, and until the end of the Hu era, there was no significant change in the use of the death penalty, and the execution number, which is showed by Graph 3.2, was still at a high level in accordance with the Amnesty International estimate report.

Although the death penalty still plays an important role in crime control and social governance, China has already amended the criminal law towards limiting its use. In 2007, a significant reforming step was taken, when, on 1 January 2007, the power to review for all death sentences was restored to SPC from the local Higher People's Courts and the Military Courts, such that the SPC can now uniformly exercise the power to review and further improve the standards and conditions of evidence and the procedure involved in sentencing someone to death. Therefore, we can see the execution number at that year in the post-deng era is the lowest. This is the first time

[39] *《中共中央加强改进新形势下党建若干重大问题的决定》[Decision of the CPC Central Committee on Major Issues on Strengthening and Improving Party Building]*, available at: 中央人民政府[Central People's Government of P.R.C.] http://www.gov.cn/jrzg/2009-09/27/content_1428158.htm (Last visited: January 18th, 2024).

China has limited the use of the death penalty in judicial practice since the passing of the 1979 Criminal Law. On the one hand, this change could be due to the inclusion in the Constitution of the statement 'the state respects and protect human rights'; on the other hand, it could be a result of a change in the criminal policy in 2006 from a policy of "*cracking down on crime(严打)*" to one of "combining leniency and severity (宽严相济)".[40]

3.1.1.4 The Death Penalty Legislation and Reform in the Period from 2011 to 2015: Abolishing the Death Penalty for Some Economic Crimes

Another significant and substantial step was taken by the Eighth Amendment. In 2011, the Eighth Amendment, which was adopted on February 25th, abolished the death penalty for 13 economic and nonviolent crimes, reducing the number of crimes punishable by death from 68 to 55, and banned capital punishment for offenders over the age of 75. Even though seven amendments were adopted before the Eighth Amendment, they did not involve any reform of the death penalty; in other words, the Eighth Amendment started a process of gradually abolishing the death penalty in China. Professor Carolyn Hoyle in the UK pointed out that "important in themselves, these reforms are emblematic of China's emerging commitment to limit the scope and practice of capital punishment in stages, with, as it stated to the UN Human Rights Council in 2007, the final aim of abolition."[41]

From the above, we can see that in the Jiang era, China did not undertake any reform of the death penalty and denied criminals human rights, but in the Hu era, the country put emphasis on the central task of putting people first, and so the concept of the 'state respects and protects human rights' was included in the Constitution in 2004. Following this, reform of the death penalty was started by limiting its use in judicial practice in 2007, and in 2011, by legislatively decreasing in a significant fashion the number of crimes punishable by death. This is one important illustration of the CPC's shifting approach to human rights and to the reform of the death penalty system, but we cannot fine any information about execution number after 2008. However, after the Eight Amendment, there were still 55 crimes punishable by death, and it is impossible to get.

[40] On October 18, 2006, the Sixth Plenary Session of the Sixteenth Central Committee of the CPC decided that China would implement the criminal policy of severity tempered with gentleness in the future. See *《中共中央关于构建社会注意和谐社会若干重大问题的决定》 [Decision of the CPC Central Committee on Certain Major Issues in the Building of a Harmonious Socialist Society]*, available at: 中国共产党新闻网[News of Communist Party of China]. http://cpc.people.com.cn/GB/64093/64094/4932424.html (Last visited: January 18th, 2024). With this Decision it also emphasized its intention to crack down heavily on severe crime by means of the law, to attempt to regulate areas with serious security problems, and to significantly rein back the upward growth in criminal activity.

[41] *The Death Penalty in China—the road to reform,* available at: Faculty of Law of Oxford University. https://www.law.ox.ac.uk/research-subject-groups/research-index/impact-index/death-penalty-china-road-reform (Last visited: January 18th, 2024).

China entered the Xi Jinping era in November 2012, and launched its first *White Paper on Judicial Reform in China (hereinafter: White Paper)* in this year.[42] This *White Paper* explicitly states that "China retains the death penalty, but strictly controls and prudently applies it."[43] This was also the first time that China had stated its opinion on the death penalty in a White Paper. *Decision of the Central Committee of the Communist Party of China on Some Major Issues Concerning Comprehensively Deepening the Reform (hereinafter, the 2013 Decision)* also stated that "we will gradually reduce the number of crimes punishable by death penalty",[44] which was also the first time China had discussed abolishing the death penalty gradually in the Party's report. However, *the CPC Central Committee Decision Concerning Some Major Questions in Comprehensively Moving Governing the Country According to the Law Forward (hereinafter: the 2014 Decision)* does not mention the death penalty, but states that it will "promote judicial reform", "comprehensively construct the rule of law", and "strengthen the judicial protection of human rights."[45] In the light of the Party's political documents and the *White Paper*, China adopted the Ninth Amendment to the Criminal Law (hereinafter, the Ninth Amendment) on 29 August 2015, which also abolished the death penalty for 9 crimes and reformed the relevant death penalty system.

The Ninth Amendment pushed reform of the death penalty further forward. The relevant steps in this process can be detailed as follows: (1) there has been a further reduction in the number of crimes punishable by death stipulated by specific provisions of the Criminal Law, from 55 to 46, i.e., the death penalty is no longer applicable for the crimes of smuggling weapons, ammunition, or nuclear materials, smuggling counterfeit currency, counterfeiting currency, raising funds by means of fraud, organizing prostitution, forcing another person to engage in prostitution, obstructing a commander or a person on duty from performing his duty, and fabricating rumors to mislead others during wartime. So, China has taken another solid step towards the final goal of entirely abolishing the death penalty de facto and *de jure* by reducing the number of crimes punishable by death. However, there are still 46 crimes punishable by death in the present Criminal Law, of which 24 are non-violent crimes, representing 52.2% of the total, and 22 are violent crimes; (2) the executive conditions are further improved in that the suspended death penalty is commuted to immediate execution, which is a reform of great significance for China's current death penalty system. In accordance with Article 2 of the Ninth Amendment, the stipulation of the

[42] Here we must note that the White Paper on Judicial Reform in China was published on October 9 2012 when China was still in the Hu era, although in effect, it had already entered the Xi era, Xi being elected as General Secretary of the Central Committee of the Communist Party of China (CPC) on November 15 2012.

[43] The Information Office of the State Council of P.R.C, *Judicial Reform in China*, available at: 中国共产党新闻网 [News of the Communist Party of China]. http://english.cpc.people.com.cn/206972/206981/8211483.html (Last visited: January 19th, 2024).

[44] *Decision of the Central Committee of the Communist Party of China on Some Major Issues Concerning Comprehensively Deepening the Reform*, above no. 5.

[45] *The CCP Central Committee Decision Concerning Some Major Questions in Comprehensively Moving Governing the Country According to the Law Forward*, above no. 33.

previous Article 50(1) that "if it is verified that he or she has committed an intentional crime, the death penalty shall be executed upon verification and approval of the SPC" is amended by the Ninth to "if he or she has committed an intentional crime the circumstances of which are flagrant, the death penalty shall be executed upon verification and approval of the SPC; if he or she has committed an intentional crime, but the death penalty is not carried out, the terms of the suspension of the carrying out of the death penalty shall be reviewed again, and reported to the SPC for the record".[46] In other words, the system of the death penalty with suspension of execution was reformed in two senses; firstly, "it raises further the thresholds of the suspension of execution of death penalty commuted to immediate execution.",[47] i.e. the previous terms of "it is verified" is amended to "circumstances are flagrant"; secondly, it increases the probation period of the suspension of execution; in other words, it appears to put the criminal onto a longer "death row"[48] once again, since the Ninth Amendment provides that if he or she has committed an intentional crime during the probation period of the suspension of execution and the circumstances are not flagrant, the death penalty shall not be carried out, but the terms of the suspension of the execution of the death penalty shall be reviewed again.

Certainly, China is still facing a difficult path to the complete abolition of the death penalty *de jure and* de facto. In the post-Deng era, following the analysis above, the CPC's outlook on human rights has undergone a great change, especially in the area of criminals' human rights, from denying criminals human rights protection to "strengthen the judicial protection of human rights", but the CPC still emphasizes the human rights and interests of the majority and the primacy of the nation and economic development; and the individual interests of the few always make way for the former. Even though *the SOD* stated the importance of "putting people first as its core principle" and the *2013 and 2014 Decisions* declared the judicial protection of human rights, they also emphasized the importance of "persisting in starting from China's reality and striving to make the people feel fairness and justice in every judicial case".[49] As far as fairness is concerned, however, different people have different perspectives. Hence it is a pseudo-perspective that every person should feel fairness and justice in every judicial case. Particularly now, judicial authorities in China have to implement all kinds of "Mass Line Campaigns" as a form of political initiative. In these kinds of political campaign, fairness and justice tend to be the

---

[46] *《中华人民共和国刑法修正案(九)》[The Ninth Amendment to the Criminal Law of the People's Republic of China],* above no. 6, Article 2.

[47] 陈丽平[CHEN Liping], *《点击中华人民共和国刑法修正案(九)草案的七大亮点》[Clicking on the 7 highlights of the Draft of the Ninth Amendment to the Penal Code of the P.R.C],* 法制日报[Legal Daily News], October 28th, 2014, 3.

[48] Here, death row is very different from the "death row" in America where the criminal spends a long time waiting for execution; some inmates even have to spend several decades awaiting execution. In China, death row is the probation period, which is not less than two years. See DREHLE David Von, *The Death of the Death Penalty: why the Era of Capital Punishment is Ending*, available at: http://time.com/deathpenalty/ (Last visited: January 19th, 2024).

[49] *The CCP Central Committee Decision Concerning Some Major Questions in Comprehensively Moving Governing the Country According to the Law Forward*, above no. 33.

property of the majority of the people; public opinion can always be involved and can react to events in the judicial sphere.[50]

The White Paper and the *2013 Decision* have already stated to strictly control and apply cautiously the death penalty, but the process they establish for this is a gradual one. Nobody knows the timetable for China's complete abolition of the death penalty. In the present situation in China, however, death penalty reform is always decided by the nation's leaders. On the one hand, the nation's leaders have to focus on the demands of the mass of the people, because they are "the subjects of and source of strength for ruling the country according to the law"[51]; on the other hand, the death penalty is still the most effective measure available to the rulers to protect national stability and public security.[52]

---

[50] It has recently become very common for public opinion to influence the judiciary, particularly in the criminal justice field, and the impact of public opinion is increasing, as can be seen in the following cases: *许霆 [XU Ting] (2007)穗中法刑二初字第196号[(2007) Hui Intermediate the Second Criminal Court First Trial. No. 196, (2008) 穗中法刑二重字第2号 [(2008) Hui Intermediate the Second Criminal Court Second Trial. No. 2; 药家鑫 [YAO Jiaxin] (2011) 西刑一初字第68号 [(2011) Xi the First Criminal Court First Trial. No. 68]; 李昌奎 [LI Changkui] (2010) 昭中刑一初字第52号 [(2010) Zhao intermediate Criminal Court First Trial. No. 52], (2010) 云高法终字第1314号 [(2010) Yun High Court Second Trial No. 1314].* All of which reflect the influence of public opinion on criminal practice. The most important impact of public opinion is to influence the judges' sentencing decisions, as, for example, in the case of Xu, where the punishment was changed from life imprisonment to a fixed term of 5 years, in the case of Yao, where public opinion was always focused on the death penalty in the two trials, and in the case of Li, where the sentence was changed from the death penalty with immediate execution to a suspended death penalty, which then became the death penalty with execution at the retrial. In all of these cases public opinion played an important role in changing sentences.

[51] *The CCP Central Committee Decision Concerning Some Major Questions in Comprehensively Moving Governing the Country According to the Law Forward*, above no. 33.

[52] We have indirect evidence of this from the legislator. The Vice-Chairmen of the Law Committee of the National People's Congress of the P.R.C., Li Shishi, when delivering the explanatory note for the Draft of the Ninth Amendment to the Criminal Law of the P.R.C. said that since the death penalty for 13 economic and nonviolent crimes had been abolished by the Eighth Amendment in 2011, the general security situation of Chinese society is within a controllable range and the number of serious crimes is stable, with a slight decline. The initiative has already indicated that the abolition of the death penalty for 13 crimes by the Eighth Amendment did not have any negative impact on society, and sections of society in China have reacted positively to the abolition and commented on this. However, we must note that the death penalty for these crimes is seldom or never applied in judicial practice, and its abolition would not cause any negative impact on public security (See 陈兴良 [CHEN Xingliang], *《减少死刑的立法路线图》[Reduction of the Legislation Road Map for the Death Penalty]*, 政治与法律 [Political Science and Law] 2015, No. 7, 71; 黄太云 [HUANG Taiyun], *《< 中华人民共和国刑法修正案(八) 解读(一) 》[Unscrambling the Amendment VIII to the Criminal Law (The First Part)]*, 人民检察[People's Procuratorial Semi-monthly] 2011, No. 6, 6.

3.1.2 The Death Penalty Legislation and Reform After 2015

The Eighth and Ninth Amendment have dramatically reduced the number of crimes punishable by death stipulated by the specific provisions; there are still 46 crimes punishable by death. And the Chinese legislature has to reduce entirely this number of crimes step by step in the future. The approaches and strategies below should be adopted for the next steps.

3.1.2.1 Strategy One: Abolishing the Death Penalty for Non-Violent Crimes

The Eighth and Ninth Amendment have abolished the death penalty for 13 economic and non-violent crimes and 9 crimes respectively. This kind of trend and style of reducing the number of crimes punishable by death will be the significant and appropriate approach and strategy for reform of the death penalty in China, and it is basic on the distributed situation of crime punishable by death in the specific provisions of Criminal Law and judicial practice. Table 3.1 shows the distributed situations of crimes punishable by death.

At the same time, in the judicial practice of China, the actual applicable rate of non-violent crimes also determines that the focus of death penalty reform in China in the future should be on abolishing the death penalty for non-violent crimes. Since the present Criminal Law was enacted in 1997, the death penalty for the crimes of impairing the interests of national defence, crimes of servicemen transgression of duties and most crimes of endangering national security have never been applied up until the present time, and it seems that this form of punishment in these cases has been put aside. The death penalty used to be frequently applied in the past for the crimes of embezzlement and bribery, but this has not been the judicial practice in recent years, including the implementation of the death penalty with immediate execution. Therefore, in accordance with the judicial practice in China, abolishing the death penalty for non-violent crimes would not have any practical negative impact.

Furthermore, non-violent crime is very substantially different from violent crime, due to the latter's infringements upon the right to life and right to health, and the former does not directly endanger another person's right to life. So, sentencing the criminal who committed extremely serious non-violent crimes to death is in fact out of keeping with the essential balance between crime and punishment. "non-violent crime does not only doesn't include the violent factor in terms of constitutive elements of a crime, but also doesn't take another person's life as the target of crime. So, the nature of social harmfulness of this kind of crime is absolutely different from such homicide as violent crime, and they could not view as the serious crime. But in accordance with the present Criminal Law, the maximum punishment prescribed is the death penalty for these two kinds of crimes, which is doubtlessly against the

Table 3.1 The distributed situations of crimes punishable by death

	The number of crimes punishable by death	The number of non-violent crimes
Crimes of endangering national security	7	6
Crimes of endangering public security	14	4
Crimes of disrupting the order of the socialist market economy	2	2
Crimes of infringing upon citizens's right of person and democratic rights	5	1
Crimes of property violation	1	0
Crimes obstructing the administration of public order	3	1
Crimes of impairing the interests of national defence	2	1
Crimes of embezzlement and bribery	2	2
Crimes of servicemen's transgression of duties	10	7
Total	46	24

The table shows that there are 46 crimes punishable by death in the present Criminal Law, of which there are 24 crimes of a non-violent nature, occupying 52.2%. Even after two reductions by the Eighth and Ninth Amendment, the percentage of non-violent crimes punishable by death is still large, which thus determines that the focus of death penalty reform in China in the future should be on the abolition of the death penalty for non-violent crimes

principle of suitable punishment for crime."[53] Non-violent crimes will become the preference for China to reform the death penalty system.

Strategy Two: Reducing the Number of Non-lethal Violent Crime Punishable by Death

Non-lethal violent crime refers to those crimes committed by violent means but which don't cause the victim's death. For example, the crime of forcing other person to engage in prostitution and the crime of obstructing a commander or a person on duty from performing his duties are non-lethal violent crime. The Ninth Amendment abolished the death penalty for economic and non-lethal violent crimes, going beyond

[53] 赵秉志[ZHAO Bingzhi], *《论中国非暴力犯罪死刑的逐步废止》[On Abolition of Death Penalty of Non-Violent Crimes in China]*, 中国刑法学年会文集(第1卷: 死刑问题研究)[Collected Works of 2004 Annual Conference of China's Criminal Law: On the Death Penalty (Volume 1)], 中国人民公安大学出版社[China's People's Public Security University Press], Beijing, 2004, 779.

the limitations of the Eighth Amendment which only abolished the death penalty for economic and non-violent crime. "It (the Ninth Amendment) has now taken a step to abolish the death penalty for non-lethal violent crime precedent, and in the future, China should keep on moving toward abolishing the death penalty for this kind of crime."[54]

After enactment of the Ninth Amendment, in the present Criminal Law there are still 22 violent crimes punishable by death, most of which are stipulated by Chapter II (10 Crimes of endangering public security) and Chapter IV (4 crimes of infringing upon citizens' right of the person) in The Specific Provisions of Criminal Law. The non-lethal violent crimes mainly include crimes of stealing or forcibly seizing any guns, ammunition or explosives, or stealing or forcibly seizing poisonous or radioactive substances, infectious disease pathogens (Article 127), crime of rape (Article 236), crime of abducting and trafficking in women or children (Article 240), crime of robbery (Article 263), crime of smuggling, trafficking in, transporting and manufacturing narcotic drugs (Article 347), and so on. According to traditional Chinese thinking, the harmful social consequences caused by these crimes are very serious and the perpetrators should be sentenced to death for committing them. And for these kinds of crimes, now, "China remains heavily dependent on the death penalty to control them."[55] To a great extent, China is still very resistant to abolishing the death penalty for these kinds of crimes. Non-lethal violent crimes, normally, are committed by violent means and cause a serious harmful social consequence, and the culpability of the perpetrator who commits this kind of crime is much more than that of the perpetrator who commits a non-violent crime. As for the value of life, the direct result of the death penalty is far more than the result caused by the non-lethal violent crime. Therefore, stipulating the death penalty for the non-lethal violent crime, to a great extent, implies that it is unsuitable punishment for the crime. So, China should abolish the death penalty for non-lethal violent crime. Abolishing the death penalty for non-lethal violent crime lays the groundwork for further abolishing the death penalty for lethal violent crime.

Strategy Three: Strictly Limiting the Application of Death Penalty for Lethal Violent Crime Until Entirely Abolishing the Death Penalty

Lethal violent crime refers to the crime of infringing or illegally depriving another person of their right to life by means of violence, such as the crime of hijacking aircraft (Article 121), and the crime of homicide (Article 232). All these kinds of crimes are punishable by death in light of the Criminal Law. The nature of the death

---

54 赵秉志[ZHAO Bingzhi], *《中国死刑立法改革新思考——以《刑法修正案(九)(草案)》为主要视角》[New Thinking on Death Penalty in China: With the Perspective of Amendment (Draft) to Criminal Law]*, 吉林大学社会科学学报[Ji Lin University Journal Social Sciences Edition] 2015, Vol. 55, No. 1, 8.

55 曲晟[QU Sheng], *《论我国死刑制度新动向及其出路:兼评《刑法修正案(八)》的死刑制度》[On the New Tendency of Death Penalty System and its Outlet in China: Reviewing the Death Penalty System in the Eighth Amendment]*, 求索[*Search*] 2012, No. 2,133.

penalty for this kind of crime is called "absolutely determinate death penalty"[56] or called mandatory death penalty. And all this time, "the death penalty is mainly applied to such homicide, crime of intentional injury as only a few types of serious crimes."[57] Abolishing the death penalty for lethal violent crime would be the last strategy of death penalty system reform in China and it will be the most difficult. On the one hand, lethal violent crime has the most serious reverse-ethic, and it also easily raises the whole society concerns and easily sparks outrage. This can be clearly seen in recent cases, such as that of Li Changkui,[58] who raped and killed his fiancée and then killed the fiancée's brother, and the case of Yao Jiaxin,[59] who cruelly killed a woman. These two cases called the public's attention to lethal violent crime and the death penalty system, and caused the society to intensively debate whether these two perpetrators shall be sentenced to death or not. Finally, however, the opponents of the death penalty really lost to the proponent. And this result was reflected in the final judgments of these two cases. On the other hand, the death penalty for lethal violent crime is in line with traditional Chinese concepts of retribution, which include "death to the killer, prison to the violence". "This traditional concept has already survived more than one thousand years in China, and until now the revenge consciousness and retribution concept remain ingrained in Chinese thinking, and the psychological expectation of retribution can distinctly be found amongst the Chinese."[60] The traditional concept of "life for a life" has a firm foundation in the whole society and it has a deep influence on the criminal legislation and also provides a strong basis for sentencing the criminal who committed lethal violent crime to death. In addition, "immediately abolishing entirely the death penalty *de jure and* de facto would be too sudden to be accepted by the current social reality in China, because social support for complete abolition is lacking. But it doesn't mean that the public security now is in a bad situation; it was deeply impacted by the large population, the model of criminal legislation and the model of social control instead."[61] The complete abolition of the death penalty for lethal violent crime is at this stage unrealistic, but it should be limited by legislation. One important step is to amend the provisions of mandatory death penalty in the Criminal Law. There

---

56 陆建红[LU Jianhong], *《"绝对"死刑条款的适用研究》[On the Application of Terms of "Absolutely Determinate Death Penalty System]*, available at: http://china.findlaw.cn/hetongfa/mianzetiaokuan/168886.html (Last visited: January 19th, 2024).

57 赵秉志[ZHAO Bingzhi], *《中国死刑立法改革新思考——以《刑法修正案(九)(草案)》为主要视角》[New Thinking on Death Penalty in China: With the Perspective of Amendment (Draft) to Criminal Law]*, above no. 260, 8.

58 *李昌奎 [LI Changkui](2010) 昭中刑一初字第52号 [(2010) Zhao intermediate Criminal Court First Trial. No. 52], (2010) 云高法终字第1314号 [(2010) Yun High Court Second Trial No. 1314].*

59 *药家鑫 [YAO Jiaxin] (2011) 西刑一初字第68号 [(2011) Xi the First Criminal Court First Trial. No. 68].*

60 霍存福[HUO Cunfu], *《复仇·报应刑·报应说——中国人法律观念的文化解说》[Vengeance, Retributive Penalty and the Theory of Retribution: Explicating Culturally the Legal Concept of Chinese]*, 吉林人民出版社[Jilin People's Publishing House], Ji Lin, 2005, 5.

61 王勇[WANG Yong],《中国死刑研究的三个误区与路径调整》[On the Three Misunderstanding Areas of the Study of Death Penalty in China and the Adjustment of Approaches], 吉林大学社会科学学报[Jilin University Journal Social Sciences Edition] 2012, Vol. 52, No. 5, 130.

are 4 crimes punishable by mandatory death penalty in the present Criminal Law, namely, the crime of hijacking aircraft (Article 121), crime of kidnapping (Article 239), crime of abducting and trafficking in a woman or child (Article 240) and crime of instigating a riot to escape from prison or gather people to raid a prison with weapons. In accordance with these provisions, "if the crime falls under any category provided by the Criminal Law, the defender shall be sentenced to death, except if he or she due to the circumstances of a crime calls for a lighter or mitigated punishment or exemption from punishment under the provisions of Criminal Law, or he or she is in the situation that the death penalty shall not be imposed on him or her."[62] To a great extent, therefore, the judicial discretion of the judge in the process of sentencing is limited. As for the policy of "strictly controlling and applying the death penalty deliberately", the terms of mandatory death penalty is nothing else but will only bring the possibility that the death policy will be ignored by the judge. This kind of provision, thus, should be amended and replaced by life-imprisonment for the sake of strictly controlling and limiting the death penalty for lethal violent crime.

3.1.3 The Death Penalty and Its Reforms in Other Countries

In according to *the Amnesty International Global Report (hereinafter: AIGR)*, as of December 31, 2016, there were 57 countries retaining the death penalty, and 104 countries abolished the death penalty for all crimes, and 141 countries totally abolished the death penalty in law or practice.[63] For these 57 retentionist, the *AIGR* states that at least 1032 people were executed in 2016, a 37% decrease in the number of executions carried out globally in 2016 against the previous year.[64] According to the *AIGR,* the Republic of Benin and the Republic of Nauru abolished the death penalty in January 21, 2016, and May 12, 2016, respectively; "several others took steps to restrict use of the death penalty; and the global trend remained towards the abolition of the death penalty as the ultimate cruel, inhuman and degrading punishment."[65] This book would like to explore the legislation of the death penalty and its potential reform in the retention states, taking United States of American, Japan, Indonesia, and other states as examples, as well as taking the abolitionist states, like European states, as the contrastively analyzing example.

---

[62] 陆建红[LU Jianhong], above no. 262.

[63] See Amnesty International Global Report, *The Death Sentences and Executions 2016*, Index: ACT 50/5740/2017, April 2017.

[64] Ibid, 4. This report covers the judicial use of the death penalty for the period Jaunuary to December 2016, and it is only on executions, death sentences and other aspects of the use of the death penalty, such as commutations and exonerations, where there is reasonable confirmation. This report's figures on the use of the death penalty are minimum figures, the true figures are likely to be higher. This numbe does not include the thousands of executions carried out in China. See ibid, 2, 4.

[65] Ibid, 3 and 9.

3.1.3.1 The Death Penalty and Its Reforms in Asia: Taking Japan and Indonesia as Examples

The Death Penalty and Its Reforms in Japan

Japan is an important country and "the only high-income democracy Asian state in the world to retain and apply the death penalty",[66] as one of the six principal punishments it applies.[67] In accordance with the Penal Code of Japan, judges are empowered to sentence the convict to death by hanging for twelve crimes,[68] which include insurrection (Article 77(1. i), instigation of foreign aggression (Article 81), assistance to the enemy (Article 82), arson of inhabited buildings (Article 108), detonating explosives (Article 117 (1)), damage to an inhabited building by flood (Article 119), overturning of trains (Article 126), endangering traffic by overturning of a train (Article 127), pollution of water supplies with poisonous materials and causing death thereby (Article 146), homicide (Article 199), robbery causing death or injury (Article 240), rape at the scene of a robbery and causing death thereby (Article 241); in addition to these twelve crimes, some scholars state that there are six crimes that are punished by death, including use of explosives, causing death as a result of a duel, causing death as a result of an aeroplane crash, causing death by hijacking an aircraft, and killing a hostage.[69] Except for the crimes provided by Articles 77 (1. i), 81, 82, 108, 117, 119, and 127, the crimes provided by Articles 126, 146, 199,240 and 241 and the other six crimes described by other scholars are all lethal crimes, for which the application circumstances for the death penalty are that the crime causes the death of another person. According to the AIGRs, for these eighteen crimes, the Japanese judicial authorities have imposed the death penalty on several convicts and executions have been carried out, as can be seen in the following Graph 3.3.[70]

---

[66] MRAE Dave, *Indonesian Capital Punishment in Comparative Perspective*, Bijdragen tot de taal, land-en volkenkunde [Journal of the Humanities and Social Sciences of Southeast Asia] 2017, Vol. 173, Issue 1, 3.

[67] *Penal Code of Japan, Act No. 45 of April 24, 1907 (日本国刑法45号,1907年4月24日)*, Article 9. These six principal punishments include the death penalty, imprisonment with work, imprisonment without work, a fine, misdemeanor imprisonment without work and a petty fine.

[68] Ibid, Article 11. However, some scholars say that the Penal Code and other special laws outline eighteen crimes that are punishable by death; in practice, death sentences have been used only for convictions of murder, robbery-murder and rape-murder. See SHER Elizabeth M, *Death Penalty Sentencing in Japan under the Lay Assessor System: Avoiding the Avoidable through Unanimity,* Pacific Rim Law & Policy Journal, 2011, Vol. 20, No. 3, 644; see also AMBLER Leah, *The People Decide: The Effect of the Introduction of the Quasi-Jury System (Saiban-In Seido) on the Death Penalty in Japan,* Northwestern Journal of International Human Rights, 2008, Vol. 6, Issue 1, 5.

[69] AMBLER Leah, above no. 274, 5.

[70] All these data are from the Amnesty International Global Report: *Death Sentences and Executions 2016* (Index: ACT 50/5740/2017), *Death Sentences and Executions 2015* (Index: ACT 50/3487/2016), *Death Sentences and Executions 2014* (Index: ACT 50/001/2015), *Death Sentences and Executions 2013* (Index: ACT 50/001/2014), *Death Sentences and Executions 2012* (Index: ACT 50/001/2013), *Death Sentences and Executions 2011* (Index: ACT 50/001/2012), *Death Sentences*

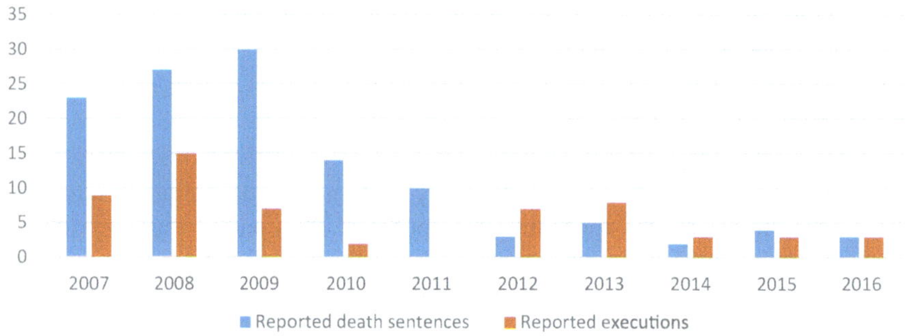

Graph 3.3 The numbers of reported death sentences and reported executions in Japan from 2007 to 2016. From the above graph, we can see that the number of reported death sentences in Japan has fluctuated, i.e. there was a slight increase from 23 in 2007 to a peak of 30 in 2009 and then a sharp decline to a low of 2 in 2014, before which there had been a slight increase from 3 in 2012 to 5 in 2013; after 2014 the number remained at its relatively low level of between 2 and 4. Similarly, the number of reported executions in Japan also fluctuated. It hit a peak of 15 in 2008, increasing from 9 in 2007, and then decreased to zero in 2011, which means that Japan did not carry out any executions in that year. However, 7 convicts were executed in 2012 and 8 in 2013; after that, Japan only executed 3 convicts a year in 2014, 2015 and 2016

From the above graph, we can see an obvious change after 2009, when the numbers of reported death sentences and reported executions show a sharp decline. This is mainly the result of the introduction of the lay assessor trials in 2009—the saiban-in ('public participants')—in which six saiban-in and three judges deliberate and make decisions together on both guilt and the sentence.[71] Before the implementation of the sailan-in seido, "each party in the new saiban-in court had appeared to directly or indirectly contemplate the prospect of de facto abolition of the death penalty".[72] Under the new trial system, "the lay judge panels impose a death sentence in approximately seventy percent of the cases where the prosecutors seek one,"[73] and so the number of the death sentences has decreased since 2009, as shown in the above graph. This is the most important reform to control the use of the death penalty in Japan to date, in the context of a retention of capital punishment.

and Executions 2010 (Index: ACT 50/ 001/2011), *Death Sentences and Executions 2009* (Index: ACT 50/001/2010), *Death Sentences and Executions 2008* (Index: ACT 50/ 003/2009), *Death Sentences and Executions 2007* (Index: ACT 50/ 001/2008).

[71] See AMBLER Leah, above no. 274, 15; see also The Justice System Reform Council, *Recommendations of the Justice System Reform Council--for a Justice System to Support Japan in the 21st Century--*, available at: http://japan.kantei.go.jp/judiciary/2001/0612report.html (Last visited: January 19th, 2024).

[72] See AMBLER Leah, above no. 274, 22.

[73] JOHNSON David T., *Retention and Reform in Japanese Capital Punishment,* University of Michigan Journal of Law Reform, 2016, Vol. 49, No. 4, 865.

3.1.3.2 The Death Penalty and Its Reform in Indonesia

The Republic of Indonesia is an important Asian state which retains the death penalty, and it has been "a persistent feature of the Indonesian legal system"[74] in a country which has a "population of 260 million people and ... is the world's fourth most populous country."[75] According to the Penal Code of Indonesia, the death penalty by shooting is provided as one of the basic punishments, along with imprisonment, light imprisonment and a fine.[76] There are 11 types of crime in the Indonesian Penal Code where the culprit can be sentenced to capital punishment, including assaulting the President or Vice President (Article 104), persuading another country to take hostile action against Indonesia (Article 111 Paragraph (2)), deliberately revealing or informing or smuggling information concerning the interests of the state to foreign powers (Article 112), voluntarily entering into military service with a foreign power (Article 123), supporting the enemy in a time of war (Article 124 Paragraph (3)), committing a fraudulent act in the delivery of materials for use of the navy or the army in time of war (Article 127 Paragraph (1)), assaulting a King or a President of another country, either as a premeditated action or where the action results in death (Article 140 Paragraph (3)), premeditated murder (Article 340), theft which results in serious injury or death (Article 365 Paragraph 4), extortion which results in serious injury or death (Article 365 Paragraph 2), and sea/river hijacking which results in death (Article 444).[77] Outside the Penal Code, the death penalty also can be used for criminal actions under specific central government laws, including economic crimes (Law No. 21 Year 1959[78]), abuse of political powers (Law No. 11 Year 1963[79]), crimes of corruption (Law No.31. 1999; and Law No. 20. Year 2001[80]), drug trafficking (Law No. 39 Year 2005[81]), acts of terrorism (Law No. 9 Year 2013[82]), and crimes involving

---

[74] MRAE Dave, above no. 272, 2.

[75] *Indonesia*, available at: https://en.wikipedia.org/wiki/Indonesia (Last visited: January 19th, 2024).

[76] Law of the Republic of Indonesia 27 of 1999 on the Penal Code, May 19, 1999, Articles 10 and 11.

[77] Ibid. See HERIYANTO Dodik Setiawan Nur and HUANG Gui, Death Penalty Legislation in China and Indonesia Under International Human Rights Law Perspective, JURNAL HUKUM IUS QUIA IUSTUM, 2016, Vol. 23, Issue 4, 589.

[78] See *Undang-Undang REPUBLIK INDONESIA NOMOR 21 TAHUN 1959*, available at: file:///C:/Users/huanggui/Downloads/UU_NO_21_1959.HTM (Last visited: April 24th, 2017).

[79] See *UNDANG-UNDANG REPUBLIK INDONESIA NOMOR 1 TAHUN 1963*, available at: http://www.dpr.go.id/dokjdih/document/uu/UU_1963_1.pdf . (Last visited: April 24th, 2017).

[80] See *UNDANG-UNDANG REPUBLIK INDONESIA NOMOR 31 TAHUN 1999*, available at: http://www.kpu.go.id/dmdocuments/UU%20PNS.pdf; see also, *UNDANG-UNDANG REPUBLIK INDONESIA NOMOR 20 TAHUN 2001*, available at: http://www.kpu.go.id/dmdocuments/UU202001.pdf (Last visited: January 19th, 2024).

[81] See, *PERATURAN PEMERINTAH REPUBLIK INDONESIA NOMOR 39 TAHUN 2005*, available at: http://peraturan.go.id/inc/view/11e44c4f0c1a8d609dee313231383331.html (Last visited: January 20th, 2024).

[82] See *UNDANG-UNDANG REPUBLIK INDONESIA NOMOR 9 TAHUN 2013*, available at: http://kesbangpol.kemendagri.go.id/files_arsip/uu_no.09-2013_.pdf(Last visited: January 20th, 2024).

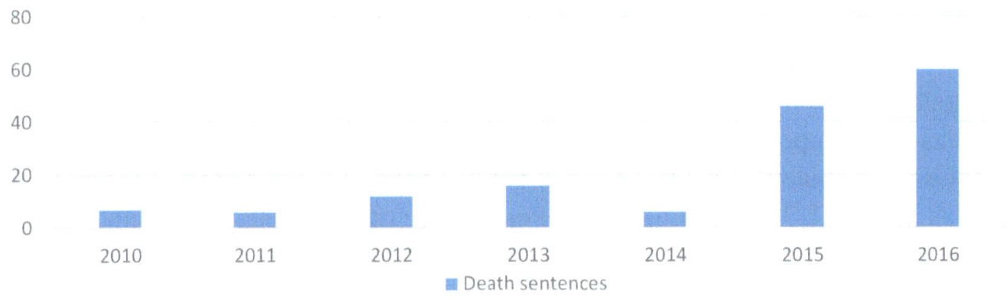

Graph 3.4 The numbers of the death sentences in Indonesia since 2010 (all these numbers are the credible minimum figure). From the above graph, we can see that the number of reported death sentences is generally increasing except in 2014, when it fell to 6, the same number as in 2011; the peak was in 2016, when approximately 60 were executed. All these data are drawn from Amnesty International Reports: *Death Sentences and Executions 2016* (Index: ACT 50/5740/2017), *Death Sentences and Executions 2015* (Index: ACT 50/3487/2016), *Death Sentences and Executions 2014* (Index: ACT 50/001/2015), *Death Sentences and Executions 2013* (Index: ACT 50/001/2014), *Death Sentences and Executions 2012* (Index: ACT 50/001/2013), *Death Sentences and Executions 2011* (Index: ACT 50/001/2012), *Death Sentences and Executions 2010* (Index: ACT 50/ 001/2011).

air transport (Law No. 4 Year 1976[83]).[84] Based on these clauses which provide for those crimes punishable by death, according to the *Amnesty International Report of 2016*, the Indonesian judicial authorities passed more than 60 death sentences and executed 4 offenders; the number of sentences being higher than in 2015 when it was 46, but the number of executions lower than in that year, when 14 people were[85] "convicted of drug-related offenses to confront 'a national emergency' in drug-related deaths."[86] However, in practice Indonesia does not execute convicts who are given death sentence in all years; for instance, it did not carry out the death penalty from 2009 to 2012 according to the AIGRs,[87] although we can see that it has imposed death sentences in every year since 2010, as can be seen in the following Graph 3.4.

From the list of crimes punishable by death mentioned above, we can see that Indonesia has not legislatively abolished or reduced the number of the crimes punishable by death, but increased it by legislation after the amendment to the Penal Code in 1999, in the cases of, for example, drug traffickers (Law No. 39 Year 2005), and the Act of Terrorism (Law No. 9 Year 2013). However, we can see that even though the number of crimes punishable by death in the legislation has increased, the number

[83] See *UNDANG-UNDANG REPUBLIK INDONESIA NOMOR 4 TAHUN 1976*, available at: http://ditjenpp.kemenkumham.go.id/arsip/ln/1976/uu4-1976.pdf (Last visited: January 20th, 2024).

[84] See HERIYANTO Dodik Setiawan Nur and HUANG Gui, above no. 283, 589.

[85] See Amnesty International Global Report: *Death Sentences and Executions 2016* (Index: ACT 50/5740/2017), Death Sentences and Executions 2015 (Index: ACT 50/3487/2016).

[86] Amnesty International Global Report: *Death Sentences and Executions 2016* (Index: ACT 50/5740/2017), 10.

[87] See Amnesty International Global Report: *Death Sentences and Executions 2012* (Index: ACT 50/001/2013); Death Sentences and Executions 2009 (Index: ACT 50/001/2010).

of death sentences in judicial practice was relatively low during the administration of the former President, Susilo Bambang Yudhoyono (2004–2014); however, with the current President of Indonesia, Joko Widodo, the number has increased two or threefold. Reacting to this, some scholars have criticized the fact that the Indonesian democratization process, including a fundamental overhaul of its legal system, which was promoted by Susilo, did not extend to revoking the death penalty[88]; and his successor, Joko Widodo, "has proven to be a staunch supporter of the death penalty".[89] Actually, under the Penal Code of Indonesia, the crimes punishable by death mentioned above are mainly crimes against the security of the state and lethal crimes which result in death where there are circumstances which can be applied to impose the death penalty. Beyond the Penal Code, the other crimes for which it is possible to impose the death sentence are not violent and lethal crimes, but for instance, economic crimes, abuse of political power, and drug trafficking, and the grounds for stipulating the death penalty for these kinds of the crimes can mainly be attributed to "political reasons, [including] actual crime control measures"[90]; in addition, the deterrence theory has a great influence on the leadership and legislators in Indonesia. For example, some Indonesian officials argue that "executions would have a deterrent effect on crime, that the most serious crimes merit the death penalty, and that unrepentant or recidivist criminals deserve death"[91]; and this is particularly strongly argued for drug-related crimes; for instance, the former President, Yudhoyono, said that "deterrence and the interests of justice justify the use of the death penalty for drug charges".[92] Just as Professor Daniel points out, "outright abolition is considered unlikely under Joko Widodo, as Indonesia's public, government, and religious institutions still favor retention."[93] Based on the aforementioned political reasons, the idea of deterrence and the interests of justice, Indonesia would not consider repealing the death penalty for the time being[94] and will even increase the use of the death penalty, as has occurred in the past two years.

---

[88] See MRAE Dave, above no. 272, 6.

[89] PASCOE Daniel, *Three Coming Legal Challenges to Indonesia's Death Penalty Regime*, The Indonesian Journal of International & Comparative Law, 2015, Vol. II, Issue. 2. 278.

[90] Ibid, 245.

[91] MRAE Dave, above no. 272, 2.

[92] LYNCH Columan, *Indonesia's Use of Capital Punishment for Drug-Trafficking Crimes: Legal Obligations, Extralegal Factors, and the Bali Nine Case*, Columbia Human Rights Law Review, 2009, Vol. 40, Issue. 2, 540.

[93] PASCOE Daniel, above no. 296, 240.

[94] Ibid, 239.

3.1.4 The Death Penalty and Its Reforms in Europe and Central Asia

The movement to abolish the death penalty was driven by theoretical controversy, in particular in Western Europe, where debates on the abolition of the death penalty took place several centuries ago and "have been going on at least since Cesar Beccaria."[95] In 1764, Beccaria in his book, *Dei Delitti et dellepene (On Crimes and punishments)*, strongly expressed his attitude against the death penalty, which gave rise to a heated discussion on the abolition of the death penalty. "During the second half of the eighteenth century, the abolition of the death penalty became an important political issue in several Western European countries"[96]; and after 1848 some clear signs of a gradual elimination of the death penalty in some Europe states were already observable[97]; for example, after 1850 the death penalty in the Netherlands was not carried out in public any more but behind prison walls due to public aversion to witnessing it.[98] And then, "in 1860, the death penalty in Netherlands was abolished de facto, and 1870 formal abolition was debated and accepted by Parliament."[99] However, the death penalty could be used under a situation of national emergency, like, for example, a war, and until 1878 it was completely repealed for crimes in peacetime.[100] The treatment of the death penalty in France had similar characteristics of gradual abolition, i.e., the number of capital crimes was gradually reduced.[101]

However, by reviewing the history of the abolition of the death penalty in Europe, it seems that the main reason driving the abolition of the death penalty from the earliest times was not concern for human rights, but other arguments. For example, in her paper, Professor Annemarieke Beijer points out that the two main objections against the death penalty in the Netherlands in the nineteenth century were that "the death penalty violates the 'evolving standard of decency' and it is not a necessary instrument to maintain public order"[102]; she noted that in 1870 the public was against the death penalty on religious grounds[103] and "they were afraid that the Bible would

---

[95] ANNERMARIEKE Beijer, *The Debate on Capital Punishment in the Netherlands and Germany*, International Criminal Justice Review, 2000, Vol. 10, Issue. 1, 99.

[96] Ibid.

[97] See ibid, 100.

[98] See ibid.

[99] Ibid, 101.

[100] See HESSING Dick J. KEIJSER Jan W., and ELFFERS Henk, *Explaining Capital Punishment Support in an Abolitionist Country: The Case of the Netherlands*, Law and Human Behavior, 2003, Vol. 27, No. 6, 606. This paper says that in 1878 the death penalty was abolished for crimes committed in peace time. But in 1983 the death penalty was formally abolished for all crimes, including war crimes.

[101] See JAMES M. Donoval, *Public Opinion and the French Capital Punishment Debate of 1908*, Law and History Review, 2014, Vol. 32, No. 3, 577.

[102] ANNERMARIEKE Beijer, above no. 302, 101.

[103] See Ibid.

lose its importance as a guide to penal policy."[104] To a great extent, the issue of human rights at that time was not a central concern with the death penalty, but referred to slavery; therefore, the concept of human rights was still not the core reason to drive the abolition of the death penalty, although it perhaps was important in some European states, such as Iceland (1928),[105] and Sweden (1921).[106]

However, with the outbreak of World Wars I and II in the first half of the twenty century and the resulting huge loss of life, the concept of human rights and human dignity become important issues for the public and even, finally, become a main value proposition from a legislative perspective. Subsequently, the death penalty was finally considered to be incompatible with the presumably humane values of modern liberal democracy.[107] Especially given that, as the ECHR was drafted in 1948 and adopted on 4 November 1950, human rights truly became the most important factor driving the movement to abolish the death penalty. This was because the ECHR is "a central reference text for the protection of fundamental rights in Europe,"[108] and it established the European Court of Human Rights (hereinafter: ECtHR); all member states have to belong to the ECHR and new members have to ratify it. However, the ECHR does not directly require member states to abolish the death penalty, but it does prohibit torture.[109] Certainly, the death penalty is by its nature classified as a form of torture. To a great extent, the ECHR acts as a foundation legal instrument against the death penalty, and its two important protocols, i.e. *Protocol No.6 to the Convention for the Protection of Human Rights and Fundamental Freedoms concerning the Abolition of the Death Penalty* (hereinafter, Protocol No.6) and *Protocol No. 13 to the Convention for the Protection of Human Rights and Fundamental Freedoms, Concerning the Abolition of the Death Penalty in All Circumstances* (hereinafter, Protocol No.13), are specific and main instruments driving member states to abolish the death penalty, as they directly require member states to abolish it.

In fact, the strategy of the abolition of the death penalty in Europe is also a gradual one. After WWII, the movement to abolish the death penalty was pushed to a peak, driven by the ECHR, but it still followed the route of gradualism, i.e., on the one hand, some member states first gradually reduced the number of capital crimes and then completely abolished the death penalty, or some member states prohibited the use of the death penalty for all crimes except in conditions of war or national emergency; on the other hand, after the ECHR, the other international Conventions proposed gradualism and allowed member states to use the death penalty in time

---

[104] Ibid.

[105] See *Capital Punishment in Iceland*, available at: https://en.wikipedia.org/wiki/Capital_punishment_in_Iceland (Last visited: January 20th, 2024).

[106] See *Capital Punishment in Sweden*, available at: https://en.wikipedia.org/wiki/Capital_punishment_in_Sweden (Last visited: January 20th, 2024). In 1921, the death penalty was abolished for crimes committed in peace time, and, in 1973, it was abolished for all crimes, including crimes committed in time of war.

[107] See JAMES M. Donovan, above no. 308, 575.

[108] MAJA Nastić, *ECHR and National Constitutional Courts*, Zbornik Radova Pravnog Fakulteta u Nisu, 2015, Issue. 71, 203.

[109] *The European Convention on Human Rights*, Article 3.

of war until 2000. For example, Article 2 of *Protocol No.6*, which was adopted in 1983, allows member states to make provision in its law for the death penalty in respect of acts committed in time of war or of imminent threat of war,[110] but this condition was only completely changed in *Protocol No. 13*, adopted in 2000 which declared that the final step should be taken to abolish the death penalty in all circumstances.[111] In addition, the Charter of Fundamental Rights of the European Union (hereinafter, the EU Charter) is another important political document in the drive towards the abolition of the death penalty. In accordance with Article 2 of the Charter, the death penalty is an absolutely prohibited punishment.[112] From the political perspective, under the requirements of the Council of the Europe, "abolition is an explicit and absolute condition to become a member of the EU, and also a prerequisite for membership in the Council of Europe."[113] Regarding this, some scholars argue that "the approach taken by the European countries to the death penalty is nearly homogeneous and shows clearly the path regional institutions follow to achieve a common understanding on human rights."[114] Meanwhile, more European states—around 27—had removed the death penalty from the penal system for crimes committed in peacetime before the adoption of Protocol No.13 in 2000, including Germany (West Germany in 1949, East Germany in 1978), Italy (1947), Portugal (1867 for peacetime, 1978 for wartime), the United Kingdom (suspended in 1965, and confirmed in 1969),[115] and Hungary(1990)[116]; some member states—around—14 repealed the death penalty for crimes committed in the peacetime after 1990. To date, almost all European states have abolished the death penalty for all crimes *de*

---

[110] *Protocol No. 6 to the Convention for the Protection of Human Rights and Fundamental Freedoms concerning the Abolition of the Death Penalty, as Amended by Protocol No. 11* (Strasbourg, 28.IV.1983), Article 2.

[111] *Protocol No. 13 to the Convention for the Protection of Human Rights and Fundamental Freedoms, concerning the Abolition of the Death Penalty in all Circumstances*, (Vilnius, 3.V. 2002).

[112] The *Charter of Fundamental Rights of the European Union (2000/C 364/01),* Article 2.

[113] *EU Lines to Take on the Policy of the Council of Europe in Relation to the Death Penalty,* (Strasbourg, 05/04/2017), available at: https://eeas.europa.eu/headquarters/headquarters-homepage/24625/eu-lines-take-policy-council-europe-relation-death-penalty_en (Last visited: January 20th, 2024).

[114] MANACORDA Stefano, *Restraints on the Death Penalty in Europe: A Circular Process,* Journal of International Criminal Justice, 2003, Vol. 1, Issue. 2, 265.

[115] YORKE Jon, *Inhuman Punishment and Abolition of the Death Penalty in the Council of Europe*, European Public Law, 2010, Vol. 16, No. 1, 81.

[116] MADAI Sándor, *《第二次世界大战后匈牙利死刑改革分析》* [*Evolution of Capital Punishment Regulations in Hungary following World War II]*, traslated by Xiao Fan, 刑法评论 [Chinese Criminal Law Review] 2016, Vol. 29, Issue. 1, 376. In this paper, Professor Madai argues that, between 1988 and 1990 no capital punishment was imposed—due to a moratorium—and later, in 1990, the Constitutional Court of Hungary abolished any and all provisions on the death penalty in Hungary, because it found the most severe sanction unconstitutional. However, some Hungarians have argued for the reintroduction of the death penalty in Hungary because they think that the death penalty would deter some potential murderers from committing their crimes and it is cheaper than life imprisonment. See also, ZOLTANT. J. Toth, *The Capital Punishment Controversy in Hungary: Frogments on the Issues of Deterrent Effect and Wrongful Convictions, European Journal of Crime,* Criminal Law and Criminal Justice, 2013, Vol. 21, Issue. 1, 39.

jure and de facto, except for Russia, Belarus, and Kazakhstan. The latter two are not the members of the Council of Europe because of the human rights concerns.

According to Belarus's Constitution, "the death penalty may be applied in accordance with the law as an exceptional penalty for especially grave crimes and only in accordance with the verdict of a court of law."[117] Therefore, there is no constitutional obstacle to abolishing the death penalty in Belarus, but the Constitution authorizes its use. Under the Criminal Code of the Republic of Belarus, the death penalty is an exclusive penal measure for some particularly serious crimes involving deliberate deprivation of a person's life with aggravating circumstances, but it cannot be applied to persons who are younger than eighteen years old before committing the crime, to women, or to a man who has reached the age of sixty-five when the sentencing judgment is pronounced; the death penalty may be replaced by a pardon with life imprisonment.[118] As of now, according to the Criminal Code of Belarus, there are 14 crimes punishable by death, including launching or conducting aggressive war (Article 122.2), murder of a representative of a foreign state or international organization in order to provoke international complications or war or destabilize public order in a foreign country (Article 124.2), acts of international terrorism (Article 126), genocide (Article 127), crimes against the safety of humanity (Article 128), use of weapons of mass destruction prohibited by an international treaty (Article 134), violation of the laws and usages of war (Article 135.3), murder committed under aggravating circumstances (Article 139.2), terrorism (Article 289.3), treason involving a murder (Article 356.2), conspiracy to seize state power (Article 357.3), an act of terrorism against a state or public figure (Article 359), sabotage (Article 360.2), and murder of an employee of law-enforcement bodies (Article 362.2).[119] Of these 14 crimes, 7 are crimes against peace, security, humanity and the military, 5 are crimes against the state and the order implemented by the authorities; and most of them take aggravating circumstances and causing death as the condition for the application of the death penalty. For these 14 crimes, Belarus authorities have imposed death sentences and executed only a few convicts in recent years, according to the AIGR. For instance, in 2016, 4 convicts had been given death sentences by April 2016, and 4 executed, and there are 2 individuals known to be under sentence of death at the end of 2016[120]; however, in 2015, only 2 convicts had a death sentence imposed, and no

---

[117] *Constitution of the Republic of Belarus of 1994 with Amendments through 2004*, Article 24, available at: https://www.constituteproject.org/constitution/Belarus_2004.pdf (Last visited: January 20th, 2024).

[118] *The Criminal Code of the Republic of Belarus No. 275-3 of 09.07.1999* (as amended by No. 60-3 of 12.07.2013) (*Уголовный кодекс Республики Беларусь № 275-З от 09.07.1999 г. (в редакции № 60-З от 12.07.2013 г.)*), Article 59.

[119] Ibid.

[120] See Amnesty International Global Report, *Death Sentences and Executions 2016*, Index: ACT 50/5740/2017, April 2017.

one was executed.[121] By contrast, in 2014, Belarus authorities executed 3 convicts after a 24 month hiatus, but no one had a death sentence imposed.[122]

Belarus, one of the two states in the Europe and Central Asia to use the death penalty, is under great pressure from the Council of Europe. The 1283rd Meeting of the Committee of Ministers of the Council of Europe explicitly states that "we call on the Belarus' authorities to commute the remaining death sentences and establish a moratorium on executions as a first step towards abolition of this practice".[123] In fact, as early as 2012, "the European Parliament adopted resolutions to call for the initiation of moratorium as a step to abolition of the death penalty in Belarus."[124] Reacting to this Resolution, however, the Belarusian government made a statement criticizing it for being "nothing but a continuation of its pressure tactic on the Belarusian authorities and interference with the domestic affairs of the country"[125]; and argued that "it [this resolution] produces the impression that European MPs care less about [the] reliability of the facts and [the] validity of [the] conclusion".[126] Belarus has not abolished the death penalty in recent years, but "has more stringent restrictions on the use of the death penalty than provided for in the international covenant"[127] according to Belarus' Deputy Minister of Foreign Affairs Valentin Rybakov, who gave a speech at the international conference on the Death Penalty in 2016, where he also argued that it is impossible to impose a moratorium on the death penalty due to "repeated opinion polls [which] suggest that the death penalty continues to be differently perceived in the society and still has a majority of supporters."[128] Moreover, on May 3, 2017, the House of Representatives set up a working group on the death penalty in the new convocation parliament, which will inform the public on different aspects of the punishment and provide a full-fledged monitoring of the situation.[129]

The Republic of Kazakhstan is another non-member state of the Council of Europe which retains the death penalty in the European and Central Asian region. The retention of the death penalty in Kazakhstan has constitutional grounds and its use is restricted by the Constitution, which provides that "the death penalty shall be established by law as an exceptional punishment for terrorist crimes which have resulted in

---

[121] See Amnesty International Global Report, *Death Sentences and Executions 2015*, Index: ACT 50/3487/2016.

[122] See Amnesty International Global Report, *Death Sentences and Executions 2014*, Index: ACT 50/001/2015.

[123] *EU Lines to Take on the Policy of the Council of Europe in Relation to Death Penalty*, (Strasbourg, 05/04/2017), above no. 320.

[124] BEHRMANN Christian and YORKE Jon, *The European Union and Abolition of the Death Penalty*, Pace International Law Review Online Companion, 2013, Vol. 4, No. 1, 32.

[125] *European MPs Unconcerned about the Real Situation in Belarus*, available at: http://law.by/news/news/2012/february/18067/?sphrase_id=156708 (Last visited: January 20th, 2024).

[126] Ibid.

[127] *Rybakov: Death Penalty is not Prohibited by International Law*, available at: http://law.by/news/news/2016/march/16502/?sphrase_id=156760 (Last visited: May 4, 2017).

[128] Ibid.

[129] *Belarus Parliament Discusses Death Penalty Issues*, available at: http://law.by/news/news/2017/may/24048/?sphrase_id=156760 (Last visited: January 20th, 2024).

fatalities, and also for especially grave crimes, committed in wartime, with granting a sentenced person a right to appeal for pardon."[130] Under the present Criminal Code of the Republic of Kazakhstan, the death penalty is stipulated as one of the five types of punishment which may be applied to a person recognized as a guilty of committing a crime,[131] and is an exceptional measure of punishment carried out by shooting for crimes of terrorism, which cause loss of life, as well as for especially grave crimes, committed in wartime. These punishments originate almost directly from the Constitution.[132]

Currently, there are 17 crimes punishable by death, i.e., unleashing or conducting aggressive war (Article 160(2)), use of weapons of mass destruction, as prohibited by international treaty signed by Kazakhstan, conduct in war (Article 163(2)), murder of a special person listed in Article 164(1) (Article 164(2)), genocide in wartime (Article 168), acting as a mercenary involved in the death of people or causing other grave consequences (Article 170 (4)), treason in wartime (Article 175(3)), an infringement on the life of the first President of Kazakhstan-leader of the nation (Article 177), an infringement on the life of the President of Kazakhstan (Article 178), sabotage (Article 184), acts of terrorism (Article 255), insubordination or other non-execution of orders in wartime (Article 437 (5)), resistance to the Head of the public association or compelling him (her) to violate official obligations in wartime (Article 438 (4)), violent actions in relation to the Head of the public association in wartime (Article 439 (4)), desertion in wartime (Article 442(4)), evasion or refusal of military service in wartime (Article 443 (3)), violation of rules regarding combat duty in a military situation or in war time (Article 444(3)), and surrendering or abandoning means of warfare to the enemy (Article 455).[133] From these crimes, we can see that one of the application conditions for 12 of these 17 crimes is explicitly provided for in wartime, and one of them is explicitly stipulated as related to terrorism. For these crimes, Kazakhstan authorities rarely use the death penalty and almost never execution; for example, in 2016 Kazakhstan imposed a death sentence on one convict charged with a terrorism-related offense, but did not execute. This is the first time that Kazakhstan has used the death penalty since 2003 when the official moratorium on execution was launched, which continues to be observed. Furthermore, if the convict has been sentenced to death, he (she) is granted a right to plead for mercy[134]; and the death penalty is not be imposed on a person who committed a crime at an age younger than eighteen years, on women and on men of sixty-three years old or over.[135] However, the current Criminal Code has already reduced the scope of the death penalty.[136] When

---

[130] *The Constitution of the Republic of Kazakhstan*, Article 15.

[131] *The Penal Code of the Republic of Kazakhstan, the Code of the Republic of Kazakhstan dated 3 July 2014, No. 226-V of the Law of the Republic of Kazakhstan*, Article 40.

[132] Ibid, Article 47 (1).

[133] Ibid.

[134] Ibid, Article 47(1).

[135] Ibid, Article 47(2).

[136] Amnesty International Global Report, *The Death Sentences and Executions 2014,* Index: ACT 50/001/2015.

compared with the Criminal Code of the Republic of Kazakhstan No. 167 of July 16, 1997 (as amended by the Law of the Republic of Kazakhstan No. 24-V of June 28, 2012) (с изменениями, внесенными Законом Республики Казахстан № 24-V от 28.06.2012 г), for the death penalty imposed on an older convict the present Criminal Code does not provide for the application condition of "by the time of the court passes judgement (и мужчинам, достигшим к моменту вынесения судом приговора шестидесятипятилетнего возраста)", and it reduces the age limitation from 65 to 63. The Criminal Code of 2012 provided for the age limitation for the death penalty imposed on an older convict; i.e. that the convict be 65 years old by the time the court passes the judgment.[137] By law, the death penalty may be commuted to life imprisonment or imprisonment for the specified period with service of the sentence in the correctional colonies under a special regime; in the case of a cancellation of the moratorium on the execution of the death penalty, the convict under the death sentence shall have a right to plead for mercy irrespective of whether they have made this plea before the moratorium or not.[138] In this sense, the Kazakhstan government states that "in the context of Kazakhstan it is the actual abolition of the death penalty."[139] However, the use of the death sentence in 2016 has to a great extent, already proved this statement to be false.

Russia is another European state which is a member of the Council of Europe and retains the death penalty in law, although it has never been carried out in judicial practice since the introduction of the Russian president's "de facto ban on executions -- or 'moratorium'-- to comply with Russia's obligations to the Council of Europe"[140] in 1996. In addition, two decisions of the Constitutional Court, i.e., temporarily barring the death penalty on procedural grounds and suspending it indefinitely, but not irrevocably, have contributed to the prohibition of executions and the use of the death penalty in Russia.[141] In accordance with the Criminal Code of Russia, the death penalty may be imposed only for especially grave crimes endangering human life, and it shall not be imposed on women, nor to persons who have committed offenses when under 18 years of age, nor to men who have reached 65 years of age by the time of adjudication; and it may be replaced by a pardon with deprivation of liberty for life or by deprivation of liberty for a term of 25 years.[142] Currently, there are 5 crimes

---

[137] See *the Criminal Code of the Republic of Kazakhstan No. 167 of July 16, 1997 (as amended up to Law of the Republic of Kazakhstan No. 24-V of June 28, 2012) (с изменениями, внесенными Законом Республики Казахстан № 24-V от 28.06.2012 г)*, Article 49(2).

[138] *The Penal Code of the Republic of Kazakhstan, the Code of the Republic of Kazakhstan dated 3 July 2014, No. 226-V of the Law of the Republic of Kazakhstan*, Article 47(5).

[139] *On the Concept of Legal Policy of the Republic of Kazakhstan for the period 2010 to 2020 (Decree of the President of the Republic of Kazakhstan dated 24 August 2009 № 858)*, available at: http://sud.gov.kz/eng/content/concept-legal-policy-republic-kazakhstan-period-2010-2020 (Last visited: January 20th, 2024).

[140] LIGHT Matthew and KOVALEV Nikolai, *Russia, The Death Penalty, and Europe: The Ambiguities of Influence*, Post-Soviet Affairs, 2013, Vol. 29, No. 6, 541.

[141] Ibid.

[142] *The Criminal Code of the Russian Federation, No. 63-Fz of June 13, 1996* (with amendments and additions of March 1, 2012), Article 59.

which may be punishable by death, i.e., murder (Article 105 (2)), an encroachment on the life of a statesman or a public figure (Article 277), an encroachment on the life of a person administering justice or engaged in a preliminary investigation (Article 295), an encroachment on the life of an officer of a law-enforcement agency (Article 317), and genocide (Article 357).[143] However, considering the anti-terrorism situation in Russia, in 2016, the AIGR points out that "some Russian politicians expressed support for the death penalty; in March (2016) they submitted a bill to the Duma to reinstate the death penalty for terrorism-related crimes; the government and the Supreme Court expressed their opposition to the bill in the same month."[144]

3.1.5 The Death Penalty and Its Reform in the USA

Considering the historical context of the death penalty in Europe and the USA, Professor Joshua Kleinfeld, in his paper "*Two Cultures of Punishment*" points out that "the European/American disagreement about capital punishment is not just an instrumental or practical disagreement about policy but a clash between two visions of justice".[145] In this paper, he further argues that if capital punishment is ever just, then the right to life must be such as to be forfeit for the worst wrongdoing[146]; if it is never just, then the right to life must be such as to never be forfeit[147]; "Europe's opposition to the death penalty reflects the belief that the right to life is never forfeit for any wrong."[148] By contrast, American capital punishment represents the belief that ultimate wrongdoing deprives wrongdoers of worth.[149] Along with Japan, "the United States is the only high-income democracy in the world to retain capital punishment".[150] Under the special federal regime of the USA, however, not all states in America retain the death penalty. As of November 9, 2016, there are 31 out of 50 states—and the Federal government and the military—which still use the death penalty, and among these 31 states, 4 states have the death penalty with gubernatorial moratoria, i.e., Colorado, Pennsylvania, Washington and Oregon[151]; 19 out of the 50 states—as well as the District of Columbia—have already abolished the death

[143] See ibid.

[144] Amnesty International Global Report, *The Death Sentences and Executions 2016*, Index: ACT 50/5740/2017.

[145] KLEINFELD Joshua, *Two Cultures of Punishment*, Stanford Law Review, 2016, Vol. 68, Issue. 5, 991.

[146] Ibid, 992.

[147] Ibid.

[148] Ibid.

[149] Ibid.

[150] MRAE Dave, above no. 272, 3.

[151] The Death Penalty Information Center, *States with and without the Death Penalty*, available at: https://deathpenaltyinfo.org/states-and-without-death-penalty (Last visited: January 20th, 2024).

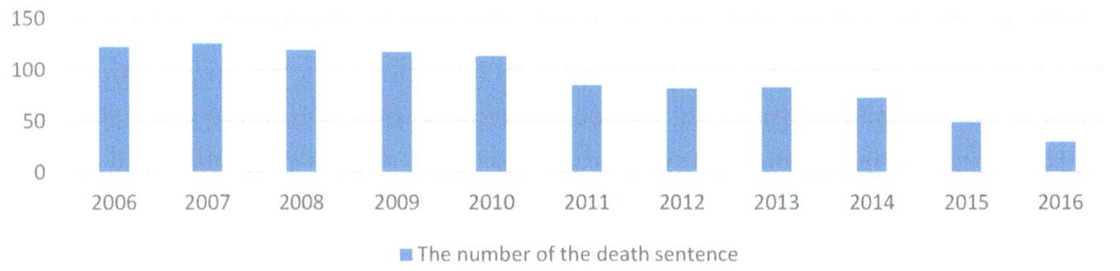

Graph 3.5 The numbers of death sentences in the USA from 2006 to 2016. From the above graph, we can see that the highest number of death sentences in the last ten years was in 2007, i.e. 126 offenders, 3 more than in 2006, while the lowest is 30 in 2016. The graph as a whole shows a significant decrease from 2006 to 2016. *Death Sentences in the United States from 1977 by State and by Year*, available at: https://deathpenaltyinfo.org/death-sentences-united-states-1977-present (Last visited: January 20th, 2024)

penalty.[152] At the federal law level, i.e. the United States Code, there are 40 clauses providing for the death penalty for 40 criminal behaviors.[153] However, most of these 40 criminal behaviors are explicitly provided to be related to murder, i.e. 30 crimes are directly related to murder,[154] the 7 crimes punishable by death are those which have causing another person to die as their circumstance of application,[155] while there are 3 other crimes, namely espionage, genocide, and treason.[156] Therefore, it can be said that "the death penalty in the United States is used almost exclusively for the crime of murder."[157] At the states' level of the Criminal Code, most of the crimes punishable by death are murder or involve causing the victim to die.[158] Under these crimes punishable by death, the number of the death sentences imposed by the federal and states' courts in the last ten years can be seen in the following Graph 3.5.

[152] Ibid.

[153] The Death Penalty Information Center, *Federal Laws Providing for the Death Penalty*, available at: https://deathpenaltyinfo.org/federal-laws-providing-death-penalty (Last visited: January 20th, 2024).

[154] Ibid.

[155] For example, destruction of aircraft, motor vehicles, or related facilities resulting in death (18 U.S.C. 32–34), civil rights offenses resulting in death (18 U.S.C. 241,242, 245, 247), death resulting from offenses involving transportation of explosives, destruction of government property, or destruction of property related to foreign or interstate commerce (18 U.S.C. 844(d), (f), (i)), mailing of injurious articles with intent to kill or resulting in death (18 U.S.C. 1716), assassination or kidnapping resulting in the death of the President or Vice President (18 U.S.C. 1751[by cross-reference to 18 U.S.C. 1111]), willful wrecking of a train resulting in death (18 U.S.C. 1992), death resulting from aircraft hijacking (49 U.S.C. 1472–1473). See ibid.

[156] Ibid.

[157] *Death Penalty for Offenses other than Murder*, available at: https://deathpenaltyinfo.org/death-penalty-offenses-other-murder (Last visited: January 20th, 2024).

[158] *Crimes Punishable by the Death Penalty*, available at: https://deathpenaltyinfo.org/crimes-punishable-death-penalty#BJS (Last visited May 16, 2017). See also the Bureau of Justice Statistics, *Capital Punishment, 2012-Statistical Tables*, available at: https://www.bjs.gov/content/pub/pdf/cp12st.pdf (Last visited: January 20th, 2024).

According to a report by the Bureau of Justice Statistics, *Capital Punishment 2014–2015-Statistical Brief*, "by the end of 2015, 33 states and the BOP (the Federal Bureau of Prisons) held 2881 inmates under sentence of death, 61 fewer that at year end 2014, which is 2942, and it was the fifteenth consecutive year in which the number of inmates under sentence of death decreased."[159] This decrease is mainly attributable to the reform and restriction of the use of the death penalty, as it has been said that "Americans have stuck with grim determination to the idea of the ultimate penalty even as other Western democracies have turned against it."[160] Drehle David Von gives five reasons for this; despite decades of effort (to use the death penalty), we are not getting better at it; the crime rate in recent years has plunged; there are dwindling justifications; governments are going broke,[161] and "the justices that themodern death penalty is a failure."[162] In recent years, some states have removed the death penalty from their states' Criminal Code; these include Connecticut, which abolished the death penalty in 2012, Illinois in 2011, Maryland in 2013, and Delaware in 2016; in this latter case the Supreme Court held that the state's capital sentencing procedures were unconstitutional and struck down Delaware's death penalty statute.[163] 4 states have the gubernatorial moratorium—Colorado, Pennsylvania, Washington and Oregon.[164] Some American scholars have said that "the momentum of death penalty abolition and reform work can be attributed largely to a combination of the accomplishments of the innocence movement, the demonstrated exorbitant cost of the sentence, and the lengthy appeals process."[165] Even though "justices all know that the modern death penalty is a failure",[166] the public in the U.S. still shows great support for the death penalty, according to a report released by Gallup in October 2016, which showed that 60% of respondents still favor the death penalty, although this is the lowest level since 1972.[167] 41% of respondents thought that the death penalty is not imposed frequently enough, and 26% thought the frequency is

---

[159] Bureau of Justice Statistics, *Capital Punishment, 2014–2015-Statistical Brief*, available at: https://www.bjs.gov/index.cfm?ty=pbdetail&iid=5908 (Last visited: January 20th, 2024).

[160] DREHLE David Von, above no. 254.

[161] Regarding this, the author said that "the American death-penalty system is so slow, inconsistent and inefficient that it costs far more than the life-without-parole alternative". Ibid. Some scholars have also argued that, "the extraordinary rise in capital costs is a very recent phenomenon, and likely a permanent one." See STEIKER Jordan M., *The American Death Penalty: Constitutional Regulation as the Distinctive Feature of American Exceptionalism*, University of Miami Law Review, 2013, Vol. 67, No. 2, 351.

[162] DREHLE David Von, above no. 254.

[163] *States with and without the Death Penalty*, available at: https://deathpenaltyinfo.org/states-and-without-death-penalty (January 20th, 2024).

[164] Ibid.

[165] NELLIS Ashley, *Tinkering with Life: A Look at the Inappropriateness of Life without Parole as an Alternative to the Death Penalty*, University of Miami Law Review, 2013, Vol. 67, Issue. 2, 440.

[166] DREHLE David Von, above no. 254.

[167] *Gallup Poll: Support for the Death Penalty at Lowest Level since 1972*, available at: https://deathpenaltyinfo.org/node/6589 (Last visited: January 20th, 2024).

right.[168] Therefore, the death penalty is still retained in the federal Criminal Code and a majority of states' Criminal Codes.

Other than the death penalty, Life imprisonment without parole, serving as a sentencing alternative, is provided in the Criminal Codes of the 31 states in which the death penalty is still applicable, as well as the Federal Statute and the Military Statute.[169] In addition, except for Alaska, the Criminal Codes of the 18 states and the District of Columbia in which the death penalty has already been abolished provide for Life imprisonment without parole. Life imprisonment without parole had great public support in the public opinion poll in September 2014, in which 45% of respondends thought that life imprisonment without parole is the best penalty for murder, while 50% preferred the death penalty, and only 5% did not have any opinion.[170] Some American scholars point out that the emergence of life imprisonment without parole as the primary alternative punishment to the death penalty for capital crimes is the major reform in contemporary capital practice[171]; and the rapid rise of its use "can partly be attributed to a desire for a reliable, terminal punishment to replace the death penalty".[172] In practice, "since the widespread adoption of life imprisonment without parole in the mid-1990s, the imposition of new capital sentences and the number of executions have declined to levels not seen since the 1970s."[173] However, we all know that life imprisonment without parole does, in fact, deprive the inmate's rights to hope for rehabilitation and violates human rights; however, "the United States has been nonchalantly condemning tens of thousands of people to the 'other death penalty' with barely a legal or political whimper".[174] Fortunately, it is criticized by many American scholars,[175] and the issues of life imprisonment without parole and the death penalty are discussed in the USA; the state of Alaska

[168] See *Gallup, Death Penalty,* available at: http://www.gallup.com/poll/1606/death-penalty.aspx (Last visited: January 20th, 2024).

[169] *Life without Parole*, available at: Death Penalty Information Center https://deathpenaltyinfo.org/life-without-parole (Last visited: January 20th, 2024).

[170] See *Gallup, Death Penalty*, available at: http://www.gallup.com/poll/1606/death-penalty.aspx (Last visited: January 20th, 2024).

[171] STEIKER Jordan M., above no. 369, 346.

[172] NELLIS Ashley, above no. 373, 445.

[173] BERRY William W. III, *Life-with-Hope Sentencing: The Argument for Replacing Life-without-Parole Sentences with Presumptive Life Sentences*, Ohio State Law Journal, 2015, Vol. 76, No. 5, 1053.

[174] GOTTSCHALK Marie, *No Way out? Life Sentences and the Politics of Penal Reform,* Life Without Parole: America's New Death Penalty? Edited by OGLETREE Charles J. and SARAT Austin, NYU Press, New York, 2012, 267.

[175] For example, NELLIS Ashley argues in her paper that it is an inappropriate alternative to the death penalty. See NELLIS Ashley, above no. 373, 454; Mare Gottschalk refers to it as the "other death penalty". See GOTTSCHALK Marie, above no. 368, 267; life imprisonment without parole "accurately reflects society's disdain for the taking of human life." See WRIGHT Julian H., *Life-without Parole: An Alternative to Death or Not Much of A Life at All*, Vanderbilt Law Review, 1990, Vol. 43, 567; "so whether life imprisonment without parole is the head of the snake or its tail, there has never been a greater need to grapple with this crucial subject. To ignore it is to be silent about the new death penalty lurking in the shadows." See OGLETREE Charles J., Jr. and SARAT Austin, *Lives on the Line: From Capital Punishment to Life without Parole*, Life Without Parole:

has repealed the death penalty and life imprisonment without parole and this will be a great example for other states in the USA to follow in the near future. All in all, Jordan M. Steiker argues, "the modern American death penalty—with its unprecedented costs, alternatives, and legal regulatory framework—seems newly vulnerable to judicial invalidation; reform of the death penalty and its abolition might well be on the same path."[176]

3.2 Conclusion

Historically, China is a capital punishment country, which has never removed the death penalty from its legal system. China will not completely abolish the death penalty de facto *and de jure* in the near future (some scholars say that it will take at least 30 years). This is the background to death penalty reform in China. In the Mao era, China was in a lawless period (even though there were some laws and regulations, they were barely used) and thus countless people were executed without any legal procedure and legal judgment; however, we cannot ignore the fact that the country implemented a policy of cautious and strict execution. Post Mao, the death penalty policy of cautious and strict execution was still taken as the effective policy. This changed a little in the Deng Xiaoping era, in which the execution legislation was expanded and the death penalty was used more frequently in judicial practice. Since the Deng era, the "strike-hard" movement—which is in fact a kind of revolution in the approach to crime—was introduced and implemented, and the death penalty in this period was deemed to be the best deterrent to curb crime. After Deng, in the Jiang Zemin era, a death penalty policy of cautious and strict execution was implemented again, but was expressed in another form, i.e. "killing cautiously and killing less". In the Jiang era, the number of crimes punishable by death was kept at a same level and this situation continued to the early period of Hu Jintao's premiership.

In the middle of the Hu era, in 2007, China took the first step to effectively control the use of the death penalty, namely, the power to review for all death sentences was restored to the SPC from the local High People's Courts and the Military Courts, such that the SPC can now uniformly exercise the power to review and further improve the standards and conditions of evidence and the procedure involved in sentencing someone to death. Actually, this was a reform conducted from the perspective of judicial practice. At the end of the Hu era, China took the second step to reduce the possibility of the use of the death penalty, namely, repealing the death penalty for 13 crimes. Then, in 2015, the Ninth Amendment removed the death penalty from a further 9 crimes. In fact, these were two great steps for the reform of China's

America's New Death Penalty? Edited by OGLETREE Charles J. and SARAT Austin, NYU Press, New York, 2012, 21; "This eternal banishment (life imprisonment without parole) means that the offender must simply wait to die; a life imprisonment without parole is worse than a death sentence as death sentences at least mark an anticipated end to suffering." See BERRY William W. III, above no. 381, 1054.

[176] STEIKEI Jordan M., above no. 369, 346.

punishment system. However, we cannot ignore the fact that the abolition of the death penalty for these 22 crimes is almost useless in reducing the possibility of the use of the death penalty, because the death penalty for these crimes was almost never used in judicial practice. At present, there are 46 crimes punishable by death, but we do not know how many people are sentenced to death and executed every year because this information is treated as a secret in China. According to the Amnesty International Report, around 1500 offenders are sentenced to the death penalty and executed annually. Even though China will not completely abolish the death penalty in the near future, the Party's political document promises that China will gradually reduce the number of charges that could lead to the death penalty. Some scholars have pointed out that China will strategically remove the death penalty from the penalty system; namely, firstly repealing the death penalty for nonviolent crimes, and then abolishing the death penalty for violent but non-lethal crimes, and finally removing the death penalty for lethal crimes. Consequently, China will be able to completely abolish the death penalty de facto and de jure.

Outside of China, at the international level, as an obviously inhuman punishment, the death penalty is gradually being abolished de jure and de facto by more and more states. Even though it is still provided for in the Criminal Law, the judicial authorities have already taken many steps to limit and control its use. In the future, we can say that the death penalty will be completely removed from the penalty system around the world under the influence of the concept human rights. Obviously, however, the moment at which a state abolishes the death penalty does not have any connection with its economic and social development, or even with its democratic development. For instance, the USA and Japan are two important and democratic developed countries, but the death penalty is still provided in their criminal laws and used frequently, and many citizens in these countries are in favor of the death penalty. Therefore, to a great extent, the abolition of the death penalty is still in process, and steps to abolish it are also being taken slowly. However, we can also see that the reform of the death penalty has already been launched in these states.

Chapter 4
The Alternative Punishment to the Death Penalty

Abstract This chapter focuses on the issue of an alternative punishment to the death penalty. It will start with a discussion of the notion of an alternative punishment to the death penalty, and establish what the alternative punishment is. This book argues that the alternative punishment to the death penalty should be the punishment that replaces the death penalty for the most heinous crimes, i.e. the most serious violent and lethal crimes. Following this, the chapter will explore factors influencing punishment options to replace the death penalty, which include human rights, the ideas behind punishment, criminal policy, and public opinion, as well as political concerns. Then this chapter will look at the issues around an alternative to the death penalty in other states. It takes some European member states as examples, where life imprisonment has already been adopted as the alternative punishment to the death penalty, and India, Japan and the USA, where the potential alternative punishment to the death penalty is under discussion. From these states' examples, this chapter establishes that life imprisonment is the ideal option to replace the death penalty.

4.1 Controversy over the Notion of an Alternative Punishment to the Death Penalty

As regards the definition of an alternative sanction to the death penalty, it seems that most Western scholars are not interested in discussing it.[1] By contrast, however, most Chinese scholars start their research with a discussion of the notion of the alternative to the death penalty for the following two reasons: firstly, the research

[1] Almost all of the limited number of research papers published by the Western scholars available on the internet or in libraries do not include any special section or chapter to explain the notion of the alternative sanction to the death penalty, or discuss the legislative and/or judicial alternative to the death penalty. See, generally, BERRY William W. III, above no. 381; WRIGHT Julian H., above no. 383; WOOD Arthur Lewis, *The Alternatives to the Death Penalty,* The Annals of the American Academy of Political and Social Science, 1952, Vol. 284, No. 1, 63; SNELLENBURG Sidney C., *Is There a Reasonable Alternative to the Death Penalty?,* Judicature, 1987, Vol. 71, No. 1, 5; MULROY Steven J., *Avoiding 'Death By Default': Does the Constitution Require a 'Life Without Parole' Alternative to the Death Penalty*, Tulane Law Review, 2004, Vol. 79, No. 2, 401.

G. Huang, *On the Alternative Punishment to the Death Penalty in China*,
https://doi.org/10.1007/978-981-97-1627-2_4

approaches adopted by Chinese scholars are different from those adopted by Western scholars. These differences could be caused by the national culture, ways of thinking and research logic, etc. Most Chinese scholars think that the notion of the criminal law mainly associates the cognitive style of criminal theory with criminal issues, the mental approach of the theory with criminal phenomenon and the methods of evaluation used by the theory with the value of criminal law.[2] Therefore, they seek to define the criminal issues on which they will focus by clarifying a relevant notion of the issues. Secondly, China's death penalty system is very different from that of other states. This is because, in accordance with Article 48 of the Criminal Law, the death penalty can be carried out in two ways, i.e., immediate execution and execution with two-year' suspension.[3] Furthermore, many serious crimes are still punishable by the death penalty under the present law, while for some of them, the death penalty is not necessary and should be removed. In other words, not all of the capital crimes provided by the present law can result in an alternative sanction to the death penalty but rather in a lighter punishment, and so the scope of crimes punishable by death needs to be made clear by discussing the notion of an alternative punishment, and my proposal in the forth section will be made on this basis.

As has already been mentioned briefly in the first section, these discussions on the notion of an alternative punishment can be divided into two elements, i.e., a judicial alternative punishment to the death penalty and a legislative alternative. Some scholars argue that the alternative sanction to the death penalty should refer to the kind of punishment which could be used to replace the death penalty with immediate execution when it is not deemed necessary.[4] This is referred to as the judicial alternative to the death penalty with immediate execution, on the following three bases. Firstly, the death penalty, which is the precondition of the existing alternative punishment, should be promulgated by China's Criminal Law for certain capital crimes and it should be the death penalty with immediate execution rather than with reprieve. In other words, in order to limit the use of the death penalty, the court should use another severe punishment to replace immediate execution when the convicted individual has committed the capital crime and should have been sentenced to immediate execution.[5] Secondly, the replacement punishment discussed here under the premise of the death penalty is still retained, and this is done with the joint aims of controlling and limiting the use of the death penalty in legislative and judicial terms. Specifically, from the legislative perspective, there is a need to amend the criminal law and improve the criminal punishment system and stipulate another appropriate punishment to replace immediate execution; from the judicial perspective, another severe punishment should be used to replace immediate execution for the convict who has

---

[2] See 刘远 [LIU Yuan], above no. 7, 47.

[3] *《中华人民共和国刑法》[Criminal Law of the People's Republic of China]*, Order No. 83, 14 March 1997, Article. 48.

[4] See 高铭暄 [GAO Mingxuan], *《略论中国刑法中的死刑替代措施》[Brief Discussion on the Alternative Measures to the Death Penalty in Chinese Criminal Law]*, above no. 13, 19.

[5] See ibid.

committed a capital crime and who should have been sentenced to immediate execution.[6] Thirdly, an alternative punishment to the death penalty should be closely tied to the nature of the offense and the specific circumstances of a concrete crime.[7] By contrast, there is a legislative alternative to the death penalty, where other scholars argue that the alternative punishment to the death penalty refers to a punishment replacing the death penalty for a crime that has already been removed from the list of the most heinous crimes punishable by death under the law.[8] According to this argument, the alternative punishment to the death penalty is applicable to lethal and serious violent offenses such as the most heinous crimes, and not for other serious crimes. In other words, even though other crimes can be punished by the death penalty under the current Criminal Law, in fact they should not be subject to the death penalty.[9] Consequently, they are beyond the scope of alternative punishment. From two basically different perspectives, these two notions of alternative punishment to the death penalty seem very different; however, they are both based on the aims of the limitation or abolition of the death penalty.

From the perspective of the judicial alternative to the death penalty, this is based on a situation in which the death penalty should be imposed on a criminal who commits the most heinous crime, but, with the aim of limiting the use of death penalty, he or she would not be immediately executed, but rather sentenced to death with a two-year suspension, or given another custodial penalty. This could be considered to be limiting the death penalty de facto rather than de jure, and it is not an effective way to fundamentally control the death penalty. Furthermore, under the punishment system provided by China's present Criminal Law, immediate execution, the death penalty with reprieve and life imprisonment are among the possible punishment options for heinous crimes, and they can substitute for each other in certain circumstances. In order to control and limit the death penalty, the SPC adopted relevant judicial interpretations to change the applicable conditions for the death penalty, such as changing the conditions of offenses punishable by death and reducing the applicable conditions for the death penalty with reprieve. The decision taken was an alternative to providing that all capital cases should be punished initially with the death penalty with two-year suspension, before later deciding whether or not this should be changed to immediate execution upon the expiry of the two-year period. It is still possible to

[6] See ibid.

[7] See ibid.

[8] See 李希惠 [LI Xihui], above no. 14, 27.

[9] For example, the death penalty was provided for 22 economic and non-violent crimes by the 1997 Criminal Law, but these were then removed from the scope of the death penalty by the Eighth and Ninth Amendments in 2011 and 2015, respectively. These kinds of offenses normally cause economic loss rather than that of a person's right to life, so they do not merit a death sentence, and in judicial practice, the death penalty was never, or only rarely, imposed on anyone convicted of them. So when the death penalty was abolished for these 22 crimes by the two amendments, they were directly downgraded to a maximum life imprisonment without any other alternative punishment. See *《关于<中华人民共和国刑法修正案(八)(草案)>的说明》[The Explanations for the Draft of the Eighth Amendment to Criminal Law of the People's Republic of China]*, above no. 8.

apply the immediate execution in judicial practice, so this does not really signify a replacement of the death penalty.

As for the notion of the alternative to the death penalty, this book tends to agree with the argument of a legislatively alternative punishment. Admittedly, the alternative punishment should be the punishment for crimes which are the most heinous and cause the most damage to society, such as the most serious lethally violent crimes of murder, and causing explosions; other less serious crimes or misdemeanors should not be punishable by this alternative punishment but by other lighter punishments.[10] Therefore, as some scholars point out, the alternative punishment to the death penalty should only be used as a last resort and when necessary, and only for crimes that should be punishable by death under the law; and it should be the most severe punishment after the death penalty is removed completely from the Criminal Law.[11] The alternative punishment to the death penalty should be the punishment that replaces the death penalty for the most heinous crimes, which should be the most serious violent and lethal crimes.

4.2 The Influencing Factors on the Punishment Options to Replace the Death Penalty

The factors influencing punishment options to replace the death penalty are varied, but this book only focuses on four important factors, i.e., human rights, the ideas behind the penalty, criminal policy, public opinion as well as the special political concern. The first factor can be explained from the perspective of the traditional Chinese penalty cultures, and the special political regimes and their views on the penalty. It can be termed the inner factor, which determines the differences between the China's penalty system and those of other states. The second concerns human rights protection, which is a kind of international obligation which needs to be fulfilled by China. Criminal policy and public opinion are two significant and typical factors involving obvious political considerations in China.

[10] See 赵秉志 [ZHAO Bingzhi], *《中国死刑替代措施要论》[On Alternative Measures to the Death Penalty in China]*, 学术交流 [Academic Exchange] 2008, No. 9, 33.

[11] See王志祥 [WANG Zhixiang], *《死刑替代措施:一个需要警惕的刑法概念》 [Alternative* Measures to the Death Penalty: A Criminal Conception Needs to be Considered], 中国法学 [China Legal Science] 2005, No. 1, 292.

4.2.1 *Human Rights*

4.2.1.1 The Development of Human Rights in China and the CPC's View on It

In the introduction, this book has already analyzed the relationship between the CPC's view and the legislation and taken the CPC's view on human rights and the death penaly legistion as an analysis example. This section would like to further explore both policy and law by examining the CPC's understanding and practice of human rights by analyzing key leaders' relevant speeches and documents and the death penalty legislation in the Maoist, the Deng Xiaoping and the post-Deng eras.

In the Mao Zedong era, a completely negative attitude was taken towards human rights theory. "For a very long time after the founding of New China, human rights were seen as a bourgeoisie slogan that had long been criticized and rejected, and the issue of human rights was an exclusion zone of theoretical research due to the influence of 'left' thought"[12]; the term 'human rights' could never be used in the policy and legal documents created by the Party and the relevant legislature. Therefore, human rights theory in this period era was at a standstill under the domination of "left" thought and the practice of understanding class struggle as the key concept in society. In practice, the period saw many social initiatives, including Land Reform, Anti-rightist activities, the Great Leap Forward, and the Cultural Revolution, in which regular violations of human rights occurred, without any legal basis. In the Maoist era, China was obviously under a "paternalistic authoritarian regime",[13] in which Mao's thought was considered "the guiding thought of the CPC and the Chinese people's spiritual treasure".[14] In other words, Mao's human rights thinking can be considered as identical to the CPC's outlook. Chinese scholars conducting research on Mao's thinking explain and comment on Mao's human rights concepts from different perspectives, but they work with two different attitudes, i.e. negativism and positivism. The negativist approach holds that Mao denied and ignored human rights due to the fact that Mao never used the notion of human rights or rarely explained human rights thinking; some scholars have pointed out that before the foundation of New China, Mao explained some of his thinking on human rights, but subsequently, he and all the whole country were trapped in a nihilistic approach to human rights.[15] However, most Chinese scholars take a positivist approach, which insists that, in

---

[12] 汪猕[WANG Mi], *《人权理论禁区是怎样突破的》[How* the Exclusion Zone of Human Rights Theory was Broken Through], 百年潮 [Hundred Year Tide] 2004, No. 5, 13.

[13] 于建嵘[YU Jianrong], *《共治威权与法治威权——中国政治发展的问题与出路》[Condominium Authoritarian Regime and the Authoritarian Regime of the Rule of Law: the Problems and Outlooks of Political Development in China],* above no. 27, 18.

[14] 郑德荣[ZHENG Derong], *《毛泽东思想的历史地位与当代价值》[The Historical Status and Contemporary Values of Mao Zedong's Thought],* 中国共产党新闻网[News of the Community of the Party of China Net] http://theory.people.com.cn/GB/13619948.html. (Last visited: January 20th, 2024).

[15] 杜钢建[DU Gangjian], *《谈克服人权虚无主义》[On Overcoming the Nihilism of Human Rights],* 法律学习与研究 [Law Study and Research] 1992, No. 1, 3.

Mao's thinking about rights, he rarely used the concept of "human rights", preferring most of time to use the term "citizen's rights". This detail is always ignored in academic circles. Mao's thinking about citizens' rights was an experiment that critically developed Western human rights theory. Chinese traditional culture, Marxism, and the experiences of the long process of rescuing China from subjugation deeply influenced Mao thinking on citizens' rights, and introduced him to the other aspect of human rights, and, consequently, to propose another form of thinking on citizens' rights, which differed from Western human rights theory. This thinking on citizens' rights emphasizes class attribution, collectivism and non-elitism. Furthermore, citizens' rights come from the people rather than god, and in a class-based society, citizens' rights can only be obtained by struggle. Furthermore collective citizens' rights should be protected as a first priority, and the right to subsistence is a fundamental citizens' right.[16] This thinking on citizens' rights was entirely incorporated in constitutional legislation.

In the Maoist period, four constitutions were passed between 1949 and 1979, namely, the Common Program of the Chinese People's Political Consultative Conference in 1949, the 1954 Constitution, and later the 1975 Constitution and the 1978 Constitution. In these constitutions, although there was no provision stipulating the need to "protect human rights" or some other similar expression, there were explicit references entitling citizens to broad, basic rights, including the rights to elect and to be elected according to law, freedom of thought, speech, and publication, and the freedom to "hold processions and demonstrations". Moreover, "women enjoy equal rights with men in political, economic, cultural, education and social life", "all nationalities have equal rights and duties', and the 'freedom to report truthful news shall be safeguarded", and so on.[17]

However, Undeniably, although citizens were entitled to the above basic rights, they were laid aside and neglected in the several decades of Mao's rule, and the state did not take on its responsibility to put the rights guaranteed in the constitution into action, due to the fact that the constitutions were not judicially actionable; indeed, the whole legal system was weakened, especially during the period of the "Cultural Revolution" launched by Mao Zedong from 1966 to 1977, when "the Cultural

[16] See 林育川[LIN Yuchuan], *《人民权利:人权的一种替代方案——从毛泽东的权利思维看》[Citizen's Rights: An Alternative to the Human Rights—With the Perspective of Mao Zedong's Thinking on Rights]*, 现代哲学 [Modern Philosophy] 2007, No. 1, 37; 戴立兴 [DAI Xingli], *《论毛泽东的人权思想》[On Mao Zedong' Thought of Human Rights]*, 马克思主义研究 [Studies on Marxism] 2014, No. 2, 29; 付子堂, 崔燕 [FU Zitang and CUI Yan], *《毛泽东早期文稿 中的人权观念》[The Human Rights Concept in Mao Zedong's Early Manuscripts]*, 毛泽东思想研究[Studies on Mao Zedong's Thought] 2012, No. 3, 26; 沈晓阳[SHEN Xiaoyang], *《论毛泽东的人权思想》[On Mao Zedong's Thought on Human Rights]*, 甘肃理论学刊 [Guansu Theory Research] 1995, No. 3, 3; 鲜开林[XIAN Kailin], *《论毛泽东人权思想的独特贡献》[On the Unique Contribution of Mao Zedong's Thought on Human Rights]*, 人权 [Human Rights] 2013, No. 6, 21.

[17] See *《中国人民政治协商会议共同纲领》[The Common Program of the Chinese People's Political Consultative Conference]*, 1949; *《中华人民共和国宪法》[The Constitution of the P.R.C.], 1954,* *《中华人民共和国宪法》[The Constitution of the P.R.C.]*, 1975; *《中华人民共和国宪法》[The Constitution of the P.R.C.]*, 1984.

Revolution made the legal construction of China nearly suffer from extinction."[18] Even the CPC publicly denied the importance and necessity of legislation. In 1958, Mao Zedong said that "we are not to rely on law to manage the majority of people; [they] should develop a habit; who can remember so many provisions contained by Laws?",[19] at the same time, the Report to the Chairman and Central Government on Some Issues of Political and Legal Affairs Since the Organization of People's Communes throughout the Country, issued by the Central Group of Political Science and Law, pointed out that "in according to China's reality, it is not necessary to make and pass Criminal Law, Civil Law, or Procedural Law."[20] Subsequently, legislation was effectively discontinued and legal nihilism became the order of the day. This led to a situation in which the legal construction of the state was completely destroyed and the ideology of one-man rule took over. In addition, the issues of the mixed functions of the political party and laws and even the existence of the political party in the place of the law, meant that at that time the emphasis was on policies rather than law. All of this meant that in the period from 1949 to 1979 there were frequent cases where the interests of citizens were ignored and their rights overridden. In the social circumstances of the time under the rule of Mao and under the impact of his political ideology, citizens' rights in the Constitutions were stipulated as a political aim, rather than an entitlement to rights and an undertaking to respect and protect them; indeed, these rights existed in name only. Meanwhile, the laws at that time were used entirely as a measure to protect dictatorship, one-man rule and privilege, even without considering legal nihilism and the prevalence of class struggle. So, any practical protection for human rights was, at that time, out of the question.

Based on the above analysis, we can see that citizen' rights were wantonly trampled on in practice, reflecting the reality that there were no human rights at all and legal vacancy at that time. As some scholars have said that, "the development of human rights in China was in fact at a standstill and regression"[21] in the period of Mao's rule. From this point of view, therefore, Mao at that time only had an awareness of rights, rather than a comprehensive concept or perspective on human rights, and so how do they protect human rights by legislation? The citizen's rights provided by the Constitutions were not able to reflect Mao's human rights view. In addition, we must note that in the Mao era and even up until the early 1980s, China rejected Western values, including the human rights concept, so it cannot be argued that Mao Zedong and even the CPC itself had a human rights approach.

---

[18] GAO Mingxuan and ZHAO Bingzhi, above no. 65, 69.

[19] 全国人大常委会办公室研究室 [Research Office of General Office of the NPC Standing Committee], *《人民代表大会制度建设40年》[The 40 year Construction of the System of National People's Congress]*, 中国民主与法制出版社 [China Democracy and Law Press], Beijing, 1991, 102, cited in 张继良 [ZHANG Jiliang], *《中共人权理论与中国人权立法研究》[On the Chinese Communist's Thesis of Human Rights and Its Legislation in China]*, 东北师范大学博士论文 [PhD Dissertation, Northeast Normal University], 2004, 30.

[20] 张继良 [ZHANG Jiliang], above no. 403, 30–31.

[21] 严冬 [YAN Dong], *《国际人权法之于中国人权法制建设的历时性研究》[A Diachronic Study on the Influence of International Human Rights Law on the Chinese Legal System Construction]*, 河北法学 [Hebei Law Science] 2014, Vol. 32, No. 2, 172.

After Mao, came Deng Xiaoping. The 3rd Plenary Session of the 11th Central of the Communist Party of China turned back to ideological guidelines which encouraged the emancipation of the mind and the search for truth derived from facts, and embarked on an attempt to turn wrongs into rights all over the country. Human rights concepts were introduced into China and widely discussed by Chinese scholars following this meeting.

Human rights were first introduced into China through the controversy on whether human rights belonged to a socialist or capitalist system. This controversy had a heavily ideological content in the early 1980s. Those who thought human rights belonged to a capitalist system considered that human rights is only a capitalist slogan, and cannot be applied to the proletariat,[22] but those who thought human rights also belong to a socialist system argued that it is not only the bourgeoisie who can have their own human rights concepts; the proletariat, too, can have their own human rights slogan.[23] In May and June 1985, Deng noted, "What are human rights? Above all, how many people are they meant for? Do those rights belong to the minority, to the majority, or to all the people in a country? Our concept of human rights is, in essence, different from that of the Western world, because we see the question from a different point of view."[24] Based on this argument, Deng pointed out that individual human rights should not be set against the human rights of the masses; in order to protect the majority's rights and security we must exercise dictatorship over a small number of criminals, and crack down severely on crimes; "since the current situation is unusual, we have to strike hard, fast and according to law…This is what we mean by strengthening the people's democratic dictatorship. So far as humanitarianism is concerned, since we are protecting the safety of the overwhelming majority of the people, we are humanitarian in the true sense of the word."[25] Deng believed that individual human rights were consistent with collective human rights, and emphasized the extreme importance of state sovereignty to human rights protection in a developing country. In other words, he thought that state sovereignty is more important than human rights. In this sense, during Deng's visit to the USA in 1989, he had explicitly pointed out that "people who value human rights should not forget the rights of the state. When they talk about human dignity,

---

[22] For example, on March 22, 1979, a paper, "Human rights isn't the slogan of the proletariat (人权不是无产阶级的口号)", was published in Beijing Ribao (Beijing Daily), and it was claimed that human rights is the slogan of bourgeoisie, not the banner of the struggling proletariat. Some scholars thought that human rights were only the slogan and ideology of bourgeoisie, and it would be interpreted as a demonstration against Communism and the government if the slogans "Respect human rights" and "Fight for human rights" were proposed. See 陈佑武, 李步云 [CHEN Youwu and LI Buyun], *《改革开放以来法治与人权关系的历史发展》[The Historical Development of the Relationship between the Rule of Law and Human Rights since the Reform and Opening-up]*, 现在法学[Modern Law Science] 2015, Vol. 37, No. 2, 4.

[23] 蓝瑛 [LAN Ying], *《"人权"从来就是资产阶级的口号吗?——同肖蔚云等同志商榷》['Is Human Rights always the Slogan of Bourgeoisie? Discussion with Comrade Xiao Weiyun, etc.]*, 社会科学 [Social Sciences] 1979, No. 3, 71.

[24] DENG Xiaoping, *Bourgeois Liberalization Means Taking the Capitalist Road*, above no. 226.

[25] Ibid.

they should not forget national dignity."[26] Based on the rights of the state view, he insisted that "stability is of overriding importance" and that the "first priority should always be given to national sovereignty and security."[27]

As for Deng's outlook on human rights, most Chinese scholars offer positive comments, and are unanimous that Deng's thinking on human rights is the latest development in Marxist human rights theory in China, and it has not only a scientific, but also an epochal, character and reality, and always guides the protection and creation of human rights in China. Deng's human rights thinking is critical to China, it illuminates the Party's basic position and perspective on human rights, and it also gives guidance on respecting and developing human rights in the country.[28]

Obviously, Deng's human rights thinking respects the CPC's human rights perspective and has had a deep influence on China's human rights development in both the Deng and post-Deng eras. On the one hand, not only general ideas about human rights, but also the specific aspects of Deng's human rights thinking, were fully incorporated in the White Paper on Human Rights in China launched by State Council of the PRC in November 1991. This document emphasizes that 'for any country or nation, the right to subsistence is the most important of all human rights, without which the other rights are out of the question', that "without national independence, there would be no guarantee for the people's lives", and that "the Chinese people had to win national independence before they could gain the right to subsistence"[29]; on the other hand, in 1997, the *Report on Hold High the Great Banner of Deng Xiaoping's Theory for an All-Round Advancement of the Cause of Building Socialism with Chinese Characteristics into the 21st Century* stated that we (i.e. the Chinese) must hold high the great banner of Deng Xiaoping's Theory and apply it to our entire cause and all our undertakings. This is an unshakable conclusion the Party

---

[26] Ibid.

[27] Ibid.

[28] See 黄惟勤 [HUANG Weiqin], *《坚持邓小平人权观;走中国特色的人权发展道路》[Insistence on Deng Xiaoping's Outlook on Human Rights; Maintain the Human Rights Development Road with Chinese Characteristics]*, available at: 中国共产党新闻网[News of Communist Party of China] http://theory.people.com.cn/GB/148980/16810107.html. (Last visited: January 20th, 2024); 李燕奇 [LI Yanqi], 《学习邓小平人权问题的思想》[Learning Deng Xiaoping's Thinking about the Issues of Human Rights], available at: 中华人民共和国国史网 [The History of the People's Republic of China] http://www.hprc.org.cn/gsyj/zzs/zzsxs/200909/t20090912_30910.html (Last visited: January 20th, 2024); 王福春[WANG Fuchun], *《邓小平人权思想初探》[Primary Studying on Deng Xiaoping's Thinking on Human Rights]*, 北京行政学院学报 [Journal of Beijing Administrative College] 2001, No. 1, 53; 袁旭川[YUAN Xuchuan], *《邓小平人权理论探析》[Theoretically Analyzing Deng Xiaoping's Human Rights Thinking]*, 毛泽东思想研究 [Mao Zedong's Thought Study] 2005, No. 6 88; 孙立 [SUN Li], *《邓小平人权思想对马克思主义的开拓创新》[Deng Xiaoping's Human Rights Thinking Pioneering and Innovating Marxism]*, 社会科学 [Journal of Social Sciences] 2005, No. 5, 40.

[29] Information Office of the State Council of the PRC, *White Papers on Human Rights in China*, available at: (China Human Rights Net) http://www.chinahumanrights.org/html/2014/WP_0724/36.html. (Last visited: January 21st, 2024).

has drawn from both history and current realities.[30] Although the Chinese government launched its first White Paper on Human Rights to show China's basic position on and its practice of human rights, to a great extent, the issue of human rights at that time served as a theme for declarations intended for foreign consumption, at least until the 15th National Congress of the Communist Party of China. At this Congress, the phrase "respect and safeguard human rights"[31] was first written into the Party's political report.

In the post-Deng Xiaoping era, "lacking a unifying figure like Deng or Mao, China's leadership today is a mostly faceless group of longtime party engineers",[32] which has been transformed from a structure dominated by one man to a collective leadership[33]; in other words, the paternalistic authoritarian regime of the Mao and Deng eras is over, and in the era of Jiang Zeming (from 1989 to 2002) and Hu Jintao (from 2002 to 2012) China has developed a condominium authoritarian regime, and is now trying to become an authoritarian rule of law regime in the era of Xi Jinping (from 2012 to present).

More than 30 years after the reforms and opening up implemented in 1979, and particularly over the last 20 years, historic changes have taken place in the Chinese people and society and in the CPC. Firstly, the way in which social and political life was completely controlled by the ideological state apparatus and its ideology has already changed dramatically. Since the 1980s, the Chinese totalitarianism regime has moved irrevocably towards limited diversification, and its ideology has become secularized because of the economic diversification and development the country has experienced; at the end of the 1990s, China had already completed the historical transformation from totalitarianism to post- totalitarianism.[34] In the transformation

[30] 江泽民[JIANG Zemin], *《高举邓小平理论伟大旗帜,把建设有中国特色社会主义事业全面推向二十一世纪》[Hold High the Great Banner of Deng Xiaoping's Theory for an All-Round Advancement of the Cause of Building Socialism with Chinese Characteristics into the 21st Century (hereinafter abbreviated to HHG-DXT)*, available at: 中央人民政府网 [The Central People's Government of the P.R.C] http://www.gov.cn/test/2008-07/11/content_1042080.htm. (Last visited: January 21st, 2024).

[31] Ibid.

[32] KURLANTZICK Joshua, *After Deng: On China's Transformation—Is Deng Xiaoping's legacy of modernization without political reform one that no contemporary Chinese official can control* available at: The Nation Instigating http://www.thenation.com/article/after-deng-chinas-transformation/ (Last visited: May 22nd, 2017).

[33] The Report on Hold High the Great Banner of Socialism with Chinese Characteristics and Strive for New Victories in Building a Moderately Prosperous Society in all Respects, delivered by Hu Jintao on Oct. 15 2007, had stated that 'we will strictly implement democratic centralism, improve the system that combines collective leadership with division of responsibilities among individuals, and oppose and prevent arbitrary decision-making by an individual or a minority of people.' See HU Jintao, *Hold High the Great Banner of Socialism with Chinese Characteristics and Strive for New Victories in Building a Moderately Prosperous Society in all Respects* (hereinafter abbreviated to RHH-GBS)' available at: China daily. http://www.chinadaily.com.cn/china/2007-10/24/content_6204564.htm (Last visited: January 21st, 2024).

[34] 萧功秦 [XIAO Gongqin], *《从发展政治学看中国转型体制》[On the Chinese Transformation Regime with a Perspective from the Politics of Development]*, 浙江学刊 [Zhejing Academic Journal] 2005, No. 5, 107.

process, freedom of personal movement is accepted and protected, which means the previous mandatory political identity and interpersonal relationships based on personal loyalty are weakened, and consequently citizens no longer believe in empty political and ideological indoctrination. Secondly, the trust in politics and the political identity of the populace have significantly weakened, and civil disorder or "mass incidents (群体性事件)"[35] have occurred frequently over these decades, and assumed an anti-institutional character. According to research, the number of civil disorder cases was 8700 in 1993, and around 10,000 in 1994; in 2003, however, it was around 60,000, while in 2005 it increased to 87,000, and reached 90,000 in 2006. According to other research, in the past 15 years the annual rate of increase in cases of civil disorder is approximately 17%; in other words, civil disorder is increasing.[36] This kind of civil disorder, which is known as a "mass incident" or "mass frustration" in China, is normally caused by dissatisfaction with a particular leader, and then gradually changes to dissatisfaction with the whole state regime and the community of democracy.

The two main reasons discussed above prompted the CPC to consider implementing political reform, and changing their approach to human rights. As regards political reform, at the 15th National Congress of the CPC, Jiang Zemin stated that "we should continue to press ahead with the reform of the political structure, further extend the scope of socialist democracy and improve the socialist legal system, governing the country according to law and making it a socialist country ruled by law"[37]; as regards the changing approach to human rights, individual human rights

[35] Incidents of civil disorder or "mass incidents (群体性事件)", refer to collectively violent confrontations occurring in a public place, including physical space and virtual collaborative space such as the internet, and are normally caused by dissatisfaction with the enforcement of government policies, crime and corruption, and environmental issues and seizures of land by local government and so on. The formation, outbreak and tailing off of these incidents have an intimate and direct relationship with important structural characteristics of the Chinese transformation, and also with the special management and control patterns of the Chinese government, and its political culture and political psychology. See 刘能 [LIU Neng], *《当代中国的群体性事件:形象地位变迁和分类框架再构》[Mass Incidents in Modern China: Change of Image and Reconstruction of the Classification Framework]*, 江苏行政学院学报 [Journal of Jiangsu Administration Institute] 2011, Vol. 56, No. 2, 53; 蒋永甫[JIANG Yongfu], *《当代中国群体性事件频发的体制性根源与发生机理——一个国家与社会关系的解释框架》[The Institutional Source and Mechanism of the Frequent Contemporary Chinese Mass Incidents—An Interpretation of the Relationship Between the State and the Social Framework]*, 湖北行政学院学报 [Journal of Hubei Administration Institute] 2012, No. 6, 86.

[36] 刘能 [LIU Neng], above no. 419, 54.

[37] Hu Jintao, RHH-GBS, above no. 417. We should note that in this report, the CPC still used the term 'rule by law', which is very different from 'rule of law'. 'A system under a rule of law system has a political and social order due to the positive nature of the stated law, whereas a system ruled by law has a political and social order that depends on already existing political laws or political interpretations of stated laws. The danger in a 'rule by law' system is that a domineering state can vindicate any action as long as it alters or interprets the rules accordingly.' See MONTHY Jeremy T., *Internal Perspectives on Chinese Human Rights Reform: The Death Penalty in the PRC*, Texas International Law Journal, 1998, Vol. 33, No. 1, 194). At the 17th CPC National Congress, Hu Jintao's report first uses the term 'rule of law'.

has received more and more attention due to the internal factors described above, as well as international considerations.

As regards the international factors, on the one hand, "human rights groups regularly issue scathing reports condemning China for widespread human rights violations",[38] which puts international pressure on the CPC and makes it change its approach to human rights and improve the human rights situation; on the other hand, the Chinese government has gradually acknowledged and accepted various international human rights covenants and started to participate in some international human rights initiatives. For example, the Chinese government signed *the Convention against Torture and other Cruel, Inhuman or Degrading Treatment or Punishment* in 1986 and ratified it in 1988), as well as other international treaties, such as the *International Convention Against Apartheid in Sports* (signed in 1984), the *Convention Concerning Vocational Rehabilitation and Employment (Disabled Persons)* (ratified in 1987), the *International Covenant on Civil and Political Rights (hereinafter: ICCPR) (signed in 1998)* and the *International Covenant on Economic, Social and Cultural Rights (*hereinafter: ICESCR*)* (signed in 1997 and ratified in 2001). In addition, China has also actively participated in international organizations; for example, China began sending observers to the UN Commission on Human Rights and became a full member in 1982. All of these require the Chinese government to fulfill its corresponding international responsibilities; in addition, the CPC has gradually begun to pay attention to the importance and value of individual human rights. We can read about these changes in the CPC's Work Reports; for example, at the 16th National Congress of the CPC in 2002, Jiang Zemin stated that "... human rights are respected and guaranteed' and he also stated that 'we should uphold and improve the system of people's congresses and ensure ... their legislation and policy decisions better embody the people's will."[39] A significant milestone in the development of human rights in China was the inclusion of the statement "the state respects and preserves human rights"[40] in the Constitution in 2004, although the state is still lagging several decades and perhaps several centuries behind the West. The Constitution of the PRC included the concept of human rights protection for the first time, and transformed human rights from a political notion into a legal concept. Furthermore, the state, rather than only the Party and the government, has become the principle means of protecting human rights, and the citizen's will and values have become an element in state construction and development as a constitutional principle. At the CPC's 17th National Congress in 2007, Hu Jintao also emphasized that "we must respect and safeguard human rights, and ensure the equal right to participation and development for all members of society in accordance with the law."[41] At the CPC's 18th National

---

[38] PEERENHOOM Randall, above no. 21, 72.

[39] 江泽民 [JIANG Zemin], *《全面建设小康社会,开创中国特色社会主义事业新局面 > [Build a Well-off Society in an All-Round Way and Create a New Situation in Building Socialism with Chinese Characteristics* (hereinafter:BWS-AWC)], available at: 人民网(People Net) http://www.people.com.cn/GB/paper39/7683/733922.html (Last visited: January 21st, 2024).

[40] *《中华人民共和国宪法》[The Constitution of the People's Republic of China.]*, 2004, Article 33 (3).

[41] HU Jintao, RHH-GBS, above no. 417.

Congress in 2012, Hu Jintao stated that "the rule of law should be fully implemented as a basic strategy, a law-based government should be a basic function, judicial credibility should be steadily enhanced, and human rights should be fully respected and protected."[42] In 2013, the 4th Plenary Session of the 18th Central Committee of the CPC launched the *2013 Decision*, and discussed "promoting the rule of law", and emphasized the importance of "improving the judicial system to protect human rights."[43] In 2014, the 4th Plenary Session of the 18th Central Committee of the CPC passed the *2014 Decision*, and once again declared its intention to, "strengthen the judicial protection of human rights; to strengthen the consciousness of the importance of respecting and protecting human rights in society, and to provide complete channels and methods to obtain relief for citizen's rights."[44] All of these developments, to a great extent, show that in the post-Deng era there has been a gradual shift in the CPC's attitude to human rights and judicial protection for all members of society.

The attitude toward human rights is accompanied by a change in approach. However, as mentioned above, Deng had a profound influence on his successors, in particular Jiang Zemin, who propounded the important concept of "*Three Representatives*",[45] which emphasizes that "to satisfy the interests and demands of the overwhelming majority of the people is the most important thing and should be given top priority", and that "the interests of the overwhelming majority of the people are the vital and most decisive factor. This has always been vital to the overall interests of keeping the Party in power",[46] and they "are also the guidebook of Chinese human rights development."[47] According to the *"Three Representatives"*, protecting the human rights of the overwhelming majority of people has priority. When Jiang

[42] 胡锦涛[HU Jintao],《坚定不移沿着中国特色社会主义道理前进, 为全面建成小康社会奋斗》[Firmly March on the Path of Socialism with Chinese Characteristics and Strive to Complete the Building of A Moderately Prosperous Society in All Respects], available at:《中国共产党第18次全国代表大会, 人民网[18th CPC National Congress; People Net] http://cpc.people.com.cn/18/n/2012/1109/c350821-19529916.html (Last visited: January 21st, 2024).

[43] *Decision of the Central Committee of the Communist Party of China on Some Major Issues Concerning Comprehensively Deepening the Reform*, above no. 5.

[44] *《中共中央关于全面推进依法治国若干重大问题的决定》[The CCP Central Committee Decision Concerning Some Major Questions in Comprehensively Moving Government of the Country According to the Law Forward*, above no. 20. Based on this Decision, we can say that China is trying to promote the "authoritarian regime of the rule of law".

[45] The main elements of the important thinking of "three representatives" are that the CPC always represents advanced social productive forces; always represents the progressive course of China's advanced culture and always represents the fundamental interests of the majority. In reality, these three representatives stand respectively for economic production, cultural development and political consensus. See 江泽民[JIANG Zemin], *BWS-AWC,* above no. 423.

[46] JIANG Zemin, Speech at the Meeting Celebrating the 80th Anniversary of the Founding of the Communist Party of China, available at: China Net. http://www.china.org.cn/e-speech/a.htm (Last visited: January 21st, 2024).

[47] 苏哲[SU Zhe], *《'三个代表' 重要思想是中国人权事业发展的指南》[The Important Thought of 'Three Representatives' is the Guidebook of Human Rights Development in China],* 人权[Human Rights] 2002, No. 5, 47.

Zemin referred to Ugandan President Yoweri Museveni's speech on January 30 1996, he said that,

> For China, to insure the people's rights to subsistence and development is the primary and the most vital human rights protection; to insure Chinese social stability, economic development and the improvement of people's living standards are the basic conditions and important content of improving human rights in China.[48]

He also pointed out that,

> The criminal who has committed crimes against the people's interest can't be contained within the scope of human rights protection; all kinds of crimes must be punished according to the law and this is for the sake of protecting the human rights of the overwhelming majority of the people.[49]

Therefore, Jiang Zemin emphasized the human rights of the majority and did not recognize the human rights of criminals.

Hu Jintao's outlook on human rights is somewhat different from Jiang's. *The SOD*, which was propounded by Hu, "takes development as its essence, putting people first as its core principle" and emphasizes that "we must respect the principal position of the people in the country's political life … and protect their rights and interests."[50] Even though *the SOD* takes development as its essence, it puts the people first as its core principle, which consequently includes two factors, namely, humanism and rights. Individual freedom and dignity should be equally respected and protected, and when the individual interest conflicts with that of the state or the overwhelming majority of the people, it should be dealt with in an all-encompassing and considered approach, and both sides should be equally considered and protected.

Since then, individual human rights have received more and more attention. The *2014 Decision* mentioned the need to "strengthen the judicial protection of human rights."[51] This was the first time in its history that the CPC had taken "the judicial protection of human rights" as one of their general objectives, together with the need to "make the people feel fairness and justice in every judicial case,"[52] and this initiative will enrich the CPC's political values.

According to the above discussion and analysis, the CPC's outlook on human rights, and in particular individual human rights, has undergone a great change. However, we need to face the fact that in China individual human rights have not received enough attention, or enough respect. The state is strong enough to force the citizen to yield to the national interest or to the interests of the majority; in other words, individual human rights always suffer when faced with state interests or the human rights or interests of the majority.

---

[48] *《江泽民论人权》[On Human Rights by Jiang Zemin]*, available at: 人民网 [People's Net] http://politics.people.com.cn/GB/8198/5139784.html (Last visited: January 21st, 2024).

[49] Ibid.

[50] Hu Jintao, RHH-GBS, above no. 417.

[51] *《中共中央关于全面推进依法治国若干重大问题的决定》[The CCP Central Committee Decision Concerning Some Major Questions in Comprehensively Moving Government of the Country According to the Law Forward]*, above no. 20.

[52] Ibid.

4.2.1.2 Human Rights and the Alternative Punishment to the Death Penalty

Undeniably, even though China has signed but not yet ratified *the ICCPR*, human rights protection is driving China to abolish the death penalty and reform its punishment system since the idea that "the state respects and preserves human rights"[53] was included in *the Constitution* in 2004. By this change, China "breaks through the exclusion zone of human rights and makes a significant progress in the construction of constitutionalism".[54] Even though the CPC has its own outlook on human rights, which emphasizes national security and stability, and correspondingly individual human rights have not been taken account of in a reasonable way, the constitutional clause of human rights protection is driving China to carry out its international responsibilities in terms of limiting the use of, and even abolishing, the death penalty. Regarding the alternative punishment to the death penalty, it should not be another form of chronic death penalty, and should fulfill constitutional requirements in that it "respects and preserves human rights", even if this punishment should be merely for the offender who commits extremely serious crimes, because the offender should be treated as an ordinary human rather than a "morally deformed person". When considering the abolition of the death penalty, based on international legislative experience and China's current legislative status, clearly two important options—i.e. LWOR and life imprisonment with the possibility of release (hereinafter: LWPR)—will be available for China's legislators to consider. LWOR is widely criticized due to its violation of human rights protection, as mentioned in the preceding paragraph. However, in the context of a full awareness that it violates the constitutional clause which "respects and preserves human rights", LWOR was still introduced by the Ninth Amendment into the penalty system for corruption crimes, which are now punishable by death. Consequently, this legislative practice naturally raises a series of concerns for the future punishment option to replace the death penalty, i.e., will China turn a deaf ear to human rights protection and adopt LWOR to replace the death penalty for other extremely serious crimes, such as crimes of endangering national security and lethal crimes? This concern is both practical and necessary because the preceding legislative practice has, to a great extent, already shown the attitudes and tendentiousness of the CPC and its legislature toward the balance between an anti-serious crime policy and human rights protection. Obviously, if China does use LWOR to replace the death penalty, this kind of legislative practice will just wrap a cloak around immediate execution and form a new chronic death penalty, which will be unconstitutional and aggravate the issues of human rights related to criminal affairs. It will also bring a great number of challenges related to issues of international cooperation in criminal matters, such as the extradition between China and member states of the EU which

[53] 《中华人民共和国宪法》*[The Constitution of the People's Republic of China], 2004,* Article 33 (3).

[54] 郭道晖 [GUO Daohui], 《人权观念与人权入宪》*[On the Concept of Human Rights and the Inclusion of Human Rights into the Constitution]*, 法学 [Law Science] 2004, No. 4, 19.

protect human rights. Furthermore, it will bring a great challenge to China's government to ratify the ICCPR. Obviously and finally, given these considerations, LWPR will be the only potential option to replace the death penalty from the perspective of human rights protection in China.

4.2.2 The Ideas Behind the Penalty

The ideas behind the punishment are embodied in all kinds of views and perspectives on the penalty, the conception behind the penalty and attitudes toward the establishment, assignment and use of the criminal punishment, and they are normally elucidated in tradition by philosophers in the context of retributive theory and utilitarian theory, and play a foundation role in the establishment and assignment of the penalty system. In the light of this, as an obvious form of change in the establishment and reassignment of the penalty system, the punishment option to replace the death penalty will consequently, of its nature, be greatly influenced by the ideas behind the penalty, which should be the basic affecting factors dominating the option. But, what kinds of ideas behind the penalty will have an influence on the punishment option to replace the death penalty? It seems that this can be easily answered by citing retributive theory or utilitarian theory, which have clearly driven China to launch its reform of the criminal punishment in recent decades.[55] Furthermore, some scholars, by discussing and analyzing the introduction of community correction and reform of the punishment system in recent years, point out that the concept of lightening the penalty is driving China to build a reasonable and mitigative penalty system[56]; and this concept will naturally influence the punishment option towards replacing the death penalty, because to choose a reasonable punishment to replace the death penalty is an important form of lightening the penalty system in China. Certainly, the retributive and utilitarian theories and the concept of lightening the penalty system are significant factors influencing the punishment option to replace the death penalty. However, based on the fact that China has not completely abolished the death penalty in recent years, and the supposition that the punishment option to replace the death penalty will be introduced in the future, this book would like to explain the ideas behind the penalty influencing the punishment option by analyzing the factors that permanently and profoundly influence China's penalty reforms, i.e., a traditional concept of the penalty system which may to a certain extent be considered the culture of punishment and the orientation of the nation-state regarding that system. Meanwhile, given that the punishments that will be chosen to replace the

---

[55] See 李晓明, 陈争尧 [LI Xiaoming and CHEN Zhengyao],*《"并合主义" 刑罚观对我国刑法立法的推动——以 < 刑法修正案(九)为视角* [On the Promotion of the "Combination Theory on the Penalty" to Criminal Legislation in China: From the Perspective of the Ninth Amendment to the Criminal Law], 政法论丛 [Journal of Political Science and Law] 2016, No. 2, 104.

[56] See 尹振国 (YING Zhenguo), *《国家治理现代化与人本主义刑法观》[Modernization of State Governance and the Humanistic Concept of the Criminal Law]*, 重庆理工大学学报 (社会科学) [Journal of Chongqing University of Technology (Social Science)] 2015, Vol. 29, No. 4, 85–86.

death penalty will be provided for the most heinous crimes, this book would like to explain the preceding two concepts by focusing on the most heinous crimes.

4.2.2.1 A Traditional Concept of the Penalty System

An undeniable fact is that "criminal justice is culture-bearing. It is the site at which cultures negotiate certain kinds of issues connected to wrongdoing and community, social order and violence…"[57] Focusing on the American and European cultures of punishment, Professor Joshua argues that America considers serious offenders as morally deformed people rather than ordinary people who have committed crimes, and so serious crime is taken by the criminal system as a justification for banishing him or her from social life.[58] Therefore, we can see that the death penalty and life imprisonment without parole is used in the American criminal system; in Europe, by contrast, the penalty system "denies that any offense marks the offender as a morally deformed person,"[59] and thus it never deprives the offender's right to hope of rehabilitation.[60] Looking to China, it seems that China is similar to America in terms of its views on serious offenders, and consequently holds that the death penalty is the extreme severe penalty. However, China is very different from the West in terms of legal culture; the traditional Chinese legal system was deeply influenced by two significant philosophical schools of thought, humanist Confucianism and rationalistic Legalism.[61] In terms of their views on human nature, Confucianism argues that humans may be inculcated, so cultivation (教化) is emphasized; it also argues that each single human has a sense of compassion, and so benevolence (仁), righteousness (义) and virtues (德) are emphasized. Based on this philosophy of human nature, in terms of punishment, Confucianism holds the position of "justice in return for injustice (以直报怨)",[62] and argues that the state should resort to "the criminal

[57] KLEINFELD Joshua, above no. 352, 940.

[58] See ibid.

[59] Ibid., 933.

[60] See ibid.

[61] Some scholars argued that the traditional Chinese legal system was created by Legalism and given life by the Confucianism. See, e.g., 吴正茂 [WU Zhengmao], *《再论法律儒家化:对瞿同祖"法律儒家化"之不同理解》[Revisiting the Confucianization of Law: A Different Understanding of the Confucianization of Law with Qu Tongzu]*, 中外法学 [Peking University Law Journal] 2011, Vol. 23, No. 3, 484. However, other than these two philosophical schools, there are other schools, such as Daoism and Mohism, and they played a key role in the issues of classical Chinese philosophical discourse; however, their importance is less than the Confucianism and Legalism. Therefore, this paper would like to take these latter two as examples.

[62] Here "直 (zhi)" means fairness and integrity, which has been accepted by the whole society and become a social consensus. Professor Zhu Suli argues that Confucianism's "justice in return for injustice" is a kind of retributive penalty concept, rather than a simple concept of revenge (an eye for an eye, 冤冤相报); and this concept of Confucianism is in basic accordance with the particular concept of justice defined by Aristotle. See 苏力 [SU Li], *《早期儒家的人性观》[Early Confucian View of Human Nature]*, 法制与社会发展 [Law and Social Development] 2015, Vol. 16, No. 5, 12–13.

punishment only after the courteous ones fail", and it should be characterized by "morality-primary, punishment-secondary". In light of this, therefore, Confucianism takes a cautious stand towards the use of the penalty, but does not deny the use of the punishment for serious crimes. And it even insists on the need "to apply severe punishment to govern the time of peace, but the light penalty for the time of chaos (治则刑重, 乱则刑轻),"[63] on the premise that the punishment is proportional to the crime.[64] Consequently, Confucianism does not reject the death penalty, but even takes the position that if the crime is "murder, the killer should receive the death penalty; if injury, the perpetrator should be given other punishment. This rule has never been changed in history."[65] This position became a significant element of the wisdom of Confucianism and a philosophical basis for those who favor in the death penalty in China, and exists now in the form of a traditional concept among the general public. This kind of traditional concept has already brought great challenges to the legal reform of the limitation and even abolition of the death penalty, and it will also have an influence on the punishment option to replace the death penalty. Under this traditional concept, many people, in particular the victim's family members, cannot accept the fact that they can see the perpetrator in the street or in their community after the latter has served in prison for a certain number of years, and they think social justice and the victim's right to life cannot be respected and their right to justice cannot be effectively protected. Therefore, some victims' family members hope the authorities will sentence the perpetrators to death, and complain to the State Bureau for Letters and Calls or other superior government or judicial organizations.[66] Therefore, in this context, especially in a situation in which judicial corruption has not been fundamentally eliminated, judicial credibility will be seriously challenged. An inappropriate but similar example can be seen in the judicial practice which involves financial compensation for leniency in death sentencing (referred to as victim-offender mediation in capital cases, 死刑案件的刑事和解), which is also vividly referred to as "cash for clemency"[67] by Susan Trevaskes. This practice has attracted great public attention and contributed to public outrage, and become an important element in the debate on the death penalty reform. Critics say

---

[63] *《荀子· 第18篇》[XUN Zi: Book 18].*

[64] See ibid. If the punishment is proportional to the crime, the society will be in a peace; if not, it will become chaos. (刑称罪, 则治; 不称罪, 则乱).

[65] See ibid.

[66] One of judges, who works in Supreme People's Court, says that "in the capital cases, the victims' family members generally hope the judges impose a heavy punishment and even the immediate execution on the perpetrators for the sake of vengeful mentality, without considering the criminal facts and legal provisions. See 刘静坤 [LIU Jingkun], *《死刑案件被害人家属信访问题研究》[On the Complain of the Family Members of the Victims in the Capital Cases],* 政法论丛 [Journal of Political Science and Law] 2009, No. 1, 95.

[67] TREVASKES Susan, *Lenient Death Sentencing and the "Cash for Clemency" Debate*, above no. 30, 38.

that "it may intensify social contradictions and causes disorder in the belief in social fairness."[68]

However, in contrast, Legalism believes that the "drive to profit (好利)" which is determined by a human being's need to survive and by physiological conditions, is a kind of basic human instinct and desire, and so it proposed "alternating rewards with punishments".[69] Rewards is a kind of commendation, and inflicting death or torture upon culprits is called chastisement or punishment; these are two handles that the intelligent ruler uses to control his ministers.[70] In the light of this, Legalism insists on the use of punishment to deter citizens so that humanity's "drive to profit" is regulated. It also argues that the state should impose "serious punishment to suppress all wickedness within the boundaries"[71]; and that "light punishment would either plunge the state into confusion or set traps for the people."[72] In the light of these ideas, Legalism is in favor of "cruel punishment" and praises highly the general prevalence of the concept of "execute one as a warning to others". This concept is deeply rooted among Chinese people, and is frequently mentioned by the rulers, especially when the social or ruling order is challenged. For instance, in the 1980s and 1990s, when "serious criminal cases happened frequently and the social order was in an abnormal state, cracking down severely on crimes became a strong voice in the country."[73] In

68 孙万怀 [SUN Wanhuai], *《死刑案件可以并需要和解吗?》[Could the Criminal Reconciliation Be Taken Place in the Capital Case? Does it need?],* 中国法学[China Legal Science] 2010, No. 1, 187. Other critics say that the public perception of the judicial justice will be, to an extreme extent, undermined and destroy the weaken rule of law which the country is building. See also 王满生 [WANG Mansheng], *《死刑案件刑事和解——法治与反法治之辩》[On Criminal Reconciliation of the Capital Cases: Debating between Rule or Law and Anti-rule of Law],* 行政与法 [Public Administration & Law] 2011, No. 11, 118.

69 Generally speaking, the order of All-under-Heaven must accord with human feelings. Human feelings have likes and dislikes, wherefore reward and punishment can be applied. If reward and punishment are applicable, prohibitions and orders will prevail and the course of government will be accomplished. As the ruler has the handles in his grip and thereby upholds his august position, what is ordered works and what is prohibited stops. The handles are regulators of life and death; the position is the means of overcoming the masses. See *《韩非子·八经》[Han Feizi: Chapter XLVIII. Eight Canons],* available at: http://www2.iath.virginia.edu:8080/exist/cocoon/xwomen/texts/hanfei/d2.48/1/0/bilingual (Last visited: January 21st, 2024).

70 See *《韩非子·二柄》[Han Feizi: Chapter VII. The Two Handles], available at:* http://www2.iath.virginia.edu:8080/exist/cocoon/xwomen/texts/hanfei/d2.7/1/0/bilingual (Last visited: June 1st, 2017).

71 *《韩非子·六反》[Han Feizi: Six Contrarieties],* available at: http://www2.iath.virginia.edu:8080/exist/cocoon/xwomen/texts/hanfei/d2.46/1/0/bilingual (Last visited: June 1st, 2017).

72 Ibid.

73 中华人民共和国最高人民法院 [The Supreme People's Court of P.R.C], *《数说人民法院审批工作60年》[Showing the People's Courts' Trail Works by Statistics Over 60 Years],* above no. 224. In accordance with this report, there were 1.4 million criminal cases dealt with by the courts throughout the country, and 1.72 million perpetrators were punished in the period from August 1983 to December 1986. According to the official report, the population of China was 1 billion, therefore the proportion of individuals sentenced was 1.72/1000 persons. See 中华人民共和国国家统计局 (National Bureau of Statistics of the People's Republic of China): *《关于1982年人口普查主要数字的公报》[A Bulletin on the Main Statistics of Population Census in 1982],* 中国统计[China Statistics] 1982, No. 6, 1.

recent years, for example, for the issues of anti-corruption, anti-terrorism, combating drug-related crimes and food safety, this concept is frequently mentioned in different ways. Supporting cruel punishment, Legalism, as a punishment culture developed and passed down through history, has provided a great philosophical ground and theoretical foundation for the retention of the death penalty, and it brings great challenges to abolition. Consequently, it will, by its nature influence the punishment option to replace the death penalty. From the perspective of legalism, to permanently isolate the offender from society by execution is a good way to achieve the specific and general prevention of crime; therefore, in this light, to permanently isolate by other means, such as LWOR rather than the death penalty, will be an appropriate punishment choice to replace the death penalty.

In terms of culture, regardless of the evolution of the nation's history, the traditional approach has always appeared in different ways. These two philosophical schools of thought have taken root in different state rulers throughout China's history, and have been transmitted through successive generations. This is because the traditional culture is a kind of feeling and value system which is formed and developed in the everyday environment and life-style of traditional Chinese society, and so it cultivates the relevant regime and legal system with which it is associated. History indicates that to venerate only one philosophical school makes it hard to maintain prolonged stability for state rulers; consequently, if rulers believe in Confucianism, they seek to adopt and integrate some arguments or measures of Legalism, and vice versa. Although China now is not the typical traditional state it was several decades and even hundreds of years ago, the views of traditional culture and the philosophical schools regarding human nature still have a very significant meanings for modern Chinese society and for the regime and legal system which are built on this foundation culture and this philosophical thinking, and they will also unconsciously influence the legislators who make the decision to choose the punishment to replace the death penalty.

4.2.2.2 The Position of the Nation-State Regarding the Penalty

Undeniably, China's penal system has always had a very strong tendency towards, and obvious characteristics of, the representation of state interests and regime supremacy. Using the penalty system to safeguard security of the State, and to defend the State power of the democratic dictatorship and the socialist system, is emphasized and takes priority among the aims of the punishments provided in the Criminal Law.[74]

Furthermore, in these two decades, the government launched the "strike hard" campaign to crack down on crime, and frequently passed many laws to stipulate new types of crime and to aggravate punishments.

[74] Specifically, the Article 2 of the Criminal Law provides that "the aim of the Criminal Law of the People's Republic of China is to use criminal punishments to fight against all criminal acts in order to safeguard security of the State, to defend the State power of the People's democratic dictatorship and the socialist system, to protect property owned by the State, and property collective owned by the working people and property privately owned by citizens, to protect citizens' rights of the

Firstly, this is because of the special nature of the Chinese regime. In a state like China, which some scholars call a "State Power Society",[75] the CPC is the sole governing party and takes Marxism-Leninism as its guiding principle. The positions, approaches and views of Marxism-Leninism are the vital theoretical tools used by the national leadership to understand, explain and then deal with the issues facing China. Under Marxism, state interests include the interests of the ruling class and social interests; the former plays the key role in this and determines the scope and degree of the latter.[76] In other words, protecting state interests is an important form of protecting the interest of the ruling class. The criminal law is considered an important instrument for protecting state interests in accordance with Marxist theory. An obvious example of this point is that some heavy punishments, such as the death penalty, life imprisonment and long-term imprisonment, are widely provided for crimes of endangering national security, endangering public security and economic crimes. This position was widely highlighted in the authoritative textbooks on criminal law and has a great influence on legislators and judicial practitioners.[77] Secondly, "the first modern criminal law of China was introduced in 1979 and derived almost entirely from the former Soviet Union Criminal Code."[78] It was characteristically Soviet, "being clad in the ideology of class struggle",[79] and showed an obvious tendency to instrumentalism, which played a dominant role for a long period in the criminal legislation and judicial practice of the 1980s and 1990s; even today some scholars have argued that the new form of criminal instrumentalism can also be found in current legislative and judicial practice.[80] Given that "a new social constraint mechanism hasn't been built yet to replace the traditional one,"[81] this instrumentalism has solid foundations for its existence, because most citizens hope to deal with social conflicts by punishment, and the

---

person and their democratic and other rights, to maintain public and economic order, and to ensure the smooth progress of socialist construction". See *《中华人民共和国刑法》[Criminal Law of the People's Republic of China]*, Order No. 83, 14 March 1997, Article 2.

[75] WANG Yunhai, *The Death Penalty and Society in East Asia—How to Understand and Compare the Death Penalty in China, Japan and South Korea*—Hitotsubashi Journal of Law and Politics, 2012, No. 24, 2.

[76] See 庞仁芝 (PANG Renzhi), *《马克思主义国家学说的一个重要范畴--国家利益 [An Important Category of Marxism Theory on the State: State Interests]*, 科学社会主义 [Scientific Socialism] 1992, No. 3, 72.

[77] The concept of penalty instrumentalism can easily be found in certain cases which are especially relative to the protection of state interests, such as the "Xu Ting case)". See 龚向和, 邓炜辉 [GONG Xianghe and DENG Weihui], *《人权视野下传统工具主义刑法观之价值超越:对"许霆案"有罪判决的批判与反思》[Beyond the Value of the Traditional Instrument of Criminal Law from the Perspective of Human Rights: The Criticism and Reflection on the Conviction of the "Xu Ting" Case]*, 时代法学 [Present Day Law Science] 2008, Vol. 6, No. 4, 74.

[78] 刘仁文 [LIU Renwen], *《中国刑法学六十年》[Criminal Law of China from 1949 to 2009]*, 浙江大学学报(人文社会科学版) [Journal of Zhejiang University (Humanities and Social Sciences)] 2010, Vol. 40, No. 1, 87.

[79] SOOTAK Jaan, *Theories of Punishment and Reform of Criminal Law [Reform as a Change of Mentality]*, Juridical International, 2000, No. V, 71.

[80] See, e.g., 魏昌东 [Wei Changdong], above no. 106, 85.

[81] 金小红, 李家兴,杨建 [Jin Xiaohong, Li Jiaxing and Yang Jian], *《社会约束体系的弱化与解构的逻辑——一项城市流动越轨未成年人生活状态的调查》[The Logic of the Weakening and*

state leadership takes "social stability as a precondition for China's economic prosperity",[82] and deems punishment an important tool to consolidate social stability and the state's power and to ensure it operates effectively.[83] Therefore, to a great extent, the prevalence of penalty instrumentalism contributed to the severity punishment doctrine, and it even became the mainstream approach, as was reflected in some policies and legislation of that time. For instance, since the launch of the policy of cracking down severely on crimes (called the "strike hard" campaign) in 1983, the central government and some local governments have already implemented further 'strike hard' campaigns, with varying targets and in vary degrees of severity, which[84] "in the post Mao China … became a particular expression of retributive justice and heavy penaltism."[85] From 1983 to 1997, China successfully adopted 25 Special Criminal Laws, according to which 33 crimes in total could be punishable by death, and increased the total number of crimes punishable by death to around 71 before the 1997 Criminal Law was passed.[86] Under the influence of penalty instrumentalism, which takes the protection of the regime and interests of the host-state as a priority, the legislator prefers to isolate the offender from social life by treating him or her in a strict manner, so that the perpetrator's threat to social and regime stability can be permanently controlled and eliminated. Therefore, the abolition of the death penalty for the crimes of endangering national security and endangering public security will face many tough challenges and accompanying political concerns. Even if the death

---

Deconstruction of the Social Constraint Mechanism: A Survey on the State of Juvenile Delinquents in the City], 中南民族大学学报(人文社会科学版)[Journal of South-Central University For Nationalities (Humanities and Social Sciences)] 2012, Vol. 32, No. 1, 85.

[82] TREVASKES Susan, *The Shifting Sands of Punishment in China in the Era of 'Harmonious Society*, above no. 71, 339.

[83] We can see this from the function of the criminal punishment provided by the 1979 Criminal Law and the present Criminal Law. The function of the 1979 Criminal Law, to a great extent, continues to this day, even if it has been modified by deleting certain words, such as "all counter-revolution" and "the socialist revolution". For example, the task of the current Criminal Law is "to use criminal punishments to fight against all criminal acts in order to safeguard the security of the State, to defend the State power of the people's democratic dictatorship and the socialist system, to protect property owned by the State, and property collectively owned by the working people and property privately owned by citizens, to protect citizens' personal rights and their democratic and other rights, to maintain public and economic order, and to ensure the smooth progress of socialist construction." See *《中华人民共和国刑法》[The Criminal Law of the People's Republic of China]*, Order No. *5, 1979*, Article 2; and *《中华人民共和国刑法》*[Criminal Law of the People's Republic of China], Order No. 83, 14 March 1997, Article 2.

[84] Thus far, the central government of China has already launched 5 rounds of national "strike hard"; the first, in 1983, the second in 1996, and then in 2001, 2010 and in 2014. The local governments of China have initiated many rounds of partial "strike hard". See *《严打》[Strike Hard]*, available at: 360百科 [360Baike] http://baike.so.com/doc/6395274-6608931.html (Last visited: January 21st, 2024).

[85] TREVASKES Susan, *The Shifting Sands of Punishment in China in the Era of 'Harmonious Society*, above no. 71, 340.

[86] See高铭暄 [GAO Mingxuan], *《死刑60年:新中国死刑立法的变迁与展望》[60 years of the Death Penalty: the Evolution of and Prospects for the Capital Legislation of New China*], above no. 210.

penalty for these crimes is abolished, a punishment option which at least has a similar function to the death penalty will be considered to replace the death penalty.

Furthermore, the issue of the punishment option to replace the death penalty is also a political concern. In China, it is not just, as Professor Trevaskes points out, that "the criminal justice policy emerges un-reflectively from the top echelons of power to the grassroots without need for fineness or negotiation between 'stakeholders'",[87] but that punishment reform, in particular reform of the death penalty, is dominated by the state leadership, who play a substantive and crucial role in its development,[88] due to it being a kind of political issue rather than a simple legal one. The punishment option to replace the death penalty is, in fact, an extension of the issue of reform of the death penalty, and this consideration is key to understanding how to control the most heinous crimes without the death penalty and what kind of punishment will prove the most suitable measure to adopt for extremely serious crimes after removing the death penalty. It is not only closely related to the protection and realization of justice from the perspective of the victim, but also to the maintenance of the regime and society stability from the perspective of the national leadership and legislator. Consequently, the issue of the punishment option to replace the death penalty goes beyond a merely legal scope and becomes an important political concern that will make the legislator inclined to protect state interests and the regime by eliminating the threats from the perpetrators of serious crimes, either for a long period, or permanently.

4.2.3 Criminal Policy

In a state power society such as China, given the special political regime, the policies declared by the Communist Party and the Central Government are normally more important than laws.[89] The criminal policy is normally issued by the CPLAC and described as the guidance of legislation and judicature,[90] and thus plays a crucial role

[87] TREVASKES Susan, *The Shifting Sands of Punishment in China in the Era of 'Harmonious Society*, above no. 71, 333–334.

[88] See 吴大华, 王飞 [WU Dahua and WANG Fei], *《限制死刑的理性思考——以100例死刑案件为视角》[Thinking Rationally on Limiting the Death Penalty: From the Perspective of 100 Death Cases]*, 政治与法律[Political Science and Law] 2005, No. 3, 92.

[89] In accordance with the Constitution of the People's Republic of China and the Constitution of the Communist Party of China, China is a one-party state and the Communist Party of China is the sole governing party of China and coexists alongside other legal parties which hold no real power or independence from the Communist Party. The Policies declared by the Communist Party are the most important means for the national leadership to run and govern the state's affairs. As for legal affairs, policies are normally decided both by the Central Communist Party of China and the Central Political and Legal Affairs Commission of the Communist Party of China and all of these policies operate as guidance and grounds for legislation and the judiciary. See 刘家征 [LIU Jiazheng], above no. 23.

[90] For example, criminal policy could function as the legal ground to deal with criminal cases in judicial practice when there was a lack of relevant criminal provisions in the early days following the founding of New China. However, after the Criminal Law was passed, criminal policy was

in criminal legislation and judicial practice. "Throughout the background to all the amendments adopted in criminal law, they are, without exception, done in accordance with the adjustment of criminal policies."[91] Obviously, punishment reform should naturally follow the requirements of criminal policy. For example, *the Explanations for the Draft of the Ninth Amendment to the Criminal Law (hereinafter: the Explanation)* emphasize that, criminal policy is "one of the important guiding concepts for the Ninth Amendment."[92] "Combining Leniency and Severity" is now an important criminal policy undertaken by China, and is referred to as a "bipolar criminal policy" by some scholars.[93] The substance of this policy is to give different punishments to different criminals under different circumstances, and to make sure that the criminal is given lenient punishment if the crime should be punished leniently, but receive a severe punishment if it should be punished heavily (该严则严, 当宽则宽), so that a unification of both the social and legal effects can be achieved.[94]

In line with the policy of "combining leniency and severity", the criminal who commits a very serious crime with great social harm which should be given a heavy punishment or the death penalty by law, must receive a heavy punishment or the death penalty. The reasoning must closely follow the principle that serious crimes should be punished heavily by law.[95] For example, the Explanation emphasizes that it "adheres to the policy of 'combining leniency and severity', safeguards social fairness and justice, and maintains a tough attitude to and severely punishes offenders who

---

not used as the legal ground to deal with criminal cases but as guidance for understanding and interpreting criminal provisions. See 高铭暄 [GAO Mingxuan], *《刑法体现宽严相济刑事政策》[The Embodiment of the Criminal Policy of Combining Leniency and Severity in Criminal Law]*, available at: 人民网 [People Net] http://opinion.people.com.cn/n/2015/0828/c1003-27525830.html (Last visited: January 21st, 2024); Susan Trevaskes notes in her paper that "the policy of balancing leniency and severity is meant to traverse the entire gamut of criminal legislation, criminal justice practice, and criminal punishment in China". See also TREVASKES Susan, *The Shifting Sands of Punishment in China in the Era of 'Harmonious Society,* above no. 71, 335.

91 陈伟 [Chen Wei], *《刑事立法的政策导向与技术制衡》[On the Policy Orientation of Criminal Legislation and its Technical Checks and Balances],* 中国法学 [China Legal Science] 2013, No. 3, 123.

92 *《关于 < 中华人民共和国刑法修正案(九)(草案) > 的说明》[The Explanations for the Draft of the Ninth Amendment to Criminal Law of the People's Republic of China],* above no. 8.

93 See 田兴洪, 马长生 [TIAN Xinghong and MA Changsheng], *《"两极化刑事政策" 之理性辨思》[Rationally Analyzing the Bipolar Criminal Policy],* 湖南师范大学社会科学学报[Journal of Social Science of Hunan Normal University] 2010, No. 4, 71. However, some scholars do not consider it a bipolar criminal policy, and argue that the criminal policy of combining leniency and severity is very different from a bipolar criminal policy. Cf 黄华生 [HUANG Huasheng], *《两极化刑事政策之批判》[Criticizing the Bipolar Criminal Policy],* 法律科学 (西北政法学院学报) [Science of Law (Journal of Northwest University of Political Science and Law)] 2008, No. 6, 71.

94 See *《全国政法工作会议召开,贯彻宽严相济刑事政策》[The National Working Conference on Politics and Law; Implementing the Criminal Policy of Combining Leniency and Severity],* available at: 新浪网 [Sina Net]. http://news.sina.com.cn/c/2006-12-04/091010677430s.shtml. (Last visited: January 21st, 2024).

95 See *《最高人民法院关于贯彻宽严相济刑事政策的若干意见, (法发 [2010]9 号)》[Opinions of the Supreme People's Court on the Implementation of the Criminal Policy of Combining Leniency and Severity (No. 9, Legal Issue, 2010)]*, February 8th, 2010).

commit the serious crimes."[96] This is known by some scholars as the policy of "harsh punishment for serious crimes", and is criticized, because "in contemporary China, the inertia of a functional intention to control the serious crimes is still maintained in the Criminal Law."[97] Undeniably, being tough on serious crimes is necessary, and its temporary effect is also obvious because, in a certain sense, it generally emphasizes the deterrent effect of severe punishment, rather than prevention or education. The tough on crimes policy has not only been appreciated by China, but it has even been adopted by the USA and Canada in recent years.[98]

A punishment replacing the death penalty will be the harshest punishment measure after the death penalty has been completely repealed, and it should only be used for the most heinous crimes that could be punishable by immediate execution under the law,[99] and it should comply with the criminal policy of "combining leniency and severity". Consequently, it should basically have the function of controlling the most heinous crimes, so that it can satisfy the severity requirement of the criminal policy. However, it is different from the death penalty because it effectively protects human rights, and can achieve both justice and punishment aim. For some long time, the death penalty has been considered an important measure for lethal and serious crimes of violence, and only the death penalty can satisfy the victim and his or her family as well as the public expectations of social justice.[100] The death penalty plays an important role in maintaining social justice and achieving punishment aims for serious crimes among the wider public. Any punishment replacing the death penalty

---

[96] *《关于<中华人民共和国刑法修正案(九)(草案)>的说明》[The Explanations for the Draft of the Ninth Amendment to Criminal Law of the People's Republic of China],* above no. 8.

[97] 刘崇亮 [LIU Chongliang], *《"重重"刑罚观对监狱行刑的效果: 以刑法修正案(八)对刑罚结构的调整为分析视角》[The Effect of the 'Harsh Punishment for Serious Crimes' Doctrine on the Execution of Punishment in Prison: An Analysis on the Adjustment of the Punishment Structure in the Eighth Amendment to Criminal Law],* 法制与社会发展[Law and Social Development] 2013, No. 6, 135.

[98] Tough on crime rhetoric has dominated the political and criminal justice sphere for decades. See CANTY Aimée Tecla, *A Return to Balance: Federal Sentencing Reform After the 'Tough on Crime' Era',* Stetson Law Review, 2015, Vol. 44, No. 3, 895. The Harper Conservative government has implemented tough on crime policies in the past decade. See ZINGER Ivan, *Human Rights and Federal Corrections: A Commentary on a Decade of Tough on Crime Policies in Canada*, Canadian Journal of Criminal Justice, 2016, Vol. 58, No. 4, 610.

[99] According to Article 48 of the Criminal Law, the death penalty is only applied to a criminal who commits an extremely serious crime; in this sense, an alternative punishment should also only be used for these kinds of extremely serious crimes. See *《中华人民共和国刑法》[Criminal Law of the People's Republic of China],* Order No. 83, 14 March 1997, Article 48.

[100] Particularly for homicides, the victims' families and the public are strongly supportive of the death penalty, and their opinions have a great influence on the courts, as for example, in the cases of Yao Jianxin, or Li Changkui. In the former case, the criminal, Yao Jiaxin (药家鑫), intentionally killed a woman; and was finally sentenced to death; in the latter case, the criminal, Li Changkui (李昌奎), intentionally killed two people, and was finally sentenced to death after three changes of judgement. In these cases, the behavior of the criminals caused great public outrage, and the victims' families and the public gave strong support to the death penalty. See *药家鑫 [Yao Jiaxin], (2011) 西刑一初字第68号 [(2011 Xi the First Criminal Court First Trial. No. 68)*; *李昌奎 [LI Changkui](2010) 昭中刑一初字第52号 [(2010) Zhao intermediate Criminal Court First Trial. No. 52] (2010) 云高法终字第1314号 [(2010) Yun High Court Second Trial No. 1314].*

is, to a great extent, expected to have these social and legal effects.[101] In addition, in the policy of "combining leniency and severity", a rational punishment system is needed, and is considered essential for this policy.[102] Before the Eighth Amendment, some scholars pointed out that the punishment system has serious defects because the number of crimes punishable by death is too high, but incarceration is too light a punishment[103]; as a whole, the punishment system is considered a severe one. The Eighth and Ninth Amendments have already removed the death penalty from 22 crimes, and so the number of crimes punishable by death is, to a great extent, reduced. However, in judicial practice, the problem that the death penalty is too severe but the incarceration is too light is still obvious,[104] because the death penalty for these 22 crimes was seldom or never used in judicial practice and its abolition does not bring any substantive change to the judicial practice. So any punishment replacing the death penalty is expected to be able to deal effectively with these issues and contribute to a rational punishment system.

4.2.4 Public Opinion

In the judicial practice of China, regarding the state political regime and legal system, "death cases are generally politically sensitive and draw significant public attention"[105]; in terms of legislation, it is more obvious and significant that, "the abolition of the death penalty is merely a political option rather than a simple legal reform, and it cannot be carried out till a majority of the public favor abolition."[106] Even though

---

[101] The Explanations for the Draft of the Ninth Amendment to the Criminal Law of the People's Republic of China states that "crimes that are no longer subject to the death penalty can be heavily punished by strengthening the punishment if the perpetrators should be severely punished; in this way, the intensity of the whole punishment is not reduced and the stability of the social order can be guaranteed. See *《关于<中华人民共和国刑法修正案(九)(草案)>的说明》[The Explanations for the Draft of the Ninth Amendment to Criminal Law of the People's Republic of China]*, above no. 8.

[102] See 陈兴良 [CHEN Xingliang], *《宽严相济刑事政策研究》[On the Criminal Policy of Combining Leniency and Severity]*, 法学杂志[Law Science Magazine] 2006, No. 1, 22.

[103] See 贾成宽 [Jia Chengkuan], *《刑罚的结构性缺陷及其化解—以宽严相济刑事政策的刑法化为视角》[On the Structural Defects of Criminal Punishment and their Solution: From the Perspective of Criminal Legislation relating to the Criminal Policy of Combining Leniency and Severity]*, 甘肃社会科学 [Gansu Social Sciences] 2009, No. 3, 41.

[104] See *《关于<中华人民共和国刑法修正案(九)(草案)>的说明》[The Explanations for the Draft of the Ninth Amendment to Criminal Law of the People's Republic of China]*, above no. 8.

[105] YANG Jie, *The Development of China's Death Penalty Representation Guidelines: A Learning Model Based on the ABA Guidelines for the Appointment and Performance of Defense Counsel in Death Penalty Cases*, Hofstra Law Review, 2013, Vol. 42, No. 2, 594.

[106] 张远煌, 徐苗 [ZHANG Yuanhuang and XU Miao], *《揭开民意与死刑关系的面纱:从民意的实质看影响死刑控制进程的症结所在》[Lifting the Veil on the Relationship Between Public Opinion and the Death Penalty: Reviewing the Factors Impacting the Process of Death Penalty Control from the Perspective of Public Opinion]*, 刑法论丛[Criminal Law Review] 2012, No. 4, 162.

the Chinese government leaders do not have to face the political risk of losing control of the government if they express different opinions on the death penalty from the public, they do need to worry about the risk of "political suicide" if they completely abolish the death penalty without paying any attention to public demands,[107] especially since the CPC has launched a "mass line education campaign"[108] and made the construction of a Socialist rule of law country a strategic objective.[109] Given this, the social effect of sentencing is constantly emphasized in judicial practice. As a significant factor reflecting these social effects, "public opinion in individual cases has already become an important assessment factor for judicial decision-making."[110]

So far, the public does not have a general pro or contra position on abolition, but the public always expresses its own opinions with simple feelings, and can somehow reach a consensus on the use of the death penalty in individual capital cases, for instance, with capital cases which spark outrage. In cases like these, such the case of Yao Jiaxin, the public normally hope that the offenders are given the extreme penalty, i.e., the death penalty with immediate execution. With capital cases which provoke public compassion, such as the case of Deng Yujiao and the case of a twin sister killing her own mentally ill sister, the pubic express their compassion for the offenders and hope that they are given lighter punishments.[111] And these simple opinions have had a great influence on judicial judgments in some cases.[112] As for these simple public opinions, a scholar has classified them as follows: public opinion

---

[107] See赵军 [ZHAO Jun], *《死刑存废的民意维度:以组织卖淫罪可罚性观念的测量为中心》[Public Opinion on the Abolition of the Death Penalty: Measurement of Ideas about Guilt Relating to the Crime of Organizing Prostitution]*, 法学研究 [Chinese Journal of Law] 2015, No. 2, 26.

[108] *Officials Urged to Promote the 'Mass Line' Campaign*, available at: 中国共产党新闻 News of the Communist Party of China. http://english.cpc.people.com.cn/206972/206976/8329485.html. This "Mass Line" education campaign requires CPC officials and members to prioritize the interests of the people and persist in representing them and working on their behalf.

[109] *《中共中央关于全面推进依法治国若干重大问题的决定》[Decisions of the Central Committee of the Communist Party of China Concerning some Major Questions in Comprehensively Moving Forward in Governing the Country According to the Law]*, above no. 20. This Decision is designed to "guarantee the popular masses' participation in the judiciary; persist in people's justice for the people, rely on the people to move judicial fairness forward.

[110] 徐阳[XU Yang], *《"舆情再审":司法决策的困境与出路》["Introspecting Retrials by Public Opinion: the Dilemma and Solution of Judicial Decision-Making]*, 中国法学[China Legal Science] 2012, No. 2, 182.

[111] See generally吴百花 [WU Baihua], *《自媒体时代死刑适用该如何回应民意》 [How to Respond to Public Opinion by the Application of the Death Penalty in the We-Media Age]*, 广州市公安管理干部学院学报 [Journal of Guangzhou Police College] 2013, No. 3, 51.

[112] Regarding this argument, a research team found from an analysis of 217 capital cases that the question of whether or not public opinion influences the judgement in individual capital cases depends on the specific case. In some cases, public opinion on the death penalty should be integrated into the judicial judgement because it correctly and comprehensively reflects the factors which should concern the judge; but in other cases, it should be ignored. In addition, the opinions of the victims, their families and the public have a strong connection with the circumstances of the sentencing of cases. See袁彬, 王奉帅等 [YUAN Bin and WANG Fengshuai] etc., *《死刑个案民意的现实性考察:基于217起死刑个案的实证分析》[A Practical Investigation on Public Opinion on Death Penalty Case: Empirical Analysis on 217 Cases of the Death Penalty]*, 刑法论丛[Criminal Law Review] 2015, No. 3, 1.

in general seems to be opposed to the abolition of the death penalty on the former level, which is in striking contrast to the strong demand for abolition of the death penalty by legal scholars and social elites. However, public opinion seems to demand a certain degree of leniency and exemption from the death penalty for some specific cases under most circumstances on the latter level, although they may also demand the death sentence for some cases.[113]

Even though these opinions are quite varied, and they cannot be considered a general opinion favoring or opposing the abolition, this approach "has already deeply influenced and even decides on the issues of death penalty reform in China."[114] On one hand, they are closely connected to the reform process; on the other hand, they even give rationality and authority to the reform.[115] Obviously, in this sense, the option of the alternative punishment to the death penalty is also influenced by public opinion. Although there has been no authoritative and scientific survey on public opinion regarding death penalty reform, nor on the alternative punishment to the death penalty,[116] undeniably, the public in China has a generally negative attitude toward abolition of death penalty, which would inevitably influence the options for alternative punishment. However, given the social formation of China, as some scholars have pointed out, most citizens are not concerned with the theoretical issues of whether the death penalty is a deterrent or retribution; they pay more attention to

---

[113] See LU Jianping, *On the Application of the Death Penalty and Public Opinion*, Chinese Sociology and Anthropology, 2009, Vol. 41, No. 4, 66.

[114] 张明楷 [ZHANG Mingkai], *《刑法学者如何为削减死刑作贡献》[How Should Criminal Scholars Contribute to Reducing the Number of Crimes punishable by the Death Penalty?]*, 当代法学[Contemporary Law Review] 2005, Vol. 19, No. 1, 10.

[115] See 赵秉志, 张伟珂 [ZHAO Bingzhi and ZHANG Weike], *《略论死刑的民意引导:以慎用死刑为视角》[Brief Comments on the Guidance of Public Opinion on the Death Penalty from the Perspective of a Careful Use of the Death Penalty]*, 国家检察官学院学报 [Journal of the National Prosecutors College] 2013, Vol. 21, No. 4, 41.

[116] Thus far, there have been four typical surveys on the death penalty reform: the Law School of Wuhan University conducted a polling survey of judicial officials and others on death penalty reform in 2004; The Research Center for Contemporary China of Beijing University was entrusted by the Max Planck Institute for Foreign and International Criminal Law to conduct an opinion survey on death penalty reform in Beijing, Hubei and Guangdong from 2007 to 2008; Professor Yuan Bing, Beijing Normal University, conducted a questionnaire survey on death penalty reform in Beijing, Guangdong, Hebei, Jiangxi and Gansu in 2008; and Professor Zhang Huifang and her team conducted an opinion survey on the death penalty in Xi An City in 2009. Although, in general, the results of these surveys have a certain representativeness, they could not comprehensively reflect all citizens' opinions on death penalty reform because the range of respondents is limited and does not represent citizens in other parts of China, especially in country areas. These surveys include: 康均心[KANG Junxin], *《理想与现实:中国死刑制度报告》[The Ideals and Realities: A Report on the Death Penalty System in China]*, 中国人民公安大学出版社[People's Public Security University of China Press], Beijing, 2005, 2–4 and 91; 何荣功[HE Ronggong], *《当代中国死刑民意的现状与解构》[Contemporary Situation and Deconstruction of Chinese Public Opinion on the Death Penalty]*, 刑法论丛[Criminal Law Review] 2010, No. 3, 264; 袁彬[YUAN Bin], *《死刑民意及其内部冲突的调查与分析》[Public Opinion on the Death Penalty and Its Internal Conflicts: An Investigation and Analysis]*, 法学[Legal Science] 2009, No. 1, 99; 张惠芳, 何小俊[ZHANG Huifang and HE Xiaojun], *《死刑民意调查研究》[Survey Report on the Death Penalty]*, 时代法学[Present Day Law Science] 2011, Vol. 9, No. 4, 59.

their environment and daily lives, because they think theoretical issues are not practical and are removed from their daily needs.[117] After abolition, if the government cannot protect their basic security and has no effective measure to control the rampant violent crime which causes serious harm to life and property, and victims and their families cannot get effective judicial remedy, most citizens will oppose abolition out of natural thoughts of revenge and self-defense. The concepts of humanity and mercy cannot, to any great extent, effectively overcome their demand for vengeance and longing for security. Most people still have faith in the deterrent and vengeance aspects of the death penalty.[118] The psychological effects of a lack of a sense of security and reliance on the death penalty will deeply influence public opinion regarding alternative punishments to it.

4.2.5 Political Concerns

As regards the relationship between law and politics, there are three characteristics of this relationship, namely politics as a goal, as a means or as an obstacle.[119] As a goal, politics defines certain predominantly legal values or institutions as its goal, and they are also the same as the values or institutions of the law; as a means, the law exists merely to fulfill certain political interests; as an obstacle, law is deemed an obstacle on the way toward the realization of certain political goals.[120] In the light of the legal development of contemporary China, the law, to a great extent, plays a key role as a means to fulfill political interests; this is particularly true for the criminal law, which, as a consequence, is determined by the country's special political regime.

According to the Preamble of the Constitution of China, the country is a one-party state, and the system is one of multiparty cooperation and political consultation led

---

[117] See黎宏 [LI Hong],《刑法学》*[Criminal Law]*, 法律出版社 [Law Press. China], Beijing, 2012, 336–337.

[118] For example, there was a rape and murder case in Qing Yang City, Gansu Province. The convict was sentenced to immediate execution for the crime of acting indecently against a child of 14 years' old and murder in the first instance, but the local Higher People's Court remanded him for retrial and the retrial court then imposed the death penalty with reprieve. Reacting to the retrial sentence, the local People's Procuratorate lodged a counterclaim against this judgement because the sentencing was so light that the sentence was not proportionate and did not give justice; the victim's family was not satisfied it and they hoped the convict would be sentenced to immediate execution, so that the victim could be given a just judgement for her death. See *《保安缓刑期内残杀14岁女孩仅判死缓,检方抗诉》[A Security Man is only Sentenced to the Death Penalty with Reprieve for the Crime of Murdering A Girl of 14 Years' Old in the Probation Period for Another Punishment, the Procuratorate Raises a Counterclaim]*, available at: 凤凰网 [IFeng] http://news.ifeng.com/a/20170116/50581315_0.shtml (Last visited: January 21st, 2024). This is only one example, and in fact, we can see many similar cases and they are frequently reported on the internet.

[119] CERAR Miro, *The Relationship between Law and Politics*, Annual Survey of International &Comparative Law, 2009, Vol. 15, No. 1, 19–41.

[120] Ibid.

by the CPC.[121] The CPC does not only play a political leadership role, but also directs legislation and law enforcement, and its view or standpoint is considered the national will and so becomes law.[122] Party-led legislation is a system with Chinese characteristics. In accordance with the Constitution of the CPC, "leadership by the Party means mainly political, ideological and organizational leadership".[123] As an important branch of the law, with the most mandatory characteristics, the criminal law, "serving as a political tool, is always highly praised,"[124] and is led by the Party and implements the Party's ruling policies and will. The penalty system, playing an important role in this, is the embodiment of this kind of mandatory nature, and is also the result of political expediency; in particular, the death penalty system "is mainly caused by the excessive politicization of the criminal law."[125] In a situation in which the crime of embezzlement and bribery is still punishable by death under Article 383 (3) of Criminal Law, stipulating LWOR for this crime is another result of political considerations.[126] On one hand, the anti-corruption initiative is now a serious political campaign in China.[127] Upon taking office in late 2012, China's President, Xi Jinping, "vowed to crack down on both 'tigers and flies' -powerful leaders and lowly bureaucrats—in his campaign against corruption and petty officialdom",[128] "with a

---

[121] *《中华人民共和国宪法》[Constitution of the People's Republic of China]*, 2004.

[122] See *《中共中央关于全面推进依法治国若干重大问题的决定》[The CCP Central Committee Decision Concerning Some Major Questions in Comprehensively Moving Government of the Country According to the Law Forward (hereinafter abbreviated to CCP-CDC)]*,above no. 20; 刘家征 [LIU Jiazheng], above no. 23.

[123] *《中国共产党章程》[Constitution of the Communist Party of China]*, 2012.

[124] 刘远 [LIU Yuan], above no. 7, 54–55.

[125] Ibid., 54.

[126] In this regard, many Chinese scholars have criticized the fact that life imprisonment without release for the crime is a political option, or emotional legislation. See 任重远 [REN Zhongyuan], *《刑法修正案九: 嫖宿幼女罪没了,终身监禁来了》[The Ninth Amendment to Criminal Law: the Crime of Prostitution Involving a Girl under the Age of 14 is Abolished and Life Imprisonment without Possibility of Release is Provided]*, available at: 大众数字报[Public Statistics News], Available at: http://paper.dzwww.com/xcb/data/20150829/html/3/content_1.html (Last visited: January 21st, 2024). In this interview, Professor Chu Huaizhi said that "it (life imprisonment without release) chiefly reflects political attitudes." See also 刘宪权 [LIU Xianquan], *《刑事立法应力戒情绪—以 < 刑法修正案(九) > 为视角》[Criminal Legislation Should Strictly Avoid Emotion: From the Perspective of the Ninth Amendment]*, 法学评论 [Law Review] 2016, No. 1, 86. In this paper, the author pointed out that "it [the government] may be 'forced' by the people to enact legislation inappropriately and emotionally in order to severely punish corruption officers.

[127] 吴建雄 [WU Jianxiong], *《怎样看待近几年的"高压反腐"》[How to View the 'Heavy Anti-corruption' of Recent Years]*, available at: 中国共产党新闻网[Communist Party of China's News Net] http://theory.people.com.cn/n1/2016/0225/c143844-28150603.html (Last visited: January 21st, 2024); See also 郑永年[ZHENG Yongnian], *《运动式反腐败符合政治理性》[The Campaign-style of Anti-corruption is Appropriate to Political Rationality]*, available at: 凤凰网[Ifeng Net] http://news.ifeng.com/exclusive/lecture/special/zhengyongnian2/ (Last visited: January 21st, 2024).

[128] *Xi Jinping Vows to Fight 'Tigers' and 'Flies' in Anti-Corruption Drive*, available at: https://www.theguardian.com/world/2013/jan/22/xi-jinping-tigers-flies-corruption (Last visited: January 21st, 2024).

determination to inflict heavy punishment for them in this special time".[129] In this political context, LWOR thus has political reasons for its existence. The Deputy Director of the Criminal Law Office of the NPC Standing Committee, Zang Tiewei, also noted that "it (LWOR) is primarily designed for the present situation of anti-corruption, [based] upon the Mass's requirements… and to implement the relative requirements of the central government."[130] And the then vice-president of SPC, Shen Deyong, also said that "it fully reflects the Party Central Committee's distinct attitude toward, and steadfast determination to severely punish, corruption crimes according to the law."[131] On the other hand, The *White Paper of Judicial Reform in China* emphasizes that "[i]t (judicial reform) sticks to the line of relying on the people, strives to meet their expectations, tackles problems of particular concern to the people, and subjects itself to their supervision and examination"[132]; LWOR meets the people's requirements regarding the anti-corruption initiative. One of the legislators, while discussing the Ninth Amendment (draft) said that the fact that a corrupt official can be released early "is one of the basic reasons why the people are not satisfied with the results of anti-corruption, and it also gives these corruption officials a chance of 'escape from prison.'"[133] All in all, the relationship between politics and law has always existed since the founding of New China in 1949, and the instrumentalism of criminal law, serving as the regulatory tool of politics, is simply manifest in a new form. LWOR is an obvious consequence of the new instrumentalism.

4.3 The Issues of Alternative to the Death Penalty in Other States

The repeal of the death penalty has already become a global tide and more and more states or territories are abolishing the death penal de facto *and de jure*, or restricting the use of death penalty in judicial practice. According to the Amnesty International report, as for December 31, 2015, 102 states had abolished the death penalty for

---

[129] 吴建雄[WU Jianxiong], above no. 511.

[130] 李婧, 刘茸[LI Jing and LIU Rong], *《臧铁伟:终身监禁不是新刑种 适用于重特大贪污受贿犯罪》[Zang Tiewei: Life Imprisonment without Possibility of Release is not a New Penalty Type, and it is Imposed for the Serious Crime of Embezzlement and Bribery]*, available at:人民网-中国人大新闻网[People Net and National People's Congress Net], available at: http://npc.people.com.cn/n/2015/0829/c14576-27531201.html (Last visited: January 21st, 2024).

[131] *《最高法谈对贪官增设终身监禁:改变无期名不副实现象》[The Supreme People's Court Talking about Adding Life Imprisonment without Possibility of Release for Corrupt Officers: Changes in the Phenomenon of Life Imprisonment are Changes in Name rather than in Reality]*, available at:凤凰网[ifeng Net] http://news.ifeng.com/a/20151105/46124190_0.shtml (Last visited: January 21st, 2024).

[132] *《< 中国的司法改革 > 白皮书》[The White Paper on Judicial Reform in China]*, above no. 4.

[133] *《专家谈刑法修正案(九):终身监禁让巨贪把牢底坐穿》[Experts Discussing the Ninth Amendment to the Criminal Law: Life Imprisonment without Possibility of Release: Let the Arch Corrupt Official Rot in Detention]*, available at: 中国新闻网[China's News Net]. http://www.chinanews.com/ll/2015/09-08/7510951.shtml (Last visited: January 21st, 2024).

all crimes and 140 states had totally abolished the death penalty in law or practice.[134]There are fewer retentionist than abolitionist states, and there are 58 states[135] which are also improving their national legal system to repeal capital punishment or restrict the use of it, so as to protect human rights. In this international context, life imprisonment is upgraded to the maximum punishment in most abolitionist states, and is also in general the best option for most retentionist states intending to replace death penalty. This section will explore the alternative punishment to death penalty in the abolitionist states, focusing on European states, and potential alternative punishment in some retentionist states, taking India, Japan and USA an example.

4.3.1 The Alternative Punishment to the Death Penalty in Abolitionist States: The European Perspective

The ECHR plays an important role in the EU and its member states, creating legal obligations under international law which are also considered elements of European states' domestic legal systems. So, the ECHR and its case law can be directly applied by the national court or by the ECtHR. Article 3 of the ECHR is one of the significant provisions protecting convicted people; it prohibits torture, inhuman and degrading treatment and punishment, and provides a framework in which the EU holds a strong and principled position against the death penalty, as it has not been shown in any way to act as a deterrent to crime as it is cruel and inhuman.[136] Life imprisonment is today the most severe punishment measure as an alternative punishment to death penalty in the EU member states' penal systems. There are now three types of life imprisonment in European states. The first is the long-term sentence. In fact, a long-term sentence is not the common understanding of life imprisonment, which, although it "is privative of freedom, ... does not have a temporary character as imprisonment ..., but a perpetual one."[137] States which only have long term sentences include Portugal—where the maximum imprisonment is 25 years,[138] Norway—where the maximum is 21 years,[139] and Spain—where the maximum is 40 years.[140] These states' criminal codes do not stipulate "life imprisonment" or provide that "the offender, who is

---

[134] Amnesty International Global Report*: Death Sentences and Executions in 2015*, Index: ACT 50/348/2016)", 65.

[135] Ibid.

[136] *World and Europe Day against the Death Penalty,* available at: *European Union External Action* https://eeas.europa.eu/headquarters/headquarters-homepage/13174/world-and-europe-day-against-death-penalty_en (Last visited: January 21st, 2024).

[137] FRÎNTU Viorica-Mihaela, *Pedeapsa Detenţiunii Pe Viaţă (Life Imprisonment Penalty)*, Annals of the Constantin Brancusi University—Juridical Sciences Series, 2013, No. 4, 94–95.

[138] *The Portuguese Criminal Code, Legislative Decree n. 4/2003 of November 18, 2003,* Article 41.

[139] *The Norway General Civil Penal Code, Act of 22 May 1902 No. 10,* with subsequent amendments, Act of 21 December 2005, No. 131, Section 17.

[140] *The Criminal Code of the Kingdom of Spain, ORGANI ACT 10/1995, 2010,* Article 76.

sentenced to life imprisonment, may be released on parole after he has served a fixed term", and the number of these states is very low. Most European states' criminal law stipulates life imprisonment with a possibility of parole after the offender has served a fixed-period. These include Germany, Austria, Luxemburg, and Switzerland, where the offender has to serve at least 15 years; and the Czech Republic, Finland, Romania and Turkey, where the offender has to serve at least 20 years. However, there are some states' or regions' criminal law which stipulates life imprisonment without parole, including Hungary,[141] the Netherlands, and the United Kingdom.[142] Therefore, the number of states with Life imprisonment without parole or whole-life sentences is also rare; the majority of European states have life imprisonment with parole.

It seems like that the direction of European states' life imprisonment policies has already been explicitly indicated by the case-law of the ECtHR and Article 3 of the ECHR. Article 3 prohibits torture and inhuman treatment or ill-treatment. The Human Rights Handbooks state that 'duration' is one of the factors referred to when discussing ill-treatment.[143] This factor, to a great extent, rejects life imprisonment without parole because it puts the offender in prison for the rest of his life without any hope of rehabilitation, and it "shares some characteristics with death sentences because both alter the offender's life by a forfeiture that is irrevocable."[144] In the case of Öcalan v. Turkey, the ECtHR commented on:

> Life imprisonment without any possibility of conditional release ... [finding that], in the absence of any review mechanism, the life prison sentence imposed on the applicant constituted an irreducible sentence that amounted to inhuman treatment.[145]

The case-law of the ECtHR, to a great extent, represents the attitude of the EU toward life imprisonment, i.e. that LWOP should be rejected and abolished *de jure* and in practice, and as regards the whole life sentence, the relevant state was prompted by the ECtHR's case-law to establish a review system of this form of punishment, such as was the case in László Magyar v. Hungary.[146] Abolition of the death penalty first occurred in Europe, as did the adoption of long-term imprisonment as the replacement for capital punishment (for example, Portugal adopted long term imprisonment as an alternative to the death penalty with the prison reforms of Sampaio e Melo in 1884). Having led the trend in the reform of the death penalty, Europe is still takes a global lead in life imprisonment reform.

---

[141] According to the Criminal Code of Hungary, Section 42, the court shall specify the earliest date for eligibility for parole, or shall preclude any eligibility for parole. See *Criminal Code of Hungary, Act C of 2012,* Section 42. See also generally, MADAI Sándor, above no. 323, 371.

[142] *The Criminal Justice Act 2003 (UK) c44,* Article 273.

[143] REIDY Aisling, *The Prohibition of Torture: A Guide to the Implementation of Article 3 of the European Convention on Human Rights*, Human Rights Handbooks, 2003, No. 1, 12.

[144] NELLIS Ashley, above no. 373, 455.

[145] *Öcalan v. Turkey* [2005] IV (European Court HR, Grand Chamber, Application No. 46221/99, May 12, 2005).

[146] *László Magyar v. Hungary* [2014] (European Court HR, Chamber, Application No. 73593/10, May 20, 2014).

4.3.2 The Potential Alternative Punishment to the Death Penalty in Retentionist States: Taking India, Japan and the United States as Examples

India is one of the world's retentionist states. In the Report of the Law Commission of India, Indian legislators and the government are urged to develop its national law to abolish the death penalty.[147] In accordance with this report, the Supreme Court states that the death penalty system operated in an arbitrary fashion, which means the current method of application of the death penalty has to end, and the death penalty should not be imposed save in the rarest of cases when the alternative option is unquestionably foreclosed; and it also states that one of the principles guiding judicial discretion in determining the appropriate sentence is that life imprisonment is the rule, and the death penalty is the exception.[148] To a great extent, it can be said that life imprisonment has functioned as an alternative punishment to death penalty in Indian judicial practice. In the Criminal Justice Reform of India, the law commission states that the "time is not ripe for abolition of death sentencing; Section 354(3) Cr.P.C. makes imprisonment for life the normal punishment."[149] In addition, in this Report, as the alternative punishment to the death penalty, the Law Committee considers that.

> It is desirable to prescribe a punishment higher than that of imprisonment for life and lower than the death penalty; Section 53 of the Indian Penal Code [should] be suitably amended to include 'imprisonment for life without commutation or remission' as one of the punishments.[150]

Life imprisonment is the second most severe punishment after death, according to Section 53 of the Indian Penal Code, and it is called imprisonment for life,[151] and "is now substituted for transportation and it means rigorous imprisonment for life", which means imprisonment till the end of life in prison.[152] In Indian judicial practice, life imprisonment is an option for the judge who can choose between the death penalty and life imprisonment, for example, in the case of Ediga Anamma vs. State of Andhra Pradesh.[153]

"Against the international backdrop of declining use, Japan is an outlier in retaining the death penalty."[154] "In Japan, as of 2012, 19 crimes are eligible for capital

---

[147] Law Commission of India Report No. 262. *The Death Penalty, August 2015. D.O. No. 6(3)263/2014-LC(LS).*

[148] Ibid., 173.

[149] Ministry of Home Affairs of Government of India, *Committee on Reforms of Criminal Justice System Report*, Vol. I, March 2003, 169.

[150] Ibid., 176.

[151] *The Indian Penal Code, Act No. 45 of 1860 1*, Section 53.

[152] YADAV Mukesh, *Life Imprisonment: Meaning and Interpretation of Law*, Journal of Indian Academy of Forensic Medicine, 2007, Vol. 29, No. 2, 54.

[153] *Ediga Anamma vs. State of Andhra Pradesh*, Equivalent citations: 1974 AIR 799, 1974 SCR (3) 329.

[154] AMBLER Leah, above no. 274, 5.

punishment,"[155] although in practice the death penalty is only imposed for offenses involving murder.[156] Regarding abolition of the death penalty in Japan, a Japanese government survey in 2009 reported that "86% of respondents favored retention,"[157] although the Japanese Supreme Court is already aware that "the abolition of the death penalty is the domain of policy and requires a legislative modification."[158] According to Articles 12 and 13 of the Penal Code of Japan, there are two kinds of imprisonment for life, namely, imprisonment for life with work and imprisonment for life without work, and the former is heavier than the latter in terms of gravity. Both of them can be reduced to a definite term imprisonment of a maximum of 30 years.[159] However, in the Japanese abolitionist movement, some have called for a moratorium or even for a compromise, with the introduction of a law replacing the death penalty with life imprisonment without parole,[160] although this is only now beginning to shape the debate.

"In the West, the US is described as 'exceptional' in its reluctance to abolish the death penalty; given that it is a rich and powerful democracy."[161] Currently, in the United States of America, there are 31 states with the death penalty, but 19 states and the District of Columbia have already abolished the death penalty.[162] As for life imprisonment, there are 31 states with the death penalty offering life imprisonment without parole and 18 non-death penalty states and the District of Columbia offering life without parole.[163] In addition, there are other offenders sentenced to extremely long specific terms of imprisonment which are so long that the sentence is a de facto life sentence. In the USA, "life imprisonment without parole is often touted as the humane alternative to the death penalty."[164] The United States is also on

---

155 The Death Penalty Project, *The Death Penalty in Japan: A Report on Japan's Legal Obligations under the International Convention on Civil and Political Rights and an Assessment of Public Attitudes to Capital Punishment*, available at: http://www.deathpenaltyproject.org/wp-content/uploads/2013/03/DPP-Japan-report.pdf (Last visited: January 21st, 2024).

156 TAGUSARI Maiko, *Death Penalty in Japan*, East Asian Law Journal, 2010, Vol. 1, No. 2, 94.

157 The Death Penalty Project, *The Death Penalty in Japan: A Report on Japan's Legal Obligations under the International Convention on Civil and Political Rights and an Assessment of Public Attitudes to Capital Punishment*, above no. 539.

158 International Federation for Human Rights, *The Death Penalty in Japan: The Law of Silence*, available at: https://www.fidh.org/IMG/pdf/japon505a2008.pdf (Last visited: January 21st, 2024).

159 *Penal Code of Japan, Act No. 45 of April 24, 1907*, Articles. 12 and 13.

160 The Death Penalty Project, *The Death Penalty in Japan: A Report on Japan's Legal Obligations under the International Convention on Civil and Political Rights and an Assessment of Public Attitudes to Capital Punishment*, above no. 539.

161 HOYLE Carolyn, *Review Essay: The Death Penalty in Japan: Will the Public Tolerate Abolition?* by Mai Sato (Springer Press, 2013), available at: Faculty of Law of University of Oxford https://www.law.ox.ac.uk/centres-institutes/centre-criminology/blog/2014/01/death-penalty-japan (Last visited: January 22nd, 2024).

162 *States with and without the Death Penalty*, available at: Death Penalty Information Center http://www.deathpenaltyinfo.org/states-and-without-death-penalty (Last visited: January 22nd, 2024).

163 *Life without Parole*, available at: Death Penalty Information Center http://www.deathpenaltyinfo.org/life-without-parole#States (Last visited: January 22nd, 2024).

164 NELLIS Ashley, above no. 373, 440.

course to repeal the death penalty and using "Life imprisonment without parole as an alternative to the death penalty."[165] However, some American scholars have already become aware of the problems of Life imprisonment without parole and are criticizing it.[166]

4.4 Conclusion

The issue of the alternative punishment to the death penalty is the core and also the main topic of this book. Due to the differences of the research approaches and habits of thought, Chinese scholars would normally prefer to start their research with a discussion of the notion of the alternative to the death penalty, which Western scholars seldom do. In the notion of the alternative punishment to the death penalty, there are two main arguments, i.e., a judicial alternative punishment to the death penalty and a legislative alternative. As to the former, some scholars argue that the alternative punishment to the death penalty should refer to the kind of punishment which could be used to replace the death penalty with immediate execution; but for the latter, scholars believe that the alternative punishment to the death penalty refers to a punishment replacing the death penalty for a crime that has already been removed from the list of the most heinous crimes punishable by death under the law. Both of these two arguments are based on the aim of reducing the use of the death penalty. However, the judicial argument is based on the fact that the death penalty is still stipulated in the criminal law and applicable in the judicial practice; in this case, the argument is about controlling or reducing the use of the death penalty rather than abolishing it; therefore, this book disagrees with this argument, but tends to agree with the argument of a legislative alternative punishment. The alternative punishment to the death penalty should be the punishment that replaces the death penalty for the most heinous crimes, which should be the most serious violent and lethal crimes. After clarifying the notion of the alternative punishment to the death penalty, we need to explore the potential factors that influence the punishment options to replace the death penalty. Actually, in China, the factors influencing punishment options to replace the death penalty are varied. However, all of these factors should be understood on the basis of Chinese realities, in particular the special political regime, culture and social development. The book focuses on four factors, i.e., human rights, the ideas behind the penalty, criminal policy, public opinion, and political concerns in terms of the anti-corruption campaign. Human rights is the most important factor influencing punishment options to replace the death penalty, and it can be said that

---

165 BERRY William W. III, above no. 381, 1061.

166 These include NELLIS Ashley, *Tinkering with Life: A Look at the Inappropriateness of Life without Parole as an Alternative to the Death Penalty*, University of Miami Law Review 2013, Vol. 67, No. 2; BERRY William W. III, above no. 381; LIEBMAN James S., *Opting for Real Death Penalty Reform*, Ohio State Law Journal, 2002, Vol. 63, No. 1, 315–342; LERNER Craig S., *Life without Parole as a Conflicted Punishment*, Wake Forest Law Review, 2013, Vol. 48, 1101–1171, and so on.

human rights has pushed the abolition of the death penalty forward in the world and now it also influences the punishment options to replace the death penalty in the retentionist states, and influences the imprisonment penalty reform in the abolitionist states. As for China, because of its special political regime, the CPC's views on human rights play a dominant role throughout the country, and have a great influence on all aspects of life. The development of human rights has a very short history in China; the CPC admits and accepts human rights, although focus is given to different aspects of these rights. The CPC always emphasizes that national development and stability are guarantees of all citizens' human rights, and consequently, protecting the majority of citizens' human rights and the people's right to subsistence and development are always the CPC's priority. However, the development and changes in the CPC's views on human rights will give correct guidance to China's legislation to choose the right punishment to replace the death penalty. The second important factor is the ideas behind the penalty, which are analyzed from the perspective of historic culture and society, as well as the political factors. The ideas behind the penalty mainly include the traditional concept of the penalty system, i.e., the foundation culture and philosophical thinking on the penalty, and the position of the nation-state regarding the penalty, i.e., China's penal system has always had a very strong tendency towards, and obvious characteristics of, the representation of state interests and regime supremacy. The third important influencing factor is the criminal policy, which plays a crucial role in criminal legislation and judicial practice. "Combining leniency and severity" is the current policy, and will greatly influence the potential punishment option to replace the death penalty for the most heinous crimes, so that it can keep the severe punishment for serious crimes. Public opinion is the fourth most important factor influencing the potential punishment option to replace the death penalty. However, so far there has been no exact social survey on the alternative punishment to the death penalty, only a few surveys on death penalty reform. In these surveys, most respondents support the death penalty. In this case, public opinion seems to present a great challenge to abolition and to the punishment option to replace the death penalty. Finally, a new factor which is found in the Ninth Amendment is the particular political concern related to corruption crimes. The fact that LWOR is stipulated for corruption crimes is mainly caused by political concerns in the context of anti-corruption campaigns.

After exploring the issues of the alternative punishment to the death penalty in China, this book looks to other states for guidance by analyzing the same issues in the abolitionist states and retentionist states. Most abolitionist states have adopted LWPR as the punishment option to replace the death penalty, and some of these states have already abolished life imprisonment, leaving only long-term imprisonment as the maximum punishment in their penalty system. In some retentionist states, there is a debate about the abolition of the death penalty, and some propose to adopt LWPR as the punishment to replace the death penalty, although some of them support LWOR as the punishment to replace the death penalty.

Chapter 5
General Issues Concerning Life Imprisonment

Abstract This chapter will explore issues surrounding life imprisonment. These include the notion of life imprisonment, i.e., what life imprisonment is. The notion of life imprisonment can refer to a penal measure imprisoning the inmate for a certain crime for the rest of the inmate's life, or until he or she is allowed to be released by law. However, only in a case in which the convict is imprisoned for the rest of his or her life, such as occurs with life imprisonment without possibility of release (hereinafter: LWOR), can this be termed life imprisonment in the real sense of the term; in a case in which the convict is sentenced to life imprisonment but will be released after a certain time on parole or commutation or other arrangement, life imprisonment is, in fact, a kind of indefinite-term imprisonment or long-term imprisonment, and is, by its very nature, indeterminate. Following this, this chapter will explore the characteristics of life imprisonment, which include lengthy incarceration, and where its severity ranks only second to the death penalty, and when it is only used for the most serious crimes. Next, the chapter will analyse the forms of life imprisonment, which include life imprisonment without release and with the possibility of release, life imprisonment with work and without work, as well as mandatory life imprisonment and discretionary life imprisonment. This chapter will also explore the effects of life imprisonment, which include the effects on the inmate, on the victims and on the public. Following this, the chapter will analyse the life imprisonment system in China and various other countries, including some abolitionist European Union (hereinafter: EU) member states, in retentionist states such as Japan and Singapore, and also long term imprisonment in Norway and Portugal. This discussion will include the prevalence of life imprisonment (or long-term imprisonment) in the related states' Criminal Codes (or Penal Codes), the conditions for passing a sentence of life imprisonment (or long-term imprisonment), and the termination mechanisms for life imprisonment (or long-term imprisonment). In addition, this chapter will focus on the international documents regarding life imprisonment.

G. Huang, *On the Alternative Punishment to the Death Penalty in China*,
https://doi.org/10.1007/978-981-97-1627-2_5

5.1 The Notion of Life Imprisonment

In Chinese the term life imprisonment (Wuqi Tuxing, 无期徒刑); semantically, "wuqi (无期)", means "indefinite term"; however, according to the official translation of the Criminal Law of China, it is "life imprisonment"[1]). In English it is also referred to as a lifelong sentence,[2] a life sentence, lifelong imprisonment,[3] lifelong incarceration,[4] or life incarceration. The term refers to a kind of severe punishment widely and generally used by many countries around the world. However, "the term of 'life imprisonment' has divergent meanings in various countries."[5] Some Western scholars argue that "it consists in the convict's deprivation of freedom for the rest of his life".[6] According to the Wikipedia website, "life imprisonment is any sentence of imprisonment for a crime under which convicted persons are to remain in prison for the rest of their lives or until paroled."[7] Some Chinese scholars have tried to explain the notion of life imprisonment based on its semantics and argued that, in Chinese, "wuqi (无期)" means that the time is indeterminate, and "tuxing (徒刑)" refers to a punishment that forces the inmate to work; consequently, life imprisonment is a kind of "punishment without definite duration of time or forever, under which the inmates are compelled to work".[8]

However, in order to make the notion of life imprisonment clear, it cannot be defined according to semantics, but rather on the basis of criminal laws as legal documents. Therefore, the provisions of some states will be taken as examples in the following paragraph. The Austrian Penal Code provides that "life imprisonment is a period of indefinite detention, but the inmate can be eligible for parole if he or she

---

[1] The Legislative Affairs Office of the State Council of the People's Republic of China, "Laws and Regulations of the People's Republic of China: Criminal Law, China Legal Publishing House, 2011, 14. For the purpose of this paper, however, an indefinite term of imprisonment implies life imprisonment. For example, it imposes long-term determinate sentences that are referred to as "life imprisonment". See The Crime Prevention and Criminal Justice Branch of United Nations Office in Vienna, *Life imprisonment*, ST/CSDHA/24, 1994, 1.

[2] See the *Criminal Code of the Kingdom of Netherlands, Act of 3 March 1881,* amended in 2012, Section 10 paragraph 3.

[3] See the *General Penal Code of Iceland, 1940 No. 19* (12 February), 1.44/2015 (took effect 2 July 2015), Article 100a.

[4] See the *Criminal Code of the Swiss Confederation of 21 December 1937* (Status as of 1 October 2016), Article 64, paragraph 1bis.

[5] The Crime Prevention and Criminal Justice Branch of United Nations Office at Vienna, *Life Imprisonment*, ST/CSHDA/24, Vienna, 1994, 1.

[6] FRÎNTU Viorica-Mihaela, above no. 521, 94. According to the Criminal Code of the Republic of Romania, life imprisonment consists of deprivation of freedom for an indeterminate duration of time and shall be served according to the Law on the Service of Penalties. See the Criminal Code of the Republic of Romania, LAW # 286 of 17 July 2009, in force as of 12 November 2012, Article 56.

[7] *Life Imprisonment*, available at: https://en.wikipedia.org/wiki/Life_imprisonment (Last visited: January 22nd, 2024).

[8] See 张秀玲 [ZHANG Xiuling], *《无期徒刑研究》[On Life Imprisonment],* 吉林大学博士论文 [Ph.D. Dissertation, Jilin University], 2010, 7.

satisfies requirements stipulated by the law"[9]; the Criminal Code of the Republic of Bulgaria provides that imprisonment for life shall be the compulsory isolation of a convict for the remaining portion of the convict's life at penitentiary institutions to serve a punishment by deprivation of liberty[10]; according to the Criminal Code of Cyprus, life imprisonment is for the remainder of the biological existence of the convicted person and not for twenty years[11]; the Hungarian Criminal Code provides that life imprisonment shall be served in a penitentiary, and when deciding to impose it, the court shall specify the earliest date of eligibility for parole, or shall preclude any eligibility for parole[12]; the Penal Code of Lithuania provides that convicted persons shall serve the penalty of life imprisonment in a prison, but may be transferred to a house of correction after serving 10 years imprisonment[13]; in Sweden, "life imprisonment is an indeterminate sentence which can theoretically last for the remainder of a person's nature life, but it may be commuted to fixed term imprisonment."[14] The above examples show various European states' provisions on life imprisonment. We also need to take some Asian states as examples, i.e., under the Penal Code of Singapore, imprisonment for life "in relation to any prescribed punishment means imprisonment for the duration of a person's natural life"[15]; in the Penal Code of Japan there is no any special clause to provide the notion of life imprisonment like that provided in the Penal Code of Singapore, but two types of imprisonment for life are provided, i.e. imprisonment for life with work and imprisonment for life without work[16]; similarly, the Criminal Law of China does not explicitly explain what life imprisonment is in the relevant provision, but it provides that "any criminal who is sentenced to life imprisonment shall serve his sentence in prison or another place for the execution [of the sentence]; anyone who is able to work shall do so to accept education and reform through labour"[17]; the Penal Code of Vietnam provides that

---

[9] The *Criminal Code of Republic of Austria (Strafgesetzbuch, StGB),* as promulgated on 13 November 1998 (Federal Law Gazette I, p. 945, p. 3322), Section 57 (a) 1.

[10] The *Criminal Code of the Republic of Bulgaria, No. 26/02.04.1968,* in force as of 01.05.1968, last amendment SG No. 32/27.04.2010, in force as of 28.05.2010, Article 38a.

[11] *KAFKARIS v. CYPRUS (Application no. 21906/04), 12 February 2008,* available at: http://hudoc.echr.coe.int/eng#{"itemid":["001-85019"]} (Last visited: January 22nd, 2024).

[12] See the *Criminal Code of Hungary, Act C of 2012,* promulgated on 13 July 2012, Section 41 and 42.

[13] *Penal Code of the Republic of Lithuania, 26 September 2000 No. VIII-1968,* Amended on 11th February 2010-No. XI-677, Article 51(3).

[14] *Life Imprisonment of Children in the European Union,* available at: Child Rights International Network https://www.crin.org/en/home/campaigns/inhuman-sentencing/problem/life-imprisonment/life-imprisonment-children-europe. (Last visited: January 22nd, 2024).

[15] *The Statutes of the Republic of Singapore: Penal Code (Chapter 224),* Original Enactment: Ordinance 4 of 1871, Revised Edition 2008, Article 54.

[16] See the *Penal Code of Japan, Act No. 45 of April 24, 1907 (日本国刑法, 明治四十年四月二十四日法律第四十五)*, the latest version is amended by Act No. 54 of June 3, 2016 (最終改正: 平成二八年六月三日法律第五四号), Article 12 and 13, available at: http://law.e-gov.go.jp/htmldata/M40/M40HO045.html (Last visited: January 22nd, 2024).

[17] *《中华人民共和国刑法》[Criminal Law of the People's Republic of China]*, Order No. 83, *2015*, Article 46.

"life imprisonment is the penalty of indefinite imprisonment applicable to persons who commit particularly serious crimes, but not so as to warrant being sentenced to death."[18] According to the Indian Penal Code, imprisonment for life is construed as "transportation for life".[19] Even though we cannot find a clause providing for life imprisonment in the Criminal Code of the USA as in other states' codes, we know that there is life imprisonment without possibility of parole in the criminal justice system in America, and the convict will be imprisoned in prison or jail for the rest of his or her life.

Based upon the brief summary above on the life imprisonment clauses provided in some states' Criminal Laws or Penal Codes, as the argument made by the Crime Prevention and Criminal Justice Branch of United Nations points out, "the term 'life imprisonment' has divergent meanings in various countries; states impose life sentences for different ranges of offenses; and states that release life-sentence prisoners do it in a variety of ways."[20] Meanwhile, we can see that life imprisonment, in fact, includes two basic concepts, i.e., the concept of time or duration and that of space. As regards duration, the punishment emphasizes that the sentence should be the convict's "life", i.e. it is life-long, which generally "denotes the life of a human being."[21] In fact, the term "life" means the rest of the convict's life or an indefinite term until he or she is released from the prison or dies there. In terms of space, it emphasizes that the punishment should be in prison, where the convict is reformed or educated or where the convict is locked away from society.[22] From this perspective, Professor Joshua argues that it is a kind of "'social banishment', which means that a system of punishment has decided that the offender is an 'other' who must be excluded 'from society'",[23] and he argues that there are four formulas, i.e., life in prison without parole, a sentence lengthy enough to constitute a stage of an offender's life, collateral consequences systematic and substantial enough to constitute an analogue to civil death, and capital punishment.[24]

According to the aforesaid analysis, the notion of life imprisonment can refer to a penal measure imprisoning the inmate for a certain crime for the rest of the inmate's life or until he or she is permitted to be released by law. However, undeniably, only in those cases where the convict is imprisoned in a prison for the rest of his or her life, such as in life imprisonment without possibility of release, can we speak of life imprisonment in the real sense of the term; in cases where the convict is sentenced to life imprisonment but will be released after a certain time on parole or commutation or other arrangement, life imprisonment is, in fact, a kind of indefinite-term imprisonment or long-term imprisonment, sentences which are, "by their very

---

[18] The *Penal Code of Socialist Republic of Viet Nam, (No. 15/1999/QH 10),* Article 34.

[19] *The Indian Penal Code, 1860, ACT No. 45 of 1860 1**, Article A53 1* (4)(a).

[20] The Crime Prevention and Criminal Justice Branch of United Nations Office at Vienna, *Life imprisonment*, ST/CSDHA/24, 1994, 1.

[21] Ibid., Article 45.

[22] BERRY William W. III, above no. 381, 1053.

[23] KLEINFELD Joshua, above no. 352, 949.

[24] Ibid., 949–950.

nature, indeterminate."[25] In this case, as some scholars have pointed out "life in prison has never really meant life in prison."[26] However, in some states, such as the USA, an offender can be sentenced to extremely long specific terms of imprisonment,[27] or multiple consecutive long terms of imprisonment, and these are deemed de facto life imprisonment sentences because they are so long that the sentence has the practical effect of being a life sentence.[28] In fact, extremely long specific terms of imprisonment or multiple consecutive long terms of imprisonment are not de jure life imprisonment terms and are not within the scope of the discussion in this book, even though the offender will spend the rest of their life behind bars. This is because this kind of punishment takes the form of a definite term of imprisonment in the law rather than being a lifetime punishment, and so should have its own terminal system.

5.2 The Characteristics of Life Imprisonment

Based on the notions explained in the preceding section, life imprisonment is, by its nature, a kind of imprisonment measure which isolates the offender from society and protects society and the public from the negative effects caused by the offenders sentenced to this punishment. It is very different from fixed-term imprisonment, the death penalty, or other custodial sentences, chiefly because it has certain special characteristics, described below, i.e. lengthy incarceration, severity, and quarantine.

5.2.1 Lengthy Incarceration

Lengthy incarceration is a by far the most obvious feature of life imprisonment, and the other characteristics derive from it. If the offender is sentenced to life imprisonment, and if, according to the law, he or she cannot be released, the incarceration

[25] The Crime Prevention and Criminal Justice Branch of United Nations Office at Vienna, *Life imprisonment*, ST/CSDHA/24, 1994, 1.

[26] *A Matter of Life and Death: The Effect of Life-without-parole Statutes on Capital Punishment*, Havard Law Review, 2006, Vol. 119, Issue 6, 1839.

[27] United States Sentencing Commission, *Life Sentences in the Federal System*, available at: http://www.ussc.gov/sites/default/files/pdf/research-and-publications/research-projects-and-surveys/miscellaneous/20150226_Life_Sentences.pdf; see also United States Sentencing Commission, *Sentencing Table*, available at: http://www.ussc.gov/sites/default/files/pdf/guidelines-manual/2016/Sentencing_Table.pdf. (Last visited: January 22nd, 2024). For example, according to the Sentencing Table of the United States Sentencing Commission, there are sentences ranging from 360 months to life imprisonment. According to "Life Sentences in the Federal System", it is reported that, in fiscal year of 2013, there were 168 offenders sentenced to imprisonment for 470 months or longer; in 2008, there were 150, and in 2005, 232; while as of January 2015, there were 1983 offenders in the BOP system serving a sentence of incarceration of 470 months or longer. They accounted for 1.1% of all federal sentenced offenders.

[28] Ibid., 10.

term of his punishment should be the rest of his or her lifetime. This is the reason why it is named "life imprisonment", and consequently some scholars deem this kind of life imprisonment "a different death penalty",[29] because it deprives the prisoner of life-long freedom, and ensures that he or she will die naturally in prison as a consequence. Just as with lengthy incarceration in general, life imprisonment without possibility of release is criticized by many scholars and is deemed a form of torture, and a brutal and inhuman punishment. However, some states' criminal law codes provide for life imprisonment without possibility of release; for instance, in the USA, life imprisonment without parole is provided for and applied in the federal legal system and in judicial practice; in England and Wales, life imprisonment and parole systems are provided for in the penal system, but certain categories of prisoners are not eligible for release[30]; in Turkey, there are two kinds of life imprisonment, i.e. life imprisonment and aggravated life imprisonment,[31] the latter lasts until the death of the convict and is enforced under a strict security regime as defined in law and legislation[32]; in China, for serious corruption crimes, if the offender is given the death penalty with a reprieve and this is commuted to life imprisonment after a two year suspension, neither parole nor commutation is granted to the convict.[33] In addition to cases where the convict serves the rest of his or her life in prison, which obviously represent the extremely lengthy incarceration of life imprisonment, life imprisonment with an indefinite term can also mean lengthy incarceration. In another word, cases in which the convict is given life imprisonment and will be released on parole

[29] DOW David R., *Life without Parole: A Different Death Penalty*, available at: https://www.thenation.com/article/life-without-parole-different-death-penalty/. (Last visited: January 22nd, 2024).

[30] LÜDTKE Florian and İDIL Aydınoğlu, "Life Imprisonment (without Parole)", Turkey's Center for Prison Studies, 2015, 30, available at: http://www.tcps.org.tr/sites/default/files/kitaplar/Life%20Imprisonment_report%20march-3.pdf. (Last visited: January 22nd, 2024). In 2012, there was a case, Vinter and Others v. United Kingdom, appealed to the European Court of Human Rights on the ground that the applicants were sentenced to life, and they could not be released; they complained imprisonment for life amounted to inhuman and degrading treatment as they had no hope of release. See Cases of *Vinter and Others v. the United Kingdom*, Applications nos. 66069/09 and 130/10 and 3896/10, Strasbourg, 17 January 2012.

[31] European Commission for Democracy Through Law, *Penal Code of Turkey, Opinion No. 831/2015,* Strasbourg, 15 February 2016, Article 46.

[32] Ibid. Article 47. However, parole is possibly granted to the offender who is given aggravated life imprisonment for most crimes, although for some special crimes, such as terrorism, parole is not granted, and the prisoner has to serve life imprisonment without possibility of parole. See LÜDTKE Florian and İDIL Aydınoğlu, "Life Imprisonment (without Parole)", Turkey's Center for Prison Studies, 2015, 30, available at: http://www.tcps.org.tr/sites/default/files/kitaplar/Life%20Imprisonment_report%20march-3.pdf. (Last visited: January 22nd, 2024). For example, in 2014, in the case of Öcalan v. Turkey, the European Court of Human Rights held that the judgement of the Ankara State Security Court had been a violation of Article 3 of the European Convention on Human Rights because the applicant, Mr. Öcalan was given life imprisonment without any possibility of conditional release. See European Court of Human Rights, *The Court Delivers its Chamber Judgment in the Case of Öcalan v. Turkey, Application nos. 24069/03, 197/04, 6201/06 and 10464/07. ECHR 077 (2014) 18.03.2014.*

[33]《中华人民共和国刑法》[Criminal Law of the People's Republic of China], Order No. 83, 2015, Article 383(3).

or commutation after he or she has served a certain number of years in prison can also embody the lengthy incarceration of life imprisonment. For instance, according to the Hungarian Criminal Code, if the court has not precluded eligibility for parole with a sentence of life imprisonment, the date of release on parole can be forty years[34]; this period (forty years) is also the maximum limited effective sentence to be served by a convict if he or she has been found guilty of two or more felonies and at least two of them are punishment by law with a prison sentence exceeding twenty years.[35] This is an extremely lengthy incarceration, effectively life imprisonment. However, most countries Criminal Law codes generally allow the convict to request parole and/or commutation after serving around 25 years, and some countries' laws allow the court to grant the convict parole after serving in prison for about 15 years, or even 10 years, as in the Republic of Korea.[36] The lengthy incarceration aspect of life imprisonment is its primary and most important character, and also creates the severity of this punishment.

5.2.2 In Its Severity Life Imprisonment Ranks Only Second to the Death Penalty

Life imprisonment is almost the most severe punishment in the world. Here I use the term "almost" because the death penalty is still provided in some states' criminal law codes, and so life imprisonment is the second most severe punishment; for abolitionist states, however, life imprisonment has become the most severe punishment. Put another way, in terms of severity, in modern punishments life imprisonment ranks only second to the death penalty. The severity of life imprisonment is, on one hand, chiefly because it deprives the convict of his or her right to freedom for a long time, by putting the convict behind bars for more than a decade, or even for the rest of his or her life. In this sense, life imprisonment does not directly impose physical pain, as corporal punishment does, but brings psychological pain to a convict. Moreover, to a certain extent it limits social survival skills and may even degrade them. On the other hand, generally, if the convict is sentenced to life imprisonment, he or she may be given another supplementary punishment by law. For example, in China, according to Article 57, any criminal who is sentenced to life imprisonment shall be deprived of his political rights for life[37]; in accordance with Article 113, whoever commits any of the crimes which involve endangering national security may concurrently be sentenced to confiscation of property[38]; according to Article 141, whoever commits the crime of

---

[34] *Act C of 2012 on the Criminal Code of Hungary*, Section 43.

[35] *Penal Code of the Kingdom of Spain, Organic ACT 10/1995, Dated 23 November, 1995*, as amended up to Law No. 4/2015 of April 27, 2015, Article 76.

[36] The *Criminal Code of the Republic of Korea*, amended as of Jan 1st, 1998, Article 72.

[37] 《中华人民共和国刑法》 *[Criminal Law of the People's Republic of China]*, Order No. 83, 2015, Article 57.

[38] Ibid., Article 113.

producing or selling bogus drugs may be sentenced to life imprisonment and a fine.[39] However, we must be aware that this phenomenon is chiefly the result of China's penalty system, which includes both a principal and a supplementary punishment. The latter may be imposed independently of the former, and can thus increase the severity of life imprisonment. Even when there is no other supplementary punishment provided for serious crimes in other states' criminal law codes, other punishments can also be concurrently imposed on the convict; for instance, under the Penal Code of Singapore, whoever wages war against the Government, or attempts to wage such war, or abets the waging of such war, shall also be fined concurrently if he or she is sentenced to imprisonment for life.[40] Under Section 43a of the German Criminal Law, the court may, collateral to imprisonment for life, impose payment of a sum of money (a property fine).[41] If the lighter punishment measure is not concurrently imposed on the convict, some conditions are imposed; for instance, according to the Section 10 of Finland's Criminal Code, a public official, a person elected to a public office or a person who exercises public authority who is sentenced to life imprisonment shall also be dismissed.[42] In addition, the Netherlands's Criminal Law provides explicitly that in cases where life imprisonment has been imposed, disqualification from certain rights, confiscation of objects seized and publication of the judgement may be imposed in conjunction with the main sentence.[43]

5.2.3 *Only for the Most Serious Crimes*

In the modern punishment system, life imprisonment is one kind of severe form of punishment, and it is provided for the most serious crimes. In retentionist states, taking Japan's Criminal Punishment as an example, life imprisonment normally serves as an alternative option to the death penalty for certain serious crimes; for instance, according to the Article 77, a ringleader of a group which commits the crime of insurrection shall be punished by death or life imprisonment without work[44]; according to Article 121 of Penal Code of Singapore, whoever commits offenses against the President's person shall be punished with death, or with imprisonment for life.[45] In other abolitionist states, like the member states of European Union,

[39] Ibid., Article 141.

[40] *The Statutes of the Republic of Singapore: Penal Code, ordinance 4 of 1871*, revised edition 2008, 30th November 2008, Article 121.

[41] The *German Criminal Code (Strafgesetzbuch, StGB), as promulgated on 13 November 1998 (Federal Law Gazette I, p. 945, p. 3322)*, Section 43a.

[42] The *Criminal Code of Finland, 39/1889*, amendments up to 766/2015 included, Section 10.

[43] The *Criminal Code of the Kingdom of Netherlands, Act of 3 March 1881*, Amended in 2012, Section 59.

[44] The *Penal Code of Japan, Act No. 45 of April 24, 1907 (日本国刑法45号，1907年4月24日)*, Article 77.

[45] *The Statutes of the Republic of Singapore: Penal Code, ordinance 4 of 1871*, revised edition 2008, 30th November 2008, Article 121A.

life imprisonment is only provided for the most serious crimes, for instance, under the Criminal Code of the Czech Republic, life imprisonment may only be imposed on an offender who has committed an especially serious felony of murder, an especially serious felony of public menace, treason, terrorist attack, genocide, an attack against humanity, cruelty in war, and so on.[46] Similarly, the Swiss Criminal Code also provides explicitly that lifelong incarceration may be only imposed on the convict who commits murder, intentional homicide, serious assault, robbery, rape, indecent assault, false imprisonment or abduction, hostage-taking, trafficking in human beings, genocide, or a felony under the heading of crimes against humanity or war crimes.[47]

These are the main three characteristics of life imprisonment. From the above analysis, it is clear that the lengthy incarceration which is implicit in life imprisonment determines its severity and its applicable scope, and also distinguishes it from other punishment measures.

5.3 The Forms of Life Imprisonment

Depending on the classification criteria, life imprisonment can be classified into the following main types: life imprisonment with possibility of release (LWPR) and without possibility of release (LWOR), life imprisonment with work and without work, mandatory life imprisonment and discretionary life imprisonment.

5.3.1 LWPR and LWOR

Regarding its means of termination, life imprisonment can be classified as life imprisonment with possibility of release (LWPR) and life imprisonment without release (LWOR). The former, LWPR, is a kind of generally applicable imprisonment, which is provided in many countries' criminal law codes. It means that the convict can be released from prison after serving a determinate or indeterminate term. It is also referred to as conditional release from life imprisonment by most states' criminal law codes, although these conditions are very different; some of them are explicitly provided by the criminal law, while for others the judge is authorized to make a decision. In addition, the methods of release are very different, and can include release on parole, probation, commutation, pardon, mercy, amnesty, and suspended execution, and so on. By contrast, LWOR is a kind of lifelong incarceration from which the convict cannot be released. This means the convict has to spend the rest of his or her life behind bars, and is, to a great extent, isolated from normal social life;

---

[46] *Law No. 40/2009 Coll., Criminal Code of the Czech Republic*, effective from 1 January 2010, Section 54(3).

[47] The *Swiss Criminal Code, of 21 December 1937* (Status as of 1 October 2016), Article 64, 1bis.

consequently, this form of punishment has been criticized as "a form of torture that renders death a mercy."[48] LWOR is not a generally applicable punishment around the world, and only a few states' criminal law codes provide for it in their penalty system, including the USA, China, Vietnam, Morocco, Laos, Israel, Indonesia, and so on.

5.3.2 Life Imprisonment with Work and Without Work

"By being forced to work within the institution, the prisoners were trained in a trade, and it was hoped that they would voluntarily flood the labour market when released."[49] In contemporary penal systems, prison work is not only carried out with the aim of inflicting punishment, but has also become a way of regulating and controlling prison life, and "become a central mode of carceral power and of penal discipline."[50] If life imprisonment, as a type of incarceration punishment, is imposed on the convict, he or she should be forced to work if able to. This requirement is directly or indirectly provided in many state's criminal law codes and has become one of the convicts' obligations; for instance, the Swiss Criminal Code provides that "the prison inmate is obliged to work. Wherever possible, the work should be appropriate to his skills, education and training and his interests."[51] This requirement is also applied to the convict who is sentenced to life imprisonment. China also has a similar provision in its Criminal Law. However, there are some differences, i.e., not all life imprisonment requires the convict to work, even when able to. According to the Japanese Penal Code, life imprisonment can be categorized as life imprisonment with work, which consists of confinement in a penal institution with assigned work, and life imprisonment without work, which consists of confinement in a penal institution.[52] The gravity of the former is greater than that of the latter.[53]

---

[48] LERNER Craig S., *Life without Parole as A Conflicted Punishment*, Wake Forest Law Review, 2013, Vol.48, 1108.

[49] LEBARON Genevieve, *Rethinking Prison Labor: Social Discipline and the State in Historical Perspective*, Working USA: The Journal of Labor & Society, 2012, Vol. 15, Issue 3, 331.

[50] HANEY Lynne A., *Working through Mass Incarceration: Gender and the Politics of Prison Labor from East to West*, Journal of Women in Culture and Society, 2010, Vol. 36, No. 1, 92.

[51] *Criminal Code of the Swiss Confederation of 21 December 1937 (Status as of 1 October 2016)*, Article 81 paragraph 1.

[52] The *Penal Code of Japan, Act No. 45 of April 24, 1907 (日本国刑法45号， 1907年4月24日)*, Articles 12 and 13.

[53] Ibid., Article 10.

5.3.3 Mandatory Life Imprisonment and Discretionary Life Imprisonment

For certain crimes, life imprisonment can be divided into mandatory and discretionary life sentences on the basis of whether it is the sole punishment or an alternative. Mandatory life imprisonment is a sentence which is the only punishment that can be imposed on a convict who commits a certain crime or "a life sentence passed in circumstances where the sentence is fixed by law."[54] For instance, in the UK mandatory life imprisonment is the only sentence that can be imposed on a convict who is aged 21 or over if he or she has committed a murder, according to the Criminal Justice Act 2003[55]; according to Article 302 of Turkey's Criminal Code, if the convict committed an act to place all or part of the territory of the state under the sovereignty of a foreign state or to disrupt the unity of the state or to weaken the independence of the state or to separate part of the territory under the sovereignty of the state, he or she shall be sentenced to a penalty of aggravated life imprisonment.[56] By contrast, discretionary life imprisonment is a punishment option which may be offered to the judge to make a choice when punishing a certain crime. It is normally provided together with other punishment measures, such as fixed term imprisonment, or the death penalty. For example, according to the Criminal Code of Romania, if a convict has committed aggravated murder, he or she may be punished by life imprisonment or no less than 15 and no more than 25 years of imprisonment, with a ban on the exercise of certain rights.[57] In another words, the provisions of discretionary life imprisonment give discretionary power to the judge when sentencing, but the provisions regarding mandatory life imprisonment do not leave any sentencing discretion to the judge, i.e., the judge does not have any other option but to give life imprisonment to the convict if the crime committed by the offender and its circumstances satisfy the requirements.

5.4 The Effects of Life Imprisonment

As a type of punishment, life imprisonment has the same, or at least similar, functions and effects to other punishment measures, in particular to incarceration. Generally, the penalty function refers to the social results or effects which are brought by the application of the penalty. Normally, it is considered that the penalty function mainly includes punishing and preventing crime in order to protect the social order, public security, the ruling order, individual rights, and so on. However, with the development of the punishment theory, some scholars believe that the application of the penalty should have learning effects in that it encourages the whole of society to learn the

[54] The *Criminal Justice Act 2003 of the United Kingdom,* Schedule 21 (1).

[55] Ibid., Schedule 21 (4).

[56] The *Criminal Code of Turkey (2011) Law No. 5237 of September 26, 2004*, as amended to Law No. 6217 of March 31, 2011, Article 302.

[57] *LAW # 286 of 17 July 2009 of the Criminal Code of Romania*, Article 189.

law and use it[58]; and the use of the penalty can make the public believe in the law and make them feel the law is being implemented[59]; furthermore, the use of the penalty should have a restorative effect such that the public can 'feel' the law and that their security is effectively protected by the imposition of an appropriate punishment on the offender.[60] However, these three penalty functions can all be deduced from the basic argument of using punishment to punish and prevent crime and to protect society. It is undeniable that life imprisonment does in fact have the functions mentioned above, which act as general functions. However, this section focuses on the functions and effects which are specific to life imprisonment due to its own special characters, by analyzing them from the perspectives of the convict, the victim and society.

5.4.1 The Effects of Life Imprisonment on the Convict

The effects of life imprisonment on the convict, including the "pains of imprisonment"[61] and the consequences of the incarceration are obvious and clear because the punishment is imposed directly on him or her. There have been studies conducted by American and British scholars attempting to assess the problems of long-term imprisonment[62]; but there is no unanimity regarding the scope of the effects of life imprisonment on the convict.[63] However, as a long-term incarceration, life imprisonment, should, on the one hand, bring many positive effects to the convict, which are also expected by the public and conform to the aims of the punishment. These kinds of positive effects include helping the convicts to recognise their criminal behaviour and lean from their mistakes; helping them to better understand the harm they have done to the victim and society; educating them to respect and obey the law; and then making them into better people by educating them. On the other hand, at the same time, it also has many obvious negative effects on convicts. Generally, the negative effects of life imprisonment on the convict are divided into two main categories, i.e., psychological problems and sociological problems. Life imprisonment puts convicts who have certain similar problems into a limited and sealed place, which isolates the convict from normal society for a long time, which thus brings serious psychological problems and sociological problems. The psychological problems are the most serious and obvious for the convict because they lose their normal social life and their freedom is greatly limited. As some scholars point out, missing

58 张秀玲 [ZHANG Xiuling], above no. 558, 18.

59 Ibid.

60 Ibid.

61 ROCHELEAU Ann Marie, *An Empirical Exploration of the 'Pains of Imprisonment' and the Level of Prison Misconduct and Violence,* Criminal Justice Review, 2013, Vol. 38, No. 3, 355.

62 See HULLEY Susie, CREWE Ben and WRIGHT Serena, *Re-examining the Problems of Long-term Imprisonment*, British Journal of Criminology, 2016, Vol. 56, Issue 4, 2.

63 See SCHNITTKER Jason, and MASSOGLIA Michael, *A Sociocognitive Approach to Studying the Effects of Incarceration,* Wisconsin Law Review, 2015, Vol. 2015, Issue 2, 349.

freedom, missing their family and the lack of privacy are the most difficult; the lack of autonomy and missing activities/possessions can be categorized as moderately negative in the list of hardships; concerns about their safety will also a serious of problem for them.[64] Furthermore, a lack of confidence and anxiety about their lives, the loss of the capacity for self-definition,[65] disappointment and loss of hope regarding their rehabilitation are also very comment problems. A Chinese empirical study shows that depression, helplessness, anxiety, hostility, fear and personal prejudice are all extreme and obvious features of the life of convicts serving long-term incarceration.[66] In particular, the lack of any sign of release from prison back to society may have a great negative impact on the convict's mental health. In addition, sociological problems are also serious and obvious effects on long-term prisoners. Long-term incarceration in fact deprives the convict's rights to liberty as long as he or she is in prison by removing him or her from the society and, to a great extent, cutting his or her contact with the outside world. In this case, the convict will gradually lose any social interaction over a long period. Consequently, long-term prisoners will suffer from isolation, indifference, loss of personal responsibility, and a lack of identity and social skills. Furthermore, an important negative result of long-term incarceration is that the convict is invisibly subject to the stigma of incarceration marking a prisoner or former inmate,[67] and this inevitably causes an increase in the prejudice the convict is subject to. Consequently, to a great extent, even though they are released from prison after a number of years in prison, they "are less likely to be hired, have slower wage growth, have more unstable relationships, and have higher rates of illness."[68] Undeniably, when a person who is removed from and isolated from society lives in a place of discipline and punishment for more than 10 years, or even for several decades, his or her behaviour and way of thinking naturally change, with some improvement, which could be viewed as the positive effects of punishment; however, its negative effects are also obvious and last for a very long time after the convict is released from prison. In addition, "family (i.e. the prisoner's family) is affected and involved in the prison sentence, [and] it affects everybody close."[69] The effect of life imprisonment on prisoners' families is very apparent and intense, in fact "it is like someone had died."[70] These effects may include the loss of the family income, strongly negative effects on marital relationships, even leading to divorce,

---

[64] See ROCHELEAU Ann Marie, above no. 611, 365.

[65] SCHNITTKER Jason, and MASSOGLIA Michael, above no. 613, 357.

[66] 符少剑, 姚乾坤, 等 [FU Shaojian, YAO Qiankun etc.], *《1120 例监狱服刑人员心理健康与人格特征分析》[Investigation on Mental Health and Personality traits of 1 120 Prisoners in Hainan Province]*, 现代预防医学 [Modern Preventive Medicine] 2012, Vol. 39, No. 23, 6194.

[67] See SCHNITTKER Jason, and MASSOGLIA Michael, above no. 613, 359. In this paper, Jason notes that, for the inmate, perhaps the most persistent challenge is how to deal with the stigma of incarceration itself.

[68] Ibid., 350.

[69] MURRAY Joseph, *The Effects of Imprisonment on Families and Children of Prisoners*, "The Effects of Imprisonment", Edited by LIEBLING Alison and MARUNA Shadd, Routledge, Oxford, 2011, 442.

[70] Ibid., 444.

and, in some cases, a prisoner's older parents cannot provide support for the children, which has a very negative impact on prisoners' children. Especially in China, long term imprisonment has an impact on the children's occupational opportunities, in areas such as the police force, and civil or public service, where political background checks may be run on the applicant. We cannot ignore the fact that the effect of life imprisonment on prisoners' families are long term and hidden.

5.4.2 The Effects of Life Imprisonment on the Victims

As a specific penal measure, it seems that there are no direct effects of life imprisonment on the victims and even their family members. However, the penalty is, to a great extent derived from the concept of private retaliation, i.e., "an eye for an eye, a life for a life". However, this right to retaliation is transferred to the sovereign, which becomes the public power, to determine and punish the crime in the name of the state. Thus, in a formal sense, contemporary punishment is no longer private revenge, but is regarded as the symbol of the power of the state, which represents the whole society, including the victims and their family members, and is entrusted to punish the crime, protect the state's legal interests and individual interests, and then achieve social justice and fairness. In the light of this, the penalty does not bring any direct and visible compensation or economic benefit to the victims and their family members; it only can bring them some kinds of spiritual solace, i.e., the victims and their families believe that the offender has received his or her just deserts. Life imprisonment plays an important role in the penalty system, and it is normally only used for the most serious crimes, which generally cause serious harm and damage to the victim's health, property and even life. For the serious harmful consequences caused by the crime, the victim and his or her family members naturally hope that the offender is given a serious penalty, so that justice can be restorative. As some scholars have said, "when a person is unjustly harmed, people experience a strong desire to punish the wrongdoer and more harm is typically accompanied with more punishment."[71] For the victims and their family members, life imprisonment, serving as the second severest punishment after the death penalty, is an appropriate penalty measure satisfying the victims and their family members' expectations, and it can, to a great extent, indirectly compensate their mental suffering.

[71] CALSEYDE Philippe P.F.M. van de, ZEELENBERG Gideon Keren Marcel, *The Insured Victim Effect: When and Why Compensating Harm Decreases Punishment Recommendations*, Judgement and Decision Making, 2013, Vol. 8, No. 2, 162.

5.4.3 The Effects of Life Imprisonment on the Public

In fact, the effects of life imprisonment on the public are also in some senses hidden and indirect, and generally include deterrence—which means the potential offender is deterred by the life sentence -, and restorative justice. Firstly, as the second severest punishment, life imprisonment should have a largely deterrent effect similar to the death penalty. Even though life imprisonment does not deprive the offender of the right to life, it deprives him or her of liberty and even the right to hope for a long time, and even for the rest of his or her life. It also means he or she will be isolated from society and forced to remain in a prison with similar people. In prison they do not have a normal social life. From this perspective, life imprisonment is a strong deterrent to the potential offender. However, this is only a theoretical prediction, lacking any exact statistics or empirical studies to show what kind of deterrence life imprisonment has. It is like the deterrence of the death penalty, on which "the question whether the death penalty actually deters is uncertain"[72]; some scholars have even cited the American Civil Liberties Union report and argued that "there is no credible proof that the death penalty in either substance or practice deters future or recidivist criminal behaviour."[73] In the light of this, the deterrence of life imprisonment is also indirect and uncertain. However, we also cannot deny and ignore its deterrence, since it is normally provided for serious crimes, and usually only for the most serious of these. A potential offender will hesitate to commit a serious crime when he or she is aware of the consequence of his or her behaviour. Secondly, it is natural that restorative justice will normally be understood to mean that the crime is punished by the relevant punishment, in order to protect legal interests. In China, restorative justice may have another important meaning, especially in cases which attract public attention and outrage. In these cases, life imprisonment normally serves to assuage the public in situations in which the relevant circumstances of the crime are not sufficient for the imposition of the death penalty, because life is the second severest punishment and can incarcerate the offender for a long term and can thus be accepted by the public. For example, in judicial practice there have been certain controversial cases which have provoked public debate and outrage, like the cases of "Tanghui"[74]

[72] WILLIAMS Kenneth, *Why and How the Supreme Court Should End the Death Penalty*, University of San Francisco Law Review, 2017, Vol. 51, Issue 2, 283.

[73] TIBBS Donald F., *Towards an Abolition Democracy: The Death Penalty, Circa 2015*, Widener Law Journal, 2016, Vol. 25, Issue 1, 89.

[74] In this case, Tang Hui was the mother of the victim, an 11-year old girl, who was forced to engage in prostitution by the perpetrators, Zhou Junhui, Qin Xing and others. Zhou and Qin were sentenced to death at the first trial and at the retrial, and at the second and final retrial they were sentenced to life imprisonment. See generally, *唐惠 [TANG Hui]*, available at: http://baike.so.com/doc/1050580-1111313.html; and 柴会群 [CHAI Huiqun], *《什么造就了唐慧》[What made Tang Hui?]*, available at: http://www.360doc.com/content/14/0617/10/4089344_387392854.shtml. (Last visited: January 22nd, 2024); See *周军辉，秦星 [ZHOU Junhui and QIN xing] (2010) 永中刑一初字第55号 [2010] Yong the First Criminal Court First Trial. No. 55; (2012) 湘高法刑三终字第31号 [2012] Xiang High Court Third Criminal Trial. No. 31; (2014) 湘高法刑重字第5号 [2014] Xiang High Court Criminal Retrial. No. 5]*. The judgement of this case can be found on

and of "Sun Weiming".[75] As a concrete measure applied by the punishment system, it protects both public and private security and legal interests, together with other penalty measures, although it is hard to say life imprisonment has a direct effect on the public.

5.5 Life Imprisonment in China and Other Countries

5.5.1 Life Imprisonment in China

After the death penalty, life imprisonment is the second most severe punishment in China's present criminal punishment system. There are currently 102 crimes punishable by life imprisonment in the present Specific Provisions of Criminal Law, accounting for 21.79% of a total of 468 crimes[76]; almost all of these 102 are provided with a fixed-term imprisonment of not less than 10 years, 46 of them are stipulated together with the death penalty,[77] 5 are provided with a fixed-term imprisonment of not less than 7 years,[78] and 1 is provided with a fixed-term imprisonment of not less than 15 years.[79] The distribution of crimes punishable by life imprisonment is shown in Table 5.1. Based on the analysis, this section intends to examine the life imprisonment system in the present Criminal Law of China).

the "China Judgements Online" website, http://wenshu.court.gov.cn/content/content?DocID=3a471b1c-dfa8-4ea0-b53f-edf0a40d5ac5&KeyWord=%E5%91%A8%E5%86%9B%E8%BE%89%7C%E5%91%A8%E5%86%9B%E8%BE%89%EF%BC%8C%E7%A7%A6%E6%98%9F. (Last visited: January 22nd, 2024).

[75] In this case, the offender, Sun Weiming, was initially sentenced to immediate execution for the crime of using other dangerous means when inflicting serious injury on 1 person and death on 4 persons, but this was reduced to life imprisonment at the second trial. See *孙伟铭 [SUN Weiming] (2009) 成刑初字第158号 [2009] Cheng the First Criminal Court First Trial. No. 158; (2009) 川刑终字第690号 [2009] Chuan the Criminal Court the Second Trial. No. 690].*

[76] *《刑法最新罪名一览表》[Chart Showing the New Crimes in the Criminal Law],* above no. 125.

[77] These 46 crimes are punishable by death; life imprisonment for these crimes is a possible option to capital punishment, and it is even the lightest punishment for some crimes, such as kidnapping (Article 239(2). See《中华人民共和国刑法》[Criminal Law of the People's Republic of China], Order No. 83, 2015.

[78] These crimes include crimes of producing or selling food that is not up to safety standards (Article 143), producing fake pesticides, fake animal pharmaceuticals or fake chemical fertilizers or selling pesticides, animal pharmaceuticals, chemical fertilizers or seeds (Article 147), forming or using superstitious sects or secret societies or 'unusual' religious organizations or using superstition to undermine the implementation of laws and administrative rules and regulations (Article 300), making arrangements for another person to illegally cross the national border (Article 318), illegally possessing narcotic drug (Article 348). See《中华人民共和国刑法》[Criminal Law of the People's Republic of China], Order No. 83, 2015.

[79] This is the crime of smuggling, trafficking in, transporting or manufacturing narcotic drugs, provided by Article 347(1). See《中华人民共和国刑法》[Criminal Law of the People's Republic of China], Order No. 83, 2015,

Table 5.1 The distribution of crimes punishable by life imprisonment[80]

Crimes and chapters in the Specific Provisions of the Criminal Law	Number of crimes punishable with life imprisonment
Crimes of endangering national security (Chapter I)	8
Crimes of endangering public security (Chapter II)	17
Crimes of disrupting the order of the socialist market economy (Chapter III)	34
Crimes of infringing upon citizens' personal and democratic rights (Chapter IV)	5
Crimes of property violation (Chapter V)	4
Crimes obstructing the administration of public order (Chapter VI)	14
Crimes of impairing the interests of national defence (Chapter VII)	3
Crimes of embezzlement and bribery (Chapter VIII)	4
Crimes of dereliction of duty (Chapter IX)	0
Crimes of servicemen's transgression of duties (Chapter X)	13
Total	102

From the above table, we can see that the greatest number of crimes involve disrupting the order of the socialist market economy provided by Chapter III (34 crimes), followed by crimes of endangering public security in Chapter II, (17 crimes); there is no crime punishable by life imprisonment in Chapter IX

5.5.1.1 Conditions for Passing a Sentence of Life Imprisonment

In the General Provisions of the Criminal Law, there is no special provision to stipulate directly the applicable condition for life imprisonment, such as is provided for the use of the death penalty in some articles.[81] However, in the light of Article 17, criminal punishment, including life imprisonment, shall not be imposed on a person who had not reached the age of 14 years old when he or she committed the crime; a person who was over 16 at the time he or she committed the crime shall be given a criminal punishment, including life imprisonment; but a person who has reached the age of 14 but not the age of 16, and has committed intentional homicide, intentionally hurts another person so as to cause serious injury or death, or commits rape, robbery, drug-trafficking, arson, explosion or poisoning, shall bear

80 《中华人民共和国刑法》[Criminal Law of the People's Republic of China], Order No. 83, 2015,.

81 These articles include Articles 48, 49, 50, 51 in Session 5 of Chapter III of the General Provisions of the Criminal Law of People Republic of China.

criminal liability.[82] According to the Specific Provisions of Criminal Law, all these 8 crimes can be punishable by life imprisonment and death, and an offender who is younger than 16 years old but has turned 14 and committed one, or more than one kind of these 8 crimes may be sentenced to life imprisonment, although in these cases the applicable conditions should be stricter than those applied to others.[83] In addition, under the present Criminal Law, a person who has reached the age of 75 may also be sentenced to life imprisonment if he has committed a crime punishable by life imprisonment and/or death, even though Article 17–1 provides that a person who has reached the age of 75 may be given a lighter or mitigated penalty if he commits an intentional crime.[84] When considering other states, we can see that their provisions for the use of life imprisonment are stricter than China's. For example, in accordance with the Article 57 of the Romanian Penal Code, life imprisonment shall not be imposed on an offender who has turned 65 years of age at the date when the judgment to convict is returned, but shall be replaced by a prison term of 30 years and a ban on the exercise of certain rights for the maximum duration of the prison sentence[85] and "life imprisonment is also not going to be applied for the minor offender"[86]; Under the Hungarian Criminal Code, only persons over the age of 20 at the time of commission of the crime shall be sentenced to life imprisonment.[87] Except for these considerations relating to age, in the Criminal Law of China, there is no specific general provision referring to the applicable conditions for life imprison. However, conditions are provided by the Specific Provisions of the Criminal Law in

---

82 *《中华人民共和国刑法》*[Criminal Law of the People's Republic of China], Order No. 83, 2015, Article 17.

83 In judicial practice, the SPC has always made a relevant judicial interpretation of this provision, based on the judicial enquiry of the Ji Lin High People's Court regarding the question of whether life imprisonment may be imposed on a criminal who is younger than 16 years old but had reached the age of 14 years when he or she committed a very serious crime. In this judicial interpretation, the SPC said that life imprisonment may be imposed on them in accordance with the Articles 44 and 14(2) of the Criminal Law 1979, but it also should be applied in the light of Article 14(3), providing that a lighter or mitigated punishment shall be given an offender who is older than 14 but younger than 16, and the applicable conditions of life imprisonment for them shall be stricter than those for others. However, this judicial decision was repealed in 2013. See《最高人民法院关于已满14岁不满16岁的人所犯罪行特别严重能否判处无期徒刑问题的电话答复》[Answer by Phone from the SPC on the Issue of Whether a Person who has Reached the Age of 14 but not the Age of 18 Commits Very Serious Crimes], 17 April 1991, available at: http://www.law-lib.com/law/law_view.asp?id=53045. (Last visited: January 22nd, 2024); and *《最高人民法院关于废止1980年1月1日至1997年6月30日期间发布的部分司法解释和司法解释性质文件(第九批)的决定》[SPC's Decision on Repealing the Partial Judicial Interpretations and Judicial Interpretative Documents (The Ninth Batch) Made in the period from 1 January 1980 to 30 June 1997], 法释〔2013〕2号 [No. 2 Legal Interpretation (2013)].*

84 Article 17-1 of the Criminal Law provides that "A person attaining the age of 75 may be given a lighter or mitigated penalty if he commits an intentional crime; or shall be given a lighter or mitigated penalty if he commits a crime of negligence.".

85 *Criminal Code of the Republic of Romania, LAW # 286 of 17 July 2009*, Article 57.

86 FRÎNTU Viorica-Mihaela, above no. 521, 97. According to Article 113 of Criminal Code of the Republic of Romania, a juvenile includes a person who is younger than 16 years old.

87 *Criminal Code of Hungary, ACT C of 2012*, Section 41.

all kinds of crimes punishable by life imprisonment, and they include the following types.

(1) Life imprisonment for action crime (行为犯). The actus reus of action crimes here is simply an act or behavior which is proved to have already been committed, the consequences of which are immaterial, and which is an important type of crime; most of these crimes are generally relatively serious and are provided with a correspondingly heavy penalty, such as the death penalty and life imprisonment. In the Criminal Law, life imprisonment is normally provided for action crime without any consideration of circumstances or any other conditions; it is normally a mandatory sentence, and in some crimes, it is the maximum legally prescribed penalty. These action crimes include treason (Article 102), aiding the enemy (Article 112), forming or leading a terrorist organization (Article 120), aircraft hijacking (Article 121), intentional homicide (Article 232) and stealing, spying into or buying military secrets for, or illegally offering such secrets to, agencies, organizations or individuals outside the territory of China (Article 431(2)). All of these six crimes are very serious crimes and all of them can be punishable by death.
(2) Life imprisonment may only be imposed on a perpetrator under some legally-prescribed circumstance according to the law. These circumstances include the crime scene, the object of the crime, the criminal consequences, the means of crime, and the position of perpetrator in a criminal organization, and so on. The crime scene is a significant legally prescribed circumstance for passing sentence in the Criminal Law of China; for example, robbing public or private property by violence, coercion or other methods carries a fixed-term imprisonment of not less than three but not more than 10 years, but if the robber intrudes into another person's residence to rob, robs on board a means of public transportation, or rapes a woman in a public place, he shall be sentenced to a fixed-term imprisonment of not less than 10 years, life imprisonment or death.[88] The object of the crime is also an important sentencing factor; for example, anyone robbing a bank or any other banking institution,[89] or stealing or forcibly seizing guns, ammunition or explosives from State organs, members of the armed forces, the police or the people's militia,[90] shall be sentenced to a fixed-term imprisonment of not less than 10 years, life imprisonment or death. Criminal consequence is another important sentence factor in a majority of provisions in the Specific Provisions of the Criminal Law. Some provisions stipulate directly the consequence of crimes, with the amount of property or illegal property involved in the crime serving as the applicable condition for life imprisonment; for example, for economic crimes in Chap. 3, the amount of property or other

---

[88] See《中华人民共和国刑法》*[Criminal Law of the People's Republic of China]*, Order No. 83, 2015, Article 263.

[89] Ibid.

[90] Ibid., Article 127(2).

goods involved in the crime serves as a sentencing factor,[91] and some provisions stipulate "causing death or serious injury, or causing heavy losses of public or private property" as the applicable condition for life imprisonment; for example, Article 236(3) provides that anyone raping a women and causing serious injury or death to the victim or any other serious consequences, the offender shall be sentenced to a fixed-term imprisonment of not less than 10 years or life imprisonment or the death penalty.[92] However, a majority of provisions, i.e. around 53 provisions, include the terms "commit major crimes" or "serious circumstance" or "especially serious circumstance" which serves as the applicable condition for life imprisonment. Generally, these kinds of terms in the provision are normally regarded as "miscellaneous provisions (兜底条款)" and in practice, it is normally interpreted by the SPC through judicial interpretation in accordance with the characteristics of different crimes, or according to mandate, by the local High People's Courts, who make this kind of interpretation according to the local economic and social situation. The means of the crime is also a sentencing element; for example, robbing with a gun,[93] or, by resorting to especially cruel means, causing severe injury to another person, or reducing the person to utter disability,[94] and using arms to protect the smuggling, trafficking in, transporting or manufacturing of narcotic drugs,[95] all bring a sentence of a fixed-term imprisonment of not less than 10 years, life imprisonment or death. The position of the perpetrator in a criminal organization is also an important applicable condition for life imprisonment; for example, anyone who is a ringleader of a gang engaged in abducting and trafficking in women and children shall be sentenced to a fixed-term imprisonment or life imprisonment.[96] Meanwhile, there are other applicable conditions for life imprisonment such as the perpetrator's attitude towards an admission of guilt, the perpetrator's criminal record and so on.

---

[91] In the Specific Provisions of the Criminal Law, only the crimes of manufacturing or selling counterfeit or inferior products, which are punishable by life imprisonment, are stipulated explicitly with the amount of property relating to the crime, namely, "if the amount of earnings from sales is more than 2 million Yuan, he shall be sentenced to a fixed-term imprisonment of 15 years or life imprisonment" (see Criminal Law of PRC 1997, Article 140); most of the other provisions use the phrase "the amount involved is large or especially large" as the applicable condition for life imprisonment; see, for example, Articles 152(3),170, 178, 192, 194, 195, 196, 197, 200, 204, 206, 207, 224, 264, 267, 382(3), 384. Based on the specific crime, the SPC makes different judicial interpretations of these vague terms. In addition, the crime of illegal drug-possessing is provided with the term "quantity" as the condition for sentencing to life imprisonment, namely, illegally possessing not less than 1 kg of opium, or not less than 50 g' heroin or methyl-aniline of, or any other large quantities of narcotic drugs". See《中华人民共和国刑法》*[Criminal Law of the People's Republic of China],* Order No. 83, 2015, Article 384.

[92] See《中华人民共和国刑法》*[Criminal Law of the People's Republic of China],* Order No. 83, 2015, Article 236(3); and Articles 115, 141, 144, 147, 234, 263, 390, 421, 422, 423 and 424.

[93] See ibid., Article 263.

[94] Ibid., Article 234(2).

[95] Ibid., Article 247(2).

[96] Ibid., Article 240; and Articles 103, 104, 105, 170, 317, 318, 328 and 347.

All in all, the applicable conditions for life imprisonment are not stipulated directly by the General Provisions of the Criminal Law, except for the object of the punishment itself, but by the provisions providing concrete crimes in the Specific Provisions. Life imprisonment in the Specific Provisions is stipulated together with the death penalty, serving as an alternative option to the latter, and the applicable conditions for both penalties are, to a great extent, the same. But the applicable conditions for the death penalty are provided by Articles 48, 49, 50 and 51 in the General Provisions, and limit the use of the death penalty. The question remains, therefore, whether it is necessary or not to provide the applicable conditions for life imprisonment in the General Provisions when the death penalty is completely removed from the Criminal Law. Looking at the criminal codes of some abolitionist states, such as the German Criminal Code, the General Penal Code of Finland (1940 No. 19 (12 February)), and the Criminal Code of Hungary (Act C of 2012), we find that there is no general applicable condition for life imprisonment. But the situation in China is very different, which the death penalty has not been completely repealed, and there are two types of life imprisonment, i.e., LWPR and LWOR. In order to protect human rights, the conditions limiting it should be provided explicitly by the General Provisions, just as is the case with the limiting conditions for the death penalty, and LWOR should not be the alternative option to the death penalty as "life imprisonment without parole is worse than a death sentenced."[97]

5.5.1.2 Terminating Mechanisms: A Twin-Track Approach

Under the present Criminal Law, a twin-track approach is adopted to terminate life imprisonment: i.e. LWPR and LWOR.

LWPR: Commutation

Considering the special penalty elimination system in China, release from prison can generally come through the commutation of punishment and parole, both of which are normally applied at the same time. According to Article 78, commutation operates in two situations; namely, discretionary commutation (酌定减刑, zhuodingjianxing) and mandatory or legally provided commutation (法定减刑, fading jiangxing). Discretionary commutation of life imprisonment refers to a situation in which the penalty "may" be commuted if the offender "conscientiously observes prison regulations, accepts education and reform through labor and shows true repentance or performs meritorious services while serving his sentence,[98] but the commutation is not certain to be granted and its likelihood is lower than with mandatory commutation, which is a situation in which the penalty "shall" be commuted, and

[97] BERRY William W. III, above no. 381, 1054.

[98] 《中华人民共和国刑法》*[Criminal Law of the People's Republic of China]*, Order No. 83, 2015, Article 78.

this is certain to be granted by law if the perpetrator performs any of the major meritorious services provided in the Criminal Law as detailed below:

(1) Preventing another person from conducting major criminal activities;
(2) Informing against major criminal activities conducted inside or outside prison and verified through investigation;
(3) Assisting judiciary authorities to arrest another major suspect/offender, including a joint offender;
(4) Having inventions or important technical innovations to his credit;
(5) Coming to the rescue of another in everyday life and activities, at the risk of losing his own life;
(6) Performing remarkable services in fighting against natural disasters or curbing major accidents; or
(7) Making other major contributions to the country and society.[99]

For the offender sentenced to life imprisonment, if his performances meet the conditions for discretionary commutation, the penalty may be commuted to a fixed-term imprisonment of 22 years after serving two years of the sentence, if the offender shows true repentance or performs meritorious services; it may be commuted to a fixed-term imprisonment of 21–22 years if he or she shows true repentance and performs meritorious services[100]; by contrast, if the offender serving life imprisonment performs major meritorious service, the sentence may be commuted to a fixed-term imprisonment of 20–21 years; it may be commuted to a fixed-term imprisonment of 19–20 years if the offender shows true repentance and performs major meritorious service.[101] These provisions have been changed significantly by the Eighth Amendment and relative judicial interpretation and are stricter than those of the 1997 Criminal Law. In accordance with the 1997 Criminal Law and its judicial interpretations, if the offender shows true repentance or performs meritorious services, his sentence might be commuted to a fixed-term imprisonment of 18–20 years, and if the offender performs major meritorious service, it might be commuted to a fixed-term imprisonment of 13–18 years.[102]

Compared with discretionary commutation, mandatory commutation seems much more merciful. While serving his sentence, the offender may be granted many commutations, but the interval between two commutations shall not be less than two years, and after one or multiple commutations, the actual term of the sentence

[99] Ibid., Article 78.

[100] *《最高人民法院关于办理减刑、 假释案件具体应用法律问题的规定》[Supreme People Court's Provisions on Several Legal Issues concerning the Specific Application of the Law in Handling Commutation and Parole Cases] 法释 (2016)23号 [Legal Interpretation No. 23, 2016]*, Articles 7and 8.

[101] Ibid., Article 7.

[102] See *《中华人民共和国刑法》[Criminal Law of the People's Republic of China*], Order No. 83, 14 March 1997, Article 78, and *《最高人民法院关于办理减刑、假释案件具体应用法律问题的规定》[Supreme People Court's Provisions on Several Legal Issues concerning the Specific Application of the Law in Handling Commutation and Parole Cases], 法释 (1997)6号 [Legal Interpretation No. 6, 1997]*, Article 6.

served by an offender sentenced to life imprisonment shall not be less than 13 years, which was also increased from the 10 years provided by the 1997 Criminal Law.[103] The commencement date is calculated from the date when the life imprisonment judgment is announced.[104] The commutation per instance for the offender who shows true repentance or performs major meritorious service shall be no more than 9 months; for the offender who shows true repentance and performs major meritorious service it shall be no more than 1 year; for those who perform major meritorious service it shall be no more than one and half years; for those who perform major meritorious service and show true repentance, it shall be no more than 2 years.[105] In order to truly prevent people engaging in malpractices for personal gain, power or corrupt financial dealings,[106] on 21 January 2014, the CPLAC, promulgated a document to strictly regulate and improve the conditions of commutation and parole for the offender who commits any crime which involves taking advantage of a duty, disrupting the order of financial administration, or forming, leading, taking an active part in, harboring, or conniving in an organization of a criminal syndicate nature. Based on this document, in the new *Provisions on Several Legal Issues concerning the Specific Application of the Law in Handling Commutation and Parole Cases*, the SPC extended the commencement date for the commutation of life imprisonment imposed on the offender who commits any of the above mentioned crimes, i.e., it may be commuted to fixed term imprisonment after the offender has served three years of the sentence, although the actual executive terms after the commutation shall not be less than 20 years. The interval between two commutations shall be two years or more, and the commutation per instance shall be no more than 1 year, although these requirements are not applied to the mandatory commutation; in other words, there is no limitation on the commencement date and interval for mandatory commutation.[107] These same restrictions on commutations are also applied to the offender who commits the crimes of endangering national security, or the crimes of terrorism, or is a ringleader of a gang engaged in drug-related crimes or recidivism

---

103 *《中华人民共和国刑法》[Criminal Law of the People's Republic of China]*, Order No. 83, 14 March 1997, Article 78(2).

104 See *《中华人民共和国刑法》*[Criminal Law of the People's Republic of China], Order No. 83, 2015, Article 78(2) and *《最高人民法院关于办理减刑、假释案件具体应用法律问题的规定》[Supreme People Court's Provisions on Several Legal Issues concerning the Specific Application of the Law in Handling Commutation and Parole Cases]*, above no. 650, Article 8.

105 *《最高人民法院关于办理减刑、假释案件具体应用法律问题的规定》 [Supreme People Court's Provisions on Several Legal Issues concerning the Specific Application of the Law in Handling Commutation and Parole Cases]*, above no. 650, Article 6.

106 *《中共中央政法委关于严格规范减刑、假释、暂予监外执行切实防止司法腐败的意见》 [The Opinions of the Central Political and Legal Affairs Commission of the Communist Party of China (CPLACCPC) on Effectively Preventing Judicial Corruption by Strictly Regulating the Commutation, Parole and the Temporary Service of Sentences Outside Prison] (People's Republic of China) Central Political and Legal Affairs Commission of the Communist Party of China 中政委(2014)5号 [No. 5, 2014, Central Political Commission]*, Article 1(3).

107 *《最高人民法院关于办理减刑、假释案件具体应用法律问题的规定》 [Supreme People Court's Provisions on Several Legal Issues concerning the Specific Application of the Law in Handling Commutation and Parole Cases]*, above no. 650, Article 9.

of drug crimes, and the offender who is a recidivist or convicted of murder, rape, robbery, abduction, arson, explosion, dissemination of hazardous substances or organized violence who is sentenced to death with reprieve.[108] There were no provisions with the same restrictions in the 1997 Criminal Law.

In addition, life imprisonment reduced from the death penalty with reprieve may be reduced to a fixed-term imprisonment of 25 years after the offender has served two years of the sentence if he/she shows true repentance or performs meritorious services. If he/she genuinely performs any major meritorious services, the sentence may be commuted to a fixed term imprisonment of 23–25 years after serving two years of the sentence. Under the 1997 Criminal Law, in this case, it may be commuted to a fixed-term imprisonment of 15–20 years.[109] After one or multiple commutations, the actual term of the sentence served by an offender sentenced to the death penalty with reprieve shall not be less than 15 years, which is 3 years more than that provided by the 1997 Criminal Law,[110] excluding the probation period for suspension of execution; and it may be commuted to a fixed term imprisonment after the offender has served three years of the sentence.[111] In addition, for a recidivist or someone convicted of murder, rape, robbery, abduction, arson, explosion, dissemination of hazardous substances or organized violence who is sentenced to death with reprieve, the court may, when sentencing, decide to put restrictions on the commutation of his sentence in the light of the circumstances of the crime committed; if he/she is granted a commutation while serving the sentence of life imprisonment commuted from the death penalty with reprieve, the court should strictly apply the conditions of the commencement date, the time interval and the commutation range.[112] Namely, the life imprisonment commuted from the death penalty with reprieve may only be commuted to fixed-term imprisonment after the offender has served five years of the sentence, and the commutation per instance shall be no more than 6 months; for the offender who performs meritorious services, it shall be no more than 1 year.[113] In fact, the restrictions on commutation have been newly provided by the Eighth Amendment and the judicial interpretation.

"The commutation of punishment provided by the Criminal Law is a kind of universal penalty implementation system with distinct characteristics, and it is unique

---

[108] Ibid.

[109] See 《中华人民共和国刑法》 *[Criminal Law of the People's Republic of China],* Order No. *83,* 14 March 1997, Article 50; and 《最高人民法院关于办理减刑、假释案件具体应用法律问题的规定》 *[Supreme People Court's Provisions on Several Legal Issues concerning the Specific Application of the Law in Handling Commutation and Parole Cases],* above no. 650, Article 9.

[110] Ibid.

[111] 《最高人民法院关于办理减刑、假释案件具体应用法律问题的规定》 *[Supreme People Court's Provisions on Several Legal Issues concerning the Specific Application of the Law in Handling Commutation and Parole Cases],* above no. 650, Article 9.

[112] See Ibid., Article 10, and see also 《中华人民共和国刑法》 [Criminal Law of the People's Republic of China], Order No. 83, 2015, Article 50(2).

[113] 《最高人民法院关于办理减刑、假释案件具体应用法律问题的规定》 *[Supreme People Court's Provisions on Several Legal Issues concerning the Specific Application of the Law in Handling Commutation and Parole Cases],* above no. 650, Articles 13 and 14.

… in the world."[114] In general terms, it is even a significant condition for the convict serving life imprisonment to be granted parole because "the conditions of parole are stricter than those of commutation."[115] Furthermore, in practice, the application rate of commutation is always higher than that of parole[116]; for example, in accordance with the SPC's report, the number of commutation cases from January to September 2014 was 370,998, while parole cases numbered only 26,904.[117] Even though it is impossible to discover the exact number of cases of commutation of life imprisonment, the statistical data above show that the possibility of commutation is much greater than that of parole. One of the important reasons for this might be that most enforcement authorities have to take supervisory responsibility if the convict commits any other crime while serving his sentence outside of prison when he is granted parole, so most enforcement authorities are against parole.[118]

LWPR: Parole

Parole is another significant method of early release from prison. In accordance with Article 81 of the Criminal Law, an offender sentenced to life imprisonment who has actually served not less than 13 years of imprisonment may be granted parole if he/she conscientiously observes the prison regulations, accepts education and reform through labor, shows true repentance and is not likely to commit any crime again. Actually, the limitations for parole are almost the same as those provided by the 1997 Criminal Law, except that the term of punishment actually to be served is longer than that provided by the 1997 Criminal Law, which was not less than 10 years.[119] If special circumstances exist, upon the verification and approval of the SPC, parole may be granted without regard to the above restrictions on the term served.[120] Here we can see that the condition of "he conscientiously observes the

---

114 徐静村 [XU Jingcun], *《减刑、假释制度改革若干问题研究》[On Several Issues on the Reform of Commutation of Punishment and Parole]*, 法治研究 [Research on the Rule of Law] 2010, No. 2, 3.

115 刘强 [LIU Qiang], *《在我国建立以"假释为主、减刑为辅"的罪犯出狱新模式》[Establishing the New Model of Criminals Being Released from Prison - 'Parole Principally, Reduction of Penalty Secondly' - in China]*, 法学杂志 [Law Science Magazine] 2012, No. 1, 45.

116 柳原 [LIU Yuan], *《扩大假释、缩小减刑的实证研究》[Empirical Research on Expanding the Application of Parole and Limiting Commutation]*, 中国司法 [Justice of China] 2014, No. 11, 67.

117 *《2014年1-9月人民法院办理减刑假释案件情况》[Report on the Commutation and Parole Cases Handled by the People's Court from January to September 2014]*, available at: 中华人民共和国最高人民法院 [Supreme People's Court of People's Republic of China] http://www.court.gov.cn/fabu-xiangqing-14014.html (Last visited: January 22nd, 2024).

118 See generally, 郎胜 [LANG Sheng], *《<刑法修正案(八)>解读》[Interpreting "the Eighth Amendment to the Criminal Law]*, 国家检察官学院学报 [Journal of the National Prosecutors College] 2011, No. 2, 157.

119 See *《中华人民共和国刑法》[Criminal Law of the People's Republic of China]*, Order No. 83, 14 March 1997, Article 81.

120 *《中华人民共和国刑法》*[Criminal Law of the People's Republic of China], Order No. 83, 2015, Article 81.

prison regulations, accepts education and reform through labor, and shows true repentance" and the minimum term to be served in prison, which is not less than 13 years, are the same as the basic condition for commutation, but the conditions of parole are higher and stricter than those of commutation because of the assessed risk of committing a crime again. Regarding this risk, it should be comprehensively evaluated based on the concrete circumstances of the crime committed by the convict, the facts of the original sentence, the convict's consistent performance while serving his/her sentence, the convict's age, physical condition, personality characteristics, and his/her source of livelihood after release from prison, as well as the supervision measures and conditions.[121] In addition, "when a parole decision is made on a convict, the impact of his/her release on parole on the community where he lives shall be considered,"[122] a provision which was added by Article 16(3) of the Eighth Amendment. Article 81(3) provides for an exception where a "special circumstance exists"; but what exactly is this circumstance? In accordance with judicial interpretation, it is a "circumstance … significantly related to the whole social and state interest",[123] but this interpretation is still not clear, and some scholars have pointed out that "the concept and scope of the specific circumstance defined by judicial interpretation is ambiguous and it results in theoretical diversity and abuse in judicial practice."[124] In addition, there is a prohibiting provision on parole for some special convicts, including "the recidivist or a convict sentenced to life imprisonment for murder, rape, robbery, abduction, arson, explosion, dissemination of hazardous substances, or organized violent crime."[125] It was amended by Article 16(2) of the Eighth Amendment. Even though those convicts falling into the categories above cannot be granted parole, they can be released early on commutation, in accordance with the present law. However, the convict who is sentenced to life imprisonment and released on parole is still supervised under the judicial authorities for a certain probation period.[126] During this probation period, the offender granted parole should observe the following requirements: (1) observing laws and administrative rules and regulations, and submitting to supervision; (2) reporting on his own activities as required by the supervising organ; (3) observing the regulations for receiving visitors stipulated by the supervising organ; and (4) reporting to obtain approval from

[121] *《最高人民法院关于办理减刑、假释案件具体应用法律问题的规定》 [Supreme People Court's Provisions on Several Legal Issues concerning the Specific Application of the Law in Handling Commutation and Parole Cases]*, above no. 650, Article 15.

[122] *《中华人民共和国刑法》* [Criminal Law of the People's Republic of China], Order No. 83, 2015, Article 81(3).

[123] *《最高人民法院关于办理减刑、假释案件具体应用法律问题的规定》 [Supreme People Court's Provisions on Several Legal Issues concerning the Specific Application of the Law in Handling Commutation and Parole Cases]*, above no. 650, Article 17.

[124] 柳忠卫 [Liu Zhongwei], *《对假释适用的例外性规定和禁止性规定的理性分析》 [Rational Analysis of the Exception Stipulations and Prohibiting Stipulations of Parole Application]*, 政法论丛 [Journal of Political Science and Law] 2006, No. 1, 58.

[125] *《中华人民共和国刑法》 [Criminal Law of the People's Republic of China]*, Order No. 83, 2015, Article 81(2).

[126] Ibid., Article 83.

the supervising organ for any departure from the city or country he lives in or for any change in residence.[127] Furthermore, he/she shall be subjected to community correction during parole, according to law.[128] The community correction system is newly established by the Eighth Amendment.[129] If he/she commits another crime during the probation period for parole, or is discovered to have committed, before the judgment is pronounced, other crimes for which no punishment has been imposed, or he/she violates any provision of the laws, administrative regulations or the relevant department of the State Council on parole supervision and management if the above do not constitute a new crime, his parole shall be revoked.[130]

LWOR: Crimes of Embezzlement and Bribery

In fact, the convict who is not sentenced to immediate execution may be released early on parole or commutation, regardless of the crime he/she committed, if the release conditions have been satisfied, even though he/she was restricted to commutation and prohibited parole before the Ninth Amendment. However, this situation was changed by the Ninth Amendment. According to Article 44(4) of the Ninth Amendment, for a convict who commits the crimes of embezzlement or bribery and is sentenced to the death penalty with reprieve, the court may, depending on the circumstances of the crime, at the same time decide, after commuting the suspension of execution to life imprisonment on the expiry of the two year period, to imprison him for life, without commutation or parole.[131] In accordance with the judicial interpretation made by the SPC and SPP on 28 March 2016, a convict who has embezzled or taken bribes of not less than 3 million Yuan (CNY), may, in a case where the circumstances are especially serious, the social impact is especially severe and heavy losses are caused to the state and people, be sentenced to the death penalty. However, if he/she surrenders voluntarily, performs any meritorious service, confesses the crime and so on, and if the immediate execution is not deemed necessary, a two year suspension of execution may be pronounced simultaneously with the imposition of the death sentence, and at the same time a decision taken to prohibit commutation and parole, according to the circumstances.[132] This decision should be made at the first and

[127] Ibid., Article 84.

[128] Ibid., Article 85.

[129] *《中华人民共和国刑法修正案(八)》[The Eighth Amendment to the Criminal Law of the People's Republic of China]*, above no. 1, Article 17.

[130] *《中华人民共和国刑法》[Criminal Law of the People's Republic of China]*, Order No. 83, 2015, Article 86.

[131] *《中华人民共和国刑法修正案(九)》[The Ninth Amendment to the Criminal Law of the People's Republic of China]*, above no. 6, Article 44(4).

[132] *《最高人民法院、最高人民检察院关于办理贪污贿赂刑事案件适用法律若干问题的解释》[The Supreme People's Court's and Supreme People's Procuratorate's Interpretation of Several Legal Issues Concerning the Specific Application of the Law in Handling Criminal Cases of Embezzlement and Bribery], 法释 (2016) 9号 [Legal Interpretation No. 9, 2016])*, Articles 3 and 4.

second trial, respectively, rather than upon the expiry of the two-year period, and therefore it emphasizes that once the decision to impose LWOR has been made, it will not be affected by the offender's performance during the period of suspension and it shall be enforced without any condition. Consequently, this is termed the systemic rigidity of LWOR.[133]

The LWOR system was first established by the Ninth Amendment after the first criminal law was passed in 1979 and was "a brand new punishment measure".[134] Thus far, it has already been applied to three convicts.[135] The Chief Editor of the SPP's Research Office of Legal Policies, Wan Chun, said that "it is a new enforcement measure of the death penalty, which is in between the death penalty with immediate execution and the general death penalty with reprieve."[136] Even though it exists only for the crimes of embezzlement and bribery, it sends a significant signal about the alternative penalties to execution in the context of gradually reducing the death penalty. Some scholars positively affirmed LWOR and said that "according to the principle of suitable punishment for a crime, trying to impose LWOR on the convict who should have been sentenced to death for the serious crime of embezzlement or bribery is a positive and prudent option."[137] "Compared with the immediate execution of the death penalty, LWOR has its own humanitarian aspect."[138]

---

[133] *《"两高"发布办理贪污贿赂刑事案件司法解释》[Interpretations Concerning the Specific Application of the Law in Handling Criminal Cases of Embezzlement and Bribery Issued by the 'Two Supreme Judicial Authorities (Supreme People's Court and Supreme Peoples' Procuratorate)']*, available at: 中华人民共和国最高人民法院 [Supreme People's Court of People's Republic of China], available at: http://www.court.gov.cn/zixun-xiangqing-19562.html. (Last visited: January 22nd, 2024).

[134] *《"巨贪"将把牢底坐穿?——聚焦刑法修正案(九)草案:对重特大贪污犯罪增设"终身监禁"》['Will the 'Corrupt Official' Continue to Rot in Detention? Focus on the Ninth Amendment to the Criminal Law (Draft): Stipulating Life Imprisonment without Possibility of Release for Serious Crimes of Embezzlement and Bribery]*, available at: 中央政府网 [Central People's Government] http://www.gov.cn/xinwen/2015-08/25/content_2919673.htm. (Last visited: January 22nd, 2024).

[135] These three convicts are Bai Enpei, Wei Pengyuan and Yu Tieyi. All of them are sentenced to the death penalty with reprieve for having committed corruption crimes, and are not allowed to be granted commutation and parole after the death penalty with reprieve is reduced to life imprisonment. See *《白恩培等三巨贪被判处终身监禁,释放出什么信号?》[Such Bai Enpei as Three Arch Corrupt Officials Are Sentenced to Life.*

Imprisonment without Release, what Kinds of Signals Are Released?], available at: 星翰新闻网 [Xinghan News] http://www.szxinghan.cn/Social/13972494.html. (Last visited: March 24th, 2017).

[136] *《最高检万春主任等专家解读贪污贿赂司法解释》[The Chief Editor of the Research Office of the Legal Policies of the Supreme People's Procurator of the P.R.C, Wan Chun and Other Experts Explaining the Judicial Interpretations of the Anti-crime of Embezzlement and Bribery]*, available at: 今日头条 [Daily News] http://www.toutiao.com/i6288100038123979265/. (Last visited: January 22nd, 2024).

[137] Ibid.

[138] *阮齐林[RUAN Qilin],《依法从严惩治贪污贿赂犯罪——解读 < 关于办理贪污贿赂刑事案件适用法 律若干问题的解释 >》[Severely Punishing Crimes of Embezzlement and Bribery by the Law: Analyzing 'Interpretation on Several Legal Issues Concerning the Specific Application of the Law in Handling Criminal Cases of Embezzlement and Bribery']*, available at: 法制网[Legal Net] http://www.legaldaily.com.cn/index/content/2016-04/18/content_6591201.htm?node=20908. (Last visited: January 22nd, 2024).

5.5.2 *Life Imprisonment in Other States*

Life imprisonment is the maximum and the severest punishment in many states' penalty system, except in the states that retain the death penalty as their ultimate punishment. However, some states have not only removed the death penalty from their criminal punishment system, but also repealed life imprisonment. Therefore, this section would like to analyse the system of life imprisonment in other states. Considering the content of the section, it does not cover all the states in the world, but take some states as examples for analysis, including retentionist states which still retain the death penalty, and abolitionist states, as well as states where the death penalty and life imprisonment have been repealed. But it must be pointed out that even though life imprisonment has been abolished by some states, long term imprisonment does exist in the states' penalty system and thus it will be taken as the object of analysis. This section intends to analyse the prevalence of life imprisonment, and the conditions for its use as a sentence, as well as its termination mechanism in the relevant states.

5.5.2.1 Life Imprisonment in the Abolitionist States: Taking Some Member States of the EU as Examples

As of now, all the member states of the EU have already completely removed the death penalty from their penalty system, and life imprisonment has been upgraded to the maximum punishment and so become the severest punishment. This section cannot cover all the member states' life imprisonment systems, but considers some states as examples; Germany, the Netherlands, Hungary and Romania. The former two states are West European states, and the latter are Central and South-eastern European states.

(1) The prevalence of life imprisonment. The prevalence of life imprisonment refers to the number of crimes punishable by life imprisonment according to the criminal law. In other words, this generally means that life imprisonment is prescribed by the criminal law for these crimes. In the German Criminal Code, 18 provisions in the Special Part provide for crimes punishable by life imprisonment, accounting for 5.02% of a total of 358 effective provisions in the Special Part of the Criminal Code.[139] 6 of 18 provisions deal with offenses causing a common

[139] See the *German Criminal Code, promulgated on 13 November 1998, Federal Law Gazette. [Bundesgesetzblatt] I p. 3322, last amended by Article 1 of the Law of 24 September 2013, Federal Law Gazette I p. 3671 and with the text of Article 6(18) of the Law of 10 October 2013, Federal Law Gazette I p 3799.* Available at: https://www.gesetze-im-internet.de/englisch_stgb/. (Last visited: January 23rd, 2024). These provisions include Section 80 (preparation of a war of aggression), Section 81 (high treason against the Federation), Section 94 (treason), Section 100 (engaging in relations that endanger peace), Section 176 (child abuse causing death), Section 176a (aggravated child abuse causing death), Section 178 (sexual assault by use of force or threat of force and rape causing death), Section 211 (murder under specific aggravating circumstances),

danger[140]; 3 of the 18 are offenses against sexual self-determination.[141] By comparison, there are 23 provisions in the Special Part of the Hungarian Criminal Code prescribing crimes punishable by life imprisonment, accounting for 7.28% of a total of 316 provisions providing for crimes in this Part.[142] This proportion is higher than in Germany. 4 of the 23 provisions providing for crimes punishable by life imprisonment are related to offenses against the State; 3 of the 23 provisions to crimes against humanity; 3 provisions to war crimes; 3 provisions to drug trafficking; 3 provisions are offenses against public security; 2 relate to offenses against personal freedom; 2 are crimes against the judicial system; and so on. In the Netherlands' Criminal Code, there are 32 provisions relating to crimes providing for life imprisonment,[143] accounting for 6.54% of a total of 489 effective provisions relating to crimes in Books Two and Three.This proportion is higher than that of Germany's Criminal Code, but lower than that of the Hungarian Criminal Code. Among these 32 provisions, 9 of them relate to serious offenses against the security of the state, and 8 sections to serious

Section 212 (murder), Section 239a (abduction for the purpose of blackmail), Section 251 (robbery causing death), Section 306 (arson), Section 306a (aggravated arson), Section 306b (additionally aggravated arson), Section 307 (causing a nuclear explosion), Section 308 (causing an explosion), Section 309 (misuse of ionising radiation), Section 316a (attacking a driver for the purpose of committing a robbery), Section 316c (attacking air and maritime traffic).

[140] These provisions include Section 306c (arson causing death), Section 307 (causing a nuclear explosion), Section 308 (causing an explosion), Section 309 (misuse of ionising radiation), Section 316a (attacking a driver for the purpose of committing a robbery), Section 316c.

[141] These provisions include Section 176 (child abuse causing death), Section 176a (aggravated child abuse causing death), Section 178 (sexual assault by use of force or threat of force and rape causing death).

[142] These 316 provisions are specially referred to in the provisions from Section 142 to Section 457. These 23 provisions include Section 142 (genocide), Section 143 (crimes against humanity), Section 144 (apartheid), Section 148 (assault against a war emissary), Section 149 (assault on protected persons), Section 155 (use of weapons prohibited by international convention), Section 160 (homicide), Section 176 (drug trafficking), Section 177 (offering or supplying narcotic drugs to a person under the age of eighteen years), Section 179, Section 190 (kidnapping), Section 192 (trafficking in human beings), Section 254 (attempting to overturn a constitutional order by force), Section 257 (destruction), Section 258 (high treason), Section 260 (aid and comfort), Section 284 (prison riot), Section 314 (acts of terrorism), Section 320 (unlawful seizure of a vehicle), Section 322 (public endangerment), Section 326 (criminal offenses with weapons prohibited by international convention), Section 442 (mutiny), and Section 445 (assault on a superior officer or representative of public authority). See *Act C of 2012 of the Criminal Code of Hungary*, promulgated on 13 July 2012.

[143] These 32 provisions include Sections 92, 93, 94, 95, 95a, 97, 97a, 98a, 102 (all of these nine sections provide for serious offenses against the security of the state), 108 and 114a (these two provisions relate to serious offenses against royal dignity), 115, 117, 120a and 121 (these four provisions relate to serious offenses against heads of friendly nations and other internationally protected persons), 140a (this provision relates to serious offenses against public order), 157, 161 quarter, 164, 166, 168, 170, 174 and 176a (these eight provisions relate to serious offenses endangering the general safety of persons or property), 282a, 282b, 288, 288a and 289 (these five provisions relate to serious offenses against personal liberty), 304a (this provision relates to assault), 385a and 415a (these two provisions relate to serious offenses against shipping and aviation). See *Act of 3 March 1881*, the *Criminal Code of Netherlands*.

offenses endangering the general safety of persons or property. Turning to the Criminal Code of Romania, the number of the crimes punishable by life imprisonment stipulated in the Special Part is less than in the preceding three states because there are only 12 stipulations providing for crimes punishable by life imprisonment,[144] accounting for 4.65% of a total of 258 stipulations related to crimes in the Special Part of the Criminal Code of Romania. 6 of these 12 provisions relate to offenses against national security, 3 to crimes of genocide, crimes against humanity and war crimes, 2 to crimes against the fighting capacity of the armed forces, and 1 provision relates to offenses against the person. In all of the 4 states discussed above the proportion of crimes punishable by life imprisonment in their Criminal Codes is very similar, and life imprisonment makes up only a small proportion in the penalty system, and is only used for felonies.

(2) Conditions for passing a sentence of life imprisonment. Based on an analysis of these four states' Criminal Codes, life imprisonment can be applied in the following two main situations. Firstly, life imprisonment can be applied for action crimes, which are proved to have already been committed and whose consequences are not material, and which are classified as felonies. For example, Section 80 of Germany's Criminal Code, which deals with the crime of preparation of a war of aggression, provides that "whosoever prepares a war of aggression…shall be liable to imprisonment for life",[145] and Sections 81 and 211.[146] By comparison, the number of action crimes punishable by life imprisonment in the Netherlands' Criminal Code is more than in the German Criminal Code. There are 20 provisions providing for life imprisonment for action crimes, accounting for 62.5% of a total of 32 provisions providing for crimes punishable by life imprisonment in the Netherlands Criminal Code.[147] The proportion of the number of provisions in the Hungarian Criminal Code providing for life imprisonment for action crimes is lower than in the Netherlands' Criminal Code, but higher than in the German Criminal Code, totalling 8 provisions applying life imprisonment for action crimes, accounting for 33.33% of a total of 24 provisions.[148] However, the proportion of provisions providing life imprisonment for

[144] These stipulations include Articles 189 (aggravated murder), 396 (treason by helping the enemy), 398 (high treason), 401 (attack that jeopardizes national security), 402 (attack against a community), 403 (diversionary acts), 408 (offenses against representatives who have international immunity), 421 (capitulation), 422 (leaving the battlefield), 438 (genocide), 439 (crimes against humanity), and 440 (war crimes against persons). See *LAW # 286 of 7 July 2009 of the Criminal Code of Romania, Amending Acts: #M1, Law # 27/ 2012; M2: Law #63/2012; M3: Law # 187/2012,* enters into force on February 1st, 2014.

[145] See *Federal Law Gazette [Bundesgesetzblatt] I p. 3322, last amended by Article 1 of the Law of 24 September 2013, Federal Law Gazette I p. 3671 and with the text of Article 6(18) of the Law of 10 October 2013, Federal Law Gazette I p 3799,* Section 80.

[146] Ibid., Sections 81 and 211.

[147] These stipulations include Sections 92, 93, 94, 95, 95a, 97, 97a, 98a, 102, 108, 114, 120a, 140a, 176a, 288, 288a, 289, 304a, and 415a. See *Act of 3 March 1881,* the *Criminal Code of Netherlands.*

[148] These provisions include Sections 142, 143, 148, 149, 155, 254, 260, and 314. See Act C of 2012 of the Criminal Code of Hungary, promulgated on 13 July 2012. Considering that Section 149 does not only provide for life imprisonment for action crimes, but also provides that life imprisonment

action crimes in the Romanian Criminal Code is higher than in the Netherlands, totalling 8 provisions, accounting for 66.67% of a total of 12 provisions in the Romanian Criminal Code.[149] Secondly, life imprisonment can be applied to an offender under certain legally-prescribed circumstances according to the law, such as causing the victim to die, having serious consequences or circumstances, or in especially serious cases. For example, 15 of the 18 sections provide for crimes punishable by life imprisonment under legally prescribed circumstances in the German Criminal Code, accounting for 83.33% of a total of 18 provisions,[150] which is more than in the Hungarian Criminal Code. There are 16 provisions providing crimes punishable by life imprisonment under legally prescribed circumstances in the Hungarian Criminal Code, accounting for 66.67% of a total of 24 provisions.[151] The proportion of the number of provisions providing for crimes punishable by life imprisonment under legally prescribed circumstances in the Netherlands' Criminal Code is less than in the Hungarian and German Criminal Codes, totaling 12 provisions, accounting for 37.5% of a total of 32 provisions.[152] By comparison, the proportion of provisions providing for crimes punishable by life imprisonment under legally prescribed circumstances in the Romanian Criminal Code is the lowest, with only 4 provisions, accounting for 33.33% of a total of 12 provisions.[153] "Legally prescribed circumstances" in these four states in most cases means that the crime causes death, and in other cases that the circumstances of the case are serious. According to the above analysis, in these four states' criminal codes life imprisonment is mainly imposed on the offender under legally prescribed circumstances.

(3) Termination Mechanisms for Life Imprisonment. As for the termination mechanism for life imprisonment, there are generally two main approaches around the world, i.e. life imprisonment with possibility of release and life imprisonment without any possibility of release. Life imprisonment without release is a punishment that "removes any uncertainty at the time of sentencing about the possibility of rehabilitation by condemning the inmate to die in prison."[154]

---

can be applied to an offender under certain legally-prescribed circumstances according to the law, here I count 24 provisions, but in fact, there are only 23.

[149] These provisions include Articles 396, 398, 401, 402, 403, 408, 421 and 422. See *LAW # 286 of 7 July 2009 of the Criminal Code of Romania.*

[150] These provisions include 94, 100, 176, 176b, 177, 212, 239a, 251, 306, 306a, 306b, 307, 308, 309 and 316. See *Federal Law Gazette [Bundesgesetzblatt] I p. 3322, last amended by Article 1 of the Law of 24 September 2013, Federal Law Gazette I p. 3671 and with the text of Article 6(18) of the Law of 10 October 2013, Federal Law Gazette I p 3799.*

[151] These provisions include Sections 144, 149, 160, 176, 177, 179, 190, 192, 257, 258, 284, 320, 322, 326, 442 and 445. See *Act C of 2012 on the Criminal Code of Hungary.*

[152] These provisions include Sections 115, 117, 157, 161 quarter, 164, 166, 168, 170, 174, 282a, 282b and 385. See *Act of 3 March 1881, The Criminal Code of Netherlands.*

[153] These provisions include Articles 189, 438, 439 and 440. See *LAW # 286 of 7 July 2009 of the Criminal Code of Romania.*

[154] VEGA Connie de la, SOLTER Amanda, KWON Soo-Ryun and ISAAC Dana Marie, *Cruel and Unusual: U.S. Sentencing Practices in a Global Context*, University of San Francisco (USF) School

Currently, according to the report "Cruel and Unusual: U.S. Sentencing Practices in a Global Context", 38 countries out of the world's 193 are "known to have life imprisonment without parole statutes (20%), and 21 countries have no discernible statutory provision allowing for such a sentence".[155] The Netherlands is one of the 21 states which has life imprisonment without release, where the Criminal Law does not stipulate any provision about terminating the inmate's life sentence. The European Committee for the Prevention of Torture and Inhuman or Degrading Treatment or Punishment (CPT) have argued that, "in the Netherlands, life imprisonment really means imprisonment for the rest of one's life."[156] In relation to life imprisonment without release, a Dutch national, Mr. James Clifton Murray, alleged that, in violation of Article 3 of the Convention for the Protection of Human Rights and Fundamental Freedoms (the Convention), the life sentence imposed on him by the Netherlands' Court was de jure *and* de facto irreducible, and complained about the Kingdom of the Netherlands to the European Court of Human Rights (ECtHR) on 22 February 2010.[157] The ECtHR concluded that "the Article 3 violation was aggravated by the existence of a discretionary and opaque pardon system"[158] According to the CPT Report, as of 13 May 2016 there were 33 persons serving a life sentence in the Netherlands' prisons.[159] However, an inmate who is sentenced to life imprisonment can be released early by a pardon granted by Royal Decree upon the recommendation of a court designated by Act of Parliament according to Article 122 of the Constitution of the Kingdom of the Netherlands[160]; this

---

of Law's Center for Law and Global Justice, May, 2012, 21. Available at https://www.cpcjalliance.org/wp-content/uploads/2013/04/Cruel-And-Unusual.pdf (Last visited: January 23rd, 2024).

[155] Ibid., 25. See also GALLIANI Davide, *The Reducible Life Imprisonment Standard from a Worldwide and European Perspective*, Global Jurist 2016, Vol. 16, Issue 1, 84. These 24 countries include: Albania, Argentina, Australia, Brunei Darussalam, Bulgaria, Burundi, China, Comoros, Cuba, Eritrea, Ethiopia, Ghana, Hungary, Israel, Kazakhstan, Kenya, Lao People's Democratic Republic, Liberia, Lithuania, Malta, Marshall Islands, Namibia, the Netherlands, New Zealand, Nigeria, Palau, Seychelles, Sierra Leone, Slovakia, Solomon Islands, Sweden, Tajikistan, Tanzania, Turkey, Ukraine, United Kingdom, and Zimbabwe. These 21 countries for which the Report could not locate statutory or case law text confirming whether life imprisonment without parole exists or not include: Barbados, Bhutan, Dominica, Equatorial Guinea, Gambia, Grenada, Guyana, Indonesia, Kuwait, Lebanon, Libya, Saint Kitts and Nevis, Saint Vincent and the Grenadines, Saudi Arabia, South Sudan, Suriname, Syria, Thailand, Trinidad and Tobago, Turkmenistan, and the United Arab Emirates.

[156] *The European Committee for the Prevention of Torture and Inhuman or Degrading Treatment or Punishment (CPT) Report about the Prison in Netherlands*, Council of Europe, CPT/Inf (2017)1, Strasbourg, 19 January 2017, 31. Available at https://rm.coe.int/16806ebb7c. (Last visited: January 23rd, 2024).

[157] *Case of Murray v. The Netherlands*, (Application no. 10511/10), Judgment, Strasbourg, 26 April 2016.

[158] Ibid., 71.

[159] *The European Committee for the Prevention of Torture and Inhuman or Degrading Treatment or Punishment (CPT) Report about the Prison in Netherlands*, Council of Europe, CPT/Inf (2017)1, Strasbourg, 19 January 2017, 31.

[160] *The Constitution of the Kingdom of the Netherlands 2008*, Article 122.

"may be granted only if there are 'changed circumstances', for instance, health reasons."[161] On June 2, 2016, Klaas Dijkhoff, State Secretary for Security and Justice, addressed a letter to the Dutch Parliament indicating his plan to introduce a review mechanism for life sentences after the offender has served 25 years of the sentence.[162] In the CPT Report, therefore, the European Committee for the Prevention of Torture and Inhuman or Degrading Treatment "recommends necessary legislative and administrative measures be taken rapidly to provide persons sentenced to life imprisonment with a clear avenue for consideration of release, based upon objective criteria, after a defined time period."[163]

By comparison, life imprisonment in the Hungarian Criminal Code is relatively more humane than in Netherlands. The Hungarian Criminal Code provides that "in the event a sentence of life imprisonment is imposed, the court shall specify the earliest date of eligibility for parole, or shall preclude any eligibility for parole"[164]; if the court does not preclude eligibility for parole with a sentence of life imprisonment, the earliest date for release on parole shall be after serving 25 years, or at least forty years, and the duration of parole shall be not less than 15 years.[165] However, the court may deny the possibility of parole for the sentence of life imprisonment when the case involves crimes provided by Section 44 of Hungarian Criminal Code.[166] This Sections was applied in the case of Törköly v Hungary (Application no. 4413/06, 5

[161] See also *The European Committee for the Prevention of Torture and Inhuman or Degrading Treatment or Punishment (CPT) Report about the Prison in Netherlands*, Council of Europe, CPT/Inf (2017)1, Strasbourg, 19 January 2017, 31.

[162] Ibid.

[163] Ibid.

[164] *Act C of 2012 in the Criminal Code of Hungary*, Section 42. See generally, GÁL ISTVÁN László, SZŰCS András, *A Büntetések [The Penalties]*, in *Új Btk. Kommentár: 2. Kötet [Commentary on New Criminal Code: Vol. 2], Általános rész [General Part]*, Edited by POLT Péter, Budapest, 2013, 9–69; JUHÁSZ Zsuzsanna, *A Büntetések [The penalties], Kommentár a Büntető Törvénykönyvhöz [Commentary on Criminal Code]*, edited by KARSAI Krisztina, Budapest, 2013, 109–163; Madai Sándor: *A Társadalmi Tulajdon Fokozottabb Büntetőjogi Védelme Egykor és Most [Increased Criminal Protection of Social Property Once and Now]*, Békés Imre emlékkötet [Remembering essays for Imre Békés], edited by GELLÉRR Balázs, CSIGE Zoltán, Budapest, 2013, 143–178; KARSAI Krisztina and ZSOLT Szomora, *Criminal Law in Hungary*, Kluwer Law International BV, the Netherlands, 2010, 28.

[165] Ibid., Section 43. See generally, GÁL ISTVÁN László, László, *Feltételes szabadságra bocsátás az életfogytig tartó szabadságvesztésből 42–45. § [Release on Parole from Life Imprisonment 42–45. §], A Büntető Törvénykönyvről szóló 2012. évi C. törvény nagykommentárja [Great Commentary on the Act C of 2012 on the Criminal Code]*, edited by POLT Péter, MISKOLCZI Barna, TÖRÖK Tímea, GASZ Péter, Budapest, 2016, 207–213.

[166] Ibid., Section 44 (1). These crimes include: (a) genocide [Subsection (1) of Section 142]; (b) crimes against humanity [Subsection (1) of Section 143]; (c) apartheid [Subsections (1) and (3) of Section 144]; (d) aggravated cases of assault against a war emissary [Subsection (2) of Section 148]; (e) assault on protected persons [Subsections (1)-(2) of Section 149]; (f) use of a weapon prohibited by international convention [Subsection (1) of Section 155]; (g) other war crimes (Section 158); (h) aggravated cases of homicide [Subsection (2) of Section 160]; (i) aggravated cases of kidnapping [Subsections (3)-(4) of Section 190]; (j) aggravated cases of trafficking in human beings [Subsection (6) of Section 192]; (k) attempt to overturn the constitutional order by force [Subsection (1)

April 2011). In this case, on 25 July 2014 the applicant, Tibor Törköly, was convicted by the Bács-Kiskun County Regional Court of multiple, recidivist attempted grave bodily assault and of aggravated murder committed with special cruelty, and given a life sentence with eligibility for release after 40 years.[167] Furthermore, if the offender is a repeat offender with a history of violence or has committed a criminal offense defined in Section 91 Subsection (1), which provides for crimes committed in the framework of a criminal organization, the court shall deny the possibility of parole for the perpetrator.[168] This means that the court has to deny parole to the perpetrator if he or she is involved in acts related to the circumstances provided in Section 44 (2); consequently, the perpetrator will not be released from prison. This section was applied in the case of László Magyar v. Hungary (application no. 73593/10, 20 May, 2014). In this case, the applicant, Mr. László Magyar, was convicted of murder, robbery and several offenses, and was sentenced to life imprisonment without eligibility for parole.[169] In fact, this "real life imprisonment" was introduced in 1998 with some modification, which is considered to be the toughest amendment."[170] The ECtHR's final judgement in this case held that "Hungary would be required to reform the system of review of whole life sentences to guarantee that life prisoners can foresee what they must do to be considered for release and under what conditions."[171] However, in 2013, the Hungarian legislature had already adopted a new Penitentiary Code (Act CCXL of 2013) to reform the penalty system by replacing the old Penitentiary Code, which was adopted in 1979, although the Act CCXL of 2013 does change the regulation of real life imprisonment.[172] This new provision on life imprisonment was changed quite soon after Act LXXII of 2014, which was adopted as a response to the judgement on the case of László Magyar v. Hungary (application no. 73593/10) and modified the new Penitentiary Code's rules on life imprisonment

---

of Section 254]; (l) aggravated cases of destruction [Subsection (2) of Section 257]; (m) aggravated cases of prison riot [Subsection (4) of Section 284]; (n) acts of terrorism [Subsection (1) of Section 314]; (o) aggravated cases of unlawful seizure of a vehicle [Subsection (2) of Section 320]; (p) aggravated cases of public endangerment [Subsection (3) of Section 322]; (q) aggravated cases of mutiny [Subsection (4) of Section 442]; (r) aggravated cases of assault on a superior officer or representative of public authority [Subsection (5) of Section 445]. See generally, MADAI Sándor, above no. 714, 143–178.

[167] See *Törköly v Hungary*, application no. 4413/06, ECtHR (Second Section), Decision of 05.04. 2011. Available at: http://hudoc.echr.coe.int/eng#{"itemid":["001-104602"]} (Last visited: January 23rd, 2024).

[168] *Act C of 2012 on the Criminal Code of Hungary*, Section 44 (2).

[169] See *László Magyar v. Hungary*, application no. 73593/10, 20 May, 2014. Available at: http:/ /hudoc.echr.coe.int/eng-press#{"itemid":["003-4764328-5797216"]} (Last visited: January 23rd, 2024).

[170] NAGY Anita, *Release from Prison and Probation in Hungary*, Juridical Current, 2016, Vol. 19, Issue 3, 65.

[171] Ibid.

[172] See PETRA Bárd, *The Hungarian Life Imprisonment Regime in front of Apex Courts I.*, available at: Blogsite of the Institute for Legal Studies http://jog.tk.mta.hu/en/blog/2015/06/the-hungar ian-life-imprisonment (Last visited: June 27th, 2017). See generally, MADAI Sándor, above no. 714,143–178.

by inserting a new subtitle on mandatory pardon proceedings for persons sentenced to life imprisonment without the possibility of conditional release.[173] The pardon process, which needs to be agreed to by the convict, is deliberated by a Pardon Committee consisting of five judges, and the final decision on pardon will be made by the President of Hungary.[174] Therefore, life imprisonment in Hungary can de jure *and* de facto be terminated earlier with a Presidential pardon, which means that in response to the criticism of the ECtHR, the presidential pardon system has made modifications.[175] Even though the Hungarian legislature amended their laws and introduced a new automatic and mandatory review system of life imprisonment after the inmate has served 40 years of his or her sentence in prison, the European Court of Human Rights, in the cases of T.P. and A.T. v. Hungary (application nos. 37871/14 and 73986/14), held that there had been a violation of Article 3 of the ECHR, because making a prisoner wait 40 years before he or she could expect to be considered for clemency for the first time is too long, and such a period was significantly longer than the maximum recommended time frame (25 years).[176]

Looking at life imprisonment in Germany, according to Section 57a of the German Criminal Code, an inmate who is sentenced to life imprisonment may be conditionally released early from prison after serving 15 years of the sentence in prison if he or she met the relevant requirements, i.e. the particular seriousness of the perpetrator's guilt does not require its continued enforcement, and the release is appropriate considering public security interests, and with the consent of the perpetrator.[177] While deciding to grant early release to the inmate sentenced to life imprisonment, Section 57(1)2nd sentence and (6) shall apply mutatis mutandis,[178] the court shall particularly consider the personality of the inmate, his or her previous history, the circumstances of his offense, the importance of the legal interest endangered should he or she re-offend, the conduct of the inmate while serving his or her sentence, his or her circumstances, his or her living conditions and the effects an early release are to be expected to have on him or her[179]; and the court may refuse to grant early release from a life sentence if the perpetrator makes insufficient or false statements, as provided in Section 57(6).[180] If imprisonment for life has been imposed as an aggregate sentence the individual

---

[173] Ibid. See generally, GÁL ISTVÁN László, Szűcs András, above no. 714, 9–69; MADAI Sándor, above no. 714, 143–178.

[174] Ibid. See also NAGY Anita, Pardon System in Hungary and European Human Rights Jurisprudence, The Lawyer Quarterly, 2016, Vol.3, Issue.3, 181–188; See generally, GÁL ISTVÁN László, above no. 715, 207–213; MADAI Sándor, above no. 714, 143–178..

[175] NAGY Anita, *Presidential Pardon and the European Court of Human Rights*, CASOPIS POLICAJNA TEORIA A PRAX, 2016, Issue.1, 69..

[176] *T.P. and A.T. v. Hungary*, application nos. 37871/14 and 73986/14. Available at: http://hudoc.echr.coe.int/eng-press#{"itemid":["003-5600221-7075341"]} (Last visited: January 23rd, 2024).

[177] See *Federal Law Gazette [Bundesgesetzblatt] I p. 3322, last amended by Article 1 of the Law of 24 September 2013, Federal Law Gazette I p. 3671 and with the text of Article 6(18) of the Law of 10 October 2013, Federal Law Gazette I p 3799,* Sections 57a (1), 57(1).

[178] Ibid., Section 57a (1) 2nd sentence.

[179] Ibid., Section 57(1) 2nd sentence.

[180] Ibid., Section 57 (6).

offenses shall be comprehensively evaluated in determining the particular seriousness of the crimes.[181] Regarding this section on aggregative life imprisonment, there were two cases in which the perpetrators were not released after serving 15 years of their sentences in prisons; both convicts appealed to the European Court of Human Rights (Streicher v. Germany and Meixner v. Germany). In the case of Streicher v. Germany, the perpetrator, Mr. Dieter Streicher, was convicted of murder and attempted murder and sentenced to life imprisonment, and the Ansbach Regional Court held that the perpetrator was emotionally cold, had a tendency to overreact, and was psychopathic and antisocial. Based on the these facts and relevant reports, on 25 March 2004, the Regensburg Regional Court refused to suspend his sentence on probation and decided that the "particular gravity" of the applicant's guilt and his personality warranted extending the sentence to at least 26 years' imprisonment in total.[182] In the case of Meixner v. Germany, the inmate, Rolf Friedrich Meixner, was convicted of a number of offenses, including triple murder, which he had committed while on probation, and sentenced to life imprisonment in 1986. In 2006, the Gießen Regional Court, the Court of Appeal and the Federal Constitutional Court subsequently refused the request from Rolf Friedrich Meixner for early release, relying on an expert's opinion which concluded that there was a high risk of the applicant committing crimes again when released, and extended the sentence to at least 25 years' imprisonment.[183]

By comparison, life imprisonment in Romania seems more lenient than in the preceding three states (the Netherlands, Germany and Hungary) because life imprisonment shall be replaced or commuted to a fixed term imprisonment of 30 years if the inmate's conditions meet the requirements of the Criminal Code; and the inmate can also be released early on parole. According to Article 57 of the Romanian Criminal Code, if the defendant has turned 65 at the date when the judgment to convict is returned, the sentence of life imprisonment shall be replaced by a prison term of 30 years and a ban on the exercise of certain rights for the maximum duration of the prison sentence[184]; furthermore, if the inmate turns 65 while serving the sentence of life imprisonment, the life imprisonment can be replaced by a term of 30 years of imprisonment and a ban on the exercise of certain rights for the maximum duration of the prison sentence.[185] The former is called the replacement of life imprisonment, and the latter can be called the commutation of life imprisonment. We therefore can see that both the replacement and the commutation of life imprisonment are mandatory when the defendant or inmate reaches the age of 65. In both of these two cases the time already served in prison by the inmate shall be deemed as a prison sentence already served.[186]

---

[181] Ibid., Section 58.

[182] *Streicher v. Germany,* application no. 40384/04, 2009. Available at: http://hudoc.echr.coe.int/fre#{"itemid":["001-91620"]} (Last visited: January 23rd, 2024).

[183] *Meixner v. Germany,* application no. 26958/07, 2009. Available at: http://hudoc.echr.coe.int/fre#{"itemid":["003-2938799-3232312"]} (Last visited: June 27th, 2017).

[184] *LAW # 286 of 7 July 2009 of the Criminal Code of Romania,* Article 57.

[185] Ibid., Article 58.

[186] Ibid., Article 59.

5.5.2.2 Life Imprisonment in the Retentionist States: Taking Japan and Singapore as Examples

As is clear from the above analysis of the death penalty around the world, Japan and Singapore are both retentionist states, which retain the death penalty in their Criminal Codes. In fact, life imprisonment in these two states' penalty systems serves as an optional punishment in place of the death penalty for some serious crimes. The following section will analyse life imprisonment in these two states' Criminal Codes in terms of its prevalence, the conditions for passing a sentence of life imprisonment and its termination mechanism.

(1) The prevalence of life imprisonment. Japan and Singapore are states which retain the death penalty, and life imprisonment is an optional punishment for it. Based on an analysis of the Japanese Criminal Code, there are 13 provisions dealing with crimes punishable by life imprisonment, accounting for 6.34% of a total of 205 provisions dealing with crimes in Part II of the Code.[187] Among these 13 provisions, there are 9 provisions dealing with crimes punishable by the death penalty where life imprisonment serves as an alternative to the death penalty.[188] We also can see that the crimes punishable by life imprisonment are distributed in different chapters. As regards life imprisonment in Singapore, there are 35 provisions in the Singapore Penal Code providing for crimes punishable by life imprisonment, accounting for 8.00% of a total of 437 provisions dealing with crimes.[189] The proportion of these crimes in the Singapore Penal Code is more

[187] Penal Code of Japan, Act No. 45 of April 24, 1907 (日本国刑法45号, 1907年4月24日). These 14 provisions include: Articles 77(1) (insurrection), 82 (assistance to the enemy), 108 (arson of inhabited buildings), 119 (damage to inhabited buildings by flood), 126 (overturning of trains), 146 (pollution of water supplied with poisonous materials and causing death thereby), 148 (counterfeiting of currency or issuing counterfeit currency), 154 (counterfeiting of imperial or state documents), 181 (forcible indecency causing death or injury), 199 (homicide), 225-2 (kidnapping for ransom), 240 (robbery causing death or injury), and 241 (rape at the scene of a robbery, causing death thereby).

[188] These provisions include Articles 77, 82, 108, 119, 126, 146, 199 and 241.See Ibid.

[189] See *the Statutes of the Republic of Singapore: Penal Code (chapter 224), Original Enactment: Ordinance 4 of 1871,* the revised edition of the Laws Act (Chapter 275), in force from 1/4/2015. These provisions include: Section 121 (waging or attempting to wage war or abetting the waging of war against the Government), 121A (offenses against the President's person), 121B (offenses against authority), 122 (collecting arms, etc., with the intention of waging war against the Government), 124 (assaulting the President, etc., with intent to compel or restrain the exercise of any lawful power), 125 (waging war against any power in alliance or at peace with Singapore), 128 (a public servant voluntarily allowing a prisoner of state or war in his custody to escape), 130 (aiding the escape of, rescuing, or harbouring such a prisoner), 130B (piracy according to the law of nations), 130E (genocide), 131 (abetting mutiny, or attempting to seduce an officer or a serviceman from his duty), 132 (abetment of mutiny, if mutiny is committed in consequence thereof), 194 (giving or fabricating false evidence with intent to procure conviction of a capital offense), 195 (giving or fabricating false evidence with intent to procure conviction of an offense punishable with imprisonment), 222 (intentional omission on the part of a public servant bound by law to apprehend a person under sentence of a court of justice), 225 (resistance or obstruction to the lawful apprehension of another person), 302 (murder), 304 (culpable homicide not amounting to murder), 305 (abetment of suicide

than in the Japanese code. Among these 35 provisions, there are 10 provisions dealing with crimes punishable by death and life imprisonment, of which the latter serves as an alternative punishment to the death penalty. And among these 35 provisions, there are 11 provisions providing for offenses affecting the human body, 8 for offenses against the state, 8 for robbery and gang-robbery, and 4 for providing false evidence and offenses against public justice.

(2) Conditions for passing a sentence of life imprisonment. In the Penal Code of Japan, life imprisonment can be applied in the following two situations: (1) life imprisonment can be applied for action crimes, for example, Article 77(1.ii) provides that "a person who participates in a plot or directs a mob" shall be punished by life imprisonment without work.[190] In addition, this penalty is dealt with in Articles 82, 108, 126(1), 148, 154, 199, 225–2, 240[191] and 241.[192] There are 10 provisions (including paragraphs with the same provision but expressed in different ways), accounting for 58.82% of a total of 17 provisions. (2) Life imprisonment can be applied to an offender under certain legally-prescribed circumstances according to the law, including when the perpetrator has a special status, such as "if he or she is a ringleader" (Article 77(1.i)),[193] or if the crime causes special circumstances, as in Article 119 which deals with "a person who causes a flood to damage a building",[194] or death to another person, as in

of a child or insane person), 307 (attempt to murder), 311 (infanticide), 313 (causing miscarriage without a woman's consent), 314 (death caused by an act done with intent to cause miscarriage), 326 (voluntarily causing grievous hurt by dangerous weapons or means), 329 (voluntarily causing grievous hurt to extort property, or to constrain someone to commit an illegal act), 364 (kidnapping or abducting in order to murder), 371 (habitual dealing in slaves), 396 (gang-robbery with murder), 400 (belonging to a gang of robbers), 409 (criminal breach of trust by a public servant, or by a banker, merchant, or agent), 412 (dishonestly receiving property stolen in the commission of a gang-robbery), 430A (mischief affecting a railway engine, train, etc.), 436 (mischief by fire or explosive substance with intent to destroy a house, etc.), 438 (mischief described in Section 437 when committed by fire or any explosive substance), and 449 (house-trespass in order to commit an offense punishable with death).

[190] The Penal Code of Japan, Act No. 45 of April 24, 1907 (日本国刑法45号, 1907年4月24日), Article 77(1.ii).

[191] See Ibid., Article 240, the first sentence of which provides that "when a person who has committed the crime of robbery causes another to suffer injury at the scene of the robbery, the person shall be punished by imprisonment with work for life or for a definite term of not less than 6 years.

[192] See ibid., Article 241, the first sentence of which provides that "when a person committing the crime of robbery rapes a female, imprisonment with work for life or for a definite term of nor less than 7 years shall be imposed.

[193] See ibid., Article 77(1.ii), which provides that if the perpetrator commits an insurrection, if he or she is a ringleader, life imprisonment may be imposed on him or her.

[194] See ibid., Article 119, which provides that "a person who causes a flood to damage a building, train, tram, or mine actually used as a dwelling or in which a person is actually present shall be punished by the death penalty or imprisonment with work for life or for a definite term of not less than 3 years.".

Articles 126(3), 146, 181, 240[195] and 241.[196] There are 7 provisions (including paragraphs with the same provision but expressed in different ways), accounting for 41.18% of a total of 17 provisions. Similarly, in the terms of the categories of the applicable conditions for life imprisonment, the Singapore Penal Code is almost the same as the Penal Code of Japan; these conditions could be divided into two main situations, i.e., life imprisonment for special action crimes and life imprisonment applied to an offender under certain legally-prescribed circumstances according to the law, and the proportion of the former is higher than that of the latter. Specifically, there are 28 provisions providing for an action crime punishable by life imprisonment, accounting for 80% of a total of 35 provisions,[197] and there are 7 provisions providing for life imprisonment applied to an offender under certain legally-prescribed circumstances according to the law, accounting for 20% of a total of 35 provisions.[198] For instance, Article 307 provides "if hurt is caused to any person by such act", Article 314 provides that "if the act done with intent to cause miscarriage is done without the consent of the woman, [the perpetrator] shall be punished … with imprisonment for life", and Article 326 provides for a crime which "causes grievous hurt by special instruments."

(3) Termination Mechanisms for Life Imprisonment. It is a fact that a perpetrator who is sentenced to life imprisonment or whose sentence is life imprisonment commuted from the death penalty can be released early from prison, rather than being held in prison for the duration of his or her natural life. According to Article 28 of the Penal Code of Japan, when a person who is sentenced to imprisonment with or without work evinces signs of substantial reformation, the person may be paroled by a disposition of a government agency after that person has served 10 years of a life sentence.[199] Therefore, the inmate may be released from prison after serving 10 years of a sentence of life imprisonment in prison if he or she satisfies the conditions for parole. However, the parole may be revoked. According to Article 29, parole may be revoked in the following cases: (i) when a further crime is committed within the period of parole and a fine or greater punishment is imposed for the crime; (ii) when a fine or greater punishment is imposed for a crime committed before the parole; (iii) when a

---

[195] See ibid., Article 240, the second sentence of which provides that "when a person who has committed the crime of robbery, in the case of causing death, the death penalty or imprisonment with work for life shall be imposed.".

[196] See ibid., Article 241, the second sentence of which provides that "when a person who has committed the crime of robbery rapes a female, in the case of causing death thereby, the death penalty or imprisonment with work for life shall be imposed.

[197] See *the Statutes of the Republic of Singapore: Penal Code (chapter 224),* Original Enactment: Ordinance 4 of 1871, the revised edition of the Laws Act (Chapter 275), in force from 01.04.2015. These 28 provisions include Articles 121, 121A, 121B, 122, 124, 125, 128, 130, 130B, 130E, 131, 132, 194, 195, 302, 305, 311, 313, 364, 371, 396, 400, 409, 412, 430A, 436, 438 and 449.

[198] See ibid. These 7 provisions include Articles 222, 225, 304, 307, 314, 326 and 329.

[199] The *Penal Code of Japan*, Act No. 45 of April 24, 1907 (日本国刑法45号, 1907年4月24日), Article 28.

fine or greater punishment is imposed for another crime before the parole is implemented; (iv) when the person fails to observe any of the conditions of the parole.[200] According to a Report issued by the Ministry of Justice of Japan, in the period from 1996 to 2015 there were 576 perpetrators newly sentenced to life imprisonment (無期刑新受刑者), and by the end of 2015, there were 1835 inmates serving their sentence of life imprisonment in prisons (年末在所無期刑者) in the State of Japan. In this decade, 71 inmates were released on parole (無期刑仮釈放者数); and in these 10 years, 53 of these 71 inmates were granted parole again after their preceding parole was revoked (無期刑新仮釈放者); 64 inmates died in prison while serving their sentence of life imprisonment (死亡した無期刑受刑者) in this decade.[201] Even though the minimum term of a life imprisonment sentence that needs to be served parole to be granted is 10 years as stipulated by the Penal Code of Japan, the average length of life imprisonment sentences served in prison before release on parole (平均受刑在所期間) is more than 10 years, indeed, it was 31 years and 6 months in 2015, 31 years and 4 months in 2014, 35 years and 2 months in 2011, 35 years and 3 months in 2010, while the lowest was 25 years and 1 months in 2006.[202] In comparison, commutation (reduction)—which is another way for the inmate to be released early from prison—seems more lenient than parole, at least, de jure. According to Articles 66 and 67, punishment may be reduced in the light of the extenuating circumstances of a crime, and it may only be reduced in the light of circumstances.[203] Article 68(ii) provides that "when there are one or more statutory grounds for reduction of punishment, in the case of imprisonment with or without work for life [being] reduced, it shall be reduced to imprisonment with or without work for a definite term of not less than 7 years.[204] This means that an inmate who is sentenced to life imprisonment can be released from prison on reduction (commutation) after serving 7 years of the sentence if all the requirements for reduction are satisfied. However, we cannot find the judicial statistical data to support this argument. Looking at Singapore, we cannot find any provision providing the details of a termination mechanism for life imprisonment in the Penal Code of Singapore because they are provided by the Criminal Procedure Code of Singapore and the Prison Act of Singapore. According to Article 333 of the Criminal Procedure Code, the inmate sentenced to life imprisonment may be released with a pardon, or on remission or on commutation. Article 333(1) provides that "where a person has been sentenced to punishment for an offense, the President may grant a pardon,

[200] Ibid., Article 29.

[201] 法務省 [Ministry of Justice of Japan], *無期刑の執行状況及び無期刑受刑者に係る仮釈放の運用状況について [The Status of Execution of Life Imprisonment and the Status of Release on Parole of Inmates Sentenced to Life Imprisonment]*, available at: http://www.moj.go.jp/content/001208315.pdf (Last visited: January 23rd, 2024).

[202] Ibid.

[203] See ibid., Articles 66 and 67.

[204] Ibid., Article 68.

reprieve or respite, on such conditions as the President thinks fit, of the execution of the sentence, or remit the whole or any part of the sentence or any penalty or forfeiture imposed by law.[205] In fact, this provision specifically interprets the Constitutional provision in the Criminal Procedure Code. Article 22P of the Constitution of the Republic of Singapore provides that the President may, on the advice of the Cabinet, grant a pardon, or any reprieve, or respite or remission to the relevant inmate.[206] The inmate sentenced to life imprisonment could be granted pardon, reprieve or respite. Where an application is made to the President, the President may require the presiding judge of the court before or by which the person is convicted to state his opinion as to whether the application should be granted or refused, and the judge shall state his opinion accordingly. Article 334 provides that "the President may commute a sentence of death for a sentence of imprisonment or fine or both, or commute a sentence of imprisonment for a sentence or fine."[207] Here the sentence of imprisonment includes life imprisonment. In another words, life imprisonment may be commuted by the President to a fine. As regards remission, Article 50F of the Prison Act of Singapore provides that "a prisoner shall be entitled to be released on the day a remission order is made in respect of him or his sentence of imprisonment is remitted.[208] A person who is released and at large under a remission order shall be deemed not to be in the legal custody of the Commissioner.[209] Division 3 of Part VB providing for the Remission of Sentences of the Prison Act specifically provides the remission orders for prisoners sentenced to life imprisonment, and Article 50O provides for its application, i.e., this Division shall apply to a prisoner who is sentenced to life imprisonment, for an offense committed on or after 21st August 1997, whether or not he is also sentenced to one or more terms of imprisonment; or a prisoner whose sentence of death for an offense committed on or after 21st August 1997 is, or has been, commuted to life imprisonment under Section 334 of the Criminal Procedure Code (Cap. 68) or Section 238 of the repealed Criminal Procedure Code (Cap. 68.1985 Ed.); or a prisoner who is sentenced to be detained during the President's pleasure under Sect. 213 of the repealed Criminal Procedure Code (Cap. 68, 1985 Ed.).[210] In accordance with Article 50P, where a prisoner to whom the Division applied has served 20 years of his sentence, the Minister shall review the prisoner's case and may, at

---

[205] *The Statutes of the Republic of Singapore: Criminal Procedure Code (Chapter 68),* original enactment: Act 15 of 2010, revised edition of the Laws Act (Chapter 275), 31st August 2012, Article 333(1).

[206] *The Statutes of the Republic of Singapore: Constitution of the Republic of Singapore (Chapter const.),* Original enactment: S 1/63, the revised edition of the Laws Act (Chapter 275), 1st July, 1999, Article 22P.

[207] *The Statutes of the Republic of Singapore: Criminal Procedure Code (Chapter 68),* Article 334.

[208] *The Statutes of the Republic of Singapore: Prison Act (Chapter 247),* original enactment: Ordinance 17 of 1933, the revised edition of *the Laws Act (Chapter 275), 30th December 2000*, Article 50F(1).

[209] Ibid., Article 50F(2).

[210] Ibid., Article 50O.

the Minister's discretion, direct the Commissioner to make a remission order in respect of the prisoner.[211] In another words, the prisoner whose sentence is life imprisonment may be granted remission and released after serving 20 years of his or her life sentence in prison. Where the Minister has refused to direct the Commissioner to make a remission order in respect of a prisoner, the Minister shall, unless the prisoner is released earlier from imprisonment, review his decision at intervals not exceeding 12 months each and may, at his discretion, direct the Commissioner to make a remission order in respect of the prisoner.[212] When a remission order is made, any default sentence to which the prisoner was sentenced shall be remitted; the sentence of life imprisonment and any other sentence of imprisonment imposed on the prisoner shall be suspended and the sentence shall be remitted when the remission order expires.[213]

5.5.2.3 Long-Term Imprisonment in Some States: Taking Norway and Portugal as Examples

Many states have not only removed the death penalty from their penal system, but also outlawed life imprisonment. According to the report "Cruel and Unusual: U.S. Sentencing Practices in a Global Context", "thirty three countries set maximum sentences at a limited number of years."[214] In addition, Norway and Iceland are also among those countries that have already abolished the death penalty and life imprisonment. Even though long-term imprisonment is not in fact life imprisonment, a joint long-term imprisonment in some cases may be beyond the duration of a person's natural life; conversely, even though a prisoner may be sentenced to life imprisonment, he or she may be released earlier after serving a certain number of years of the sentence; in other words, he has served a long-term imprisonment de facto rather than imprisonment for life. Therefore, this section will analyse long-term imprisonment and take long-term imprisonment in Norway and Portugal as an example.

(1) The prevalence of long-term imprisonment. Long-term imprisonment in these three states is the maximum penalty and also the severest punishment, and, generally, it is only provided for the serious crimes. The Penal Code of Norway

---

211 Ibid., Article 50P(1).

212 Ibid., Article 50P(2).

213 Ibid., Article 50Q.

214 VEGA Connie de la, SOLTER Amanda, KWON Soo-Ryun and ISAAC Dana Marie, above no. 692. In this Report, these 33 states include Andorra (the maximum sentence is 30 years), Angola (30 years), Bolivia (30 years), Bosnia (45 years), Brazil (30 years), Cape Verde (25 years), Colombia (50 years), Costa Rica (50 years), Croatia (40 years), Dominican Republic (30 years), Ecuador (35 years), El Salvador (75 years), Guinea Bissau (25 years), Honduras (30 years), Italy (30 years), Maldives (25 years), Mauritius (60 years), Mexico (70 years), Montenegro (30 years), Mozambique (30 years), Nepal (30 years), Nicaragua (30 years), Panama (50 years), Paraguay (25 years), Peru (35 years), Portugal (25 years), San Marino (40 years), Serbia (40 years), Spain (40 years), Macedonia (20 years), Timor-leste (30 years), Uruguay (30 years), Venezuela (30 years).

provides that the ordinary penalties include imprisonment, preventive detention, detention, community sentences, fines and the loss of such rights as are referred to in Sections 29 and 33.[215] Imprisonment may be imposed for a term ranging from 14 days to 15 years, or in the cases dealt with in Sections 60a, 61 and 62 for a term not exceeding 20 years, and in cases in which it is specially provided, for a term not exceeding 21 years.[216] Imprisonment in this Penal Code means imprisonment for a limited period unless it is otherwise expressly stated.[217] Section 62 provides that "if any person has by one or more acts committed more than one felony or misdemeanour punishable by imprisonment or detention, a joint custodial sentence shall be imposed which must be more severe than the highest minimum penalty prescribed for any of the felonies or misdemeanors and must in no case be more than twice the highest penalty prescribed for any of them."[218] In another words, the joint sentence of imprisonment cannot be more than 42 years for these special cases. Based on a thorough analysis of the Norwegian Penal Code, the longest term of imprisonment dealt with by various provisions for some felonies is described in two ways, i.e. "not exceeding 15 years" and/or "not exceeding 21 years". These two expressions will be taken as the standard when analyzing long-term imprisonment in the Penal Code of Norway, in which there are 33 provisions providing for felonies punishable by long term imprisonment.[219] These account for 9.42% of a total of 350 provisions dealing with felonies and misdemeanors in Parts II and III of the Penal Code. Among these 34 provisions, there are 8 providing for felonies against the independence and security of the State, 8 for felonies against public safety, and 6 for felonies in the public service.

Turning to the Penal Code of Portugal, the duration of imprisonment is also strictly provided for, i.e. the "imprisonment penalty usually has the minimum duration of one month and the maximum duration of 20 years and in the cases prescribed by law the maximum limit of imprisonment is 25 years and in no case should be exceeded."[220] In this case, it seems that the maximum duration of imprisonment in Portugal is longer than in Norway. Furthermore, the Portuguese Penal Code provides that if the perpetrator has committed several crimes before the sentence for any of them has become definite, he or she will be sentenced to a single penalty, and the applicable penalty will be the sum of the penalties concretely applied to the various crimes as a maximum limit, without exceeding 25 years in the case of imprisonment.[221] Under

---

[215] *The Norwegian General Civil Penal Code, Act of 22 May 1902 No. 10, with subsequent amendments, Act of 21 December 2005, No. 131*, Section 15.

[216] Ibid., Section 17.

[217] Ibid.

[218] Ibid., Section 62.

[219] These provisions include Articles 83, 84, 86, 86b, 88, 97, 98, 99, 99a, 100, 101, 102, 110, 117, 117a, 147a, 148, 151a, 152, 152b, 153, 154, 162, 169, 192, 196, 225, 231, 232, 233, 245, 268, and 317.

[220] *The Portuguese Criminal Code, Legislative Decree n. 4/2003 of November 18, 2003*, Article 41.

[221] Ibid., Article 77.

this provision, the maximum duration of a joint sentence of imprisonment is 25 years, in another words, if the perpetrator is given a joint sentence of imprisonment for his or her various crimes, he or she will be released after serving 25 years of the sentence in prison. In the Portuguese Penal Code, there are four long terms, serving as the maximum penalty, stipulated respectively for various relatively serious crimes, i.e., "less than 15 years", "less than 16 years", "less than 20 years" and "less than 25 years". It therefore may be argued that a prison sentence of more than 15 years counts as long term imprisonment. Under these standards, we can see there are 21 provisions dealing with crimes punishable by imprisonment for more than 15 years in the Portuguese Penal Code,[222] which account for 8.20% of a total of 256 provisions dealing with crimes in the Specific Part of the Penal Code. Among these 21 provisions, there are 5 provisions dealing with crimes against national independence and integrity (Dos crimes contra a independência e a integridade nacionais), 3 with crimes against national military and defence capabilities (Dos crimes contra a capacidade militar e a defesa nacionais), 3 with crimes against humanity (Dos crimes contra a humanidade), and 3 with crimes against personal liberty (Dos crimes contra a liberdade pessoal).

(2) Conditions for passing a sentence of long-term imprisonment. In the Norwegian Penal Code long-term imprisonment not exceeding 21 years cannot be imposed on a perpetrator who is younger than 18 years when he or she commits the crime, and the penalty should be reduced to lighter one. Section 55 states that "for criminal acts committed before reaching 18 years of age imprisonment ... an imprisonment for a term exceeding 21 years cannot be imposed, and the penalty may without altering the form thereof be reduced below the minimum prescribed for the act, and when circumstances so indicate, to a milder form of penalty.[223] In Parts II and III of the Norwegian Penal Code, long-term imprisonment is mainly imposed on the perpetrator in two cases: (1) long term imprisonment can be applied for action crimes. This situation is also the same with the above-mentioned life imprisonment in the abolitionist and retentionist states. In this case, long term imprisonment may be imposed on the perpetrator

[222] Ibid., these provisions include Articles 131 (Homicídio, Murder), 132 (Homicídio qualificado, assigned homicide), 158 (Sequestro, kidnapping), 159 (Escravidão, slavery), 160 (Rapto, abduction), 210 (Roubo, theft), 214 (Dano com violência, damage with violence), 223 (Extorsão, extortion), 239 (Genocídio, genocide), 241 (Crimes de guerra contra civis, war crime against civilians), 244 (Tortura e outros tratamentos cruéis, degradantes ou desumanos graves, torture and other cruel, inhuman or degrading treatment or punishment), 287 (Captura ou desvio de aeronave, navio, comboio ou veículo de transporte colectivo de passageiros, capture or diversion of aircraft, ship, train, or transport vehicle, collective bus), 300 (Organizações terroristas, terrorist organization), 308 (Traição à pátria, treason of the homeland), 309 (Serviço militar em forças armadas inimigas, military service in enemy armed forces), 310 (Inteligências com o estrangeiro para provocar guerra, intelligence with a foreigner to provoke war), 313 (Ajuda a forças armadas inimigas, helping enemy military forces), 317 (Espionagem, espionage), 325 (Alteração violenta do Estado de direito, violent change in the rule of law), 326 (Incitamento à guerra civil ou à alteração violenta do Estado de direito, incitement to civil war or violent change of the rule of law), and 327 (Atentado contra o Presidente da República, attach on the President of the Republic).

[223] *The Norway General Civil Penal Code, Act of 22 May 1902 No. 10, with subsequent amendments, Act of 21 December 2005, No. 131*, Section 55.

if he or she has committed certain criminal behaviour prescribed in the relative provisions in the Penal Code; for example, Section 83 provides that any person who unlawfully attempts to cause Norway or any part of the realm to be brought under foreign rule or incorporated into another State, or any part of the realm to be detached, or who aids and abets thereto, shall be liable to imprisonment for a term of not exceeding 21 years.[224] In addition, this case can also include Sections 86, 100, 117a (not exceeding 15 years), 148, 151a, 153 and 225. These account for 24.24% of a total of 33 provisions dealing with crimes punishable by long term imprisonment. They also concentrate mainly on felonies against the independence and security of the State, felonies against the constitution of Norway and the head of state, felonies concerning the exercise of civil rights and felonies in the public service. (2) Long term imprisonment can be applied to an offender under certain legally-prescribed circumstances according to the law. The circumstances may include criminal behaviour causing heavy damage to the country or death, or resulting in severe damage to the defence of the realm, or the death of or serious injury to the body, or causing other results, as, for instance, described in Sections 84, 86b, 88, 102, 110, 117a, 147a, 152, 153, 154, 231, 268 and 317. It can also be applied to criminal behaviour which obstructs public authority, or causes serious interference with public servants, as, for example in Section 97; and where the criminal behaviour is committed by the use of special instrument or methods, such as armed force or by exploiting fear of intervention by a foreign power as, for example, in Sections 98; 232, 233 and 245.[225] As for crimes punishable by long term imprisonment in the Portuguese Penal Code, the applicable conditions for long term imprisonment can also be divided into two cases: (1) long term imprisonment can be applied for action crimes. This kind of action crime, generally, includes serious crimes, for example, murder as provided in Article 131, slavery (keeping another person in the state or condition of a slave) as provided in Article 159, genocide (intent to destroy, in whole or in part, a national, ethnic, racial or religious group) as provided in Article 239, and 5 other provisions.[226] These account for 38.10% of a total of 21 provisions. (2) Long term imprisonment can also be applied to an offender under certain legally-prescribed circumstances according to the law. These legally-prescribed circumstances include criminal behaviour resulting in the victim's death or causing other danger or harm to another person or to the public. Article 132, for example, provides for the crime of homicide where another person is killed in circumstances that show perversity[227]; Article 158

224 Ibid., Section 83.

225 Ibid.

226 See *The Portuguese Criminal Code, Legislative Decree n. 4/2003 of November 18, 2003*. Furthermore, this case includes Articles 244 (torture and other cruel, inhuman or degrading treatment or punishment), 287 (capture or diversion of aircraft, ship, train or transport vehicle), 300 (promoting or establishing a terrorist group), 309 (military service in enemy armed forces), and 327 (attack on the President of the Republic).

227 Ibid., Article 132.

provides that "if deprivation of liberty results in the death of the victim".[228] These kinds of legally-prescribed circumstances also include the criminal means; for example Article 160 deals with a crime committed "by means of violence, or threat",[229] and Article 214 with "damage with violence".[230] In all, there are 12 provisions legally prescribing circumstances as the applicable conditions for long term imprisonment, accounting for 57.14% of a total of 21 provisions.

(3) Termination Mechanisms for long-term imprisonment. With long-term imprisonment the prisoner or inmate can normally be released from the institution where they serve their sentence when the period of the sentence expires. However, there is another circumstance in which the inmate or prisoner can be released early. Section 39 provides that "release before expiry of the period of preventive detention shall be effected on probation with a probation period of from one to five years"[231]; when the convicted person or the prison and probation service applies for release on probation, the prosecuting authority shall submit the case to the District Court, which will decide it by a judgment[232]; if the prosecuting authority consents to a release on probation, the prison and probation service may decide on such a release[233]; when a release on probation is effected by the court such conditions may be imposed as in the case of a conditional sentence prescribed in the Penal Code; the court may also impose a condition to the effect that the convicted person shall be followed up by the prison and probation service.[234] Section 42 of the Norwegian Execution of Sentences Act makes a further regulation, which prescribes that "the Correctional Service may release a convicted person on probation when the said person has served two-thirds of the sentence and not less than 60 days, including any period spent remanded in custody."[235] According to this provision, the inmate or prisoner who is sentenced to long-term imprisonment may be released early after serving two-thirds of the sentence in the prison or in custody. If half the sentence of imprisonment and not less than 60 days in prison has been served, including any period spent remanded in custody, the Correctional Services may release a convict on probation if there are special reasons for doing so.[236] However, a convict who has been sentenced abroad to imprisonment for a term exceeding 21 years, and who is transferred to Norway to serve the sentence there, may be released on probation after serving a

[228] Ibid., Article 158.

[229] Ibid., Article 160.

[230] Ibid., Article 214.

[231] *The Norwegian General Civil Penal Code, Act of 22 May 1902 No. 10, with subsequent amendments, Act of 21 December 2005, No. 131*, Section 39 f.

[232] Ibid.

[233] Ibid.

[234] Ibid., Section 38g.

[235] *The Execution of Sentences Act*, Section 42. Available at: http://www.kriminalomsorgen.no/getfile.php/2018208.823.ytdxsvbtbe/Straffegjennomf%C3%B8ringsloven+engelsk.pdf (Last visited: January 23rd, 2024).

[236] Ibid.

term of not less than 14 years' imprisonment.[237] According to the Annual Report 2015, 12 inmates or prisoners were released from prison after serving 10—15 years of their sentences; and 51 inmates or prisoners, accounting for 0.8% of the total prison population, were released after serving 5—10 years of their sentence in prisons.[238] In the same year, 24 convicted persons were sentence to imprisonment for 15—17 years, according to the Annual Report 2015.[239] In comparison, the Portuguese Penal Code provides that "until two months before reaching the minimum limit of the relatively undetermined penalty, the prison administration sends the court its grounded opinion about the concession of conditional release;"[240] and, with the convict's consent, the court sets him or her at conditional liberty when two-thirds of the penalty, and a minimum of six months, has been fulfilled. This can only occur if, considering the circumstances of the case, the perpetrator's previous life, and his or her personality and its evolution during the time of imprisonment, it is reasonable to expect that when at liberty the convict will live his or her life in a responsible social way, without committing crimes.[241] If the conditional release is not granted, or is revoked, provisions dealing with security measures, such as cessation and prorogation of internment, and liberty on probation will apply.[242] Furthermore, under Article 127, the penalty may also be annulled by amnesty, by general pardon and by indult. According to the Portuguese Constitution, the Assembly of the Republic of Portugal has the power to grant generic amnesties and pardons.[243] According to the Portuguese Annual Internal Security Report 2016 (Relatório Anual de Segurança Interna 2016), as of 31st December 2016, there were 13,799 prisoners serving their sentences in different Portuguese prisons, and around 5% of the 13,799 prisoners were sentenced to imprisonment for more than 12 years but less than 20 years, with 2.5% of them serving sentences of between 20 and 25 years.[244]

---

[237] Ibid.

[238] Kriminalomsorgen, *Kriminalomsorgens årsstatistikk – 2015*, 6. Available at: http://www.kriminalomsorgen.no/publikasjoner.242465.no.html (Last visited: January 23rd, 2024).

[239] Ibid., 39.

[240] *The Portuguese Criminal Code, Legislative Decree n. 4/2003 of November 18, 2003*, Article 90.

[241] Ibid., Article 61.

[242] Ibid., Articles 90, 92 and 94.

[243] *Portugal's Constitution of 1976 with Amendments through 2005*, Article 161.

[244] Ministry of Justice of the Republic of Portugal (Ministra da Justiça), *Relatório Anual de Segurança Interna 2016 [Annual Internal Security Report 2016]*, 133. Available at: http://www.portugal.gov.pt/pt/pm/documentos/20170331-pm-rasi-2016.aspx (Last visited: January 23rd, 2024).

5.5.3 International Documents Relating to Life Imprisonment

Life imprisonment is, to a great extent, the most serious punishment after the death penalty because it removes the offender's right to hope for rehabilitation. Although there is no international convention, covenant or treaty directly stating that life imprisonment violates human rights, as Justice Kennedy said in the case of Graham v. Florida, "by denying the defendant's the right to reenter the community, the State makes an irrevocable judgment about that person's value and place in society."[245] In the light of the judgments of the ECtHR, life imprisonment, in particular life imprisonment without possibility of release, may appear to be a torture and so violate the convention, covenant or treaty on human rights. Article 5 of the *Universal Declaration of Human Rights* provides that:

> No one shall be subjected to torture or to cruel, inhuman or degrading treatment or punishment.[246]

In addition, the first part of Article 7 of the *ICCPR* states the same. Article 3 of the ECHR also provides that:

> No one shall be subjected to torture or to inhuman or degrading treatment or punishment.[247]

Based on Article 3, the ECtHR has already dealt with several cases involving life imprisonment. In these cases, LWOR is considered to violate Article 3 and to be inhuman, and, to a great extent, this reflects the development of thinking on life imprisonment in Europe, and even around the world. As for juveniles, Article 37a of the *UN Convention on the Human Rights of the Child* (hereinafter: CHRC) directly prohibits Life imprisonment without parole for a criminal who is younger than 18.

> No child shall be subjected to torture or other cruel, inhuman or degrading treatment or punishment. Neither capital punishment nor life imprisonment without possibility of release shall be imposed for offenses committed by persons below eighteen years of age.[248]

This is the only prohibition on life imprisonment for a child, and so far, there is no international provision prohibiting life imprisonment for adult criminals, although Article 110(3) of the Rome Statute of the International Criminal Court (hereinafter: ICC) provides that:

---

[245] *Graham v. Florida*, 982 So. 2d 43, 52(Fla, Dist, 2010). See also LERNER Craig S., *Life without Parole as a Conflicted Punishment,* Wake Forest Law Review, 2013, Vol. 48, 1101–1171.

[246] *Universal Declaration on Human Rights, GA Res 217 A (III), UN GAOR, 3rd sess, 183rd plen mtg, UN Doc A/810* (10 December 1984).

[247] *Convention for the Protection of Human Rights and Fundamental Freedoms*, opened for signature November 4, 1950, 2013 UNTS 221, entered into force 3 September 1953.

[248] *UN Convention on the Rights of the Child,* General Assembly Resolution 44/25 of 20 November 1989, Article 37a.

> When the person has served two thirds of the sentence, or 25 years in the case of life imprisonment, the Court shall review the sentence to determine whether it should be reduced. Such a review shall not be conducted before that time.[249]

This therefore shows that LWOR is not favored by the ICC. In all, based on the above analysis, life imprisonment without possibility of parole or reduction, or a long-term penalty (de facto life imprisonment), is not favored by the international community, and protecting an offender's right to hope will dominate international thinking.

5.6 Conclusion

The book believes that life imprisonment will be the most appropriate punishment option to replace the death penalty. Except for a few states which have abolished life imprisonment, most states provide life imprisonment in their criminal laws for serious crimes. Compared with other punishment measures, life imprisonment, generally, is a punishment which incarcerates the inmate in prison for the rest of his or her natural life, which thus removes the inmate's right to hope, and so it is almost the severest punishment. In the light of this, we also can observe that the fact that it involves lengthy incarceration, that it is almost the severest penalty, and that it is only used for the most serious crimes represent three obvious and important characteristics of life imprisonment. Based on different criteria, life imprisonment includes three main types, LWOR and LWPR, (relating to the terminating mechanism of life imprisonment), life imprisonment with work and without work, as well as mandatory life imprisonment and discretionary life imprisonment, (relating to whether life imprisonment is the only or an alternative punishment for the crimes). Even though there are different types of life imprisonment, its effects are almost the same, and it normally and mainly impacts on three kinds of people, i.e., directly impacting on the inmate and his or her family, indirectly impacting on the victims and their family, and indirectly impacting on the public. All of these are the basic and brief theories about life imprisonment. In practice, most states stipulate life imprisonment in their Criminal Laws for serious crimes. In fact, three important factors need to be examined when we examine life imprisonment in the penalty system, i.e., the prevalence of life imprisonment in the criminal law, the conditions for passing a sentence of life imprisonment, as well as the terminating mechanism. This book does not only examine life imprisonment in China, but also analyzes life imprisonment in other states, including retentionist states such as Japan and Singarpore and in some abolitionist states such as various members of the EU; in addition, this book also examines long term imprisonment in some states. After analyzing life imprisonment in the law, this book also looks to the facts of its application in judicial practice. In addition, it also discusses various international conventions or treaties and other documents concerning life

[249] *Rome Statute of the International Criminal Court, A/CONF. 183/9 of 17 July 1998,* Article 110(3).

imprisonment, which mainly include the ECHR, the ICCPR and the Rome Statute of the International Criminal Court.

Chapter 6
The Approaches of Life Imprisonment as an Alternative to the Death Penalty in China

Abstract This chapter will explore the approaches to life imprisonment as an alternative to the death penalty in China. This chapter will analyse the present theoretical debates among Chinese scholars on alternatives to the death penalty. Even though these debates are very limited, there are some suggestions for alternative punishments, i.e., life imprisonment, the death penalty with reprieve and multiple alternative punishments. Then this chapter will explore the legislative changes related to life imprisonment introduced by the Eighth Amendment and the Ninth Amendment. Based on these theoretical debates and legislation, this chapter intends to offer my proposal, which is that aggravated life imprisonment, which puts many more restrictions on commutation, could be chosen to replace immediate execution, with no parole granted. This chapter will also consider the potential changes to the alternative punishment to the death penalty in China, which include changes being made in the substantive criminal law and the procedural criminal law. Theoretical debates among Chinese scholars on alternatives to the death penalty are quite limited, but, thus far, there are three main theoretical suggestions for alternative punishments, i.e., life imprisonment, the death penalty with reprieve and multiple alternative punishments.

6.1 In theory

Life imprisonment has always been favored and proposed by many scholars as an alternative to the death penalty because it does not directly execute the offender, and furthermore, from an international perspective, it has already become the preferred punishment to replace the death penalty in many states' criminal systems. However, different scholars have different opinions on life imprisonment because it has two forms, i.e., life imprisonment with possibility of release and life imprisonment without release. LWOR, which cannot be granted commutation or parole, is preferred by some scholars as the alternative punishment to the death penalty, and "is favored especially by the scholars who focused earlier on this issue."[1] In these researches,

[1] 赵秉志 [ZHAO Bingzhi], *《中国死刑替代措施要论》[On Alternative Measures to the Death Penalty in China]*, above no. 394, 35.

G. Huang, *On the Alternative Punishment to the Death Penalty in China*,
https://doi.org/10.1007/978-981-97-1627-2_6

most scholars take the USA as a special example. They argue that the death penalty has not been removed from some states' criminal systems in the USA and life imprisonment without parole is considered to be the alternative punishment, and is also in line with public demands. They think that LWOR will narrow the large gap between the death penalty with reprieve and immediate execution, and will classify the degrees of the various offenses and limit the use of immediate execution, as well as satisfying the requirements of the principle of proportional justice, which is interpreted as the relationship between the gravity of the offense and the sanction provided; and it can correct the erroneous judgement.[2] However, many scholars argue that LWOR may be no less cruel than the death penalty, and that it violates human rights and ignores the correction of the criminal; in this light, they argue for the LWPR as the replacement for the death penalty.[3] However, different scholars have different opinions on the possibility of release. Some scholars propose that during the process of limiting and abolishing the death penalty, the life imprisonment system (before the Eighth Amendment was adopted) is sufficient as an alternative punishment, and China does not need LWOR, and does not need to increase the maximum of the fixed-term imprisonment.[4] A criminal sentenced to life imprisonment could be released on commutation and parole. Other scholars, on the other hand, argue that the prison term is too short to indicate the severity of life imprisonment, and they propose that life imprisonment could be the alternative punishment; for this kind of life imprisonment, the criminal may be granted parole after serving 25 years in prison, or the term of punishment actually to be served by those sentenced to life imprisonment should not be less than 25 years after commutation.[5] Other scholars suggest removing commutation for life imprisonment and retaining parole, which may only be granted to the criminal sentenced to life imprisonment after he or she has served not less than 25 years for a serious crime, or not less than 15 years for a less serious crime.[6] All in all, considering human rights and international trends, most scholars argue that

[2] See 张新甦 [ZHANG Xinsu], *《终身自由刑替代死刑制度研究》[On Life Imprisonment as a Substitution for the Death Penalty]*, 吉林大学博士论文 [Ph.D. Dissertation, Jilin University], 2013, 160–163.

[3] See, e.g., 高铭暄, 楼伯坤 [GAO Mingxuan and Lou Bokun], *《死刑替代位阶上无期徒刑的改良》[Ways to Reform the Life Sentence: An Alternative to the Death Penalty]*, 现代法学 [Modern Law Science] 2010, No. 6, 89.

[4] See especially 张明楷 [ZHANG Mingkai], *《死刑的废止不需要终身刑替代》[The Abolition of Capital Punishment Does Not Need Life-Long Liberty Punishment]*, 法学研究[Chinese Journal of Law] 2008, Vol. 13, No. 2, 94; see also 王志祥 [WANG Zhixiang], above no. 395, 201–303. This paper was published in 2015, after the Eighth Amendment to the Criminal Law in 2011, which had already increased the minimum prison sentence; the author argues that it is not necessary to change the punishment currently used to replace the death penalty as the requirements of punishing the crime and protecting the social order have already been fully satisfied.

[5] See especially 李希惠 [LI Xihui], *above no. 14*, 29. Even though the term of punishment actually to be served by those sentenced to life imprisonment may be around 25 years, some scholars argue that the criminal may only be granted commutation or parole after serving no less than ten years in prison. See also 高铭暄, 楼伯坤 [GAO Mingxuan and Lou Bokun], above no. 802, 94.

[6] See, e.g., 张秀玲 [ZHANG Xiuling], above no. 558, 141–146.

LWPR should be the alternative to the death penalty rather than LWOR, and this has become the dominant opinion.

The death penalty with reprieve is a special kind of execution, and is favored by some scholars as the alternative to the death penalty. According to Article 50 of the current Criminal Law, a criminal who is sentenced to the death penalty with reprieve will be executed only if he or she is found to have intentionally committed a further crime, and its circumstances are heinous, during the two years following the sentence; otherwise, the sentence will be commuted to life imprisonment.[7] Even though this is not a real legislative alternative punishment to the death penalty, in the context of China not abolishing the death penalty de facto *and* de jure within a short time, some scholars recommend this as the replacement punishment for the death penalty with immediate execution, in the interests of limiting the use of the death penalty. Some believe that before removing immediate execution from the Criminal Law, the death penalty with reprieve should replace immediate execution in judicial practice, and then gradually replace it completely in law. Before it is replaced by LWOR, the death penalty with reprieve could be considered an independent type of punishment.[8] However, others argue that the death penalty with reprieve should function as a necessary legal process before the offender is sentenced to immediate execution.[9] In this way, the offender could have at least two years' probation and the number of executions could be reduced. In reality, the death penalty with reprieve is not within the scope of alternative punishments to the death penalty as discussed in this book, and it is dependent on the pre-condition of the abolition of the death penalty de jure *and* de facto. However, it could be a possible method of eliminating any public concerns and popular opposition caused by the "sudden death of the death penalty system".[10]

The idea of multiple alternative punishments to the death penalty has been proposed by Professor Gao Mingxuan. He argues that three approaches should be adopted in harmony to replace the death penalty, i.e., changing the death penalty to reprieve, increasing the maximum served sentence of life imprisonment and establishing long term imprisonment with economic compensation.[11] Professor Gao points out that the conditions for parole and commutation for the death penalty with reprieve should be strictly limited, i.e., parole can only be granted after serving not less than 20 years and, after commutation, the term shall be not less than 20 years. Furthermore, a strict life imprisonment sentence should be set to not less than 15 years, and a

---

[7] *《中华人民共和国刑法》[Criminal Law of the People's Republic of China]*, Order No. 83, 14 March 1997, Article 50.

[8] See 钊作俊 [ZHAO Zuojun], *《中国死刑之现状与走向》[On the Reality and Trends of the Death Penalty in China]*, 郑州轻工业学院学报 (社会科学版) [Journal of Zhengzhou University of Light Industry (Social Science)] 2004, Vol. 5, No. 2, 45.

[9] See, e.g., 张文, 黄伟明 [ZHANG Wen and HUANG Weiming], *《死缓应当作为死刑执行的必经程序》[The Death Sentence with Reprieve Should Be Introduced as A Necessary Procedure of Immediate Execution]*, 现代法学 [Modern Law Science] 2004, Vol. 26, No. 4, 75.

[10] Ibid, 78.

[11] See 高铭暄 [GAO Mingxuan], *《略论中国刑法中的死刑替代措施》[Brief Discussion on the Alternative Measures to the Death Penalty in Chinese Criminal Law]*, above no. 13, 20.

long-term sentence could be established with a maximum of more than 15 years but less than 20 years, with economic compensation introduced because it compensates the victim for emotional distress.[12]

Regarding the above arguments, this book believes that LWPR will be the legislatively possible alternative punishment to the death penalty in the future when the death penalty is abolished de facto *and* de jure. LWOR will not be the ideal alternative punishment to the death penalty because it breaches human rights and "it is not much of a life at all".[13] LWPR still gives the convict the right to hope and the possibility of returning back to society, and it respects the convict's human rights. In addition, most abolitionist states, such as Austria, Hungary, Germany, France, the Netherlands, Italy, Norway, Portugal among others, have adopted LWPR as the alternative punishment to the death penalty. It will be analyzed in the following section. However, the alternative punishment to the death penalty should balance the need to control crimes and severely punish serious crime.

6.2 In Practice

It seems that the issue of the alternative punishment to the death penalty is not limited to a theoretical debate, and has already become a controversial legislative reality, as the abolition of the death penalty is gradually being achieved through the Eighth and Ninth Amendments. Judging from the two amendments, it seems that the legislation has, to a certain extent, already admitted that life imprisonment is the alternative punishment to the death penalty. However, this assertion is untenable and groundless for the follow reasons. Firstly, for these 22 crimes, from which the death penalty is removed by the Eighth and Ninth Amendments, life imprisonment served as the optional punishment, together with the death penalty, and was the second heaviest punishment after the death penalty; so, it has naturally been upgraded to the maximum and heaviest punishment for these crimes when the death penalty was removed. Secondly, these 22 crimes are all economic and non-violent crimes, and "the damage they cause to society is generally less than that caused by those crimes that violate the right to life, or endanger national and public security, and so the death penalty for them is too heavy,"[14] and also substantially violates the principle of the proportionality

[12] See ibid, 20–21. This argument is also supported by Professor Chen Xingliang, who argues that one of the important factors favoring the death penalty is the enormous pressure faced by the court from the victim's family who ask for the offender to be sentenced to death. The alternative measure proposed by Prof. Gao, can, to a great extent, make the victim's family understand and accept that it is not necessary to use the death penalty, and so reduce the pressure on the court. He believes that this proposal is feasible. See also 陈兴良 [CHEN Xingliang], *《犯罪范围的扩张与刑罚结构的调整》[On the Expansion of the Scope of the Crime and the Adjustment of the Punishment Structure: Comment on the Ninth Amendment],* 法律科学 (西北政法大学学报) [Science of Law (Journal of Northwest University of Political Science and Law)] 2016, No. 4, 187–188.

[13] WRIGHT Julian H., above no. 383, 529.

[14] 高铭暄, 苏惠渔, 于志刚[GAO Mingxuan, SU Huiyu and YU Zhigang], above no. 2, 4.

between punishment and crime (principle of proportional justice). In this sense, they should not have been subject to the death penalty; furthermore, in judicial practice, according to the official *Explanations for the Eighth and Ninth Amendments*, the death penalty for all of these 22 crimes was rarely and even never used,[15] so the death penalty in fact existed for them in name only. *The Explanation* also points out that, as the most second severe punishment, the current life imprisonment is fair enough as a punishment, and where there are special flagrant circumstances or cases, and if the offender is convicted of more than one crime or he violates other criminal provisions, it can impose other more severe punishments on them under the law.[16] Therefore, directly removing the death penalty from them without providing any replacement punishment is thus appropriate, reasonable and necessary, and lightens the punishment for them and make the punishment system more rational and humane. In this light, no alternative punishment has in fact been adopted to replace the death penalty in these two amendments.

However, it is undeniable that the Eighth and Ninth amendments have already changed the penal system in particular the use of life imprisonment and fixed-term imprisonment in the interest of taking further steps to repeal the death penalty. These changes include: (1) putting restrictions on the commutation of a death sentence with reprieve. Article 4 of the Eighth Amendment provides that if a convict commits any significant meritorious act, the sentence shall be commuted to imprisonment of 25 years upon expiry of the two-year period,[17] which is almost 10 more years than that provided by the previous Criminal Law.[18] Article 50 also provides that, for a recidivist or an offender convicted of murder, rape, robbery, abduction, arson, explosion, dissemination of hazardous substances or organized violence who is sentenced to death with reprieve, the people's court may, in sentencing, decide concurrently to put restrictions on the commutation of his sentence in the light of the circumstances of the crime committed.[19] (2) Increasing the maximum of the combined punishment for several crimes, i.e., if an offender is sentenced to several fixed-term imprisonments for more than one crime, the fixed-term imprisonment shall not exceed 25 years if the sum of the fixed-terms of imprisonment is 35 years or more,[20] which is five more years than that provided by the previous Criminal Law. (3) Extending

---

[15] See *关于< 中华人民共和国刑法修正案(八)(草案) > 的说明》[The Explanations for the Draft of the Eighth Amendment to Criminal Law of the People's Republic of China], 《关于< 中华人民共和国刑法修正案(九)(草案) > 的说明》[The Explanations for the Draft of the Ninth Amendment to Criminal Law of the People's Republic of China]*, above no. 8.

[16] See *《关于< 中华人民共和国刑法修正案(九)(草案) > 的说明》[The Explanations for the Draft of the Ninth Amendment to Criminal Law of the People's Republic of China]*, above no. 8.

[17] *《中华人民共和国刑法修正案(八)》[The Eighth Amendment to the Criminal Law of the People's Republic of China]*, above no. 1, Article 4.

[18] According to the 1997 Criminal Law, if a convict performs any significant meritorious act, the sentence shall be commuted to imprisonment of no less than 15 years but no more than 20 years upon expiry of the two-year period. See *《中华人民共和国刑法》[Criminal Law of the People's Republic of China]*, Order No. 83, 14 March 1997, Article 50.

[19] Ibid.

[20] Ibid., Article 10.

the punishment term after parole and/or commutation. Specifically, where a convict sentenced to fixed-term imprisonment has actually served not less than 13 years of imprisonment, which is an increase from the 10 years provided by the previous criminal law, he or she may be paroled if he satisfies the parole requirements.[21] For a recidivist or an offender convicted of murder, rape, robbery, abduction, arson, explosion, dissemination of hazardous substances or organized violence who is sentenced to death with reprieve, the people's court may, in sentencing, decided to put restrictions on commutation of his sentence in the light of the circumstances of the crime committed. After commutation, the actual punishment term shall not be less than 25 years if the death penalty with reprieve imposed on a convict is legally commuted to life imprisonment upon expiry of the reprieve period, or less than 20 years if it is commuted to imprisonment of 25 years upon expiry of the reprieve period.[22] This is a new provision that extends punishment terms after parole and commutation. (4) Increasing the conditions of the death penalty, moving from reprieve to immediate execution, but extending the probation term. In accordance with Article 2 of the Ninth Amendment, where a convict receives a suspended death sentence, if, during the enforcement of the suspended sentence, an intentional crime is committed and the circumstances are heinous, the death penalty will be carried out; where there is an intentional crime but the death penalty is not carried out, the period of the suspended death sentence is calculated.[23] From this provision, it is clear that the conditions under which the death penalty moves from reprieve to immediate execution have been increased, as can be seen from the phrase "if it is verified that he has committed an intentional crime"[24] in the 1997 Criminal Law to the phrase that "if an intentional crime is committed and the circumstances are heinous", i.e., by the addition of the requirement that "the circumstances are heinous" in the Ninth Amendment. The probation term will be extended by another two-year suspension upon the expiry of that firth two-year suspension, if the convict commits an intentional crime but the circumstances are not heinous and he would not be executed. (5) LWOR is prescribed for the crime of embezzlement and bribery, for the first time. This punishment has been introduced by the Ninth Amendment and only for the crime of corruption. Article 44 of the Ninth Amendment provides that if a person is convicted of crimes of corruption, and the amount is especially large and the nation and people suffer especially large losses, life imprisonment or death may be the punishment. If a suspended death sentence is given, the people's court may concurrently decide, based on the circumstances of the crime and other circumstances, that after the completion of the two-year suspended sentence and commutation to life imprisonment in accordance

[21] 《中华人民共和国刑法修正案(八)》*[The Eighth Amendment to the Criminal Law of the People's Republic of China]*, above no. 1, Articles 14 and 16.

[22] Ibid, Articles 4 and 15.

[23] 《中华人民共和国刑法修正案(九)》[The Ninth Amendment to the Criminal Law of the People's Republic of China], above no. 6, Article 2.

[24] 《中华人民共和国刑法》*[Criminal Law of the People's Republic of China]*, Order No. 83, 14 March 1997, Article 50.

with law, the offender will be imprisoned for life and must not be awarded commutation or parole.[25] Therefore, the death penalty and LWOR may be legally applied to anyone guilty of serious corruption.[26] In addition, the provisions limiting commutation and parole for some crimes were further altered by these two amendments. Namely, for a recidivist or an offender convicted of murder, rape, robbery, abduction, arson, explosion, dissemination of hazardous substances or organized violence who is sentenced to death with reprieve, the people's court may, in sentencing, decide to put restrictions on the commutation of his sentence in the light of the circumstances of the crime committed[27]; and no parole shall be granted to a recidivist or an offender sentenced to not less than 10 years or life imprisonment for the above crimes, nor to a convict whose life imprisonment or fixed-term imprisonment is commuted from the death penalty with reprieve for the above crimes.[28] In accordance with Article 7 of the Eighth Amendment, anyone convicted of jeopardizing national security, terrorist activities or organized crime of a gangland nature shall be punished as a recidivist for any of such crimes committed again at any time after he has finished serving his sentence or is pardoned.[29] According to the above provisions, a recidivist who is sentenced to the death penalty with reprieve for the crimes of jeopardizing national security, terrorist activities or organized crime of a gangland nature and an offender convicted of murder, rape, robbery, abduction, arson, explosion, dissemination of hazardous substances or organized violence who is sentenced to death with reprieve, may not be granted parole, and there may be a restriction put on commutation after commutation from the death penalty with reprieve. However, these offenders may finally be released after serving a long-term sentence commuted from the death penalty with reprieve. To a great extent, all these changes are made with the aims of limiting the use of the death penalty and preparing for the abolition of the death penalty in the near future.

---

[25] Ibid, Article 44.

[26] 《中华人民共和国刑法》 *[Criminal Law of the People's Republic of China]*, Order No. 83, 14 March 1997, Article 383.

[27] 《中华人民共和国刑法修正案(八)》 *[The Eighth Amendment to the Criminal Law of the People's Republic of China]*, above no. 1, Article 4.

[28] Ibid, Articles 16 and 《最高人民法院关于办理减刑、假释案件具体应用法律若干问题的规定》 [The Judicial Interpretations of the Supreme People's Court of the People's Republic of China on the Issues of Commutation and Parole adopted by the Supreme People's Court], 法释 [2012]2 号 [Legal Interpretation, No. 2, 2012], Article18. Available at: 法律图书馆 [Law Library] http://www.law-lib.com/law/law_view.asp?id=376011. (Last visited: January 23rd, 2024).

[29] 《中华人民共和国刑法修正案(八)》 *[The Eighth Amendment to the Criminal Law of the People's Republic of China]*, above no. 1, Article 7.

6.3 My Proposals

As it has already been discussed above, from the theoretical perspective, many scholars recommend LWPR as an alternative punishment to the death penalty; in the legislative practice, the current life imprisonment, which could be terminated early because of commutation and/or parole, was upgraded to the maximum punishment for 22 crimes after the death penalty was removed. Undeniably, the scholars' proposals are in line with the international trends and satisfy the requirements of anti-torture and protecting human rights; actually, the upgrade of the present life imprisonment to the maximum punishment for these 22 crimes is reasonable and made with the aims of making up for deficiencies caused by the removal of the death penalty from the less serious crimes. However, 46 crimes, including non-violent crimes, such as crime of embezzlement and bribery and crimes of impairing the interests of national defence, and violent and lethal crimes, are still punishable by death under the present law. Therefore, my proposal for an alternative punishment should focus on the violent and lethal crimes among the 46 capital crimes.

Considering the present punishment system, the death penalty can be carried out in two ways, i.e., the death penalty with immediate execution and with reprieve, in accordance with Article 48 of the Criminal Law. Even though the general applicable condition for these two means of execution is the same, i.e., "the death penalty shall only be applied to criminals who committed extremely serious crimes",[30] the results they cause are completely different, i.e., the former will kill the convict but the latter will give him life and hope. There is only one different and indistinct condition for them, i.e., "if the immediate execution of a criminal punishable by death is not deemed necessary".[31] Except for this, "there is no a specific criterion or interpretation for these two applicable conditions of the death penalty."[32] In most cases, the death penalty with immediate execution is only imposed on convicts who have committed the most heinous crimes and are extremely dangerous; for convicts who have committed the most heinous crimes but are not particularly personal dangerous, the death penalty with reprieve will be imposed on them.[33] If the convict is sentenced to the death penalty with reprieve, the death sentence can be commuted to life imprisonment or imprisonment for 25 years upon the expiry of the two-year period in accordance with Article 50,[34] and he or she could be released after completing a sentence of not less

---

[30] *《中华人民共和国刑法》[Criminal Law of the People's Republic of China]*, Order No. 83, 14 March 1997, Article 48.

[31] Ibid.

[32] 储怀值 [CHU Huaizhi], *《死刑司法控制:完整解读刑法第四十八条》[Judicial Control of Death Penalty: A Comprehensive Understanding of Article 48 of Penal Code]*, above no. 234, 1015.

[33] See 劳东燕 [LAO Dongyan], *《死刑适用标准的体系化构造》[System of the Standards on the Application of the Death Penalty]*, 法学研究 [Chinese Journal of Law] 2015, No. 1, 185.

[34] *《中华人民共和国刑法》[Criminal Law of the People's Republic of China]*, Order No. 83, 14 March 1997, Article 50.

than 13 years. In effect, the punishment for them is general life imprisonment.[35] If a convict has restrictions placed on the commutation of the death penalty with reprieve, the death penalty could be commuted to life imprisonment or imprisonment for 25 years, and he can be released after a term of imprisonment of not less than 25, and not less than 20 years, respectively.[36] In this sense, the present crimes punishable by death can be classified into three levels, i.e., crimes punishable by general life imprisonment, crimes punishable by life imprisonment with restrictions on commutation (life imprisonment with restriction), and crimes punishable by death with immediate execution. Based on these categories and the present criminal justice and punishment system in China, in accordance with the principle of proportional justice, the alternative punishment to the death penalty should be lighter than the death penalty with immediate execution but more severe than the present life imprisonment, including life imprisonment with restrictions. So, I think an aggravated life imprisonment,[37] which puts many more restrictions on commutation, could be chosen to replace immediate execution, with no parole granted. The reasons for this proposal could be explained as follows: (1) crimes which should be sentenced to immediate execution are more heinous and serious than crimes where the sentence is death with reprieve; (2) even though the death penalty with reprieve and death with immediate execution are both forms of the death penalty, their degrees of severity are completely different, because the former deprives the convict of his right to life; (3) the death penalty with reprieve will be legally commuted to life imprisonment or a fixed term imprisonment of 25 years upon expiry of the reprieve period; in this sense, it is in fact a form of life imprisonment or long term imprisonment.

However, not all the capital crimes provided in the present Criminal Law are eligible for death sentences and so they do not deserve an alternative punishment. Therefore, I need to give a further proposal on the basis of a discussion of abolition. Thus far, "there are 46 capital crimes, of which there are 24 crimes of a non-violent nature, occupying 52.2%."[38] The social harm the non-violent crimes cause is absolutely different from that which violent crimes cause, because the latter infringes upon the right to life and the right to health, while the former does not directly endanger the right to life of another person.[39] In this sense, "sentencing the criminal who committed extremely serious non-violent crimes to death is in fact out of keeping with the essential balance between crime and punishment."[40] Therefore, the death penalty for these 24 non-violent crimes should be directly repealed without any alternative punishment, and the present general life imprisonment should be upgraded to

---

[35] Ibid, Article 78.

[36] Ibid.

[37] The term "an aggravated life imprisonment" is from the Turkey's Criminal Code. According to Turkey's Criminal Code, aggravated life imprisonment lasts until the death of the convict and is enforced under the strict security regime measures as defined in law and legislation. See *Criminal Code of Turkey (2011) Law No. 5237 of September 26, 2004,* as amended to Law No. 6217 of March 31, 2011, Article 47.

[38] Huang Gui, above no. 114, 3.

[39] Ibid., 4.

[40] Ibid.

the maximum punishment for them. For the other 22 violent crimes, they could be divided into two situations. One is that, if the nature of the crime involves violence but is non-lethal, the death penalty for it should be directly repealed and life imprisonment with restrictions should be upgraded to the maximum available punishment; but if nature of the crime involves serious violence and is lethal, the death penalty for it should be replaced by aggravated life imprisonment, i.e., the convict who is sentenced to this sentence can be released after serving in prison for not less than 30 years on commutation. And in the last two cases, no parole would be granted.

6.4 The Potential Changes Caused by the Alternative Punishment to the Death Penalty

Even though the final alternative punishment to the death penalty for other serious capital crimes has not yet been really adopted by China's legislator, a relevant tendency has emerged in which LWPR or long fixed-term imprisonment have been upgraded to the maximum punishment for the crimes from which the death penalty was removed in accordance with the above analysis. Therefore, a series of potential legislative changes involving the whole criminal system have to be made by the legislator. This section will explore these changes from two perspectives, i.e., substantive criminal law and criminal procedure law.

6.4.1 Substantive Perspective

If the death penalty is completely repealed de jure *and* de facto, the penal system will provide four types of punishment in China's criminal law, i.e., life imprisonment (including general life imprisonment, life imprisonment with restrictions and aggravated life imprisonment), fixed-term imprisonment, criminal detention and public surveillance; life imprisonment will naturally become the most severe punishment. The punishment system, as a whole, will become "mainly imprisonment and fine oriented,"[41] and will be lighter than the present punishment system. However, problems will still remain and need to be solved.

Firstly, the number of crimes punishable by life imprisonment is too great. Thus far, in the present Criminal Law of China, there are 102 crimes punishable by life imprisonment, accounting for 21.79% of the total of 468 crimes,[42] and life imprisonment is now the second most severe punishment after the death penalty for 46

---

41 储怀植 [CHU Haizhi], 《刑事一体化》 *[Criminal Science Integration]*, 法律出版社 [Law Press·China], Beijing, 2004, 281.

42 《刑法最新罪名一览表》 *[Chart Showing the New Crimes in the Criminal Law]*, above no. 125.

crimes,[43] and the maximum legal punishment for 56 crimes. It is also stipulated as a fixed-term imprisonment of not less than 7 years for five crimes,[44] and as a fixed-term imprisonment of not less than 15 years for 1 crime.[45] Based on the above data, if the death penalty is removed completely from the Criminal Law, having life imprisonment as the maximum legal punishment for around 102 crimes still means that the penalty system in the Specific Provisions is excessively heavy, and this will also apply to the penal system as a whole. In this sense, some scholars point out that "it runs counter to the efficiency of the criminal punishment, and deviates from the penal goal"[46]; "The number of crimes punishable by life imprisonment is so high that the disadvantage to its seriousness and deterrence is fairly obvious."[47] Excessive recourse to life imprisonment in law will consequentially lead to its abuse in practice, and it will inevitably reduce the penal effect of life imprisonment. Reducing the number of crimes punishable by general life imprisonment, therefore, is necessary because it is a kind of punishment depriving the prisoner of liberty for a long period, even for the rest of his or her life, and its seriousness and deterrence are, to a great extent, as great as the death penalty. So, life imprisonment should be only provided for serious crimes after the abolition of the death penalty. There are 34 crimes involving the disruption of the order of the socialist market economy which can be punishable by life imprisonment.[48] Even though these crimes can cause serious social harm, imposing severe punishment, such as life imprisonment, on an offender who commits these crimes violates the principle of proportional justice. As some scholars argue, "these kinds of crimes could be prevented by improving the regulatory system, rather than relying

[43] These 46 crimes are punishable by death; life imprisonment for these crimes is a possible alternative to capital punishment, and is even the lightest punishment for some crimes, such as kidnapping (Article 239(2)). See *《中华人民共和国刑法》[Criminal Law of the People's Republic of China*], Order No. 83, 14 March 1997, Article 239(2).

[44] These crimes include crimes of producing or selling food that is not up to safety standards (Article 143), producing fake pesticides, fake animal pharmaceuticals or fake chemical fertilizers or selling pesticides, animal pharmaceuticals, chemical fertilizers or seeds (Article 147), forming or using superstitious sects or secret societies or 'unusual' religious organizations or using superstition to undermine the implementation of laws and administrative rules and regulations (Article 300), making arrangements for another person to illegally cross the national border (Article 318), and illegally possessing narcotic drugs (Article 348). See *《中华人民共和国刑法》[Criminal Law of the People's Republic of China*], Order No. 83, 14 March 1997.

[45] This is the crime of smuggling, trafficking in, transporting or manufacturing narcotic drugs, provided by Article 347 (1). See *《中华人民共和国刑法》[Criminal Law of the People's Republic of China*], Order No. 83, 14 March 1997, Article 347(1).

[46] 李晓欧 [LI Xiaoou], *《中国重刑化弊端及其限制路径——以 < 中华人民共和国刑法修正案(八) > 为观照》[The Drawbacks of Heavy Punishment in China and the Road to Limit them: Based on the Eighth Amendment to the Criminal Law of the P.R.C.]*, 当代法学 [Contemporary Law Review] 2010, No. 6, 40.

[47] 曾亚杰 [ZENG Yajie], *《我国无期徒刑制度改革探析》[On the Reformation of the Life Imprisonment System in China]*, 时代法学 [Presentday Law Sciences] 2008, Vol. 6, No. 2, 74.

[48] See *《中华人民共和国刑法》[Criminal Law of the People's Republic of China*], Order No. 83, 14 March 1997.

too much on criminal punishment."[49] Life imprisonment should be removed from these crimes so that the total number of crimes it punishes will be reduced.

Secondly, there is a need to clearly demarcate the circumstances and degrees of crimes and their corresponding punishments. In 2014, the SPC launched *the Sentencing Guidance for 15 Common Crimes (the Sentencing Guidance),*[50] and later added another 8 crimes to these 15 crimes, to make a total of 23 crimes by 2016.[51] Based on this *Sentencing Guidance*, the local High People's Courts are authorized to make their more specific sentencing guidance according to the context of the local social, economic and criminal environment. This *Sentencing Guidance* only clearly demarcates the sentencing circumstances of 23 crimes and their punishments, including fixed-term imprisonment, criminal detention, fines and suspensions of sentence. However, it does not cover all crimes and punishments. Furthermore, this *Sentencing Guidance* is just a pilot project in some places rather than a nationwide practice. The lack of clarity in applicable conditions for punishment for crimes generally leads to disproportion between the crime and its corresponding punishment, and reduces the justice of the punishment. Therefore, after completely abolishing the death penalty, a distinct *Sentencing Guidance* should be prepared for all crimes and their corresponding punishments, which should cover all the sentencing circumstances and their impact factors. A database should be set up for cases, which could provide reference and comparison between similar cases. For crimes punishable by the death penalty under the present criminal law, after abolishing the death penalty, special attention should be paid to clearly demarcating the applicable conditions of general life imprisonment, life imprisonment with restrictions and aggravated life imprisonment, so that these three levels of life imprisonment could properly be applied to these crimes. This *Sentencing Guidance* could refer to and compare the applicable conditions for the death penalty as stipulated by the present criminal law and their relevant judicial interpretations, but it should demarcate clearly the differences of the applicable conditions between life imprisonment with restrictions and aggravated life imprisonment.

Thirdly, the applicable objects of life imprisonment with restrictions and aggravated life imprisonment should be limited. Under the present criminal law, the death penalty cannot be imposed on criminals who had not reached the age of 18 at the time the crime was committed or on women who are pregnant at the time of trial, or on persons attaining the age of 75 at the time of trial unless they have caused the death of

---

49 高铭暄, 苏惠渔,于志刚 [GAO Mingxuan, SU Huiyu and YU Zhigang], above no. 2, 6.

50 See *《最高人民法院关于常见犯罪的量刑指导意见》 [The Sentencing Guidance of The Supreme People's Court for the Common Crimes]*, available at: 最高人民法院网 [The Supreme People's Court of the People's Republic of China] http://www.court.gov.cn/shenpan-xiangqing-6622.html. (Last visited: January 24th, 2024).

51 See 陈学勇 [CHEN Xueyong], *《最高人民法院扩大量刑规范化罪名和刑种试点: 将危险驾驶罪等8种罪名纳入规范范围》 [The Supreme People's Court Increasing the Number of Crimes and Their Corresponding Punishments and Adding Pilot Locations for Sentencing Standardization: Adding the Crime of Dangerous Driving to the Other 8 Crimes in the Scope of Sentencing Standardization]*, available at: 中国法院网 [China Court Internet] http://www.chinacourt.org/article/detail/2016/05/id/1884273.shtml. (Last visited: January 24th, 2024).

another person by especially cruel means.[52] On this basis, the applicable objects of life imprisonment with restrictions and aggravated life imprisonment should also be limited. For example, life imprisonment with restrictions and aggravated life imprisonment should not be imposed on convicts who were younger than 18 years old when committing the crime or on women who are pregnant at the time of trial, or on persons who are older than 70 at the time of trial. These limitations are stricter than those on the death penalty as stipulated by the present criminal law.

6.4.2 Procedural Perspective

Once the death penalty is abolished completely, de facto *and* de jure, there will be certain problems that need to be dealt with from the procedural perspective, especially the jurisdiction of courts of first and second instance and reviews of cases involving crimes punishable by life imprisonment, which will be discussed in this section. Namely, a decision must be made about which level of the people's courts will be empowered to handle cases of crimes punishable by life imprisonment after the death penalty has been repealed, and which level of the people's courts will be empowered to review cases of crimes punishable by life imprisonment where cases need to be reviewed. Under Articles 20, 21 and 22 of the present Criminal Procedure Law of the People's Republic of China, all the intermediate people's courts, the Higher People's Courts and the SPC have jurisdiction as courts of the first instance over crimes punishable by life imprisonment and the death penalty. However, the Higher People's Courts and the SPC handle major criminal cases relating to an entire province and the whole nation, respectively.[53] The Higher People's Court is empowered to review the death sentence and then submit it to the SPC for approval; and the SPC is empowered to review and approve the death sentence.[54] Based on the present judicial system, after abolishing the death penalty, I think it will be possible to maintain the jurisdiction of the courts of the first instance over crimes punishable by life imprisonment as is the case with the present system, but with some differences. Firstly, a case of the first instance where an Intermediate People's Court has imposed life imprisonment and the defendant does not appeal should be reviewed by a Higher People's Court. Secondly, a case of the first instance where an Intermediate People's Court has imposed life imprisonment with restrictions or aggravated life imprisonment and the defendant does not appeal should be reviewed by a Higher People's Court and submitted to the SPC for approval. Thirdly, a case of the first instance where a Higher People's Court has imposed life imprisonment with restrictions or aggravated life imprisonment and the defendant does not appeal should

---

[52] 《中华人民共和国刑法》 *[Criminal Law of the People's Republic of China]*, Order No. 83, 14 March 1997, Article 49.

[53] See 《中华人民共和国刑事诉讼法》 *[The Criminal Procedure Law of the People's Republic of China],* Order No. 64, 1July 1979, Articles 20, 21 and 22.

[54] See ibid, Articles 235–240.

be reviewed and approved by the SPC. Fourthly, a case of the first instance where an Intermediate People's Court has imposed life imprisonment with restrictions or aggravated life imprisonment and the defendant appeals to a Higher People's Court which affirms the original judgement should be reviewed and approved by the SPC. Fifthly, the judgement on the commutation of life imprisonment with restrictions or aggravated life imprisonment should be made by a Higher People's Court on the basis of the written recommendation submitted by the organ of execution; but for the commutation of life imprisonment, an Intermediate People's Court could make the decision, according to the written recommendation.

6.5 Conclusion

This chapter focuses on the core issue of the alternative punishment to the death penalty, i.e., what kind of potential punishment could be chosen to replace the death penalty, and how to replace are the questions that the book has to answer. In the limited theoretical debates, except for the suggestion from the judicial perspective which proposes the death penalty with reprieve as the multiple alternative punishment, most scholars have favored and proposed life imprisonment as an alternative punishment to the death penalty; however, as regards its terminating mechanism, different scholars have different opinions. Some scholars propose LWOR, but some propose LWPR. As regards LWPR, different scholars have different arguments in terms of the length of incarceration before release. Some scholars argue for 15 years, some argue for 25 and some for 30 years, and so on. However, in legislative practice, the legislator, on one hand, extends the punishment term for an inmate who is sentenced to a fixed term imprisonment and so serves life imprisonment in prison; on the other hand, the legislator stipulates LWOR for corruption crimes. From my perspective, I propose that an aggravated life imprisonment which puts many more restrictions on commutation, could be chosen to replace immediate execution, with no parole granted, i.e., if the nature of the crime involves serious violence and is lethal, the death penalty for it should be replaced by aggravated life imprisonment, i.e., a convict who is sentenced to this sentence can be released after serving in prison for not less than 30 years on commutation. And no parole would be granted. Meanwhile, the penalty system, in particular the imprisonment system needs to be reformed; on one hand, it is necessary to reduce the number of crimes punishable by life imprisonment; on the other hand, it is necessary to clearly demarcate the circumstances and degrees of crimes and their corresponding punishments. And from the procedural perspective, the jurisdiction of the courts of the first instance over crimes punishable by life imprisonment and the review courts should be changed to a certain extent.

Chapter 7
Conclusion

Obviously, the death penalty is a kind of torture and cruel sanction that deprives the convict of the right to life in the name of the law, and violates human rights, and thus should be removed directly from the penalty system without being replaced by any other inhuman and cruel punishment. As for capital crimes, they should be downgraded to a lighter punishment, such as life imprisonment, in the context of human rights protection and the international trend towards a lightening of penalties. In this sense, there is no point discussing the issues of alternative punishments to the death penalty. However, when considering how to control crime and organize the punishment system, according to the requirements of the principle of proportional justice, there is a need to explore whether there is an appropriate sanction which could fill the potential shortfalls caused by the abolition of the death penalty. This sanction could involve reforming or upgrading the current imprisonment penalty, or introducing a new measure. Furthermore, an important goal for our scholars could be to focus on issues relating to alternative punishments to the death penalty.

The issues of alternative sanctions to the death penalty in China is an important but hidden topic among Chinese scholars, compared with the issue of how to abolish the death penalty. Based on the materials available, most scholars have so far focused merely on the issue of the abolition of the death penalty rather than paying much attention to the issue of an alternative punishment to it, and it has only been discussed specifically by a few research papers or in a special section in others. In other words, the issue of alternative punishments to the death penalty does not receive the same attention as is devoted to the death penalty. China is now trying to control the use of the death penalty and is also moving towards gradually abolishing it. In this context, different scholars have different opinions on the notion of alternative punishments to the death penalty. From the perspective of controlling the use of the death penalty in judicial practice, an alternative punishment could be understood as something that attempts to control its use. An alternative could replace and/or suspend the death penalty with immediate execution while it is still retained. However, from the perspective of abolition, an alternative punishment should replace the death penalty

G. Huang, *On the Alternative Punishment to the Death Penalty in China*,
https://doi.org/10.1007/978-981-97-1627-2_7

de jure and de facto, rather than only in the judicial practice. The latter point is accepted by most Chinese and international scholars. The factors influencing the choice of the punishment option to replace the death penalty are complex and varied, and include the traditional punishment culture, penalty concepts, the political system, the punishment system, public opinion and human rights, etc. Given the differences between China and developed Western democratic states, when we examine these influencing factors, we cannot ignore the culture of the punishment and the special political and legislation system in China, in which *the Constitution of China* and *the Constitution of the Communist Party of China* emphasize the principle of the "leadership of the Communist Party",[1] with the Communist Party leading the legislation. In this light, this book examined and analyzed the factors that influence the choice of punishment option to replace the death penalty in this special political system with its clearly Chinese characteristics. Criminal policy and public opinion are two significant and typical factors involving obvious political considerations in China. The former normally reflects and carries out the will of the Party as expressed to the national management; the latter responds to the majority of citizens' view on the current legal system and it is, to a great extent, the basis for national leadership's running of the country. Even though LWOR has recently been stipulated by the Ninth Amendment for the crime of corruption, it should not be the preferable option as the alternative sanction to the death penalty because it is a kind of cruel torture and violates the constitutional principle of human rights protection. On the contrary, LWPR would be an option, but the termination mechanisms for inmates should be set out in accordance with the principle of proportional justice; aggravated life imprisonment, which can be terminated after serving no less than 30 years in prison, can be chosen to replace the death penalty in China. In addition, there needs to be improvements made to the relevant criminal systems.

[1] 《中华人民共和国宪法》*[The Constitution of the People's Republic of China]*, 2004; 《中国共产党党章》*[The Constitution of the Communist Party of China]*.

References

Legal Documents

Non-Chinese Legal Documents

1. *United States Code.*
2. *The European Convention on Human Rights.*
3. *The Constitution of the Republic of Kazakhstan.*
4. *Criminal Justice Act 2003 of the United Kingdom.*
5. *The Indian Penal Code, 1860, ACT No. 45 of 1860 1*.*
6. *Law No.40/2009 Coll., Criminal Code of Czech Republic.*
7. *The Constitution of the Kingdom of the Netherlands 2008.*
8. *Portugal's Constitution of 1976 with Amendments through 2005.*
9. *Penal Code of Socialist Republic of Viet Nam, (No. 15/1999/QH 10).*
10. *Criminal Code of the Republic of Korea, amended as of Jan, 1, 1998.*
11. *Charter of Fundamental Rights of the European Union (2000/C 364/01).*
12. *The Criminal Code of Finland, 39/1889, amendments up to 766/2015 included.*
13. *Law of the Republic of Indonesia 27 of 1999 on the Penal Code, May 19, 1999.*
14. *Rome Statute of the International Criminal Court, A/CONF. 183/9 of 17 July 1998.*
15. *The Portuguese Criminal Code, Legislative Decree n. 4/2003 of November 18, 2003.*
16. *Criminal Code of the Kingdom of Netherlands, Act of 3 March 1881,* Amended in 2012.
17. *Act C of 2012 on the Criminal Code of Hungary,* promulgated on 13 July 2012.
18. *General Penal Code of Iceland, 1940 No. 19* (12 February), 1.44/2015 (took effect 2 July 2015).
19. *Criminal Code of the Swiss Confederation of 21 December 1937* (Status as of 1 October 2016).
20. *UN Convention on the Rights of the Child,* General Assembly Resolution 44/25 of 20 November 1989.
21. Law Commission of India Report No. 262. *The Death Penalty, August 2015. D.O. No.6(3)263/2014-LC(LS).*
22. *Penal Code of the Republic of Lithuania, 26 September 2000 No. VIII-1968,* Amended on 11 February 2010–No. XI-677.
23. *Criminal Code of Turkey (2011) Law No.5237 of Septermber 26, 2004,* as amended up to Law No.6217 of March 31, 2011.
24. *The Criminal Code of the Russian Federation, No. 63-Fz of June 13, 1996* (with Amendments and additions of March 1, 2012).
25. European Commission for Democracy Through Law, *Penal Code of Turkey, Opinion No. 831/2015,* Strasbourg, 15 February 2016.

G. Huang, *On the Alternative Punishment to the Death Penalty in China*,
https://doi.org/10.1007/978-981-97-1627-2

26. *Universal Declaration on Human Rights,* GA Res 217 A (III), UN GAOR, 3rd sess, 183rd plen mtg, UN Doc A /810 (10 December 1984).
27. *The Norway General Civil Penal Code,* Act of 22 May 1902 No.10, with subsequent amendments, Act of 21 December 2005, No. 131.
28. *Penal Code of Kingdom of Spain,* Organic ACT 10*/1995, Dated 23 November, 1995*, as amended up to Law No. 4/2015 of April 27, 2015.
29. *Criminal Code of Republic of Austria (Strafgesetzbuch, StGB),* As promulgated on 13 November 1998 (Federal Law Gazette I, p. 945, p. 3322).
30. *Criminal Code of the Republic of Bulgaria, No. 26/02.04.1968,* in force as of 01.05.1968, Last amendment SG No. 32/27.04.2010, in force as of 28.05.2010.
31. *The Penal Code of the Republic of Kazakhstan, the Code of the Republic of Kazakhstan dated 3 July 2014, No. 226-V of the Law of the Republic of Kazakhstan.*
32. *Convention for the Protection of Human Rights and Fundamental Freedoms*, opened for signature November 4, 1950, 2013 UNTS 221, entered into force 3 September 1953.
33. *Statutes of the Republic of Singapore: Penal Code (chapter 224), Original Enactment: Ordinance 4 of 1871,* the revised edition of the Laws Act (Chapter 275), in force from 1/4/2015.
34. *The Statutes of the Republic of Singapore: Criminal Procedure Code (Chapter 68)*, original enactment: Act 15 of 2010, revised edition of the Laws Act (Chapter 275), 31st August 2012.
35. *LAW # 286 of 7 July 2009 of the Criminal Code of Romania, Amending Acts: #M1, Law # 27/2012; M2: Law #63/2012; M3: Law # 187/2012,* enters into force on February 1st, 2014.
36. *The Statutes of the Republic of Singapore: Prison Act (Chapter 247),* original enactment: Ordinance 17 of 1933, the revised edition of *the Laws Act (Chapter 275), 30th December 2000.*
37. *Protocol No. 13 to the Convention for the Protection of Human Rights and Fundamental Freedoms, concerning the Abolition of the Death Penalty in all Circumstances,* (Vilnius, 3.V.2002).
38. *Statutes of the Republic of Singapore: Constitution of the Republic of Singapore (Chapter const),* Original enactment: S 1/63, the revised edition of the Laws Act (Chapter 275), 1st July, 1999.
39. *Protocol No. 6 to the Convention for the Protection of Human Rights and Fundamental Freedoms concerning the Abolition of the Death Penalty, as Amended by Protocol No. 11* (Strasbourg, 28.IV.1983).
40. *The Criminal Code of the Republic of Belarus No. 275–3 of 09.07.1999* (as amended by No. 60–3 of 12.07.2013) (*Уголовный кодекс Республики Беларусь № 275–3 от 09.07.1999 г. (в редакции № 60–3 от 12.07.2013 г.).*
41. *Penal Code of Japan, Act No.45 of April 24, 1907* (*日本国刑法, 明治四十年四月二十四日*法律第四十五), the latest version is amended by Act No.54 of June 3, 2016 (最終改正:平成二八年六月三日法律第五四号).
42. *Criminal Code of the Republic of Kazakhstan No. 167 of July 16, 1997 (as amended up to Law of the Republic of Kazakhstan No. 24–V of June 28, 2012) (с изменениями, внесенными Законом Республики Казахстан № 24–V от 28.06.2012 г).*
43. *German Criminal Code, promulgated on 13 November 1998, Federal Law Gazette.*
44. *[Bundesgesetzblatt] I p. 3322, last amended by Article 1 of the Law of 24 September 2013, Federal Law Gazette I p. 3671 and with the text of Article 6(18) of the Law of 10 October 2013, Federal Law Gazette I p 3799.*

Chinese Legal Documents

45. 《中国共产党党章》*[Constitution of the Communist Party of China], 2012.*
46. 《中华人民共和国宪法》 *[Constitution of the People's Republic of China]*, 1954.

47. 《中华人民共和国宪法》*[Constitution of the People's Republic of China]*, 1975.
48. 《中华人民共和国宪法》*[Constitution of the People's Republic of China]*, 1984.
49. 《中华人民共和国宪法》*[Constitution of the People's Republic of China]*, 2004.
50. 《中华人民共和国刑法》*[The Criminal Law of the People's Republic of China], Order No. 5, July 6, 1979.*
51. 《中华人民共和国刑法》*[Criminal Law of the People's Republic of China]*, Order No. 83, 14 March 1997.
52. 《中国人民共和国刑法》*[Criminal Law of the People's Republic of China]*, Oder No. 30, February 25th, 2015.
53. 《中华人民共和国刑事诉讼法》*[The Criminal Procedure Law of the People's Republic of China]*, Order No. 64, 1 July 1979.
54. 《中国人民政治协商会议共同纲领》*[The Common Program of the Chinese People's Political Consultative Conference]*, 1949.
55. 《中华人民共和国刑法修正案(八)》*[The Eighth Amendment to the Criminal Law of the People's Republic of China]*, Order No. 41, February 25th, 2011.
56. 《中华人民共和国刑法修正案(九)》*[The Ninth Amendment to the Criminal Law of the People's Republic of China]*, Order No. 30, August 29th, 2015.
57. 《最高人民法院关于贯彻宽严相济刑事政策的若干意见, (法发 [2010]9 号)》*[Opinions of the Supreme People's Court on the Implementation of the Criminal Policy of Combining Leniency and Severity (No. 9, Legal Issue, 2010)].*
58. 《最高人民法院关于授权高级人民法院核准部分死刑案件的通知》 *[The Supreme People's Court's Notification on the Authorization the High People's Courts to Verify and Approve some Death Sentence Cases]*, on September 7th, 1983.
59. 《最高人民法院关于已满14岁 不满16岁的人所犯罪行特别严重能否判处无期徒刑问题的电话答复》[Answer by Phone from the SPC on the Issue of Whether a Person who has Reached the Age of 14 but not the Age of 18 Commits Very Serious Crimes], 17 April 1991.
60. 《最高人民法院关于办理减刑, 假释案件具体应用法律问题的规定》*[Supreme People Court's Provisions on Several Legal Issues concerning the Specific Application of the Law in Handling Commutation and Parole Cases], 法释 (1997)6号 [Legal Interpretation No.6, 1997].*
61. 《最高人民法院关于办理减刑、假释案件具体应用法律问题的规定》*[Supreme People Court's Provisions on Several Legal Issues concerning the Specific Application of the Law in Handling Commutation and Parole Cases] 法释 (2016)23号 [Legal Interpretation No.23, 2016].*
62. 《最高人民法院关于办理减刑、假释案件具体应用法律若干问题的规定》[The Judicial Interpretations of the Supreme People's Court of the People's Republic of China on the Issues of Commutation and Parole adopted by the Supreme People's Court], 法释[2012]2号[Legal Interpretation, No. 2, 2012].
63. 《全国人民代表大会常务委员会关于死刑案件核准问题的决定》*[The Decisions of the NPC Standing Committee on the Issues of Verifying and Approving Death Sentences]*, adopted by the 19th Session of Standing Committee of China's National Fifth National People's Congress (NPC), on June 10th, 1981.
64. 《最高人民法院关于废止1980年1月1日至1997年6月30日期间发布的部分司法解释和司法解释性质文件 (第九批) 的决定》*[SPC's Decision on Repealing the Partial Judicial Interpretations and Judicial Interpretative Documents (The Ninth Batch) Made in the period from 1 January 1980 to 30 June 1997], 法释〔2013〕2号 [No.2 Legal Interpretation (2013)].*
65. 《中共中央政法委关于严格规范减刑、假释、暂予监外执行切实防止司法腐败的意见》*[The Opinions of the Central Political and Legal Affairs Commission of the Communist Party of China (CPLACCPC) on Effectively Preventing Judicial Corruption by Strictly Regulating the Commutation, Parole and the Temporary Service of Sentences Outside Prison] (People's Republic of China) Central Political and Legal Affairs Commission of the Communist Party of China中政委(2014)5号[No. 5, 2014, Central Political Commission].*

Books and Dissertations

English Books

66. FRANK Jerome, *Law & the Modern Mind*, Transaction Publishers, St. Louis, 1963.
67. STITH Kate and CABRANES Jose A., *Fear of Judging. Sentencing Guidelines in Federal Courts*, University of Chicago Press, Chicago, 1998.
68. MURRAY Joseph, *The Effects of Imprisonment on Families and Children of Prisoners*, "The Effects of Imprisonment", Edited by LIEBLING Alison and MARUNA Shadd, Routledge, Oxford, 2011.
69. GOTTSCHALK Marie, *No Way out? Life Sentences and the Politics of Penal Reform,* Life Without Parole: America's New Death Penalty? Edited by OGLETREE Charles J. and SARAT Austin, NYU Press, New York, 2012.
70. OGLETREE Charles J., Jr. and SARAT Austin, *Lives on the Line: From Capital Punishment to Life without Parole*, Life Without Parole: America's New Death Penalty? Edited by OGLETREE Charles J. and SARAT Austin, NYU Press, New York, 2012.
71. Gao Mingxuan and Zhao Bingzhi, *The Evolution of Chinese Criminal Legislation*, Law Press. China, Beijing, 2007.
72. The Legislative Affairs Office of the State Council of the People's Republic of China, "*Laws and Regulations of the People's Republic of China: Criminal Law*", China Legal Publishing House, 2011.
73. JUHÁSZ Zsuzsanna, *A Büntetések [The penalties], Kommentár a Büntető Törvénykönyvhöz [Commentary on Criminal Code],* edited by KARSAI Krisztina, Budapest, 2013.
74. Madai Sándor: *A Társadalmi Tulajdon Fokozottabb Büntetőjogi Védelme Egykor és Most [Increased Criminal Protection of Social Property Once and Now],* Békés Imre emlékkötet [Remembering essays for Imre Békés], edited by GELLÉRR Balázs, CSIGE Zoltán, Budapest, 2013, 143–178.
75. GÁL ISTVÁN László, László, *Feltételes szabadságra bocsátás az életfogytig tartó szabadságvesztésből 42–45. § [Release on Parole from Life Imprisonment 42–45. §], A Büntető Törvénykönyvről szóló 2012. évi C. törvény nagykommentárja [Great Commentary on the Act C of 2012 on the Criminal Code],* edited by POLT Péter, MISKOLCZI Barna, TÖRÖK Tímea, GASZ Péter, Budapest, 2016.
76. GÁL ISTVÁN László, SZŰCS András, *A Büntetések [The Penalties],* in *Új Btk. Kommentár: 2. Kötet [Commentary on New Criminal Code: Vol. 2], Általános rész [General Part],* Edited by POLT Péter, Budapest, 2013.
77. KARSAI Krisztina and ZSOLT Szomora, *Criminal Law in Hungary*, Kluwer Law International BV, the Netherlands, 2010.

Chinese Books and Dissertations

78. *《荀子·第18篇》[Xun Zi: Book 18].*
79. 黎宏 [LI Hong], *《刑法学》[Criminal Law],* 法律出版社 [Law Press. China], Beijing, 2012.
80. 沈宗灵 [SHEN Zongling], *《法理学》[Jurisprudence],* 北京大学出版社 [Beijing University Press], Beijing, 2000.
81. 储怀值 [CHU Haizhi], *《刑事一体化》[Criminal Science Integration],* 法律出版社 [Law Press·China], Beijing, 2004.
82. 赵秉志 [ZHAO Bingzhi], *《刑罚总论问题探索》[Exploring the Issues of Punishments in the General Provisions of Criminal Law],* 法律出版社 [Law Press], Beijing, 2002.
83. 李荣 [LI Rong], *《公正量刑机制研究》[Research on the Guaranteeing System of Sentencing Justly],* 中央民族大学出版社 [Minzu University of China Press], Beijing, 2013.

84. 《中华人民共和国最高人民法院公报》*[The Bulletins of the Supreme People's Court of the People's Republic of China]*, 2013年卷 [Vol. 2013], 人民法院出版社 [People's Court Press], Beijing, 2014.
85. 康均心 [KANG Junxin], *《理想与现实:中国死刑制度报告》[The Ideals and Realities: A Report on the Death Penalty System in China]*, 中国人民公安大学出版社 [People's Public Security University of China Press], Beijing, 2005.
86. 全国人大常委会办公室研究室 [Research Office of General Office of the NPC Standing Committee], *《人民代表大会制度建设40年》[The 40 year Construction of the System of National People's Congress]*, 中国民主与法制出版社 [China Democracy and Law Press], Beijing, 1991.
87. 霍存福 [HUO Cunfu], *《复仇·报应刑·报应说——中国人法律观念的文化解说》[Vengeance, Retributive Penalty and the Theory of Retribution: Explicating Culturally the Legal Concept of Chinese]*, 吉林人民出版社 [Jilin People's Publishing House], Ji Lin, 2005.
88. 赵秉志 [ZHAO Bingzhi], *《论中国非暴力犯罪死刑的逐步废止》[On Abolition of Death Penalty of Non-Violent Crimes in China]*, 中国刑法学年会文集(第1卷:死刑问题研究) [Collected Works of 2004 Annual Conference of China's Criminal Law: On the Death Penalty (Volume 1)], 中国人民公安大学出版社 [China's People's Public Security University Press], Beijing, 2004.
89. 汪明亮 [WANG Mingliang], *《论死刑量刑社会学模式——以"刘涌案"为分析视角》[On the Sociological Model of the Death Sentence: From the Perspective of the Case of liu Yong]*, 中国刑法学年会文集(第1卷:死刑问题研究) [Collected Works of 2004 Annual Conference of China's Criminal Law: On the Death Penalty (Volume 1)], 中国人民公安大学出版社 [China's People's Public Security University Press], Beijing, 2004.
90. 张秀玲 [ZHANG Xiuling], *《无期徒刑研究》[On Life Imprisonment]*, 吉林大学博士论文 [Ph.D. Dissertation, Jilin University], 2010.
91. 张新甦 [ZHANG Xinsu], *《终身自由刑替代死刑制度研究》[On Life Imprisonment as a Substitution for the Death Penalty]*, 吉林大学博士论文 [Ph.D. Dissertation, Jilin University], 2013.
92. 刘耀彬 [Liu Yaobin], *《马克思主义犯罪学思想研究》[On the Marxist Thought on the Criminology]*, 南京航空航天大学博士论文 [Ph.D. Dissertation, Nanjing Univeristy of Aeronautics and Astronautics] 2010.
93. 袁江华 [YUAN Jianghua], *《马克思主义刑罚思想中国化论纲》[On the Sinicization the Marxism Penalty Thought]*, 扬州大学博士论文 [Ph.D. Dissertation, Yang Zhou University] 2011.
94. 张继良 [ZHANG Jiliang], *《中共人权理论与中国人权立法研究》[On the Chinese Communist's Thesis of Human Rights and Its Legislation in China]*, 东北师范大学博士论文 [Ph.D. Dissertation, Northeast Normal University], 2004.

Periodical Journal Papers

English Periodical Journal Papers

95. TREVASKES Susan, *Using Mao to Package Criminal Justice Discourse in 21st-century China*, The China Quarterly, 2016, No. 226.
96. TREVASKES Susan, *Lenient Death Sentencing and the "Cash for Clemency" Debate*, The China Journal, 2015, Vol. 73.
97. TREVASKES Susan, *The Shifting Sands of Punishment in China in the Era of 'Harmonious Society'*, Law & Policy, 2010, Vol. 32, No. 3.
98. IULIANO Jason, *Why Capital Punishment is no Punishment at All*, Americal University Law Review, 2015, Vol. 64, Issue. 6.

99. HUANG Gui, *On the Problems of Just Sentencing in China*, Acta Juridica Hungarica [Hungarian Journal of Legal Studies], 2015, Vol. 56, Issue 2–3.
100. HUANG Gui, *Death Penalty in China after the Ninth Amendment: Legislative Abolishing and Judicially Limiting*, Journal of Forensic Science & Criminology, 2016, Vol. 4, Issue 3.
101. HERIYANTO Dodik Setiawan Nur and HUANG Gui, Death Penalty Legislation in China and Indonesia Under International Human Rights Law Perspective, JURNAL HUKUM IUS QUIA IUSTUM, 2016, Vol. 23, Issue 4.
102. PAVEL Nicolae, *Defining the Concept of Human Rights in the Light of Juridical Values Theory*, Contemporary Readings in Law and Social Justice, 2012, Vol. 4, No. 1.
103. PEERENHOOM Randall, *Assessing Human Rights in China: Why the Double Standard?*, Cornell International Law Journal, 2005, No. 38.
104. SHETTY Salil, *The Value of International Standards in the Campaign for Abolition of the Death Penalty*, The Brown Journal of World Affairs, 2014, Vol. XXI, No. 1.
105. GARDINER Gerald, *The Purposes of Criminal Punishment*, The Mondern Law Review, 1958, Vol. 21, No. 2.
106. FLORIA Ryan, *The Capital Punishment Fits the Crime: A Comparative Analysis of the Death Penalty and Proportionality in the United States of America and the People's Republic of China*, University of Miami International and Comparative Law Review, 2008, Vol. 16, No. 1.
107. CHAI Winberg, *China after Deng Xiaoping: Some Encouraging-and Not-So-Encouraging-Signs*, Asian Affairs: An American Review, 1997, Vol. 24, Issue 2.
108. BRUDNER Alan, *Retributivism and the Death Penalty*, The University of Toronto Law Journal, 1980, Vol. 30, No. 4.
109. NEUMAYER Eric, *Death Penalty: The Political Foundations of the Global Trend towards Abolition*, Human Rights Review, 2008, Vol. 9, No. 2.
110. MRAE Dave, *Indonesian Captial Punishment in Comparative Perspective*, Bijdragen tot de taal, land-en volkenkunde [Journal of the Humanities and Social Sciences of Southeast Asia] 2017, Vol. 173, Issue 1.
111. SHER Elizabeth M, *Death Penalty Sentencing in Japan under the lay Assessor System: Avoiding the Avoidable through Unanimity*, Pacific Rim Law & Policy Journal, 2011, Vol. 20, No. 3.
112. AMBLER Leah, *The People Decide: The Effect of the Introduction of the Quasi-Jury System (Saiban-In Seido) on the Death Penalty in Japan*, Northwestern Journal of International Human Rights, 2008, Vol. 6, Issue 1.
113. JOHNSON David T., *Retention and Reform in Japanese Capital Punishment*, University of Michigan Journal of Law Reform, 2016, Vol. 49, No. 4.
114. PASCOE Daniel, *Three Coming Legal Challenges to Indonesia's Death Penalty Regime*, The Indonesian Journal of International & Comparative Law, 2015, Vol. II, Issue 2.
115. LYNCH Columan, *Indonesia's Use of Capital Punishment for Drug-Trafficking Crimes: Legal Obligations, Etralegal Factors, and the Bali Nine Case*, Columbia Human Rights Law Review, 2009, Vol. 40, Issue 2.
116. MANACORDA Stefano, *Restraints on Death Penalty in Europe: A Circular Process*, Journal of International Criminal Justice, 2003, Vol. 1, Issue 2.
117. HESSING Dick J. KEIJSER Jan W., and ELFFERS Henk, *Explaining Capital Punishment Support in an Abolitionist Country: The Case of the Netherlands*, Law and Human Behavior, 2003, Vol. 27, No. 6.
118. YORKE Jon, *Inhuman Punishment and Abolition of the Death Penalty in the Council of Europe*, European Public Law, 2010, Vol. 16, No. 1.
119. BEHRMANN Christian and YORKE Jon, *The European Union and Abolition of the Death Penalty*, Pace International Law Review Online Companion, 2013, Vol. 4, No. 1
120. LIGHT Matthew and KOVALEV Nikolai, *Russia, The Death Penalty, and Europe: The Ambiguities of Influence*, Post-Soviet Affairs, 2013, Vol. 29, No. 6
121. KLEINFELD Joshua, *Two Cultures of Punishment*, Stanford Law Review, 2016, Vol. 68, Issue 5.

122. STEIKER Jordan M., *The American Death Penalty: Constitutional Regulation as the Distinctive Feature of American Exeptionalism*, University of Miami Law Review, 2013, Vol. 67, No. 2.
123. NELLIS Ashley, *Tinkering with Life: A Look at the Inappropriateness of Life without Parole as An Alternative to the Death Penalty,* University of Miami Law Review, 2013, Vol. 67, Issue 2.
124. BERRY William W. III, *Life-with-Hope Sentencing: The Argument for Replacing Life-without- Parole Sentences with Presumptive Life Sentences*, Ohio State Law Journal, 2015, Vol. 76, No. 5.
125. WRIGHT Julian H., *Life-without Parole: An Alternative to Death or Not Much of A Life at All*, Vanderbilt Law Review, 1990, Vol. 43.
126. WOOD Arthur Lewis, *The Alternatives to the Death Penalty,* The Annals of the American Academy of Political and Social Science, 1952, Vol. 284, No. 1.
127. SNELLENBURG Sidney C., *Is There a Reasonable Alternative to the Death Penalty?*, Judicature, 1987, Vol. 71, No. 1.
128. MULROY Steven J., *Avoiding Death By Default: Does the Constitution Require a 'Life Without Parole' Alternative to the Death Penalty*, Tulane Law Review, 2004, Vol. 79, No. 2.
129. MONTHY Jeremy T., *Internal Perspectives on Chinese Human Rights Reform: The Death Penalty in the PRC*, Texas International Law Journal, 1998, Vol. 33, No. 1.
130. WANG Yunhai, *The Death Penalty and Society in East Asia—How to Understand and Compare the Death Penalty in China, Japan and South Korea—*, Hitotsubashi Journal of Law and Politics, 2012, No. 24.
131. SOOTAK Jaan, *Theories of Punishment and Reform of Criminal Law (Reform as a Change of Mentality),* Juridical International, 2000, No. V.
132. CANTY Aimée Tecla, *A Return to Balance: Federal Sentencing Reform After the 'Tough on Crime' Era',* Stetson Law Review, 2015, Vol. 44, No. 3.
133. ZINGER Ivan, *Human Rights and Federal Corrections: A Commentary on a Decade of Tough on Crime Policies in Canada*, Canadian Journal of Criminal Justice, 2016, Vol. 58, No. 4.
134. YANG Jie, *The Development of China's Death Penalty Representation Guidelines: A Learning Model Based on the ABA Guidelines for the Appointment and Performance of Defense Counsel in Death Penalty Cases*, Hofstra Law Review, 2013, Vol. 42, No. 2.
135. FRÎNTU Viorica-Mihaela, *PedeapsaDetenţiuniiPeViaţă (Life Imprisonment Penalty)*, Annals of the Constantin Brancusi University—Juridical Sciences Series, 2013, Nr. 4.
136. REIDY Aisling, *The Prohibition of Torture: A Guide to the Implementation of Article 3 of the European Convention on Human Rights*, Human Rights Handbooks, 2003, No. 1.
137. YADAV Mukesh, *Life Imprisonment: Meaning and Interpretation of Law*, Journal of Indian Academy of Forensic Medicine, 2007, Vol. 29, No. 2.
138. TAGUSARI Maiko, *Death Penalty in Japan*, East Asian Law Journal, 2010, Vol. 1, No. 2.
139. LIEBMAN James S., *Opting for Real Death Penalty Reform*, Ohio State Law Journal, 2002, Vol. 63, No. 1.
140. LERNER Craig S., *Life without Parole as a Conflicted Punishment*, Wake Forest Law Review, 2013, Vol. 48.
141. *A Matter of Life and Death: The Effect of Life-without parole Statutes on CapitalPunishmen*, Havard Law Review, 2006, Vol. 119, Issue 6.
142. LEBARON Genevieve, *Rethinking Prison Labor: Social Discipline and the State in Historical Perspective*, Working USA: The Journal of Labor & Society, 2012, Vol. 15, Issue 3.
143. HANEY Lynne A., *Working through Mass Incarceration: Gender and the Politics of Prison Labor from East to West*, Journal of Women in Culture and Society, 2010, Vol. 36, No. 1.
144. ROCHELEAU Ann Marie, *An Empirical Exploration of the 'Pains of Imprisonment' and the Level of Prison Misconduct and Violence,* Criminal Justice Review, 2013, Vol. 38, No. 3.
145. HULLEY Susie, CREWE Ben and WRIGHT Serena, *Re-examining the Problems of Long-term Imprisonment*, British Journal of Criminology, 2016, Vol. 56, Issue 4.
146. SCHNITTKER Jason, and MASSOGLIA Michael, *A Sociocognitive Approach to Studying the Effects of Incarceration,* Wisconsin Law Review, 2015, Vol. 2015, Issue 2.

147. CALSEYDE Philippe P.F.M. van de, ZEELENBERG Gideon Keren Marcel, *The Insured Victim Effect: When and Why Compensating Harm Decreases Punishment Recommendations,* Judgement and Decision Making, 2013, Vol. 8, No. 2.
148. WILLIAMS Kenneth, *Why and How the Supreme Court Should End the Death Penalty*, University of San Francisco Law Review, 2017, Vol. 51, Issue 2.
149. TIBBS Donald F., *Towards an Abolition Democracy: The Death Penalty, Circa 2015*, Widener Law Journal, 2016 Vol. 25, Issue 1.
150. GALLIANI Davide, *The Reducible Life Imprisonment Standard from a Worldwide and European Perspective*, Global Jurist, 2016, Vol. 16, Issue 1.
151. CERAR Miro, *The Relationship between Law and Politics*, Annual Survey of International &Comparative Law, 2009, Vol. 15, No. 1.
152. ANNERMARIEKE Beijer, *The Debate on Capital Punishment in the Netherlands and Germany*, International Criminal Justice Review, 2000, Vol. 10, Issue 1.
153. NAGY Anita, *Release from Prison and Probation in Hungary*, Juridical Current, 2016, Vol. 19, Issue 3.
154. NAGY Anita, Pardon System in Hungary and European Human Rights Jurisprudence, The Lawyer Quarterly, 2016, Vol. 3, Issue 3.
155. NAGY Anita, *Presidential Pardon and the European court of Human Rights*, CASOPIS POLICAJNA TEORIA A PRAX, 2016, Issue 1.
156. JAMES M. Donoval, *Public Opinion and the French Capital Punishment Debate of 1908*, Law and History Review, 2014, Vol. 32, No. 3.
157. MAJA Nastić, *ECHR and National Constitutional Courts*, Zbornik Radova Pravnog Fakulteta u Nisu, 2015, Issue. 71.
158. ZOLTANT. J. Toth, *The Capital Punishment Controversy in Hungary: Frogments on the Issues of Deterrent Effect and Wrongful Convictions, European Journal of Crime*, Criminal Law and Criminal Justice, 2013, Vol. 21, Issue 1.
159. HUANG Gui: *On the Problem of Just Sentencing in China,* Acta Juridica Hungarica, Vol. 56, Issue 2–3, 2015, pp. 177–190.
160. HUANG Gui, *On Recent Changes to Life Imprisonment in the Context of the Gradual Reduction in the Use of the Death Penalty in China*, University of Bologna Law Review, Vol. 3, Issue 1, 2018, pp. 24–63.
161. HUANG Gui: *On the Alternative Punishment to the Death Penalty in China,* Lawasia Journal, Vol. 2017, pp. 19–48.
162. HUANG Gui: *The Communist Party of China's Approach to Human Rights and the Death Penalty,* Asia-Pacific Journal on Human Rights and the Law, Vol. 18, Issue 2, 2017, pp. 117–154.
163. HUANG Gui: *Life Imprisonment System in Continental Europe and Asia: Examples from Various States,* Jura: A Pecsi Tudomanyegyetem Allam-es Jogtudomanyi Karanak Tudomanyos Lapja, Vol. 2018, Issue 1, 2018, pp. 269–279.

Chinese Periodical Journal Papers

164. 高铭暄, 苏惠渔, 于志刚[GAO Mingxuan, SU Huiyu and YU Zhigang], *《从此踏上废止死刑的征途—《刑法修正案(八)草案》死刑问题三人谈》 [Setting Out on the Journey to the Abolition of the Death Penalty—The Trialogue on the Issues of the Death Penalty of the 'The Eighth Amendment to the Criminal Law (Draft)],* 法学 [Law Science] 2010, No. 9.
165. 高铭暄 [GAO Mingxuan], *《略论中国刑法中的死刑替代措施》 [Brief Discussion on the Alternative Measures to the Death Penalty in Chinese Criminal Law],* 河北法学 [Law Science] 2008, Vol. 26, No. 2.
166. 高铭暄, 王秀梅 [GAO Mingxuan and WANG Xiumei], *《死刑替代利弊分析》 [Advantages and Disadvantages of Replacing the Death Penalty*], 江苏行政学院学报 [Journal of the Jiangsu Administration Institute] 2008, No. 1.

167. 高铭暄, 楼伯坤 [GAO Mingxuan and Lou Bokun], *《死刑替代位阶上无期徒刑的改良》 [Ways to Reform the Life Sentence: An Alternative to the Death Penalty]*, 现代法学 [Modern Law Science] 2010, No. 6.
168. 刘远 [LIU Yuan], *《刑法的道德性与政治性》 [On the Morality of the Criminal Law and its Politic]*, 华东政法大学学报 [Journal of East China University of Political Science and Law] 2007, No. 5.
169. 赵秉志 [ZHAO Bingzhi], *《中国刑法改革新思考——以<刑法修正案(八)(草案)>为主要视角》 [New Thinking on the Reform of Criminal Law of China: With the Perspective of the Eighth Amendment (Draft) to the Criminal Law]*, 北京师范大学学报(社会科学版) [Journal of Beijing Normal University (Social Sciences)] 2011, No. 1.
170. 赵秉志[ZHAO Bingzhi], *《中国死刑立法改革新思考——以《刑法修正案(九)(草案)》为主要视角》 [New Thinking on Death Penalty in China: With the Perspective of Amendment (Draft) to Criminal Law]*, 吉林大学社会科学学报[Ji Lin University Journal Social Sciences Edition] 2015, Vol. 55, No. 1.
171. 赵秉志 [ZHAO Bingzhi], *《中国死刑替代措施要论》 [On Alternative Measures to the Death Penalty in China]*, 学术交流 [Academic Exchange] 2008, No. 9.
172. 赵秉志, 张伟珂 [ZHAO Bingzhi and ZHANG Weike], *《略论死刑的民意引导: 以慎用死刑为视角》 [Brief Comments on the Guidance of Public Opinion on the Death Penalty from the Perspective of a Careful Use of the Death Penalty]*, 国家检察官学院学报 [Journal of the National Prosecutors College] 2013, Vol. 21, No. 4.
173. 田中重好, 朱安新 [TIANZHONG Chonghao and ZHU Anxin], *《中国社会结构变动和社会性调节机制的弱化》 [The Changes of the Social Structure in China and the Weakening of the Social Regulating Mechanism]*, 学习与探索 [Study & Exploration] 2010, No. 4.
174. 李希惠 [LI Xihui], *《论死刑的替代措施: 以我国刑法立法为基点》 [Study on the Alternative Measures to the Death Penalty: Standpoint on the Ground of Criminal Law Legislation in Our Country]*, 河北法学 [Hebei Law Science] 2008, Vol. 26, No. 2.
175. 吴雅凌 [WU Yaling], *《卢梭 <社会契约论> 的汉译及其影响》 [Chinese Translation of the Social Contract by Jean-Jacques Rousseau and its influences]*, 现代哲学 [Modern Philosophy] 2009, Vol. 104, No. 3.
176. 赵小波 [ZHAO Xiaobo], *《近代中国"民权"内涵演变考论: 从维新到革命的话语转换》 [On the Evolution of the Concept of Civil Rights in Modern China: The Discussion on Conversion from Restoration to Revolution]*, 法学家 [The Juris] 2015, No. 2.
177. 郭道晖, 陶威 [GUO Daohui and TAO Wei], *《人权禁区是怎样突破的—建国以来法学界重大事件研究》 [How Could the Exclusion Zone for Human Rights be Broken? On Significant Cases Occurring in the Field of Jurisprudence after the Foundation of the PRC]*, 法学 [Law Science] 1999, No. 5.
178. 郭道晖 [GUO Daohui], *《人权观念与人权入宪》 [On the Concept of Human Rights and the Inclusion of Human Rights into the Constitution]*, 法学[Law Science] 2004, No. 4.
179. 于建嵘 [YU Jianrong], *《共治威权与法治威权—中国政治发展的问题与出路》 [Condominium Authoritarian Regime and the Authoritarian Regime of the Rule of Law: the Problems and Outlooks of Political Development in China]*, 当代世界社会主义问题 [Issues of Contemporary World Socialism] 2008, Vol. 98, No. 4.
180. 于建嵘 [YU Jianrong], *《从刚性稳定到韧性稳定—关于中国社会秩序的一个分析框架》 [From Stiff Stability to Flexible Stability: An Analysizing Framwork on the Social Order in China]*, 学习与探索 [Study & Exploration] 2009, No. 5.
181. 蒋传光, 王逸飞 [JIANG Chuangang and WANG Yifei], *《论社会主义意识形态对当代法治发展的主导作用》 [On the Leading Role of the Socialism Ideology in the Development of Rule of Law in the Contemporary of China]*, 学习与探索 [Study & Exploration] 2011, No. 5.
182. 邓定一, 康松林 [DENG Dingyi and KANG Songlin], *《马克思的犯罪概念是刑法理论的根本变革》 [The Marx Notion of the Offerce is a Foundamental Change of the Criminal Theory]*, 现代法学 [Modern Law Science] 1983, No. 2.
183. 赵延光 [ZHAO Yanguang], *《论"犯罪是孤立的个人反对统治关系的斗争"》 [On the Argument that "crime is a struggle done by an isolative individual against the rule relationship]*, 贵州大学学报: 社会科学版[Journal of Guizhou University (Social Sciences)] 1984, No. 1.

184. 袁江华 [YUAN Jianghua], *《马克思主义刑罚思想中国化研究综述》[Literature Review on the Maxism Thought on the Criminal Punishment with Chinese Characters]*, 毛泽东邓小平理论研究 [Studies on Mao Zedong and Deng Xiaoping Theories] 2010, No. 5.
185. 江礼华 [JIANG Lihua], 《毛泽东的刑罚思想》 [On Mao Zedong's Thought on Criminal Punishment], 中央检察官管理学院学报 [Journal of Central Collegue of the Procurator] 1993, No. Z1.
186. 徐增文, 房博 [XU Zengwen and FANG Bo], *《社会主导意识形态变迁与中国经济发展: 1978–2008》[The Changes of the Social Dominant Ideology and the Development of the Economic in China: From 1978 to 2008]*, 南京政治学院学报 [Journal of PLA Nanjing in Stitute of Politics] 2008, No. 6.
187. 董方, 徐建 [DONG Fang and XU Jian], *《对改革开放以来我国刑事犯罪增减变化的评析》[Analyzing the Changes of the Criminal Cases since the Reform and Openning-up in China]*, 青少年犯罪问题 [Issues on Juvenile Crimes and Delinquency] 1995, No. 2.
188. 夏菲 [XIA Fei], *《观念误区与犯罪现象关联的分析: 我国改革开放进程中犯罪问题的回顾与反思》[Analysizing the Relationship between Wrong Concepts and Crime Phenomena: Reviewing and Rethinking the Crime Issues in the Process of the Reform and Openning up in China]*, 犯罪研究 [Criminou Reserch] 2001, No. 2.
189. [SHI Dandun], *《2001年第三次 '严打': '打黑除恶' 再掀高潮》[The Third "Strike Hard" Campaign in 2001: The Campaign of Cracking down on Criminal Syndicates Had Another Major Shift]*, 国家人文历史 [National Humanity History] 2013, No. 16.
190. 黎宏 [LI hong], *《刑事和解:一种新的刑罚改革理念》[Criminal Reconciliation: A New Penalty Refrom Notion]*, 法学论坛 [Legal Forum] 2006, Vol. 21, No. 4.
191. 黎宏 [LI Hong], *《终身监禁的法律性质及适用》[On the Legal Nature of Life Imprisonment without Release and its Application]*, 中国检察官 [The Chinese Procurators] 2016, No. 17.
192. 许晓龙 [XU Xiaolong], *《从"统治"到"治理": 中国行政思维的历史嬗变》[From 'Ruling' to 'Governance': The Historical Evolution of the Administration Logic of China]*, 观察与思考 [Observation and Ponderation] 2014, No. 6.
193. 胡联合, 胡鞍钢, 魏星 [HU Lianhe, HU Angang and WEI Xing], *《国家治理: 社会矛盾的实证研究》[National Governance: Empirical Study of National Social Contradition]*, 新疆师范大学学报(哲学社会科学版) [Journal of Xinjiang Normal University (Philosophy and Social Sciences)] 2014, Vol. 35, No. 3.
194. 王学荣 [WANG Xuerong, *《从统治到治理: 国家政治理念的上升——以十八届三中全会的相关论述为起点》[From Ruling to Governance: The Increase of the Political Idea of the State—Starting with the Relevant Point of the Third Plenary Session of 18th CPC]*, 机构与行政 [Organizations and Administration] 2015, No. 4.
195. 孔繁斌 [KONG Fanbin], *《 治理对话统治:一个政治发展范式的阐释》 [Conversation between Governance and Ruling: An Explornation on the Approach of the Political Development]*, 南京社会科学 [Social Sciences in Nanjing] 2006, No. 11.
196. 徐光华 [XU Ganghua], *《个案类型特征视阈下的刑事司法与民意——以2005至2014年130个影响性刑事案件为研究范本》[Criminal Justice and the Public Opinion from the Perspective of the Type-features of the Individual Cases: Taking 130 Criminal Cases Having Great Impact from 2005 to 2014 As the Study Example]*, 法律科学 (西北政法大学学报) [Science of Law (Journal of Northwest University of Political Science and Law)] 2015, No. 5.
197. 魏昌东 [WEI Changdong], *《新刑法工具主义批判与矫正》[Criticizing and Correcting the New Criminal Instrumentalism]*, 法学 [Law Science] 2016, No. 2.
198. 王海军 [WANG Haijun], *《拒不支付劳动报酬罪的规范性解读—基于"双重法益"的新立场》[Normatively Analyzing the Crime of Refusing to Pay Labor Remuneration: On the New Basis of the Dual Legal Interests]*, 法学评论 [Law Review] 2013, No. 5.
199. 王超强, 周宏, 倪晓一[WANG Chaoqiang, ZHOU Hong and NI Xiaoyi], *《胡锦涛刑法思想探析》[Examing the Criminal Thought of Hu Jintao]*, 学理论[Theory Research] 2012, No. 16.
200. 周少华 [ZHOU Shaohua], *《刑罚目的观之理论清理》[Theoretically Reviewing the Opinions on the Penalty Aims]*, 东方法学 [Oriental Law] 2012, No. 1.

201. 李永升, 冯文杰 [LI Rongsheng and FENG Wenjie], *《刑罚目的新界说》[New Definitions of the Purposes of the Criminal Punishment]*, 湖南警察学院学报 [Journal of Hunan Police Academy] 2016, Vol. 28, No. 2.
202. 王文华 [WANG Wenhua], *《"法外复仇"传统与"仇恨犯罪"的抗制——以中国传统复仇文化为视角》['Extrajudicial Revenge' and the Prevention of Hate Crime: From the Perspective of the Culture of Revenge in Chinese Tradition]*, 法学论坛[Legal Forum] 2011, Vol. 26, No. 6.
203. 王世洲 [WANG Shizhou], *《危害国家安全罪的信条学考察》[Dogmatically Review the Crimes of Endangering National Security]*, 中国刑事法杂志 [Criminal Science] 2012, No. 8.
204. 李华 [LI Hua], *《论我国刑法中的绝对确定法定刑》[On the Absolutely Determinate Statutory Punishment Provided in the China's Criminal Law]*, 法律适用 [Law Application] 1995, No. 9.
205. 樊文 [FAN Wen], *《犯罪控制的惩罚主义及其效果》[The Punitivism of the Crime Control and its Effectiveness]*, 法学研究 [Chinese Journal of Law] 2011, No. 3.
206. 高永明 [GAO Yongming], *《罚金刑的基底性批判——罚金刑执行难的另一种解读》[Thorough Animadversion to the Penal Fine: Another Understanding the Difficualties in the Execution of the Penal Fine]*, 河北法学[Hebei Law Science] 2014, Vol. 32, No. 10.
207. 王衍松, 吴优[WANG Yansong and WU You], *《罚金刑适用研究——高适用率与低实执率之二律背反》[On Application of the Penal Fine: The Antinomy of High Rate of the Application and the Low Rate of Implementation]*, 中国刑事法杂志 [Criminal Science] 2013, No. 6.
208. 劳佳琦 [LAO Jiaqi], *《累犯从严量刑适用实证研究》[Empirically Study on the Sentencing Application of A Heavier Punishment for A Revidivist]*, 中国法学 [Chinese Legal Science] 2016, No. 1.
209. 贾宇, 舒洪水 [JIA Yu and SHU Hongshui], *《累犯制度研究》[On the Revidivist System]*, 山东警察学院学报 [Journal of Shandong Public Security College] 2005, No. 5.
210. 苏彩霞 [SU Caixia], *《累犯制度设立根据之探究》[Exploring the Basis for the Establishment of the Revidivist Systm]*, 中国法学 [Chinese Legal Science] 2002, No. 5.
211. 尤金亮 [YOU Jinliang], *《刑罚裁量中法律效果与社会效果的比较与选择》[On the Comparision and the Choice between the legal Effect and Social Effect during the Penalty Sentencing]*, 学术界 [Academics] 2013, No. 3.
212. 吕方 [LV Fang], *《穿行于理想和现实之间的平衡——从法律文化的视角解读"法律效果和社会效果的统一"》[The Balance Which Across the Ideal and the Reality: Reviewing the Unity of the Effect and the Social Effect from the Perspective of Legal Culture]*, 法学论坛 [Legal Forum] 2005, Vol. 20, No. 3.
213. 黄晓亮, 王霖 [HUANG Xiaoliang and WANG Lin], *《死刑适用法律效果与社会效果问题研究》[On the Problems of the Legal Effect and the Social Effect of the Use of the Death Penalty]*, 法治研究 [Research on Rule of Law] 2013, No. 1.
214. [FENG Jun], *《评最高人民法院再审刘涌案刑事判决书》[Review on the Supreme People's Court's Judgement on the Case of Liu Yong]*, 刑事法评论 [Criminl Law Review], edited by 陈兴良 [CHEN Xingliang], 中国政法大学出版社 [China University of Political Science and Law Press], Beijing, 2004, Vol. 14.
215. [MAO Li], *《从许霆案透视法律效果与社会效果的统一> [Reviewing the Unity of the Legal Effect and the Social Effect from the Case of Xu Ting]*, 天水行政学院学报 [Journal of Tianshui College of Administration] 2009, No. 5.
216. 顾培东 [GU Peidong], *《能动司法若干问题研究》[On the Problems of the Acitive Judiciary]*, 中国法学 [China Legal Science] 2010, No. 4.
217. 姚莉 [YAO Li], *《当代中国语境下的"能动司法"界说》[On the Definition of the Active Judiciary in the Content of the Contempary China]*, 法商研究 [Studies in Law and Business] 2011, No. 1.
218. 陈金钊 [CHEN Jinzhao], *《被社会效果所异化的法律效果及其克服——对两个效果统一论的反思》[On the Alienation of the Legal Effect Conducted by the Society Effect and its Overcoming: Rethinking the Unity of the Two Effects]*, 东方法学 [Oriental Law] 2012, No. 6.

219. 杜月秋 [DU Yueqiu], *《论裁判的正当性基础: 以法律效果和社会效果的相互关系为视角》[On the Legitimate Base of the Judgment: From the Perspective of Interrelation of the Legal Effect and the Social Effect],* 法律适用 [National Judges College Law Journal (Journal of Law Application)] 2007, No. 3.
220. 刘正强 [LIU Zhengqiang], *《信访的"容量"分析——理解中国信访治理及其限度的一种思路》[Analyzing the 'Capacity' of People's Complaints vis Letters or Visits: Towards Understanding the Handling of People's Camplaints and its Limits],* 开放时代 [Open Times] 2014, No. 1.
221. 张守文, 米传勇 [ZHANG Shouwen and MI Chuanyong], *《中国死刑政策的过去、现在及未来》[The Past, Present and Future of the Death Policy in China],* 法学评论 [Law Review] 2006, No. 2.
222. 陈兴良 [CHEN Xingliang], 《死刑政策之法理解读》[Death Penalty Policies: A Jurisprudential Perception], 中国人民大学学报 [Journal of Renmin University of China] 2013, No. 6.
223. 陈兴良 [CHEN Xingliang], *《减少死刑的立法路线图》[Reduction of the Legislation Road Map for the Death Penalty],* 政治与法律 [Political Science and Law] 2015, No. 7.
224. 陈兴良 [CHEN Xingliang], *《宽严相济刑事政策研究》[On the Criminal Policy of Combining Leniency and Severity],* 法学杂志 [Law Science Magazine] 2006, No. 1.
225. 陈兴良 [CHEN Xingliang], *《犯罪范围的扩张与刑罚结构的调整》[On the Expansion of the Scope of the Crime and the Adjustment of the Punishment Structure: Comment on the Ninth Amendment],* 法律科学 (西北政法大学学报) [Science of Law (Journal of Northwest University of Political Science and Law)] 2016, No. 4.
226. 李洁 [LI Jie], *《慎重修改刑法论》[On Modifying Cautiously the Criminal Law],* 刑事法评论 [Criminl Law Review], edited by 陈兴良 [CHEN Xingliang], 中国政法大学出版社 [China University of Political Science and Law Press], Beijing, 2002, Vol. 11.
227. 葛平, 王洪谷[GE Ping and WANG Honggu], *《谈死刑》[On the Death Penalty],* 法学研究 [Chinese Journal of Law] 1980, No. 1.
228. [LI Kangtai], *《正确认识和适用死刑》[Understanding and Applying Correctly the Death Penalty],* 北京政法学院学报 [Tribune of Beijing Colleague on Political Science and Law] 1983, No. 2.
229. 张远煌 [ZHANG Yuanhuang], *《我国死刑适用标准的缺陷及其弥补方法》[On* the Defects of Applicable Standards of the Death Penalty in China and their Solution], 法商研究 [Studies in Law and Business] 2006, No. 6.
230. [ZHANG Yuanhuang and XU Miao], *《揭开民意与死刑关系的面纱:从民意的实质看影响死刑控制进程的症结所在》[Lifting the Veil on the Relationship Between Public Opinion and the Death Penalty: Reviewing the Factors Impacting the Process of Death Penalty Control from the Perspective of Public Opinion],* 刑法论丛 [Criminal Law Review] 2012, No. 4.
231. 储怀值 [CHU Huaizhi], *《死刑司法控制: 完整解读第四十八条》[Judicial Control of Death Penalty: A Comprehensive Understand*ing of Article 48 of Penal Code], 中外法学[Bejing University Law Journal] 2012, No. 5.
232. 黄太云 [HUANG Taiyun], *《<中华人民共和国刑法修正案(八)>解读(一)》[Unscrambling the Amendment VIII to the Criminal Law (The First Part)],* 人民检察 [People's Procuratorial Semi-monthly] 2011, No. 6.
233. 曲晟 [QU Sheng], *《论我国死刑制度新动向及其出路: 兼评《刑法修正案(八)》的死刑制度》[On the New Tendency of Death Penalty System and its Outlet in China: Reviewing the Death Penalty System in the Eighth Amendment],* 求索[*Search*] 2012, No. 2.
234. 王勇 [WANG Yong], 《中国死刑研究的三个误区与路径调整》[On the Three Misunderstanding Areas of the Study of Death Penalty in China and the Adjustment of Approaches], 吉林大学社会科学学报 [Jilin University Journal Social Sciences Edition] 2012, Vol. 52, No. 5.
235. 王志祥 [WANG Zhixiang], *《死刑替代措施:一个需要警惕的刑法概念》[Alternative* Measures to the Death Penalty: A Criminal Conception Needs to be Considered], 中国法学 [China Legal Science] 2005, No. 1.

236. 汪猕 [WANG Mi],《*人权理论禁区是怎样突破的*》*[How* the Exclusion Zone of Human Rights Theory was Broken Through], 百年潮 [Hundred Year Tide] 2004, No. 5.
237. 杜钢建 [DU Gangjian],《*谈客服人权虚无主义*》*[On Overcoming the Nihilism of Human Rights]*, 法律学习与研究 [Law Study and Research] 1992, No. 1.
238. 林育川 [LIN Yuchuan],《*人民权利: 人权的一种替代方案——从毛泽东的权利思维看*》*[Citizen's Rights: An Alternative to the Human Rights—With the Perspective of Mao Zedong's Thinking on Rights]*, 现代哲学 [Modern Philosophy] 2007, No. 1.
239. 戴立兴 [DAI Xingli],《*论毛泽东的人权思想*》*[On Mao Zedong' Thought of Human Rights]*, 马克思主义研究 [Studies on Marxism] 2014, No. 2.
240. 付子堂, 崔燕 [FU Zitang and CUI Yan],《*<毛泽东早期文稿>中的人权观念*》*[The Human Rights Concept in Mao Zedong's Early Manuscripts]*, 毛泽东思想研究 [Mao Zedong Thought Study] 2012, No. 3.
241. 沈晓阳 [SHEN Xiaoyang],《*论毛泽东的人权思想*》*[On Mao Zedong's Thought on Human Rights]*, 甘肃理论学刊 [Guansu Theory Research] 1995, No. 3.
242. 鲜开林 [XIAN Kailin],《*论毛泽东人权思想的独特贡献*》*[On the Unique Contribution of Mao Zedong's Thought on Human Rights]*, 人权 [Human Rights] 2013, No. 6.
243. 严冬 [YAN Dong],《*国际人权法之于中国人权法制建设的历时性研究*》*[A Diachronic Study on the Influence of International Human Rights Law on the Chinese Legal System Construction]*, 河北法学 [Hebei Law Science] 2014, Vol. 32, No. 2.
244. 陈佑武, 李步云 [CHEN Youwu and LI Buyun],《*改革开放以来法治与人权关系的历史发展*》*[The Historical Development of the Relationship between the Rule of Law and Human Rights since the Reform and Opening-up]*, 现在法学 [Modern Law Science] 2015, Vol. 37, No. 2.
245. 蓝瑛 [LAN Ying],《*"人权"从来就是资产阶级的口号吗?—同肖薇云等同志商榷*》*['Is Human Rights always the Slogan of Bourgeoisie? Discussion with Comrade Xiao Weiyun, etc.]*, 社会科学 [Social Sciences] 1979, No. 3.
246. 王福春 [WANG Fuchun],《*邓小平人权思想初探*》*[Primary Studying on Deng Xiaoping's Thinking on Human Rights]*, 北京行政学院学报 [Journal of Beijing Administrative College] 2001, No. 1.
247. 袁旭川 [YUAN Xuchuan],《*邓小平人权理论探析*》*[Theoretically Analyzing Deng Xiaoping's Human Rights Thinking]*, 毛泽东思想研究 [Mao Zedong's Thought Study] 2005, No. 6.
248. 孙立 [SUN Li],《*邓小平人权思想对马克思主义的开拓创新*》*[Deng Xiaoping's Human Rights Thinking Pioneering and Innovating Marxism]*, 社会科学 [Journal of Social Sciences] 2005, No. 5.
249. 萧功秦 [XIAO Gongqin],《*从发展政治学看中国转型体制*》*[On the Chinese Transformation Regime with a Perspective from the Politics of Development]*,浙江学刊 [Zhejing Academic Journal] 2005, No. 5.
250. 刘能[LIU Neng],《*当代中国的群体性事件: 形象地位变迁和分类框架再构*》*[Mass Incidents in Modern China: Change of Image and Reconstruction of the Classification Framework]*, 江苏行政学院学报 [Journal of Jiangsu Administration Institute] 2011, Vol. 56, No. 2.
251. 蒋永甫 [JIANG Yongfu],《*当代中国群体性事件频发的体制性根源与发生机理——一个国家与社会关系的解释框架*》*[The Institutional Source and Mechanism of the Frequent Contemporary Chinese Mass Incidents—An Interpretation of the Relationship Between the State and the Social Framework]*, 湖北行政学院学报 [Journal of Hubei Administration Institute] 2012, No. 6.
252. 苏哲 [SU Zhe],《*"个代表" 重要思想是中国人权事业发展的指南*》*[The Important Thought of "Three Representatives" is the Guidebook of Human Rights Development in China]*, 人权 [Human Rights] 2002, No. 5.
253. 李晓明, 陈争尧 [LI Xiaoming and CHEN Zhengyao],《*"并合主义" 刑罚观对我国刑法立法的推动——以<刑法修正案(九)为视角*》*[On the Promotion of the "Combinatio*n Theory on the Penalty" to Criminal Legislation in China: From the Perspective of the Ninth Amendment to the Criminal Law], 政法论丛 [Journal of Political Science and Law] 2016, No. 2.

254. 尹振国 (Ying Zhenguo),《国家治理现代化与人本主义刑法观》*[Modernization of State Governance and the Humanistic Concept of the Criminal Law]*, 重庆理工大学学报 (社会科学) [Journal of Chongqing University of Technology (Social Science)] 2015, Vol. 29, No. 4.
255. 吴正茂 [Wu Zhengmao],《再论法律儒家化: 对瞿同祖"法律儒家化"之不同理解》*[Revisiting the Confucianization of Law: A Different Understanding of the Confucianization of Law with Qu Tongzu]*, 中外法学 [Peking University Law Journal] 2011, Vol. 23, No. 3.
256. 苏力 [Su Li],《早期儒家的人性观》*[Early Confucian View of Human Nature]*, 法制与社会发展 [Law and Social Development] 2015, Vol. 16, No. 5.
257. 刘静坤 [Liu Jingkun],《死刑案件被害人家属信访问题研究》*[On the Complain of the Family Members of the Victims in the Capital Cases]*, 政法论丛 [Journal of Political Science and Law] 2009, No. 1.
258. 孙万怀 [SUN Wanhuai],《死刑案件可以并需要和解吗?》*[Could the Criminal Reconciliation Be Taken Place in the Capital Case? Does it need?]*, 中国法学 [China Legal Science] 2010, No. 1.
259. 王满生 [WANG Mansheng],《死刑案件刑事和解——法治与反法治之辩》*[On Criminal Reconciliation of the Capital Cases: Debating between Rule or Law and Anti-rule of Law]*, 行政与法 [Public Administration & Law] 2011, No. 11.
260. 中华人民共和国国家统计局 (National Bureau of Statistics of the People's Republic of China):《关于1982年人口普查主要数字的公报》*[A Bulletin on the Main Statistics of Population Census in 1982]*, 中国统计 [China Statistics] 1982, No. 6.
261. 庞仁芝 (PANG Renzhi),《马克思主义国家学说的一个重要范畴---国家利益》*[An Important Category of Marxism Theory on the State: State Interests]*, 科学社会主义 [Scientific Socialism] 1992, No. 3.
262. 龚向和, 邓炜辉 [GONG Xianghe and DENG Weihui],《人权视野下传统工具主义刑法观之价值超越: 对"许霆案"有罪判决的批判与反思》*[Beyond the Value of the Traditional Instrument of Criminal Law from the Perspective of Human Rights: The Criticism and Reflection on the Conviction of the "Xu Ting" Case]*, 时代法学 [Present Day Law Science] 2008, Vol. 6, No. 4.
263. 刘仁文 [Liu Renwen],《中国刑法学六十年》*[Criminal Law of China from 1949 to 2009]*, 浙江大学学报(人文社会科学版) [Journal of Zhejiang University (Humanities and Social Sciences)] 2010, Vol. 40, No. 1.
264. 金小红, 李家兴, 杨建 [Jin Xiaohong, Li Jiaxing and Yang Jian],《社会约束体系的弱化与解构的逻辑——一项城市流动越轨未成年人生活状态的调查》*[The Logic of the Weakening and Deconstruction of the Social Constraint Mechanism: A Survey on the State of Juvenile Delinquents in the City]*, 中南民族大学学报(人文社会科学版) [Journal of South-Central University For Nationalities (Humanities and Social Sciences)] 2012, Vol. 32, No. 1.
265. 陈伟 [Chen Wei],《刑事立法的政策导向与技术制衡》*[On the Policy Orientation of Criminal Legislation and its Technical Checks and Balances]*, 中国法学[China Legal Science] 2013, No. 3.
266. [HUANG Huasheng],《两极化刑事政策之批判》*[Criticizing the Bipolar Criminal Policy]*, 法律科学 (西北政法学院学报) [Science of Law (Journal of Northwest University of Political Science and Law)] 2008, No. 6.
267. 田兴洪, 马长生 [TIAN Xinghong and MA Changsheng],《"两极化刑事政策"之理性辨思》*[Rationally Analyzing the Bipolar Criminal Policy]*, 湖南师范大学社会科学学报 [Journal of Social Science of Hunan Normal University] 2010, No. 4.
268. 刘崇亮 [LIU Chongliang],《"重重"刑罚观对监狱行刑的效果: 以刑法修正案(八)对刑罚结构的调整为分析视角》*[The Effect of the 'Harsh Punishment for Serious Crimes' Doctrine on the Execution of Punishment in Prison: An Analysis on the Adjustment of the Punishment Structure in the Eighth Amendment to Criminal Law]*, 法制与社会发展[Law and Social Development] 2013, No. 6.
269. 赵军 [ZHAO Jun],《死刑存废的民意维度: 以组织卖淫罪可罚性观念的测量为中心》*[Public Opinion on the Abolition of the Death Penalty: Measurement of Ideas about Guilt Relating to the Crime of Organizing Prostitution]*, 法学研究 [Chinese Journal of Law] 2015, No.2.

270. 徐阳 [XU Yang],《"舆情再审": 司法决策的困境与出路》*["Introspecting Retrials by Public Opinion: the Dilemma and Solution of Judicial Decision-Making]*, 中国法学 [China Legal Science] 2012, No. 2.
271. 吴百花 [WU Baihua],《自媒体时代死刑适用该如何回应民意》*[How to Respond to Public Opinion by the Application of the Death Penalty in the We-Media Age]*, 广州市公安管理干部学院学报 [Journal of Guangzhou Police College] 2013, No. 3.
272. 袁彬, 王奉帅等 [YUAN Bin and WANG Fengshuai] etc.,《死刑个案民意的现实性考察: 基于217起死刑个案的实证分析》*[A Practical Investigation on Public Opinion on Death Penalty Case: Empirical Analysis on 217 Cases of the Death Penalty]*, 刑法论丛 [Criminal Law Review] 2015, No. 3.
273. 袁彬 [YUAN Bin],《死刑民意及其内部冲突的调查与分析》*[Public Opinion on the Death Penalty and Its Internal Conflicts: An Investigation and Analysis]*, 法学 [Legal Science] 2009, No. 1.
274. 张明楷 [ZHANG Mingkai],《刑法学者如何为削减死刑作贡献》*[How Should Criminal Scholars Contribute to Reducing the Number of Crimes punishable by the Death Penalty?]*, 当代法学 [Contemporary Law Review] 2005, Vol. 19, No. 1.
275. 张明楷 [ZHANG Mingkai],《死刑的废止不需要终身刑替代》*[The Abolition of Capital Punishment Does Not Need Life-Long Liberty Punishment]*, 法学研究 [Chinese Journal of Law] 2008, Vol. 13, No. 2.
276. 何荣功 [HE Ronggong],《当代中国死刑民意的现状与解构》*[Contemporary Situation and Deconstruction of Chinese Public Opinion on the Death Penalty]*, 刑法论丛 [Criminal Law Review] 2010, No. 3.
277. 张惠芳, 何小俊 [ZHANG Huifang and HE Xiaojun],《死刑民意调查研究》*[Survey Report on the Death Penalty]*, 时代法学 [Present Day Law Science] 2011, Vol. 9, No. 4.
278. 刘宪权 [LIU Xianquan],《刑事立法应力戒情绪—以<刑法修正案(九)>为视角》*[Criminal Legislation Should Strictly Avoid Emotion: From the Perspective of the Ninth Amendment]*, 法学评论 [Law Review] 2016, No. 1.
279. 贾成宽 [Jia Chengkuan],《刑罚的结构性缺陷及其化解—以宽严相济刑事政策的刑法化为视角》*[On the Structural Defects of Criminal Punishment and their Solution: From the Perspective of Criminal Legislation relating to the Criminal Policy of Combining Leniency and Severity]*, 甘肃社会科学 [Gansu Social Sciences] 2009, No. 3.
280. 符少剑, 姚乾坤, 等 [FU Shaojian, YAO Qiankun etc.],《1120 例监狱服刑人员心理健康与人格特征分析》*[Investigation on Mental Health and Personality Traits of 1 120 Prisoners in Hainan Province]*, 现代预防医学 [Modern Preventive Medicine] 2012, Vol. 39, No. 23.
281. 徐静村 [XU Jingcun],《减刑、假释制度改革若干问题研究》*[On Several Issues on the Reform of Commutation of Punishment and Parole]*, 法治研究 [Research on the Rule of Law] 2010, No. 2.
282. 刘强 [LIU Qiang],《在我国建立以"假释为主、减刑为辅"的罪犯出狱新模式》*[Establishing the New Model of Criminals Being Released from Prison - 'Parole Principally, Reduction of Penalty Secondly'—in China]*, 法学杂志 [Law Science Magazine] 2012, No. 1
283. 柳原 [LIU Yuan],《扩大假释、缩小减刑的实证研究》*[Empirical Research on Expanding the Application of Parole and Limiting Commutation]*, 中国司法 [Justice of China] 2014, No. 11.
284. 郎胜 [LANG Sheng],《<刑法修正案(八)>解读》*[Interpreting "the Eighth Amendment to the Criminal Law]*, 国家检察官学院学报 [Journal of the National Prosecutors College] 2011, No. 2.
285. 柳忠卫 [Liu Zhongwei],《对假释适用的例外性规定和禁止性规定的理性分析》*[Rational Analysis of the Exception Stipulations and Prohibiting Stipulations of Parole Application]*, 政法论丛 [Journal of Political Science and Law] 2006, No. 1.
286. 钊作俊 [ZHAO Zuojun],《中国死刑之现状与走向》*[On the Reality and Trends of the Death Penalty in China]*, 郑州轻工业学院学报 (社会科学版) [Journal of Zhengzhou University of Light Industry (Social Science)] 2004, Vol. 5, No. 2.
287. 张文, 黄伟明 [ZHANG Wen and HUANG Weiming],《死缓应当作为死刑执行的必经程序》*[The Death Sentence with Reprieve Should Be Introduced as A Necessary Procedure of Immediate Execution]*, 现代法学 [Modern Law Science] 2004, Vol. 26, No. 4.

288. 劳东燕 [LAO Dongyan], *《死刑适用标准的体系化构造》[System of the Standards on the Application of the Death Penalty]*, 法学研究 [Chinese Journal of Law] 2015, No. 1.
289. 李晓欧 [LI Xiaoou], *《中国重刑化弊端及其限制路径——以<中华人民共和国刑法修正案(八)>为观照》[The Drawbacks of Heavy Punishment in China and the Road to Limit them: Based on the Eighth Amendment to the Criminal Law of the P.R.C.]*, 当代法学 [Contemporary Law Review] 2010, No. 6.
290. 曾亚杰 [ZENG Yajie], *《我国无期徒刑制度改革探析》[On the Reformation of the Life Imprisonment System in China]*, 时代法学 [Presentday Law Sciences] 2008, Vol. 6, No. 2.
291. MADAI Sándor, *《第二次世界大战后匈牙利死刑改革分析》[Evolution of Capital Punishment Regulations in Hungary following World War II]*, traslated by Xiao Fan, 刑法评论 [Chinese Criminal Law Review] 2016, Vol. 29, Issue. 1.
292. 吴大华, 王飞 [WU Dahua and WANG Fei], *《限制死刑的理性思考——以100例死刑案件为视角》[Thinking Rationally on Limiting the Death Penalty: From the Perspective of 100 Death Cases]*, 政治与法律 [Political Science and Law] 2005, No. 3.

Internet

Non-Chinese Websites

293. *World and Europe Day against the Death Penalty,* available at: *European Union External Action.* https://eeas.europa.eu/headquarters/headquarters-homepage/13174/world-and-europe-day-against-death-penalty_en.
294. The Death Penalty Project, *The Death Penalty in Japan: A Report on Japan's Legal Obligations under the International Convention on Civil and Political Rights and an Assessment of Public Attitudes to Capital Punishment*, available at: http://www.deathpenaltyproject.org/wp-content/uploads/2013/03/DPP-Japan-report.pdf.
295. International Federation for Human Rights, *The Death Penalty in Japan: The Law of Silence*, available at: https://www.fidh.org/IMG/pdf/japon505a2008.pdf.
296. HOYLE Carolyn, *Review Essay: The Death Penalty in Japan: Will the Public Tolerate Abolition?* by Mai Sato (Springer Press, 2013), available at: Faculty of Law of University of Oxford. https://www.law.ox.ac.uk/centres-institutes/centre-criminology/blog/2014/01/death-penalty-japan.
297. *Life Imprisonment*, available at: https://en.wikipedia.org/wiki/Life_imprisonment.
298. *Life Imprisonment of Children in the European Union*, available at: Child Rights International Network. https://www.crin.org/en/home/campaigns/inhuman-sentencing/problem/life-imprisonment/life-imprisonment-children-europe.
299. United States Sentencing Commission, *Life Sentences in the Federal System*, available at: http://www.ussc.gov/sites/default/files/pdf/research-and-publications/research-projects-and-surveys/miscellaneous/20150226_Life_Sentences.pdf.
300. United States Sentencing Commission, *Sentencing Table*, available at: http://www.ussc.gov/sites/default/files/pdf/guidelines-anual/2016/Sentencing_Table.pdf.
301. DOW David R., *Life without Parole: A Different Death Penalty*, available at: https://www.thenation.com/article/life-without-parole-different-death-penalty/.
302. LÜDTKE Florian and İDIL Aydınoğlu, "Life Imprisonment (without Parole)", Turkey's Center for Prison Studies, 2015, 30, available at: http://www.tcps.org.tr/sites/default/files/kitaplar/Life%20Imprisonment_report%20march-3.pdf.
303. *Decision of the Central Committee of the Communist Party of China on Some Major Issues Concerning Comprehensively Deepening the Reform*, available at: China Net. http://www.china.org.cn/china/third_plenary_session/2014-01/16/content_31212602.htm.

304. *The CPC's Decision of the Central Committee of the Communist Party of China on Some Major Issues Concerning Comprehensively Deepening the Reform,* available at: China.org.cn. http://www.china.org.cn/china/third_plenary_session/2014-01/16/content_31212602_9.htm.
305. *Alternatives to the Death Penalty Information Pack (Second edition 2015),* available at: https://cdn.penalreform.org/wp-content/uploads/2015/03/PRI_Alternatives_to_death_penalty_info_pack_WEB.pdf.
306. MAO Zedong (Mao Tse-tung), *On the Struggle against the 'Three Evils' and the 'Five Evils',* "Selected Works of Mao Tse-tung: Vol. 5", available at: https://www.marxists.org/reference/archive/mao/selected-works/volume-5/mswv5_17.htm.
307. MAO Zedong, *On the People's Democratic Dictatorship,* Selected Works of Mao Tse-tung: Vol.7, available at: https://www.marxists.org/reference/archive/mao/selected-works/volume-4/mswv4_65.htm.
308. MAO Zedong, *The Situation in the Summer of 1957,* Selected Works of Mao Tse-tung: Vol.5, available at: https://www.marxists.org/reference/archive/mao/selected-works/volume-5/mswv5_66.htm.
309. MAO Zedong, *On the Correct Handling of Contradictions among the People,* Selected Workds of Mao Tse-tung: Vol. 5", available at: https://www.marxists.org/reference/archive/mao/selected-works/volume-5/mswv5_58.htm#v5_89.
310. MAO Zedong, *Fight for A Fundamental Turn for the Better in the Nation's Financial and Economic Situation,* Selected Workds of Mao Tse-tung: Vol. 5", available at: https://www.marxists.org/reference/archive/mao/selected-works/volume-5/mswv5_06.htm.
311. MAO Zedong, *The Party's Mass Line Must Be Followed in Suppressing Counter-revolutionaries,* Selected Works of Mao Tse-tung: vol.5, available at: https://www.marxists.org/reference/archive/mao/selected-works/index.htm.
312. *After Mao: The Rise of Deng Xiaoping,* available at: Facts and Details http://factsanddetails.com/china/cat2/sub7/entry-5537.html.
313. DENG Xiaoping, *Uphold the Four Cardinal Principles", Selected Works of Deng Xiaoping: Volume II,* available at: https://dengxiaopingworks.wordpress.com/2013/02/25/uphold-the-four-cardinal-principles/.
314. DENG Xiaoping, *The Present Situation and the Tasks before Us,* Selected Works of Deng Xiaoping: Volume II, available at: https://dengxiaopingworks.wordpress.com/2013/02/25/the-present-situation-and-the-tasks-before-us/.
315. DENG Xiaoping, *Talk at a Meeting of the Standing Committee of the Political Bureau of the Central Committee,* Selected Works of Deng Xiaoping, available at: https://dengxiaopingworks.wordpress.com/2013/03/18/talk-at-a-meeting-of-the-standing-committee-of-the-political-bureau-of-the-central-committee/.
316. DENG Xiaoping, *The Overriding Need is for Stability,* Selected Works of Deng Xiaoping: Volume III, available at: https://dengxiaopingworks.wordpress.com/2013/03/18/the-overriding-need-is-for-stability/.
317. DENG Xiaoping, *Take A Clear-Cut Stand against Bourgeois Liberalization,* Selected Works of Deng Xiaoping, available at: https://dengxiaopingworks.wordpress.com/2013/03/18/take-a-clear-cut-stand-against-bourgeois-liberalization/.
318. DENG Xiaoping, *Crack down on Crime,* Selected Works of Deng Xiaoping, available at: https://dengxiaopingworks.wordpress.com/2013/03/08/crack-down-on-crime/.
319. DENG Xiaoping, *Bourgeois Liberalization Means Taking the Capitalist Road,* The Selected Works of Deng Xiaoping, available at: https://dengxiaopingworks.wordpress.com/2013/03/18/bourgeois-liberalization-means-taking-the-capitalist-road/.
320. *The Death Penalty in China—the road to reform,* available at: Faculty of Law of Oxford University. https://www.law.ox.ac.uk/research-subject-groups/research-index/impact-index/death-penalty-china-road-reform.
321. The Justice System Reform Council, *Recommendations of the Justice System Reform Council—for a Justice System to Support Japan in the 21st Century—,* available at: http://japan.kantei.go.jp/judiciary/2001/0612report.html.
322. *Indonesia,* available at: https://en.wikipedia.org/wiki/Indonesia.

323. DREHLE David Von, *The Death of the Death Penalty: why the Era of Capital Punishment is Ending*, available at: http://time.com/deathpenalty/.
324. *Undang-Undang REPUBLIK INDONESIA NOMOR 21 TAHUN 1959*, available at: file:///C:/Users/huanggui/Downloads/UU_NO_21_1959.HTM.
325. *UNDANG-UNDANG REPUBLIK INDONESIA NOMOR 1 TAHUN 1963*, available at: http://www.dpr.go.id/dokjdih/document/uu/UU_1963_1.pdf.
326. *UNDANG-UNDANG REPUBLIK INDONESIA NOMOR 31 TAHUN 1999*, available at: http://www.kpu.go.id/dmdocuments/UU%20PNS.pdf.
327. *UNDANG-UNDANG REPUBLIK INDONESIA NOMOR 20 TAHUN 2001*, available at: http://www.kpu.go.id/dmdocuments/UU202001.pdf.
328. *PERATURAN PEMERINTAH REPUBLIK INDONESIA NOMOR 39 TAHUN 2005*, available at: http://peraturan.go.id/inc/view/11e44c4f0c1a8d609dee313231383331.html.
329. *UNDANG-UNDANG REPUBLIK INDONESIA NOMOR 9 TAHUN 2013*, available at: http://kesbangpol.kemendagri.go.id/files_arsip/uu_no.09-2013_.pdf.
330. *UNDANG-UNDANG REPUBLIK INDONESIA NOMOR 4 TAHUN 1976*, available at: http://ditjenpp.kemenkumham.go.id/arsip/ln/1976/uu4-1976.pdf.
331. *EU Lines to Take on the Policy of the Council of Europe in Relation to Death Penalty*, (Strasbourg, 05/04/2017), available at: https://eeas.europa.eu/headquarters/headquarters-homepage/24625/eu-lines-take-policy-council-europe-relation-death-penalty_en.
332. *Capital Punishment in Iceland*, available at: https://en.wikipedia.org/wiki/Capital_punishment_in_Iceland.
333. *Capital Punishment in Sweden*, available at: https://en.wikipedia.org/wiki/Capital_punishment_in_Sweden.
334. *European MPs Unconcerned about the Real Situation in Belarus*, available at: http://law.by/news/news/2012/february/18067/?sphrase_id=156708.
335. *Rybakov: Death Penalty is not Prohibited by International Law*, available at: http://law.by/news/news/2016/march/16502/?sphrase_id=156760.
336. *Belarus Parliament Discusses Death Penalty Issues*, available at: http://law.by/news/news/2017/may/24048/?sphrase_id=156760.
337. *On the Concept of Legal Policy of the Republic of Kazakhstan for the period 2010 to 2020 (Decree of the President of the Republic of Kazakhstan dated 24 August 2009 №. 858)*, available at: http://sud.gov.kz/eng/content/concept-legal-policy-republic-kazakhstan-period-2010-2020.
338. The Death Penalty Information Center, *States with and without the Death Penalty*, available at: https://deathpenaltyinfo.org/states-and-without-death-penalty.
339. *Constitution of the Republic of Belarus of 1994 with Amendments through 2004*, Article 24, available at: https://www.constituteproject.org/constitution/Belarus_2004.pdf.
340. The Death Penalty Information Center, *Federal Laws Providing for the Death Penalty*, available at: https://deathpenaltyinfo.org/federal-laws-providing-death-penalty.
341. *Death Penalty for Offenses other than Murder*, available at: https://deathpenaltyinfo.org/death-penalty-offenses-other-murder.
342. *Crimes Publishable by the Death Penalty*, available at: https://deathpenaltyinfo.org/crimes-punishable-death-penalty#BJS.
343. Bureau of Justice Statistics, *Capital Punishment, 2012-Statistical Tables*, available at: https://www.bjs.gov/content/pub/pdf/cp12st.pdf.
344. *Death Sentences in the United States from 1977 by State and by Year*, available at: https://deathpenaltyinfo.org/death-sentences-united-states-1977-present.
345. Bureau of Justice Statistics, *Capital Punishment, 2014–2015-Statistical Brief*, available at: https://www.bjs.gov/index.cfm?ty=pbdetail&iid=5908.
346. *States with and without the Death Penalty*, available at: https://deathpenaltyinfo.org/states-and-without-death-penalty.
347. *Gallup Poll: Support for the Death Penalty at Lowest Level since 1972*, available at: https://deathpenaltyinfo.org/node/6589.
348. *Gallup, Death Penalty,* available at: http://www.gallup.com/poll/1606/death-penalty.aspx.

349. *Life without Parole*, available at: Death Penalty Information Center https://deathpenaltyinfo.org/life-without-parole.
350. KURLANTZICK Joshua, *After Deng: On China's Transformation—Is Deng Xiaoping's legacy of modernization without political reform one that no contemporary Chinese official can control* available at: The Nation Instigating http://www.thenation.com/article/after-deng-chinas-transformation/.
351. HU Jintao, *Hold High the Great Banner of Socialism with Chinese Characteristics and Strive for New Victories in Building a Moderately Prosperous Society in all Respects,* available at: China daily. http://www.chinadaily.com.cn/china/2007-10/24/content_6204564.htm.
352. JIANG Zemin, Speech at the Meeting Celebrating the 80th Anniversary of the Founding of the Communist Party of China, available at: China Net. http://www.china.org.cn/e-speech/a.htm.
353. *Officials Urged to Promote the 'Mass Line' Campaign*, available at: 中国共产党新闻 News of the Communist Party of China. http://english.cpc.people.com.cn/206972/206976/8329485.html.
354. VEGA Connie de la, SOLTER Amanda, KWON Soo-Ryun and ISAAC Dana Marie, *Cruel and Unusual: U.S. Sentencing Practices in a Gloabal Context*, University of San Francisco (USF) School of Law's Center for Law and Global Justice, May, 2012, 21. Available at https://www.cpcjalliance.org/wp-content/uploads/2013/04/Cruel-And-Unusual.pdf.
355. *The European Committee for the Prevention of Torture and Inhuman or Degrading Treatment or Punishment (CPT) Report about the Prison in Netherlands*, Council of Europe, CPT/Inf (2017)1, Strasbourg, 19 January 2017, 31. Available at https://rm.coe.int/16806ebb7c.
356. PETRA Bárd, *The Hungarian Life Imprisonment Regime in front of Apex Courts I.*, available at: Blogsite of the Institute for Legal Studies http://jog.tk.mta.hu/en/blog/2015/06/the-hungarian-life-imprisonment.
357. 法務省 [Ministry of Justice of Japan], *無期刑の執行状況及び無期刑受刑者に係る仮釈放の運用状況について [The Status of Execution of Life Imprisonment and the Status of Release the Inmates Imposed on Life Imprisonment on Parole]*, available at: http://www.moj.go.jp/content/001208315.pdf.
358. *The Execution of Sentences Act,* Section 42. Available at: http://www.kriminalomsorgen.no/getfile.php/2018208.823.ytdxsvbtbe/Straffegjennomf%C3%B8ringsloven+engelsk.pdf.
359. Kriminalomsorgen, *Kriminalomsorgens årsstatistikk—2015*, 6. Available at: http://www.kriminalomsorgen.no/publikasjoner.242465.no.html.
360. Ministry of Justice of Republic of Portugual (Ministra da Justiça), *Relatório Anual de Segurança Interna 2016 [Annual Internal Security Report 2016]*, 133. Available at: http://www.portugal.gov.pt/pt/pm/documentos/20170331-pm-rasi-2016.aspx.
361. 张维炜 [ZHANG Weiwei]), *《"刑八": 宽严相济保护民生》['The Eighth Amendment': The Leniency and Severity Protecting Welfare], available at:*中国人大网[The National People's Congress of the People's Republic of China]. http://www.npc.gov.cn/npc/zgrdzz/2011-03/15/content_1668354.htm.
362. *Xi Jinping Vows to Fight Tigers and Flies in Anti-Corruption Drive*, available at: https://www.theguardian.com/world/2013/jan/22/xi-jinping-tigers-flies-corruption.

Chinese Websites and Newspapers

363. *《<中国的司法改革>白皮书》[The White Paper on Judicial Reform in China], available at:* 中央政府门户网站[The Central People's Government of the People's Republic of China] http://www.gov.cn/jrzg/2012-10/09/content_2239771.htm.
364. *《关于<中华人民共和国刑法修正案(八)(草案)>的说明》[The Explanations for the Draft of the Eighth Amendment to Criminal Law of the People's Republic of China]*, available at: 中国人大网 [The National People's Congress of the People's Republic of China]. http://www.npc.gov.cn/huiyi/cwh/1116/2010-08/28/content_1593165.htm.

365. *《关于<中华人民共和国刑法修正案(九)(草案)>的说明》[The Explanations for the Draft of the Ninth Amendment to Criminal Law of the People's Republic of China]*, available at: 中国人大网 [The National People's Congress of the People's Republic of China]. http://www.npc.gov.cn/npc/lfzt/rlys/2014-11/03/content_1885123.htm.
366. 彭真 [PENG Zhen], *《关于七个法律草案的说明》[An Explanatory note to the Seven Draft Laws]*, available at: 中国共产党新闻网 [News of Communist Party of China]. http://cpc.people.com.cn/GB/69112/99985/100003/9739230.html.
367. 王汉斌 [WANG Hanbin], *《关于<中华人民共和国刑法(修订草案)的说明》[Introduction on the Draft to the Criminal Law of P.R.C]*, available at: Law library. http://www.law-lib.com/fzdt/newshtml/20/20050812041456.htm.
368. 苏永通, 任重远 [SU Yongtong and REN Zhongyuan], *《152份死刑复核裁定书分析报告公开的死刑密码》[Death Sentence Code Disclosed by the Analysis Report on 152 Judgments of Death Case Review]*, available at: 凤凰网 [ifeng Net]. http://ent.ifeng.com/a/20141016/40331612_0.shtml.
369. *《中共中央关于全面推进依法治国若干重大问题的决定》[The CCP Central Committee Decision Concerning Some Major Questions in Comprehensively Moving Government of the Country According to the Law Forward (hereinafter abbreviated to CCP-CDC)]*, available at: 中国社会科学网 (China Social Science Net). http://www.cssn.cn/fx/fx_ttxw/201410/t20141030_1381703.shtml.
370. 刘家征 [LIU Jiazheng], *《党的领导和依法治国高度统一》[On the High Unity of the Party's Leadership and Rule by Law]*, available at: 求是网 (Qiu Shi Net). http://www.qstheory.cn/laigao/2015-02/10/c_1114315500.htm.
371. 聂辉华 [NIE Huihua], *《郑永年先生站着说话不腰疼》[Mr. Zheng Yongnian Spoke Irresponsibly and Sarcastically]*, available at: 新浪博客 (Sina blog). http://www.21ccom.net/html/2016/gqmq_0129/1317.html.
372. 陈翼平 [Chen Yiping], *《坚持党的领导》[Upholding the Leadership of the Party]*, available at: 求是网(Qstheory.cn). http://www.qstheory.cn/dukan/qs/2014-11/16/c_1113228486.htm.
373. 顾培东 [GU Peidong], *《当代中国法治共识的形成及法治再启蒙》[On the Formation of the Consensus of Rule of Law and its Re-enlightenment in Contemporary China]*, available at: 中国社会科学网 (Chinese Social Sciences Net). http://ex.cssn.cn/fx/201708/t20170830_3624561.shtml.
374. *《马克思恩格斯全集》[The Collected Works of Marx And Engels]*, Vol. 3 (391), available at: http://cpc.people.com.cn/GB/64184/180145/180168/10864948.html.
375. *《列宁全集》[The collected Works of Vladimir Lenin]*, Vol. 18 (259), available at: http://cpc.people.com.cn/GB/64184/180146/180248/10899743.html.
376. MAO Zedong (Mao Tse-tung), *Contradtictions under Socialism, in Selected Works of Mao Tse-tung: Vol. 7*, available at: https://www.marxists.org/reference/archive/mao/selected-works/volume-7/mswv7_466.htm.
377. 毛泽东 [MAO Zedong], *《关于镇压反革命》[Comment on Suppressing and Liquidating Counterrevolutionaries]*, 毛泽东选集 [Selected Works of Mao Tse-tung: Vol. 6], available at: http://cpc.people.com.cn/GB/64184/64185/189966/11568071.html.
378. 于建嵘 [YU Jianrong], *《当前压力维稳的困境与出路——再论中国社会的刚性稳定》[The Problems and the Solution of the Present Pressure Stability: Reviewing again the Stiff Stability in China's Society]*, available at: 爱思想 [Aisixing.com]. http://www.aisixiang.com/data/58296.html.
379. 江泽民 [JIANG Zemin], *《坚决打击走私犯罪活动》[Resolutely Crack down the Smuggling Crime Activities]*, 江泽民选集 [Selected Works of Jiang Zemin], available at: http://cpc.people.com.cn/GB/64184/64185/180138/10818637.html.
380. 江泽民 [JIANG Zemin], *《切实加强社会治安工作》[Practically Improving the Works of Public Security]*, 江泽民选集 [Selected Works of Jiang Zemin], available at: http://cpc.people.com.cn/GB/64184/64185/180139/10818572.html.
381. 王庆德 [WANG Qingde], *《人民内部矛盾并非仅是利益问题》[The Internal Contradictions among the People are not only the Interest Problems]*, available at: http://theory.people.com.cn/GB/49154/49156/13467113.html.

382. 黄凯峰 [HUANG Kaifeng], *《关于改革开放以来意识形态建设的几点认识》 [Some Understandings on the Developments of the Ideology since the Reform and Openning-up]*, available at: 中国社会科学网 [Chinese Social Science Net]. http://www.cssn.cn/ddzg/ddzg_ldjs/ddzg_wh/201105/t20110514_812709.shtml.
383. *《习近平: 打好反恐人民战争》 [XIN Jinping: Making a Good People War on Terror]*, available at: http://money.163.com/14/0504/08/9RD094QG00253B0H.html.
384. *最高人民法院:中国相当时期内不具备废除死刑条件》 [Supreme People's Court: China Does Not Have Any Conditions to Abolish the Death Penalty in A Considerably Long Time]*, available at: 人民网 [People Net]. http://society.people.com.cn/GB/42735/6979231.html.
385. 沈寅飞 [SHEN Yinfei, *《徐玉玉案9900元追回, 徐父: 如骗子判死刑, 我不要钱》 [9900 Yuan was got back in the Case of Xu Yuyu, the Father of Xu said I Do not Want Money if the Perpetrator is Sentenced to Death]*, available at: 南方网 [South Net]. http://news.southcn.com/china/content/2016-10/12/content_157394962.htm.
386. *《复旦投毒案今日宣判, 受害人家属称不判死刑就抗诉》 [The Poisoning Case in Fudan was Pronounced Judgement Today, the Victim's Family Said That They Will Make a Counterappeal if the Death Penalty was not imposed]*, available at: SOHU Net. http://news.sohu.com/20140218/n395162155.shtml.
387. *《刑法最新罪名一览表》 [Chart Showing the New Crimes in the Criminal Law]*, available at: http://www.zuiming.net/51.html.
388. 余文唐 [YU Wentang], *《终身监禁逆用之法理辨思》 [Juridically Reviewing the Reversal Use of the Life Imprisonment without Release]*, available at: http://ywt0207.fyfz.cn/b/876139.
389. *《全国民事案件审判质量工作座谈会纪要》 [The Work Syposium Summary of National Trial Quality of Civil Cases]*, 1999 (法[1999]231号) [Legal No. 231], available at: http://www.lawlib.com/law/law_view.asp?id=17091.
390. 李国光 [LI Guoguang], *《办案的重要标准:法律效果与社会效果的统一》 [An Important Standard of Handling the Case: the Unity of the Legal Effect and Social Effect]*, available at: 光明新闻 [News.gmw.cn]. http://www.gmw.cn/01gmrb/2000-01/25/GB/01%5E18312%5E0%5EGMB1-210.htm.
391. *《最高人民法院再审刘涌案刑事判决书》 [The SPC's Criminal- retrying Judgement on the Case of liu Yong]*, (2003) 刑提字第5号 [Criminal Interrogation No. 5, 2003], available at: 中国法院网 (China Court). http://old.chinacourt.org/public/detail.php?id=96393.
392. *《沈德咏与人大代表、政协委员座谈强调司法审判工作必须坚持群众路线》 [Shen Deyong Emphasizes "Judicial Works Must Uphold Mass Line" when He Holds a Symposium with Members of National People's Committee]*, available at: 中华人民共和国最高人民法院 [The Supreme People's Court of the People's Republic of China]. http://www.court.gov.cn/zixun-xiangqing-1755.html.
393. *《全面贯彻党的群众路线, 让人民群众在每一个司法案件中都感受到公平正义》 [Completely Emplemented the Party's Mass Line, Ensure that the People are Satisfied with the Equality and Justice in Every Court Verdict]*, available at: 中华人民共和国最高人民法院 [The Supreme People's Court of the People's Republic of China]. http://www.court.gov.cn/zixun-xiangqing-6149.html.
394. 马艾地 [MA Aidi and WU Cunzai], *《从法律规则的局限性谈法律效果与社会效果》 [On the Legal Effect and Social Effect from the Perspective of the Limitation of the Legal Rules]*, 人民法院报 [People's Court Daily], February 21st, 2004.
395. *《最高法:审判故意杀人等案件要注重法与社会效果的统一》 [Supreme People's Court: It Should Pay Attention to the Unity of Legal Effect and the Social Effect when Handling the Murder and other Crimes]*, available at: 中华人民共和国最高人民法院 [The Supreme People's Court of the People's Republic of China]. http://www.court.gov.cn/zixun-xiangqing-728.html.
396. *《沈德咏: 让热点案件成为全民共享法治公开课》 [Shen Deyong: To Make a Hot Case become an Open Cours for the Public to Share the Rule of Law]*, available at: 中华人民共和国最高人民法院 [The Supreme People's Court of the People's Republic of China]. http://www.court.gov.cn/zixun-xiangqing-39292.html.

397. 吕忠梅 [LV Zhongmei], *《论实现法律效果和社会效果的有机统一》 [Reanlizing the Organic Unity of the Legal Effect and the Social Effect],* 人民法院报 [People's Court Daily], Version 5, November 4, 2008.
398. 李昌奎案 [LI Changkui An] [The Case of Li Changkui], available at: <http://baike.so.com/doc/5430314-5668573.html>.
399. *许霆案 [The Case of XU Ting],* available at: 广州审判网 [Guangzhou Judgement Net]. http://www.gzcourt.gov.cn/cpws/wsjs/.
400. *药家鑫 [Yao Jiaxin An] [The Case of Yao Jiaxin],* available at: http://baike.so.com/doc/7016976-7239865.html.
401. *《最高法通知要求进一步扩大量刑规范化范围》 [Supreme Court Requires to Further Extent the Scop of the Standarization of the Sentencing],* available at: 中华人民共和国最高人民法院 [The Supreme People's Court of the People's Republic of China]. http://www.court.gov.cn/zixun-xiangqing-39112.html.
402. 最高人民法院司法改革办公室 [The Office of Judicial Reform of the Supreme People's Court of P.R.C.], *The Guiding Opinions of the People's Court for Sentencing on Trial*, available at: 中国法院网 [China Court Net]. http://www.chinacourt.org/article/detail/2013/04/id/948052.shtml.
403. 高铭暄 [GAO Mingxuan], *《死刑60年: 新中国死刑立法的变迁与展望》[60 years of the Death Penalty: the Evolution of and Prospects for the Capital Legislation of New China*], available at: 人民网[People Net]. http://history.people.com.cn/n/2014/1030/c372326-25936904.html.
404. 中华人民共和国最高人民法院 [The Supreme People's Court of P.R.C], *《数说人民法院审批工作60年》[Showing the People's Courts' Trail Works by Statistics Over 60 Years],* available at: 最高人民法院网 [Supreme People's Court Net]. http://www.court.gov.cn/fabu-xiangqing-119.html.
405. *《中共中央发出<关于严厉打击刑事犯罪活动的决定>》[CPC's Decision on Cracking Down Severely On Crimes],* available at: 中国共产党新闻网 [News of the Communist Party of China]. http://cpc.people.com.cn/GB/64162/64165/68640/68665/4739396.html.
406. *《江泽民论人权》[On Human Rights by Jiang Zemin],* available at: 人民网 [People's Net]. http://politics.people.com.cn/GB/8198/5139784.html.
407. *《中共中央加强改进新形势下党建若干重大问题的决定》[Decision of the CPC Central Committee on Major Issues on Strengthening and Improving Party Building],* available at: 中央人民政府 [Central People's Government of P.R.C.]. http://www.gov.cn/jrzg/2009-09/27/content_1428158.htm.
408. *《中共中央关于构建社会注意和谐社会若干重大问题的决定》 [Decision of the CPC Central Committee on Certain Major Issues in the Building of a Harmonious Socialist Society],* available at: 中国共产党新闻网 [News of Communist Party of China]. http://cpc.people.com.cn/GB/64093/64094/4932424.html.
409. 陈丽平 [CHEN Liping], *《点击中华人民共和国刑法修正案(九)草案的七大亮点》 [Clicking on the 7 highlights of the Draft of the Ninth Amendment to the Penal Code of the P.R.C],* 法制日报 [Legal Daily News], October 28th, 2014.
410. 陆建红 [LU Jianhong], *《"绝对"死刑条款的适用研究》[On the Application of Terms of Absolutely Determinate Death Penalty System],* available at: http://china.findlaw.cn/hetongfa/mianzetiaokuan/168886.html.
411. 郑德荣 [Zheng Derong], *《毛泽东思想的历史地位与当代价值》[The Historical Status and Contemporary Values of Mao Zedong's Thought],* 中国共产党新闻网 [News of the Community of the Party of China Net]. http://theory.people.com.cn/GB/13619948.html.
412. 黄惟勤 [HUANG Weiqin], *《坚持邓小平人权观;走中国特色的人权发展道路》[Insistence on Deng Xiaoping's Outlook on Human Rights; Maintain the Human Rights Development Road with Chinese Characteristics]*, available at: 中国共产党新闻网 [News of Communist Party of China]. http://theory.people.com.cn/GB/148980/16810107.html.
413. 李燕奇 [LI Yanqi], 《学习邓小平人权问题的思想》 [Learning Deng Xiaoping's Thinking about the Issues of Human Rights], available at: 中华人民共和国国史网 [The History of the People's Republic of China]. http://www.hprc.org.cn/gsyj/zzs/zzsxs/200909/t20090912_30910.html.

414. 江泽民 [JIANG Zemin],《高举邓小平理论伟大旗帜, 把建设有中国特色社会主义事业全面推向二十一世纪》*[Hold High the Great Banner of Deng Xiaoping's Theory for an All-Round Advancement of the Cause of Building Socialism with Chinese Characteristics into the 21st Century (hereinafter abbreviated to HHG-DXT)*, available at: 中央人民政府网 [The Central People's Government of the P.R.C]. http://www.gov.cn/test/2008-07/11/content_1042080.htm.
415. 江泽民 [JIANG Zemin],《全面建设小康社会, 开创中国特色社会主义事业新局面> *[Build a Well-off Society in an All-Round Way and Create a New Situation in Building Socialism with Chinese Characteristics (BWS-AWC)]*, available at: 人民网 (People Net). http://www.people.com.cn/GB/paper39/7683/733922.html.
416. 胡锦涛 [HU Jintao],《坚定不移沿着中国特色社会主义道理前进, 为全面建成小康社会奋斗》[Firmly March on the Path of Socialism with Chinese Characteristics and Strive to Complete the Building of A Moderately Prosperous Society in All Respects], available at: 《中国共产党第18次全国代表大会, 人民网 [18th CPC National Congress; People Net]. http://cpc.people.com.cn/18/n/2012/1109/c350821-19529916.html.
417. 韩非子·八经》*[Han Feizi: Chapter XLVIII. Eight Canons]*, available at: http://www2.iath.virginia.edu:8080/exist/cocoon/xwomen/texts/hanfei/d2.48/1/0/bilingual.
418. 《韩非子·二柄》*[Han Feizi: Chapter VII. The Two Handles], available at:* http://www2.iath.virginia.edu:8080/exist/cocoon/xwomen/texts/hanfei/d2.7/1/0/bilingual.
419. 《韩非子·六反》*[Han Feizi: Six Contrarieties]*, available at: http://www2.iath.virginia.edu:8080/exist/cocoon/xwomen/texts/hanfei/d2.46/1/0/bilingual.
420. 《严打》*[Strike Hard]*, available at: 360百科 [360Baike]. http://baike.so.com/doc/6395274-6608931.html.
421. 高铭暄 [GAO Mingxuan],《刑法体现宽严相济刑事政策》*[The Embodiment of the Criminal Policy of Combining Leniency and Severity in Criminal Law]*, available at: 人民网 [People Net]. http://opinion.people.com.cn/n/2015/0828/c1003-27525830.html.
422. 《全国政法工作会议召开, 贯彻宽严相济刑事政策》*[The National Working Conference on Politics and Law; Implementing the Criminal Policy of Combining Leniency and Severity]*, available at: 新浪网 [Sina Net]. http://news.sina.com.cn/c/2006-12-04/091010677430s.shtml.
423. 任重远 [REN Zhongyuan],《刑法修正案九: 嫖宿幼女罪没了, 终身监禁来了》*[The Ninth Amendment to Criminal Law: the Crime of Prostitution Involving a Girl under the Age of 14 is Abolished and Life Imprisonment without Possibility of Release is Provided]*, available at: 大众数字报 [Public Statistics News], Available at: http://paper.dzwww.com/xcb/data/20150829/html/3/content_1.html.
424. 吴建雄 [WU Jianxiong],《怎样看待近几年的"高压反腐"》*[How to View the 'Heavy Anti-corruption' of Recent Years]*, available at: 中国共产党新闻网 [Communist Party of China's News Net]. http://theory.people.com.cn/n1/2016/0225/c143844-28150603.html.
425. 郑永年 [ZHENG Yongnian],《运动式反腐败符合政治理性》*[The Campaign-style of Anti-corruption is Appropriate to Political Rationality]*, available at: 凤凰网 [Ifeng Net]. http://news.ifeng.com/exclusive/lecture/special/zhengyongnian2/.
426. 李婧, 刘茸 [LI Jing and LIU Rong],《臧铁伟: 终身监禁不是新刑种 适用于重特大贪污受贿犯罪》*[Zang Tiewei: Life Imprisonment without Possibility of Release is not a New Penalty Type, and it is Imposed for the Serious Crime of Embezzlement and Bribery]*, available at: 人民网-中国人大新闻网 [People Net and National People's Congress Net], available at: http://npc.people.com.cn/n/2015/0829/c14576-27531201.html.
427. 《最高法谈对贪官增设终身监禁: 改变无期名不副实现象》*[The Supreme People's Court Talking about Adding Life Imprisonment without Possibility of Release for Corrupt Officers: Changes in the Phenomenon of Life Imprisonment are Changes in Name rather than in Reality]*, available at: 凤凰网 [ifeng Net]. http://news.ifeng.com/a/20151105/46124190_0.shtml.
428. 《专家谈刑法修正案(九): 终身监禁让巨贪把牢底坐穿》*[Experts Discussing the Ninth Amendment to the Criminal Law: Life Imprisonment without Possibility of Release: Let the Arch Corrupt Official Rot in Detention]*, available at: 中国新闻网 [China's News Net]. http://www.chinanews.com/ll/2015/09-08/7510951.shtml.

429. *唐惠 [TANG Hui]*, available at: http://baike.so.com/doc/1050580-1111313.html.
430. 柴会群 [CHAI Huiqun], *《什么造就了唐慧》[What made Tang Hui?]*, available at: http://www.360doc.com/content/14/0617/10/4089344_387392854.shtml.
431. *《2014年1–9月人民法院办理减刑假释案件情况》[Report on the Commutation and Parole Cases Handled by the People's Court from January to September 2014]*, available at: 中华人民共和国最高人民法院 [Supreme People's Court of People's Republic of China]. http://www.court.gov.cn/fabu-xiangqing-14014.html.
432. *《"两高"发布办理贪污贿赂刑事案件司法解释》[Interpretations Concerning the Specific Application of the Law in Handling Criminal Cases of Embezzlement and Bribery Issued by the 'Two Supreme Judicial Authorities (Supreme People's Court and Supreme Peoples' Procuratorate)']*, available at: 中华人民共和国最高人民法院 [Supreme People's Court of People's Republic of China], available at: http://www.court.gov.cn/zixun-xiangqing-19562.html.
433. *《"巨贪"将把牢底坐穿?——聚焦刑法修正案(九)草案: 对重特大贪污犯罪增设"终身监禁"》['Will the 'Corrupt Official' Continue to Rot in Detention? Focus on the Ninth Amendment to the Criminal Law (Draft): Stipulating Life Imprisonment without Possibility of Release for Serious Crimes of Embezzlement and Bribery]*, available at: 中央政府网 [Central People's Government]. http://www.gov.cn/xinwen/2015-08/25/content_2919673.htm.
434. *《白恩培等三巨贪被判处终身监禁, 释放出什么信号?》[Such Bai Enpei as Three Arch Corrupt officials Are Sentenced to Life Imprisonment without Release, what Kinds of Signals Are Released?]*, available at: 星翰新闻网 [Xinghan News]. http://www.szxinghan.cn/Social/13972494.html.
435. *《最高检万春主任等专家解读贪污贿赂司法解释》[The Chief Editor of the Research Office of the Legal Policies of the Supreme People's Procurator of the P.R.C, Wan Chun and Other Experts Explaining the Judicial Interpretations of the Anti-crime of Embezzlement and Bribery]*, available at: 今日头条 [Daily News]. http://www.toutiao.com/i6288100038123979265/.
436. *阮齐林 [RUAN Qilin]*, *《依法从严惩治贪污贿赂犯罪——解读<关于办理贪污贿赂刑事案件适用法 律若干问题的解释>》[Severely Punishing Crimes of Embezzlement and Bribery by the Law: Analyzing 'Interpretation on Several Legal Issues Concerning the Specific Application of the Law in Handling Criminal Cases of Embezzlement and Bribery']*, available at: 法制网 [Legal Net]. http://www.legaldaily.com.cn/index/content/2016-04/18/content_6591201.htm?node=20908.
437. *《最高人民法院关于常见犯罪的量刑指导意见》[The Sentencing Guidance of The Supreme People's Court for the Common Crimes]*, available at: 最高人民法院网 [The Supreme People's Court of the People's Republic of China]. http://www.court.gov.cn/shenpan-xiangqing-6622.html.
438. 陈学勇 [CHEN Xueyong], *《最高人民法院扩大量刑规范化罪名和刑种试点: 将危险驾驶罪等8种罪名纳入规范范围》[The Supreme People's Court Increasing the Number of Crimes and Their Corresponding Punishments and Adding Pilot Locations for Sentencing Standardization: Adding the Crime of Dangerous Driving to the Other 8 Crimes in the Scope of Sentencing Standardization]*, available at: 中国法院网 [China Court Internet]. http://www.chinacourt.org/article/detail/2016/05/id/1884273.shtml.

Cases

439. *Streicher v. Germany,* application no. 40384/04, 2009.
440. *Meixner v. Germany,* application no. 26958/07, 2009.
441. *Graham v. Florida*, 982 So. 2d 43,52(Fla, Dist, 2010).
442. *László Magyar v. Hungary,* application no. 73593/10, 20 May, 2014.
443. *T.P. and A.T. v. Hungary,* application nos. 37871/14 and 73986/14.

444. *KAFKARIS v. CYPRUS (Application no. 21906/04), 12 February 2008.*
445. *Murray v. The Netherlands*, (Application no. 10511/10), Judgment, Strasbourg, 26 April 2016.
446. *Törköly v Hungary*, application no. 4413/06, ECtHR (Second Section), Decision of 05.04. 2011.
447. *Vinter and Others v. the United Kingdom*, Applications nos. 66069/09 and 130/10 and 3896/ 10.
448. *Ediga Anamma vs. State of Andhra Pradesh*, Equivalent citations: 1974 AIR 799, 1974 SCR (3) 329.
449. *Magyar v. Hungary* [2014] (European Court HR, Chamber, Application No 73593/10, May 20, 2014).
450. *Öcalan v. Turkey* [2005] IV (European Court HR, Grand Chamber, Application No. 46221/ 99, May 12, 2005).
451. *Öcalan v. Turkey, Application nos. 24069/03, 197/04, 6201/06 and 10464/07. ECHR 077 (2014) 18.03.2014.*
452. *李启铭 [LI Qiming] (2010) 河望刑初第10号 [(2010) Hewang Criminal Trial. No. 10].*
453. *药家鑫 [Yao Jiaxin], (2011) 西刑一初字第68号 [2011 Xi the First Criminal Court First Trial. No. 68].*
454. *高晓松 [Gao Xiaosong] (2011) 东刑初字第 438 号 [(2011) East Destrict the Second Criminal Court First Trial. No. 438].*
455. *李昌奎 [Li Changkui] (2010) 昭中刑一初字第52号 [(2010) Zhao intermediate Criminal Court First Trial. No. 52; (2010) 云高法终字第 1314 号* [*(2010 Yun High Court Second Trial No. 1314*).
456. *吴英 [WU ying], (2009) 浙金刑二初字第 1 号 [(2009) Zhejin the Second Criminal Court First Trial. No. 1]; (2010) 浙刑二终字第7 号 [(2010) Zhe the Second Criminal Court Second Trial. No. 27].*
457. *孙伟铭 [SUN Weiming] (2009) 成刑初字第 158 号 [2009] Cheng the First Criminal Court First Trial. No. 158; (2009) 川刑终字第690 号 [2009] Chuan the Criminal Court the Second Trial. No. 690].*
458. *于欢 [YU Huan] 山东省聊城中级人民法院刑事附带民事判决书 [The Criminal Incidental Civil Judgment of Liao Cheng Intermediate People's Court, Shandong Province], (2016) 鲁 15 刑初 33 号 [Lu No. 5 Criminal First Trial, No. 33, 2016].*
459. *许霆案 [The Case of XU Ting], (2007) 穗中法刑二重字第 196 号 [Hui Intermediate Court The Second Criminal Court Second Trial No.196, 2007; (2008) 穗中法刑二重字第2 号 [Hui Intermediate Court The Second Criminal Court Second Trial No. 2 2008], (2008) 穗法高刑重审字第 197 号 [Hui Intermediate Court The Second Criminal Court Second Trial No. 2 2008]].*
460. *黄光裕 [Huang Guangyu]《北京市第二中级人民法院刑事裁定书》[Criminal Ruling of Beijing Second Intermediate People's Court],* (2015) 二中刑减字第 1634 号 [*The Second Intermediate Criminal Commutation*, No. 1634, 2015].
461. *周军辉, 秦星 [ZHOU Junhui and QIN xing] (2010) 永中刑一初字第 55 号 [2010] Yong the First Criminal Court First Trial. No. 55; (2012) 湘高法刑三终字第 31 号 [2012] Xiang High Court Third Criminal Trial. No. 31.; (2014) 湘高法刑重字第5号 [2014] Xiang High Court Criminal Retrial. No. 5].*
462. *刘勇 [LIU Yong],《最高人民法院再审刘涌案刑事判决书》[The SPC's Criminal-retrying Judgement on the Case of Liu Yong], (2003) 刑提字第 5 号 [Criminal Interrogation, No. 5, 2003].*
463. *郝卫东 [HAO Weidong],《中华人民共和国最高人民法院公报》[The Bulletins of the Supreme People's Court of the People's Republic of China], 2013年卷 [Vol. 2013], 人民法院出版社 [People's Court Press], Beijing, 2014, 463. (2009) 刑核字第 41 号 Criminal Approval, No. 41, 2009].*

Official Reports

464. Amnesty International, *The Death Penalty Worldwide: Developments in 1996*, AI Index: ACT 50/05/97.
465. Amnesty International, *The Death Penalty Worldwide: Developments in 1997*, AI Index: ACT 50/04/98.
466. Amnesty International, *Death Sentences and Executions in 1998*, AI Index: ACT 51/01/99.
467. Amnesty International, *Amnesty International Death Sentences and Executions in 1999*, AI Index: ACT 50/08/00.
468. Amnesty International, *Amnesty International Death Sentences and Executions in 2000*, AI Index: ACT 50/001/2001.
469. Amnesty International, *Amnesty International Death Sentences and Executions in 2001*, AI Index: ACT 50/001/2002.
470. Amnesty International, *Amnesty International Death Sentences and Executions in 2002*, AI Index: ACT 50/002/2003.
471. Amnesty International, *Amnesty International Death Sentences and Executions in 2003*, AI Index: ACT 50/007/2004.
472. Amnesty International, *Amnesty International Death Sentences and Executions in 2004*, AI Index: ACT 50/005/2005.
473. Amnesty International, *Amnesty International Death Sentences and Executions in 2005*, AI Index: ACT 50/002/2006.
474. Amnesty International, *Amnesty International Death Sentences and Executions in 2006*, AI Index: ACT 50/004/2007.
475. Amnesty International, *Amnesty International Death Sentences and Executions in 2007*, AI Index: ACT 50/001/2008.
476. Amnesty International, *Amnesty International Death Sentences and Executions in 2008*, AI Index: ACT 50/003/2009.
477. Amnesty International Global Report: *Death Sentences and Executions 2009*, Index: ACT 50/001/2010.
478. Amnesty International Global Report: *Death Sentences and Executions 2010*, Index: ACT 50/001/2011.
479. Amnesty International Global Report: *Death Sentences and Executions 2011*, Index: ACT 50/001/2012.
480. Amnesty International Global Report: *Death Sentences and Executions 2012*, Index: ACT 50/001/2013.
481. Amnesty International Global Report: *Death Sentences and Execution 2013*, Index: ACT 50/001/2014.
482. Amnesty International Global Report: Death Sentences and Execution 2014, Index: ACT 50/001/2015.
483. Amnesty International Global Report: *Death Sentences and Executions* 2015 (Index: ACT 50/3487/2016).
484. Amnesty International Global Report, *The Death Sentences and Executions 2016*, Index: ACT 50/5740/2017.
485. Ministry of Home Affairs of Government of India, *Committee on Reforms of Criminal Justice System Report*, Vol. I, March 2003.
486. The Crime Prevention and Criminal Justice Branch of United Nations Office at Vienna, *Life imprisonment*, ST/CSDHA/24, 1994.
487. *The European Committee for the Prevention of Torture and Inhuman or Degrading Treatment or Punishment (CPT) Report about the Prison in Netherlands*, Council of Europe, CPT/Inf (2017) 1, Strasbourg, 19 January 2017.

SPRINGER NATURE

GPSR Compliance

The European Union's (EU) General Product Safety Regulation (GPSR) is a set of rules that requires consumer products to be safe and our obligations to ensure this.

If you have any concerns about our products, you can contact us on ProductSafety@springernature.com

In case Publisher is established outside the EU, the EU authorized representative is:

Springer Nature Customer Service Center GmbH
Europaplatz 3
69115 Heidelberg, Germany

The manufacturer's authorised representative in the EU is Springer Nature Customer Service Centre GmbH, Europaplatz 3, 69115 Heidelberg, Germany. If you have any concerns regarding our products, please contact ProductSafety@springernature.com

Printed and bound by CPI Group (UK) Ltd, Croydon, CR0 4YY
01/10/2026
02225864-0007